POLICE COMMUNITY RELATIONS

A Conflict Management Approach

PATRICK J. SOLAR, M.P.A., PH.D.
Assistant Professor, Criminal Justice
Chief of Police (Ret.) FBINA 188
University of Wisconsin-Platteville

Foreword by
Christopher Cooper
Author of "Afrocentric Perspectives on the Police"

With Contributions by
Amy Nemmetz, Ph.D., Restorative Justice
Danny McGuire, Ed.D., Police Perspectives

Editorial Support from
Dr. James Banovetz, Ph.D.
Professor Emeritus, Northern Illinois University

444 Cedar Street, Suite 700
St. Paul, MN 55101
1-877-888-1330

Printed in the United States of America

ISBN: 978-1-64020-154-5

This book is dedicated to the men and women of law enforcement who take it upon themselves to uphold the rule of law and protect our increasingly indifferent society from those, both foreign and domestic, who would cause us harm. It is my hope that what is contained herein will provide useful insight that will make their work easier.

Acknowledgments

I am exceedingly grateful for the invaluable assistance of Dr. James Banovetz, Ph.D., Professor Emeritus, Northern Illinois University a great friend and mentor who edited this volume and provided critical insight and advice. Dr. Banovetz has served as a teacher, advisor, and mentor for more than 35 years. Most importantly, he has served as a profound example of excellence in public service as well as a foremost role model.

I would like to acknowledge the support of Chancellor Dennis Shields, University of Wisconsin–Platteville for his taking the time to offer commentary and valuable suggestions to the chapter on African American perspectives. Despite a notoriously busy schedule, he cared enough about the work of a junior faculty member to read and offer his personal insight and suggestions.

I would also like to acknowledge the assistance of Dr. Frank King, Assistant Professor University of Wisconsin–Platteville who also provided important insight on this chapter. The relationship between the police and African Americans is a difficult, but is a critical topic to address today, Dr. King was generous with his time and his suggestions provided a point-of-view that any policing professional will value.

Dr. Amy Nemmetz authored the chapter on Restorative Justice. Dr. Nemmetz is a tireless advocate for crime victims and our point person on this topic. As criminal justice practitioners we tend to focus our attention on the perpetrators of crime, restorative justice seeks to re-focus our attention on the victims of crime who are often neglected in our relentless pursuit of crime control.

Danny McGuire, Jr. Ed.D. Program Director, Public Safety Programs, Calumet College of St. Joseph authored the chapter on policing perspectives. Scholars have struggled, with varying degrees of success, to understand the practical realities of policing. The function is incredibly ambiguous and fraught with nuances that defy any attempts to structure, standardize, and "improve" it. Dr. McGuire takes us into the heart of a major city police agency that has been under attack and demoralized by individuals and groups in pursuit of a political agenda that ignores the practical realities of policing.

I would also like to thank my wife "Sam" whose love and support sustain my efforts in this, my encore career. After over thirty years of public service she was looking forward to a relaxing retirement only to find me miserable, lacking a sense of purpose. Her acceptance of my need to remain productive has not come without cost and sacrifice that I can only hope I am able to make up for in other ways.

Foreword

Conflict Management and Policing
The Core of the Police Officers' Skill Based Problem Solving Tool Box[1]

by Christopher Cooper, J.D., Ph.D.

After more than 180 years of policing in the United States,[2] after decades of law enforcement trial and error, the craft of policing should have achieved perfection by the first day of the new millennium. But we all know better.

After all the advances in understanding human behavior, and all the emphasis on human rights and responsibilities on the one hand; and after all the advances in technology with its compelling and powerful sway over so much of our physical and mental activity, of our social interactions with others, and of our ability to structure our environment—with all of this change—it is hard to imagine that the industry of policing has not been perfected. But it has not.

In an ever-changing society, policing has a duty to be dynamic. We should expect—we should *demand*—that policing adapt to changing circumstances and expectations, that it update its policies and crime fighting approaches, that it more effectively advance and apply our understanding of the policing role. To be sure, policing in America has made many accommodations to our changing world. Witness, for example, the adjustment in car pursuit policies that take into account the possibility that innocent by-standers may be run-down by fleeing vehicles and their police pursuers.

But even with technologies of 21st century policing at their disposal—from body cameras to devices which detect the location of gun shots—many police agencies have not made significant strides in improving their relationship with the communities they serve. In many parts of the United States, police-citizen relations appear as troublesome as they were 50 years ago. As the nation becomes an ever-greater home to diverse cultures, the melting pot objective requires that "the cop on the beat" have a far more sophisticated set of skills and strategies with which to address the problems confronting people in their community.

---

1 The author of this Forward, Christopher C. Cooper, Ph.D., has also authored "An Afrocentric Perspective on Policing" in the 7th edition of the book, *Critical Issues in Policing*, 2015.

2 The first modern Police Department in the U.S. was established in Boston in 1838.

Only with such sensitivities, skills, and strategies will the cop on the beat be properly equipped to keep the peace, maintain domestic tranquility, and enhance the sense of community in ever more diverse and changing neighborhoods.

And that is what this book is all about: it is intended to serve as a first step in giving individual cops on the beat a "tool box" of the social and conflict management skills needed to face and resolve conflicts that are a part of the daily pattern of life in today's neighborhoods.

A major ingredient in improving police-citizen relations are cops who are armed with an appropriate, skill-based, Problem Solving Tool Box (PSTB). Such a box would consist of:

Tool #1: Exceptional Social Interaction Skills.

Tool #2: Exceptional Dispute/Conflict Management Skills (including a systematic De-escalation Skill Set).

Tool #3: Exceptional, Analytically Based Problem-Solving Skills; and

Tool #4: Training in the skills needed to apply all of these skills in a time of potential real crisis and chaos.

All police officers, from those who work routine patrol, to detectives, to those who work behind a desk, can benefit from these skills, but the primary emphasis has to be placed on giving and maintaining these skills to the police officers assigned to routine patrol duties. Like an athlete, such officers must be given continuous training so that their skills will always be at their peak of readiness for instant application in real-life situations.

Social Interaction Skills

When uniformed [patrol] police officers are interacting with citizens, they must continuously demonstrate consideration and respect. This includes:

- Listening; proper word usage and delivery; introspection; attention to one's own body language and to the body language of all others at the scene;
- An ability to control their personal feelings and emotions;
- Emotional Intelligence, which includes self-control of what may be justified frustration and anger;
- The ability to be conciliatory or assertive when necessary, and the knowledge of which is appropriate in what circumstances.

- Knowing what to say and what not to say under different, varying circumstances.

An officer's shortcomings in using social interaction skills appropriate to the situation at hand can be accurately described as a demonstration of poor social interaction skills, which, in turn, is one of the indicators of incompetent policing. All officers will sometimes choose or use tactics inappropriate to the situation at hand. It is the patterns of success or failure in multiple such situations that must be monitored.

Dispute\Conflict Management Skills

For a police officer to use his or her conflict management skills appropriately and competently, the officer must be made proficient with social interaction tools. Each officer must, therefore, be given a systematic De-escalation Skill-Set.

First and foremost, the officer's general "gift of gab" must be developed. Muir described cops as "street-corner politicians" where the importance of great communication, storytelling, and interpersonal skills cannot be understated (see Muir, 1977).[3]

Second, is the ability to be objective. In the 21st Century, an applicant to a police department must be evaluated on their ability to function as a neutral and objective party.

The third tool is the ability to empower others to help themselves. Police officers accomplish little where they exit a scene after only having superficially addressed an interpersonal dispute. The benefits of empowering disputing parties to help themselves reduces the likelihood of a re-occurrence and this, in turn, reduces the likelihood of a repeat call-for-service.

Ultimately, where PSTB approaches are employed, citizen appreciation for the police and mutual respect can be cultivated. Such a landscape enables many positive outcomes that are important to the police mission, such as reductions in the need to use force, more citizen cooperation, higher levels of citizen satisfaction, and improved police community relations overall.

Exceptional Analytically Based Problem-Solving Skills

All sorts of police calls-for-service impose on the responding uniformed officer an obligation to address a problem analytically. The old adage of shoot first and ask questions later, while intended as a safety chute, has no place in modern American policing.

---

[3] Muir, William. (1977). *Police: Streetcorner politicians.* Chicago: University of Chicago.

Analyses can and sometimes must occur in a split second. But that must be the responding officer's first obligation before any action is taken. Actions taken in haste should be avoided; they can result in shooting a fellow cop or the victim.

In social interaction, it is the officer's analytical skill set (including foresight and forward thinking) that makes him a superb problem solver. Officers who earn the mark of exceptional problem solvers are able to de-escalate scenes methodically, whether by verbal skills, conflict management, or even knowing exactly where to position a police cruiser before alighting and then positioning themselves at the scene. When citizens equate police officers with de-escalation expertise, citizens and police have more productive and collective relationships.

An Exceptional and Atypical Ability to Apply All of the Aforementioned in a Moment of Crisis and Chaos

The "cop's cop" can employ tools 1–3 effectively and with precision, when sirens are blaring and people are shouting, venting, and dictating their emotions. Said another way, the best example of a 21st Century cop is one who is able to manage a chaotic scene (inclusive of de-escalating) while keeping a cool head. *This is the type of police performance and example setting which contributes to improved citizen-police interaction.*

Going Forward

This book is about being a cop. It is written by cops for use by cops, by those who aspire to be cops, and for those who are not cops, but who want to know more about what cops think and do while out "on the street."

This book provides a starting point from which potential future cops—and veteran cops who want to upgrade their performance—can grasp an informed and sophisticated understanding of what it takes to be a police officer in the world of today and tomorrow. The book provides an overview of the best contemporary knowledge about what it takes to be a cop; about how cops are expected to conduct themselves out "on the street" facing tense and challenging circumstances.

The book also seeks to provide a reference point to help veteran cops evaluate their own performance at the end of a difficult day "on the street."

It is, in short, an effort to put into a very readable format the best current thinking about how to be a *good cop.*

Summary of Contents

Table of Contents

PART 3. MANAGING CONFLICT BY BUILDING BETTER RELATIONSHIPS

POLICE COMMUNITY RELATIONS

A Conflict Management Approach

PART 1

History, Conflict & Community

■ ■ ■

Chapter 1: Introduction: Why Do We Need the Police?

In this first part the question of why the police are necessary in a democratic society is explored. The police function is examined including the necessity of the Rule of Law, the justification for violence on the part of the police, and the problem of differing perceptions regarding the police role.

Enlightened thinkers such as Rousseau, Locke and Hobbes provided lengthy works on what is now referred to as the *social contract,* the idea that all members of society agree and surrender certain natural rights to the government in return for security. In order to provide that security, the government is invested with limited powers, such as the use of force and coercion to maintain social stability and protect the individual interests of societal members. Individuals, in turn, give up the right to use physical force except in their own defense and in their efforts to secure the necessities for survival. The government, finally, is expected to provide an effective system for regulating conduct and to create forums for resolving conflict.

The term "state of nature" refers to the hypothetical conditions experienced by people before societies came into existence. In such a hypothetical condition, all people would have been subject to what is observable in nature, to natural conditions such as the supremacy of the physically and mentally strong and the subjugation of the weak. Conversely, Rousseau believed that the nobility of the state of nature was corrupted by the unnatural limitations of civilization. He believed in the nobility of the state of nature and that man, free from the unjust societal institutions, would pursue the social good as the highest virtue.

The police exist to provide a sense of security. The idea that people may go about their normal lives without fear of being attacked, without fear of having their property taken from them, and, in the Unites States, the ability to enjoy constitutionally protected rights from governmental intervention has been a fundamental characteristic of American life since the colonial period.

Rational objectivity is introduced as a concept that defines how the law works as opposed to subjective perceptions that form the basis upon which many "social justice" arguments are formed. The police subculture is introduced as a framework for understanding why the police often come into conflict with various individuals and groups. Simply stating the police need to improve ignores the complexity and ambiguity of what the police actually do.

Chapter 2: The History of the Police Function

This chapter examines the basic mission of the police and the historical context of how the police have developed throughout history. The early beginnings of the police, how policing developed in the United States, the emergence of preventative patrol, and the various developmental eras of the police such as the political era, the professional era, the community oriented era, and a new-humanistic-era of policing are explored. The police were driven to change through each of these eras, what drove that change is explored.

The police subculture is discussed with particular attention to the *dark side* of policing, those cultural norms that speak to the more troubling aspects of the work. How the police view themselves is an important aspect of police behavior, understanding this self-image provides clues to why the police have relationship troubles and conflict today. Proactive policing is explored as an instrument of injustice in the eyes of those who are victimized by it.

The concept of Community Oriented Policing developed and continues to be heralded as a cure for the evils of the professional policing era. Civil unrest in the 1960s, 1970s and a growing crime problem in the 1980s resulted in an ill-conceived effort to re-build the vary linkages that precipitated some of the worst abuses of the rule of law attributed to the political era. Armed with a shallow understanding of history, advocates of community oriented policing preach the need for the police to embark upon "relationship building" in an effort to build trust and legitimacy. The wise individual police officer is fully aware of the value of their own credibility and the need to hold public trust as a crime fighting tool, none-the-less advocates have embarked upon an incredible array of outlandish programs and public expense that has not resulted in what Peel envisioned as the ultimate indicator of effective policing, lower levels of crime and disorder.

Community Guardianship is a concept that has been developed as an alternative to the dysfunctional aspects of community oriented policing. COP stressed a proactive response to crime problems and this breeds a warrior mentality that allows officers to view some individuals, by virtue of their behavior, as something less than human. The way that the police view themselves, by virtue of their demeanor, cultural traits, symbols, and attitudes shape the context of police community relations. How we judge police effectiveness is the basis upon which officers can draw a self-image as either warriors or guardians.

The conflicting views of justice are explored as a source of conflict between the police and various groups and between the various groups that exist in society. *Social justice* refers to how the resources of a society are distributed, unequal distributions of wealth or a criminal justice system that cerates disparate impacts based on racial groups are a sign of social injustice. However, the police are not in the social justice business, the business of the police is *criminal justice* and this focuses on the individual, whether the correct laws have been applied and the correct procedures followed. To expect the police to engage in social justice initiatives undermines the basic tenants of law enforcement.

Chapter 3: Historical Approaches to Police Community Relations

This chapter examines the historical approaches to police community relations. The police are the most visible representatives of government authority, they need to be mindful of the need to earn and maintain the consent of the governed. The way the police do this is through constant attention to police community relations.

Police officers tend to categorize individuals based upon their demeanor and their attitudes. These categories, amounting to a cognitive shorthand, are ways that the officer makes sense of his or her world but can be counterproductive to maintaining good police community relations.

The police recognition of the value of maintaining good police community relations began with the idea that the police should always seek ways to work in cooperation with the public because in some cases the police need to be able to call on public assistance in times of crisis. Professional policing had the underlying theme to establish policing as a legitimate enterprise that served the needs of all citizens. The need to elevate the image of the police away from the unprofessional and amateurish past was accomplished with public relations programs, some of which survive through today. These programs were intended to "sell" the police as elite crime fighting experts who employ the latest scientific methods to identify, apprehend, and convict the criminal perpetrators.

Recognizing that a great deal of police work is actually social work provides a better framework for which a new vision of police community relations programming and philosophy has flowed. A problem oriented approach to the job emerged as an early recognition that the police occupy a unique space in democratic societies, this new outcome based focus provided the foundation for what is now called problem oriented policing.

The community relations approach to police community relations provides a framework for a new operational philosophy generally referred to as Community Oriented Policing. Rather than dominating the community as the experts in crime suppression and prevention, the police work in cooperation with citizens and groups, promoting a "people's police" attitude that internalizes the need for trust building and working in cooperation with the community. The emphasis is upon great service, rather than pure crime fighting. The professional police agency is internally focused, the community oriented agency is externally focused making community oriented policing one of the best ways to build great police community relations and to manage conflict.

Police community relations is a new philosophical point-of-view that is distinct from the professional policing model and the programs approach to building trust and legitimacy. It involves constant attention to transparency of operations, community awareness of crime problems and the development of alternative methods and strategies that will increase police productivity and make more effective use of certified officers. At the heart of the community relations approach, and what makes it distinct from the ambiguous community oriented policing philosophy is the focus on stakeholders-those who are directly impacted by the actions, or lack of action, by the police. These are the individuals who have a willingness to engage with the police in pursuit of mutual goals such as neighborhood crime reduction and safety.

A common enemy now exists to both the efforts to promote community oriented policing and police community relations, that enemy is the specter of international and domestic terrorism. The police officer working the street is the first line of defense and the first responder to terrorism threats and this realization has led some to demand equipment and training that has taken some in the opposite direction from the traditional and accepted policing role. Police Militarization presents a clear and present danger to police community relations when it is taken to the extreme in providing equipment to officers that is not needed given the reality of the modern service orientation.

Barking at the heels of the best efforts in police community relations is the issue of police deviance. Police crime refers to violations of the law committed or facilitated by sworn officers. Occupational deviance refers to both criminal and non-criminal behavior that is committed under the guise of police authority, a kind of deviance only made possible because of the officers position. Corruption refers to the acceptance of a reward or favor by officers for engaging in a duty or behavior that they are obligated to engage in my virtue of their employment. Abuse of authority is any action by a police officer that injures, insults, or undermines the basic human dignity of any person. Police deviance is rare but it strikes at the heart of what is meant by the "police problem."

A new approach to police community relations centers around the technology of human relations. Technical skills are simply not enough in an era where police officers are called upon to handle a myriad of humanities problems. Interpersonal skills are now, and have always been, at the forefront of the capabilities of great police officers. Treating others with sensitivity, making the right ethical choices, emotional control, and the ability to work with others constitute the next level of skill development needed to promote great police community relations and conflict management.

Chapter 4: The Nature of Conflict

In this chapter, we explore conflict from a number of different perspectives. The idea that all conflict is bad is set aside in favor of various concepts illustrating the value of positive conflict. Most conflict situations are confrontations over power. The unequal distribution of power in society and between individuals can lead to either cooperative arrangements, as actors seek cooperation and order, or conflict, as the actors struggle for a more equal distribution of power and resources in a zero-sum game where one party gains advantage by diminishing the other in some way.

Conflict situations can be either constructive or dysfunctional. Most view conflict negatively and, because of this, tend to engage in one of the most dysfunctional forms of conflict resolution, which is avoidance. Dysfunctional conflict most often results from rigid competitive systems that pit individuals or groups against each other. The behaviors that follow can generate anger, resentment, and depression. Constructive conflict is process-focused as opposed to outcome-focused. The parties seek to build on the relationship rather than gain advantage by diminishing the other in some way.

The functionalist perspective sees society as a system of interconnected parts that work together in harmony to maintain a state of balance and social equilibrium for the whole. The functionalist perspective emphasizes the interconnectedness of society by focusing on how each part influences and is influenced by other parts. This perspective offers a distinction between functional and dysfunctional societal elements in that the former contributes to social stability and the latter disrupts it.

The conflict perspective views society as a collection of different parts engaged in a competition for power and resources. It is often best understood through the work of Karl Marx who suggested that society becomes divided into two distinct classes as the result of economic advantage.

The symbolic interactionist perspective relates to the meaning individuals attach to situations, rather than the objective situation itself. Individuals use these assumptions to develop their own self-concept. They imagine how they look to another person by stepping out of themselves and viewing themselves as they believe others view them (through the "looking glass" self).

Many scholars have observed a growing trend today in that more and more people, typically young people, have a worldview that is often not supported by factual information. Conflict results when offered facts go against their life narrative and their reaction is to become angry and indignant. The concept of the pristine self refers to an individual who believes that the world around them should offer them nothing but love and that they are entitled to live in a world that validates their own worldview. When challenged with contradictory ideas or actual facts, they interpret them as incorrect and even acts of aggression.

Managing conflict situations effectively requires interdependence, where both parties are dependent on the other for something in some way. When the needs of one party are not being met, the parties can seek a cooperative resolution, as in the functionalist perspective, or they can engage in competition, where one party seeks to prevail at the expense of the other. The goal of constructive competition is for both parties to acquire a deeper understanding of the others point-of-view, to value the differences in attitudes and perspectives, and to enrich mutual understanding. Cooperative competition is civilized, thought provoking, exhilarating, and even fun, but there needs to be a level of wisdom on the part of both parties that enables them to overcome the passion that often stands in the way of reason and civilized discourse.

Most understand justice as fundamental fairness, but what is considered fair is typically based upon one's point-of-view. Without a solid foundation in the rule of law and its focus on objective rationality, we are free to pursue our own interpretation of justice based on subjective criteria. This is a profound source of conflict between individuals, between individuals and groups, and between groups that the police are often called on to mediate.

A sense of injustice generally takes the form of oppression. Injustice can take the form of unfair treatment such as discrimination, disparate impact, and other perceived collective wrongs. It can take the form of harassment, breach of contract, a personal injury, and other forms of personal wrongs. These forms of injustice are often perpetrated by those who are insensitive to the feelings and perceptions of others, sometimes because they don't care and sometimes out of ignorance. Managing conflict with regard to the various perspectives on justice requires a deeper understanding of where the sense of injustice originates.

The difference between constructive and destructive conflict is often a matter of trust. Advocates for police reform often point to the trust issue as a major impediment to police community relations and charge the police with *trust building* in the community. The glib implication is that the police are responsible for the erosion of trust among poor people and people of color and, therefore, it is the police who need to fix the problem. The factors that contribute to the level of trust one enjoys include:

1. The individual disposition toward trusting others
2. The context or situational parameters; and
3. The history of the relationship.

Chapter 5: The Nature of "Community"

The term "community" encompasses a plurality of concepts and meanings. To engage with the community often implies behavioral interactions where interpersonal relationships are developed, nurtured and maintained. People engage in patterns of behavior that can be attributed to the circumstances and conditions that they find themselves in. They naturally seek comfort and security by seeking relationships with others who are like themselves in term of conditions, values, and characteristics.

Social organization can be understood as a function of the behavior of individuals. Common patterns of behavior emerge as a function of social interaction, when the actions of one individual affect another individual in some way.

A social group—a kind of community—is a type of human organization that is created by a pattern of commonly accepted interactions. It can be defined by a common culture, e.g., ethnic, religious, nationalistic, etc.; a way in which people within the group define themselves, e.g., gay, lesbian, outlaw, etc.; or it can be defined by what the group values or what they do, e.g., occupation, political allegiance, etc. Primary and secondary groups are another group distinction separated by the level of intimacy and involvement group members enjoy.

The term "community" encompasses a plurality of concepts and meanings. To engage with the community often implies behavioral interactions where interpersonal relationships are developed, nurtured and maintained. The term often involves differentiating among groups with regard to unique habits, social norms, and roles of members; communities and groups can often be defined by a unique culture that separates and defines them as unique among other social groups and actors, e.g., the police subculture, the liberal-elite culture, the working class subculture, etc.

A defining characteristic of all social groups is the demand for members to adhere to a common set of behavioral expectations or norms. Religious communities often specify these expectations in the form of commandments, rules, or covenants. To violate these standards of conduct is to be sanctioned in some way. Some of the most effective forms of social control are informal in nature. Some examples of how groups and communities maintain order in informal ways include the use of gossip, folkways, mores, custom, and religion.

When the term "community" is used it usually means the society at large, making this term of little use for a police chief or police officer seeking a better relationship with his or her customers. The community consists of many groupings of individuals who are brought together by way of culture, geography, or common interest. These subgroupings may join together in cooperation or they may compete with each other for attention and resources. The key to success rests in the ability to facilitate a balance between the interests of competing groups, and to build cooperation among groups with common interests.

The Nature of Man is usefully described as a continuum between what is called the Constrained Vision and the Unconstrained Vision. In the constrained vision man is viewed as egocentric and self-centered. "By nature, men are self-deceptive, self-centered and when given a choice will always take the path of least resistance" (Enter, 2006). Adam Smith proposed that rather than trying to change the nature of man we simply accept it and seek out the most efficient way (least costly) to produce the desired social benefits within this vision.

The Unconstrained Vision provides a contrast to Smith's philosophy in that it relies on man's ability to reason and to seek virtuous outcomes. William Godwin (1793) identified the intention to benefit others as the essence of virtue and virtue or a virtuous life as being the road to human happiness (Godwin, 1793). In this view of human nature, man is capable of feeling the needs of other people and viewing them as more important than their own. Godwin did not put this forth as a statement of what actually occurs but rather as a statement of human potential.

Traditional policing has been reactive in nature. The measure of law enforcement effectiveness in the professional policing era was rapid response to calls for service: how quickly the police arrived. Officers learned to behave like automated machines, collecting the facts, conducting perfunctory interviews, treating citizens with often callous indifference, documenting information and getting back on patrol as quickly as possible in order to be ready to quickly respond to the next call for.

The foundation of the Community Oriented Policing philosophy is based on the idea of community collaboration with the police in pursuit of crime prevention. The police and the "community" work together to identify and solve crime problems. In this scheme, the community becomes a co-producer of public safety. The theoretical foundation for Community Oriented Policing stresses the importance of shifting the focus from police practices that concentrated on process—procedure—in favor of focusing on end results. Focusing on process, it was argued, made the police blind to the problems they were meant to solve.

CHAPTER 1

Introduction: Why Do We Need the Police?

■ ■ ■

This introductory chapter addresses the influence and importance of the rule of law in building and making modern society possible. What would the world be like without it?

"Solitary, Poor, Brutish and Short." —Thomas Hobbes

Thomas Hobbes, 1588–1679*

Widely recognized as the founder of political philosophy, Thomas Hobbes is best known for his book Leviathan that outlines what is meant by the *Social Contract.* He developed many fundamental principles of liberal thought including rights of the individual, the natural equity of man, and the artificial character of the political order. He developed the premise that men should be free to pursue their own

* John Michael Wright [Public domain], via Wikimedia Commons.

cooperative self-interest and that society should leave people free to do whatever they wish unless it is forbidden by law.

Learning Outcomes

Upon successful completion of this chapter the student will be able to:

- Discuss the need for the police in general.
- Describe what the world would be like without the police.
- Describe the primary function and orientation of the police.
- Describe the difference between Social Justice and Criminal Justice.

Important Concepts

- The State of Nature and the Social Contract
- Social Justice
- Rule of Law
- Perception
- Objective Rationality vs. Subjectivity
- Objective Bias
- Subjective Bias

Questions for Discussion

- Describe what is meant by "the social contract."
- What is the "rule-of-law" and why is it important?
- What do you want from the police?
- Discuss an event or situation where the different perceptions of individuals or groups caused conflict.
- Provide an example of a subjective interpretation of an event. Provide an example of an objective interpretation of an event. Describe the difference.
- What is meant by culture? What are a few characteristics of the police subculture?

INTRODUCTION—THE SOCIAL CONTRACT & THE SOCIAL WARRIOR

What is the legitimate role of government in a Democratic society? This question has dogged scholars for centuries. Throughout history, governments have existed to restrict, regulate, and, in a general sense, put controls on people. In short, government is, by its very nature, a repressive entity.

Enlightened thinkers such as **Rousseau, Locke and Hobbes** provided lengthy works on what is now referred to as the *social contract,* the idea that all members of society agree and surrender certain natural rights to the government in return for security. In order to provide that security, the government is invested with limited powers, such as the use of force and coercion to maintain social stability and protect the individual interests of societal members. Individuals, in turn, largely give up the right to use physical force in their own defense and in their efforts to secure the necessities for survival. The government, finally, is expected to provide an effective system for regulating conduct and to create forums for resolving conflict (Gaines, 2011, p. 2).

Discuss the social contract in light of recent mass shooting events. Is the government holding up its end of the bargain?

The legal authority for the police to use force is the manifestation of the power of the state and the foundation of the police function. In the Unites States, the idea of limited government has been put to the test. The U.S. constitution is not an enabling document; it is one intended and designed to limit government, the most notable example of this being the Bill of Rights without which the constitution would not have been ratified in 1789. This document goes to great length to specify what the government, i.e., the police, cannot do. The Fourth Amendment restricts the police (search & seizure) and the Fifth and Sixth Amendments specify, through case law, what police officers must do in certain situations to preserve the rights of citizens who have been accused of crimes.

Jean-Jacques Rousseau*

French philosopher Jean-Jacques Rousseau (1712–1778). In 1762 he published 'The Social Contract' arguing that all men are born free and equal, the basis of both the French and American revolutions. Rousseau proposed that in the state of nature man holds "uncorrupted morals" in contradiction to Hobbes who maintained that man is wicked and wholly self-interested, lacking any virtue. If it were not for the corrupting influence of civilization men, would be free, wise and virtuous, living the good life.

The conflict between how Hobbes and Rousseau view man's nature, savage and wholly self-interested (Hobbes), noble and virtuous (Rousseau), continues even today. Beyond Hobbes belief in the need for collective protection, a *Leviathan* to ward-off the primitive savage nature of man against man and Rousseau's belief in the "noble savage" uncorrupted by the influence of civilization a new idea has recently crept into collective public consciousness. That idea seeks to empower government to do things *for* people, e.g., the social safety net. Hobbes believed in the need for government to protect members of society from the state of nature, Rousseau believed that the nobility of the state of nature was corrupted by the unnatural limitations of civilization.

Caught in the middle of this role dichotomy are those who are charged with maintaining public order—even using force if necessary to do so—the police. Some believe in the police as the righteous defenders of the rule-of-law, others see the police as agents of *social justice*. The problem for the police, however, is that

* Maurice Quentin de La Tour [Public domain], via Wikimedia Commons.

they are not in the social justice business; they are in the criminal justice business.[1] The idea that the police can and should do more to promote social welfare, do things for people, is at the heart of police-community relations problems today.

> What does the term "Social Justice" mean to you? Can you define it? How would your best friend define it, how about a co-worker or a parent? Would all these definitions and meanings be consistent?

Photo of Riot Police (2005)*

THE NECESSITY FOR THE RULE OF LAW

The ability for human beings to pursue their own self-interest is regulated by the rule of law.

> Freedom is constrained by laws in both the state of nature and political society. Freedom of nature is to be under no other restraint but the law of nature. Freedom of people under government is to be under no restraint apart from standing rules to live by that are common to everyone in the society and made by the lawmaking power establishment in it. Persons have a right to liberty, first, to follow their own will in all things that the law has not prohibited, and, second, to not be subject to

[1] Social Justice generally refers to the fair and equitable distribution of advantages and disadvantages within a society. The mission of Criminal Justice, conversely, is to uphold social control, through the rule of law.

* By Dave Herholz.

the inconsistent, uncertain, unknown, and arbitrary wills of others (Locke, 1680).

John Locke, 1632–1704*

> Widely recognized as the father of Liberalism, John Locke, a British philosopher, had great influence over the American revolutionaries with regard to his concept of natural rights of man. He was well known for his advancement of empiricism whereby nothing can stand as true without the capability of being tested and falsified. Nothing is exempt from being disproven.

The term "**state of nature**" refers to the hypothetical conditions experienced by people before societies came into existence. In such a hypothetical condition, all people would have been subject to what is observable in nature, to natural conditions such as the supremacy of the physically and mentally strong and the subjugation of the weak. In such an environment, and with neither commonly accepted behavioral expectations nor a system for controlling those who would take advantage of others, any expectations that existed regarding human behavior toward others would be arbitrary and subject to the irrational whims of the most powerful individuals and groups. The result would be the subjugation of the weak by the strong, as in the case of gangs of young thugs intimidating neighborhood residents and causing them to live in constant fear.

---

* By Godfrey Kneller—State Hermitage Museum, St. Petersburg, Russia, Public Domain, Courtesy wikimedia.org.

To provide an alternative to such a state of nature, evolved social systems that established rules to control relationships among and between individuals. Over time, and in different places, a common set of expected behavioral expectations for all people did evolve along with a social structure (today called government) for codifying and publishing the rules; for establishing a means (called police) to enforce the rules; and, finally, for providing a process (called courts) to prevent the arbitrary and unintended abuse of the rules. Such a social structure today is called "**the rule of law**."

As might be expected, different cultures have evolved structures and systems to perform these tasks that vary in the rules established and in the systems for rule making, enforcement, and adjudication, but all cultures have a common set of expected behavioral expectations to which no person can claim exemption; their laws all establish that no person may be punished except for a breach of law; and they all provide that the law is subject to uniform interpretation as the result of judicial decisions (Clark, 1998).

Without the rule of law there would be no common set of behavioral expectations. The rules would be arbitrary and subject to the irrational whims of the most powerful individuals and groups. When the rule of law breaks down we see the subjugation of the weak by the strong as in the case of gangs of young thugs intimidating neighborhood residents, causing them to live in constant fear.

Provide an example of the application of the rule of law to a current social problem. What are the implications and likely consequences of such action? What would happen if the rule of law did not exist in this situation?

THE POLICE FUNCTION

This book deals with the process of enforcing the laws that have been established; it deals with the *police* and the relationship the police have with the communities they serve. What, exactly, is it that society wants from its police? Law and order has been at the heart of the police function but the law itself is not universally perceived as legitimate and just. The ultimate exercise of lawful authority, police use of force, is now being challenged as an expression of societal injustice further complicating an already ambiguous function.

Police officers on high alert*

Violence and Use of Force

The police exist to provide a sense of security. The idea that people may go about their normal lives without fear of being attacked, without fear of having their property taken from them, and, in the Unites States, the ability to enjoy constitutionally protected rights from governmental intervention has been a fundamental characteristic of American life since the colonial period. **Bitner** identifies two fundamental aspirations of Western society: first, to *abolish violence* as a means of settling disputes and, second, to *instill peace* as a stable and permanent condition of everyday life. The underlying morality of this expectation speaks to the duty of societal members to sacrifice self-gratification for the benefit of the greater and common good, a utilitarian perspective. The implication for public policy is that those within society who are unwilling to sacrifice their personal gratification for the common good are to be punished (retribution), incapacitated, and then rehabilitated. The criminal justice system, beginning with the police, exist to do just that (Bitner, 1970, p. 17).

Does the presence of highly visible and heavily armed police officers give you comfort, intimidate you or make you afraid? Why?

At the heart of the policing function is **the capacity to use force and coercion**, albeit as a last resort, to fulfill this basic mission. Civilized society in the United States, and in the western world generally, has rejected the idea of individuals using force with the exception of self-defense and has legitimized the use of repressive force by the police out of necessity.

> Police intervention means above all making use of the capacity and authority to overpower resistance. This thought is always in the mind of

* Image labeled for unrestricted use.

those who "call the cops," with every police intervention projecting the message that force may be used to achieve a desired result (Bitner, 1970, p. 40).

An argument has been made that the police are no longer necessary because there are real-world alternatives that are now available to all people. These alternatives include:

- Community patrols and unarmed mediation and intervention teams that roam neighborhoods and reduce instances of disorder such as "cat-calling," partner violence and even gang murder.
- Crime decriminalization aimed at eliminating the injustice of mass incarceration.
- Restorative Justice where accountability is reinforced as a community issue through a process of transforming those impacted by crime and violence.
- Direct democracy at the community level where a more healthy political culture is produced when people feel more involved.
- Mental health care as opposed to institutionalized social control (Martin, 2014).

This perspective completely abandons the need for force as a controlling element for human behavior, as if the coercive aspect of the power of the state is no longer necessary due to the perceived injustice that its use sometimes provokes. It also serves to provide a contrasting viewpoint with regard to the importance of the use of force and coercion in the concept of the policing function.

> Do you think society can function without the police and their ability to bring physical force and violence to bear in critical situations? Discuss.

The use of physical force is actually a rare event in police work, especially when the function is carried out wisely. Police officers today understand that violence is never pretty and are fully aware that their every move can be recorded, reviewed, taken out of context, and debated. The difficulty of this function relates to the ambiguity created by the viewpoints of diverse groups regarding what they perceive as correct. Policing has always been an ambiguous function, but, given the impact of modern technology, every cop knows that his or her actions will be subjected to intense and often unfair criticism. This makes the use of force by police today a risky endeavor; individual officers do not fear confronting a violent offender, they fear how it will look to an uninformed public on you-tube. The implications of this fear, disincentive to the legally correct application of force, results in the current trend of de-policing (FBI, 2017).

In a homogeneous[2] community, everyone seems to understand the rules. The job of a police officer is more straightforward because everyone agrees on the basic application of the law and, more importantly, the informal standards of correct behavior. The police officer provided a visible symbol of the coercive force that could be employed to correct behavior perceived as a violation of the formal rules, such as theft, or the informal standards, such as not hitting a woman. Police officers in such communities are also much more willing to weigh-in on situations that they perceived as a threat to the accepted social order and are generally trusted in their judgement.

> Does the general availability of video recording technology make the job of the police more difficult? Why?

The righteous focus on diversity as a tool to better understand each other and promote social justice has changed the world for police. The law is open to much broader interpretation and those informal standards of conduct have broken down making police intervention in what was once considered appropriate situations now risky endeavors. Police officers are generally comfortable intervening in very dangerous situations such as threatening and violent encounters. Their training and experience give them a tactical edge. They are not comfortable, however, in having their actions in response to threats filmed and uploaded to you-tube to be critiqued and criticized by those with an agenda that does not include the maintenance of peace and order. As a result, the police are not engaging in the kind of pro-active work that they once did (Roy, 2016).

> The impact of diversity has also caused people generally to retract from social contact. "Diversity triggers a tendency to hunker down and have less confidence in local government, community leaders, and the news media" (Putnam, 2007).

A strong sense of community is a sought-after goal in policing and a benchmark of great police community relationships. However, the trust necessary to achieve better relationships has been undermined by a relentless focus on diversity. **James Q. Wilson**, in reviewing Putnam's book in his article "Bowling Alone" (2000), puts it this way:

> "America, and perhaps the Western world as a whole, has become increasingly disconnected from family, friends, and neighbors. We once

2 Homogeneous refers to sameness, people who are alike and share a common culture and set of behavioral expectations. Uniform, identical and consistent.

> bowled in leagues, now we bowl alone. We once flocked to local chapters of the PTA, the NAACP, or the Veterans of Foreign Wars: now we stay home and watch television. As a result, we have lost our '**Social Capital**'—by which Putnam meant both the associations themselves and the trustworthiness and reciprocity they encourage. For if tools (physical capital) and training (human capital) make the modern world possible, social capital is what helps people find jobs and enables neighborhoods and other small groupings of society to solve problems, control crime, and foster a sense of community" (Wilson, Bowling with Others, 2007).

We value diversity in the hope that bringing different people together will undermine ethnocentricity, racism, and discrimination, and increase acceptance and respect. We value this so much that we now use coercion to bring it about and the results are not good. Those who are forced into diversity training come away resenting the very groups that they are being encouraged to accept (Leibowitz, 2016).

> Compare the level of social interaction between individuals of your generation to your parents and grandparents. Is the level of social interaction generally increasing or decreasing in your opinion?
>
> When interacting in social situations do you tend to seek out those who are similar to yourself or those who are different-from yourself? Why?
>
> Do you think this was any different for your parents and grandparents?

The problem is that force-feeding can activate bias rather than stamp it out. People rebel against rules because they want to assert their personal autonomy. Better programs involve positive engagement such as mentoring that "chips-away" at long held or ingrained bias. When we believe one thing about a group of people but our experience with them shows us something else (cognitive dissonance) our views of that group will change (Dobbin, 2016). The implication is that our continued efforts at promoting diversity will, at some point in the future, reduce the bias felt by the police toward those who are different from themselves.

The President's Task Force on 21st Century policing states "Trust between law enforcement agencies and the people they protect and serve is essential in a democracy" (President's Task Force on 21st Century Policing, 2015). While law enforcement is certainly not wholly responsible for the erosion of trust many people feel toward local government, they must take responsibility for practices that further undermine it. Examples include the lack of transparency in operations. The policies and procedures that govern the actions of police officers in high-risk areas such as the use of force should be readily available and open for criticism and review. Doing so opens a municipality to higher levels of risk, but it also creates an incentive for standardization, effective training, enhanced supervision, and effective discipline. The use of force by police has done more to undermine trust and legitimacy than any other thing that the police do. This is so unfortunate because the use of force is so seldom a part of what the police actually do.

THE PERCEPTION PROBLEM

Perception is not the actual sensory input we receive from our eyes, ears, hands, etc. It is the process of creating meaning from those sensory inputs. Have you ever met someone who can make you angry just by showing up? Certainly, police officers can generate anxiety through their mere presence and the wise police officer understands how to mitigate, or enhance this affect. The best cops know how to manipulate emotion to their own advantage and emotion is often based on perception. The problem is that what is in the advantage of a typical police officer may not be conducive to great police community relationships; they may, in fact, cause conflict. The wise police officer is self-aware and knows how to manipulate perceptions.

> No two people will experience the same event in the same way. Our minds are not video recorders and the inaccuracy of eyewitness accounts of events is the stuff of legendary injustices (Loftus, 1996) (Zalman, 1999). The problem rests in the need to make judgements and this depends upon experience, knowledge, present motives and yes, bias and stereo-typing (Hunter, 2011, p. 32).

Perceptive Filters

The process of perceiving events, situations or individuals is governed by just a few psychological processes.

Generalization allows us to draw quick conclusions about what we are perceiving based on our past experience. Take, for example, a child who sticks their finger into an electrical outlet. If they survive the experience they are quite likely to be resistant to placing their finger into anything that even remotely resembles an electrical receptacle.

Deletion is when we pay selective attention to certain sensory stimuli. We filter out everything that interferes with what we wish to focus on. This often manifests itself as "selective hearing." It commonly occurs when a wife asks her husband to take out the trash during the ball game.

Distortion occurs when we filter sensory experience through our filters and then alter them due to intentional or unintentional cognitive processes. One of the best examples of this today is the issue of *micro-aggression*.[3] As an example, imagine a police officer who was called to the scene of a disturbance and encounters a group of young African Americans engaged in a dispute. The police officer states to the group "Y'all need to settle-down." In this true example, at least one individual, from Chicago, took this as disrespectful due to the phrase's common usage in the racist South. What that individual did not know is that this officer was actually from the South, did not intend any disrespect and commonly used the phrase.

> Can you provide an example of when you or someone else was misunderstood due to how verbal and non-verbal messages were perceived by others? What could have been done differently to prevent the misunderstanding?

Distortion is a common problem in policing as the police officer is likely to have very different experiences than anyone else that they are likely to encounter on the street. Citizens are equally likely to perceive the behavior of an officer quite differently than the officer intends and lack any other frame of reference. This does not stop people, particularly those who feel that they are not well served by the police, to perceive an officer as rude, antagonistic and condescending when, in fact, the officer is performing exactly as they were trained.

A recent example out of Madison, Wisconsin, provides an excellent illustration of this problem.

> ***Horrifying. Gut-wrenching. Crazy.*** *That's how elected leaders describe the arrest of 18-year-old Genele Laird by Madison police officers outside of East Towne Mall early Tuesday evening. A cellphone video of the violent encounter between police and the African American teenager was posted on Facebook shortly after the incident. By nightfall, community leaders, state and local elected officials, protesters and Laird's family were gathering outside the Public Safety Building demanding answers.*
>
> *According to police, officers responded to a call at 5:15 p.m. from mall security about a woman described as "out of control and making threats" in the food court. Laird allegedly confronted an employee at Taco Bell claiming that her phone had been*

---

[3] Webster defines a micro-aggression as a comment or action that subtly and often unconsciously or unintentionally expresses a prejudiced attitude toward a member of a marginalized group.

stolen. Security claims she then displayed a knife and made threats to the Taco Bell employee. When asked to leave, Laird allegedly threatened to kill the security staff.

The video recorded by "RichBoy Robinson" begins with an officer confronting and then restraining Laird after she exits the mall. Laird appears to try to break free from the officers but is unsuccessful. "Get your hands behind your back," says the officer. "Arrest me then, bitch," replies Laird. A second officer pulls up in a squad car with its sirens on. He exits the vehicle and joins the struggle, which quickly escalates. The second officer strikes Laird in the leg several times with his knee, as the officers bring her to the sidewalk.

As the struggle continues, one of the officers punches and then Tasers Laird as she begins to shriek. After the officers subdue her, Laird complains about being unable to breathe. She threatens to bite an officer who in turn threatens to Taser her again. The police then place a "spit sock hood" over her head.

Laird can be heard weeping, saying "I don't want you to see me like this." The teenager is then deadlifted by four officers and placed in a squad car.

Laird was taken to jail, tentatively charged with "disorderly conduct while armed (a knife has been recovered), resisting police (causing injury), battery to police officer, and discharge of bodily fluids," according to the police report. Two officers were treated and released at the hospital for injuries (Brogan, 2016).

The two Madison police officers were found to have acted correctly, consistent with their training given the situation they faced. That did not stop the community outrage as the results of the viral video of a 17 year old black woman being struck, kicked and tazered by two white police officers.[4]

> What could the officers have done differently in this situation to avoid the bad publicity? What would be the implications of the different officer actions you identify?

Clearly this case provides a good example of individual or subjective need to demonstrate the injustice of police action. First, the actions of the police were generalized to reflect the commonly held perception that police officers treat blacks more aggressively. Second, the totality of the situation was diminished in that the message did not include information that this 17 year old woman had a weapon or that she was violently resisting the police. Third, the fact that no citizen has a legal right to resist the efforts of any police officer once they have been informed that they are under arrest was not mentioned or implied in any way.

Perceptions are powerful, especially today with technology that enables individuals and groups to present events in a light most favorable to themselves.

---

4 As reported in the Wisconsin State Journal, September 2nd, 2016.

Police officers do not have this capability and are therefore at a huge disadvantage regarding public perceptions of their role.

So why is it that reasonable people can perceive situations so differently? Some reasons include:

- Differences in past experience.
- Knowledge.
- Individual needs relative to the situation in question that result from the modeling process of generalization, distortion and deletion.

African Americans, especially poor blacks, have very *different experiences* with the police than do middle class whites. The importance of these differences will be covered in a subsequent chapter. Their collective experiences are likely to predispose them to certain attitudes regarding an individual police officer. The wise police officer will be aware of these attitudes and will take steps to mitigate their impact, when possible.

Citizens generally have incomplete, partial or no *knowledge* concerning correct police practices and lawful procedure when faced with a violent confrontation. The significance of case law regarding police use of force, *Graham v. Connor*, and the legal reasoning behind it is not commonly known or understood.[5]

RATIONAL OBJECTIVITY AS PART OF OUR LEGAL TRADITION

The police function is in a world governed by the law; the law in-turn is governed by the world of *fact and objective reason*. The law governing use of force is a prime example. In the case of *Graham v. Connor*, 490 U.S.386 (1989), the Supreme Court ruled that a police officer's use of force in a given situation (context) is to be judged by the "**objectively reasonable**" standard. In the language of the court this means: "In light of the facts and circumstances confronting the officer at that time, without regard to any potential underlying intent or motivation." Our subjective feelings, attitudes, experiences and point-of-view are not to be considered. When police officers reasonably feel they, or someone else, is threatened with death or great bodily harm, the law allows that officer to use deadly force. The fact that the weapon was actually a non-

[5] U.S. Supreme Court Graham v. Connor, 490 U.S. 386 (1989) Graham v. Connor No. 87–6571 Argued February 21, 1989 490 U.S. 386. Established the objectively reasonable standard for police use of force.

lethal BB gun is irrelevant under the law. The police subculture or administrative policy may even punish an officer in such a situation for not doing so (Solar, 2016).

Subjective information is based on personal opinions, interpretations, points of view, emotions and judgment, whereas objective information or analysis is fact-based, measurable and observable. As an example, the Police Executive Research Forum's proportionality principle ignores fundamental aspects of the law and the police subculture. This new standard ignores the objective perspectives of the officer. The implication is that a cop faced with an imminent threat must now consider the subjective viewpoint of an unspecified general public asking themselves the question "How would my use of force actions in this case be viewed by the public?" In at least one instance, this push towards this "proportionality" standard resulted in a cop hesitating and second-guessing how to act in a life-threatening situation resulting in severe injury to the officer (ABC News, 2016).

> Should the police constrain their actions to what is acceptable to the general population? Why or why not?

Some argue that the police should "conform their uses of force, especially deadly force, with our wishes" (Couper, 2016). The incident about which Couper writes involved the arrest of a violently resisting black teenager. It was a shocking example of police using force in a way that complies with policy but that constitutes what has become known as a "lawful but awful" use of force; but here's the rub: individuals' wishes are **subjective**, based upon personal opinions, interpretations, points of view, emotions, and judgment. The police officer with a duty to arrest a belligerent and dangerous citizen is likely to have a different point of view. Others' points of view are worth considering, too—the officer's wife, friends, co-workers, and parents, to name a few. How about the crime victim? It is unlikely that a consensus would arise among the many stakeholders as to the proportionality of the use of force in this case. This raises a new question, whose subjective point-of-view takes precedence? The only fair, just, and reasonable, standard rests with the legal and objective reasoning of *Graham v. Connor*. However, other points of view are important to consider in light of the police community relationship.

"You need laws to survive and you need law enforcement to have an intelligent, peaceful society; but we have to live in these places and suffer the type of conditions that exist from (police) officers who lack understanding and who lack any human feeling, or lack any feeling for their fellow human being . . ."

—Malcom X (Breitman, 1965)

The above quote from Malcom X provides insight for the modern police officer committed to improving police community relations. Even the most radical and antagonistic proponents of social justice recognize the need for law enforcement. At the same time, there is a pressing need for the police to be sensitive, sympathetic and even possess the ability to empathize with the subjective viewpoints of those who are most impacted by police action, or lack thereof.

THE POLICE SUBCULTURE

Culture is the way of life shared by members of a society. It includes language, values, symbolic meanings, technology, and material objects (Crank, 2015). Policing has a unique sub-culture characterized with symbols that include the uniform, badge, gun, and squad car as well as the unique language (such as, coded communications, acronyms, euphemisms) that are rarely understood by those outside of the police subculture. Organizational arrangements, such as rank, specialized positions and status indicators, are also powerful symbols of the "cop" culture as well as the stories characterizing what is really means to be a "cop's cop." These stories are passed from officer to officer and teach young recruits how they are expected to respond, creating a sense of lore and engraining core police values.

> Do you identify with a unique cultural identity with its own symbols, language and values? Examples may include student, employee of a specific enterprise, boy scout or girl scout. How does this unique identity impact your perceptions of other individuals and cultures?

Any effort to change the police should recognize the profound influences of the **police subculture**, which is much more powerful than the law, ethical guidelines, training, discipline and even leadership. An important element of the police subculture is the need to maintain a façade of strength, independence, and invincibility. These characteristics are reinforced through socialization that begins when a police recruit receives their badge (Crank, 2015). The recruits' new roles as authority figures transform them, and they immediately begin looking for affirmation, acceptance, and role models. Popular culture supports a view of the police that is consistent with these general attributes of strength, independence, and invincibility. Recruits and veteran officers alike can find themselves at the center of a highly charged political environment that views behaviors associated with these attributes as racist, unfair and unjust.

Is this unique culture of the police a good thing or a bad thing? Discuss.

Deeply embedded in the police subculture is the idea that effective cops control their assigned territories. This idea takes the form of a moral imperative in the socialization of a police officer: cops do what they must to control their turf in face-to-face encounters with the public. This typically results in using more force than necessary in any given situation (i.e., if the suspect uses his fists, the cop uses his or her baton; if the suspect uses a knife, the cop uses a gun). The idea is to minimize potential resistance through the use of overwhelming force (Crank, 2015).

"Bumper" Morgan, The Blue Knight*

Socialization into this cultural aspect of policing takes the form of locker-room stories shared and repeated by veteran cops. These stories become part of the police ethos and establishment. The militarization of the police speaks to this cultural aspect; again, the cultural belief is that overt display of overwhelming force is useful in minimizing resistance. To the cop, it is "their" territory and "it exists to be controlled. To do less is to fail utterly" (Crank, 2015).

* By CBS Television Public Domain, https://commons.wikimedia.org/w/index.php?curid=18227554.

"The overt display of overwhelming force is useful in minimizing resistance." Do you agree or disagree?

In the heart of every cop is a unique sense of morality, existing in varying degrees in individual officers, but always present. One of the most common reasons police applicants give for wanting to join the profession is to help others, but this altruistic tendency evolves with time on the job. To the experienced police officer, "helping" others comes to mean holding them accountable for their unacceptable behavior. Cop culture endures in large part because cops start out with a common residue of moral values that are strengthened by the police subculture. They take the form of shared occupational experiences that help define the craft and unify its members. This "*us vs them*" ethos is not suitable for everyone, but these unique and shared experiences unify cops with a common perception of doing right by their fellow cops. Assigned to a territory for which they are responsible, they take on a shared and powerful vision of justice (Crank, 2015).

A shared sense of morality is built upon **territorial control**. To not exert complete and total control of the physical wellbeing of their territory is to fail as a police officer. Maintaining territorial control justifies the use of what can easily be perceived as excessive force—defined as a level of force in excess of that which would be considered reasonable under the *Graham v. Connor* standard and also referred to as "street justice." The use of excessive force is morally justified by the police subculture due to its deterrent effect in maintaining territorial control. From the viewpoint of the police subculture, to raise the standard for police use of force to a level greater than the objective reasonableness standard of *Graham v. Connor,* a standard that has been vaguely defined as "proportional," is to completely ignore the deterrent effect of "street justice" (Crank, 2015).

The police exist as a means to protect communities from the menacing aspects of an increasingly violent society. A quest for peace through peaceful means is at the very heart of the United States democratic tradition. Nonetheless, the police are given the authority to use force when the need arises. This presents a profound dilemma: how can the public ever judge the use of force by police as acceptable when the activity itself is morally unacceptable? The legal system has established strict guidelines, based on reason, where police uses of force are to be consistently reactive. It is the actions of citizens reasonably categorized as a danger to others, a danger to the police officer, or any action that is resistive to an arrest that legally authorizes the police to use force. The U.S. legal system then charges the police themselves with enforcing these rules. The courts have no direct concerns unless and until offended citizens seek redress (Bitner, 1970).

Prior to the development of technology that allows easy recording of police-citizen interactions, the use of force was a behind-the-scenes phenomenon only visible to individuals who are impacted by it directly, in stories told by others, in newspaper accounts, and in entertainment media. Our collective ignorance and general acceptance of violent police behavior ended in 1992 with the video recording of the Rodney King beating. This incident initiated a change in thinking about the police and how they should interact with the public, especially in use of force situations.

Police are the one-stop-shop for settling many disputes between citizens, particularly when one feels that an authoritarian or coercive presence is needed. Consider the teacher who does not know how to deal with an out-of-control child, a citizen who is offended by the neighbor's inoperable, junk vehicle, or a community that is bothered by the young people who hang-out on the corner drinking, smoking, making inappropriate comments, and being generally intimidating. "Calling the cops" means making use of the capacity and authority to overpower resistance to achieve a desired objective (Bitner, 1970).

Perhaps nowhere is this more profound than in the case of how to deal with the mentally ill. Mentally ill persons live quiet and unobtrusive lives but are perceived as to occasionally constitute a serious hazard to themselves and others. Why do those with superior knowledge and skill, when compared to the police, in areas such as psychiatry, social work and education call the cops when interactions do not go as planned? Because, as Bittner puts it, "on the periphery of the rationally ordered procedures of medical and social work practice lurk exigencies that call for the exercise of coercion" (Bitner, 1970, p. 43). There is a need for intervention that cannot be resisted because there lies a possibility, however remote, that to not intervene forcefully would result in great harm.

Society asks that cops deal with its most profound social problems by using whatever force is necessary to shelter citizens from the criminal and the uncivilized (Bitner, 1970), yet the public complains when the police do exactly what they are asked to do. Even cases of perfectly justified use of force are now questioned because "they just look bad" (Couper, 2016). Up to this point, society reconciled the offensive nature of routine violence on the part of the police by concealing what the police do (Bitner, 1970). The existence of video recording and online sharing technology makes this no longer possible.

> Social Justice is a type of justice that relates to the distribution of wealth, opportunity, and privilege within a society.

To a police officer who feels compelled to employ force while engaging with an individual the question is not one of social justice but rather criminal justice. Those who resist the authority of the police are challenging the established rule of law and need to be corrected. It is the behavior, not the race, age, gender, sexual orientation, religious affiliation, or national origin that matters in the police subculture. The societal problem (i.e., a social justice issue) stems from the fact that there are cultural differences related to race, age, gender, religion, national origin that conflict with those of the police:

> The use of force is not a philosophical issue for the policeman. It is not a question of would or whether, but of when and how much. Therefore, the amount of force a policeman uses does not depend solely on himself but also on the character of the people he polices and the politics of his department (Bittner as cited in Crank, 2004, p. 97).

This is not to say, however, that the decision to use force (and how much force to use) has nothing to do with the individual characteristics of the resisting subject. It certainly does, but not in a manner the public may assume. The decision is often based on the officers own **"objective" bias**, which is a product of traditional police subculture. Imagine two separate groups of "suspicious" looking young men gathered on an inner-city street corner in a high crime neighborhood. The responding police officer has very limited information based on a dispatch record or his or her own observations. The officer must rely on stereotypes and even personal prejudice, based on their past experience, as tools of survival. One image is a group of males dressed in neat slacks and polo shirts standing next to a late model BMW looking like they are lost. The other image is of a group, on the same street corner, dressed in dirty blue jeans and hoodies, wearing ball caps on backwards and making aggressive/obscene gestures. When encountering these two situations, the police officer's behavior and perception, which impacts their decision to use force, are likely very different.

The question is why? Notice that race is not a factor here, but the reader's own implicit bias might have kicked-in when picturing each of these scenes in the mind. When one adds in the cultural socialization that occurs with a police officer one is better equipped to relate to the police subculture and the idea of *objective bias*, that being a bias that is not merely the product of one's personal experiences, attitudes and point-of-view.

Objective bias refers to stereo-typical attitudes or even prejudice that is based upon actual experience or empirical data.

Danger is a constant companion in policing, but according to Kappler (1993) law enforcement is not a particularly dangerous occupation. Some dismiss danger as something that is overblown by the police themselves. To truly understand the element of danger within the police subculture one must experience it for oneself. One can begin to understand the police subculture by simply requesting a ride-along with a local police department. During a ride-along, a citizen can note how the behavior of people changes as they observe police driving slowly down a residential street or watch the reaction of bystanders as the squad car approaches a disturbance.

One might experience the apprehension, uncertainty, and fear that cops live with every day. The same people cops are sent to protect might also have negative views of police officers, further adding to these feelings. Simply being affiliated or associated with a cop in these brief moments may make one aware of the animosity the animosity that is directed at the police regularly.

The uncertain nature of police work heightens the feelings of danger and fear in the police subculture. There have been rare but widely publicized cases of people actively seeking to injure, fight, or kill police officers for no other reason that the authority that the police represent. Current knowledge and training capacities make it difficult for police to determine who is actually a danger so police often rely on objective bias to gain some measure of personal security when dealing with the multitude of ambiguous situations and unknowable individual motivations. It is a way for the cop to control his or her own fear of the unknown:

> Police officers, because their work requires them to be occupied continually with potential violence, develop a perceptual shorthand to identify certain kinds of people as **symbolic assailants**, that is, as persons who use gesture, language and attire that the police have come to recognize as a prelude to violence (Skolnik, 2011).

The original examples of the characteristics of *"symbolic assailants"* from Skolnick's first edition, published in 1965, include "a youth dressed in a black leather jacket and motorcycle boots." Today the clothing has changed but not the behavior as described by Skolnick: "A young man may suggest the threat of violence to the police by his manner of walking or 'strutting,' the insolence in the demeanor being registered by the police as a possible preamble to later attack" (Skolnick, 2011, p. 43).

> What kinds of clothing and behaviors displayed by others make you apprehensive or even fearful? Why?

Because police officers have been cast in such a negative light, police now experience profoundly disrespectful treatment in some areas. As a result, police perceive many citizens as symbolic assailants. There is little comfort in the knowledge that the truly dangerous—those who will actually kill an officer if they get the chance—rarely communicate the threat openly, like the symbolic assailant. The truly dangerous will be the quiet ones; the symbolic assailant, on the other hand, may attack or resist but will merely be showing-off for his or her friends. If the symbolic assailant happens to badly injure or kill an officer, the result is usually the result of luck or accident.

The common theme of danger is a tremendously powerful cultural element, a stimulus for cultural identity (Van Maanen, 1973). Through training and socialization, danger—and the fear strongly linked to it—is controlled for by the use of force. **Force is not an analytical construct for cops—it is a way to deal with fear.** The police socialization process weeds out those who are unable or unwilling to use force. Rookie cops, who are hesitant in the use of force, are viewed as a danger to themselves and others who work with them. If they make it through probation they will soon find themselves isolated from their fellow cops. This makes the use of force a powerful stimulus for socialization and acceptance into the police subculture. Crank (2004) notes that officers who use as much force as they can get away with, as opposed to what is reasonably necessary, are described as a "cop's cop" in traditional police subculture (p. 106).

In the context of racial disparities in police contacts, the concept of the symbolic assailant gains strength:

> The patrolman believes with considerable justification that teenagers, Negros, and lower income persons commit a disproportionate share of all reported crimes; being in those population categories at all makes one, statistically, more suspect than other persons but to be in those categories and to behave unconventionally is to make oneself a prime suspect (Wilson, 1968).

When suspect descriptions are broadcasted over a police scanner to units in an urban area, the suspects are often described as being in the ages of 14 to 20. More often than not, a racial description of black or Hispanic is also included. These descriptions are merely relayed by the dispatch center based on caller, victim, and witness descriptions. They are not a product of police bias. Consider a black teenager who engages in what Wilson refers to as "unconventional" behavior. This reflects Skolnick's "insolence in behavior" and translates into hostile, disrespectful, antagonistic, and even threatening behavior directed at the police. Such behavior makes them prime targets for police attention. This is what can be considered objective bias on the part of the police. It is not based primarily on race, as there are actually many young male whites who behave in a hostile, disrespectful, antagonistic, and threatening manner toward the police and are equally viewed as symbolic assailants. Given the context of the police subculture it is not reasonable to fault the police for bias that is a product of their socialization, training, experiences, and available information; police are merely responding to the conditions and situations that they face, just as any rational human being would.

However, there are also many who do not display the "insolence in behavior" that is characteristic of the symbolic assailant. Treating them as such reflects *subjective bias* on the part of a police officer. Intentional acts that are a product of subjective bias, i.e., behavior that rises to the level of "**objectively offensive**," should be condemned for it is this kind of behavior that undermines public trust and police legitimacy.

> Subjective bias is prejudice based on one's personal point-of-view, opinion and attitude. It comes with a tendency to group people into categories based upon their characteristics such as race, religion, national origin, age or gender. This is the foundation for racism.

> Racism is a belief that race is the primary determinant of human traits and capacities and that racial differences produce an inherent superiority of a particular race. www.merriam-webster.com/
>
> The belief that all members of each race possess characteristics or abilities specific to that race, especially so as to distinguish it as superior or inferior to another race or races. en.oxforddictionaries.com

The victims of **historic marginalization**, predominantly African Americans, also have a right to their own sense of objective bias regarding the police. Cops routinely display what can easily be interpreted as "insolence of behavior" with regard to citizens. This manifestation of what Skolnick calls the symbolic assailant can also be applied to the police themselves, when viewed through the perspective of a black, male teenager in communities traditionally experiencing poor police-community relations. Given these experiences and the unique cultural attributes of ghetto life, it is also not reasonable to fault them for this bias as it too is a product of their socialization. A compassionate, cooperative, and service-oriented police department has the capacity to recognize their own biases as well as the lens through which their constituents view them.

The legacy of the professional reforms places a high value on efficiency. To the police officer, working and living within the police sub-culture, coercion and force are the most efficient means of gaining compliance and maintaining order. To take this further, the concept of efficiency is likely to encourage a professionally minded police officer to use as much force as they can get away with, as opposed to what is objectively reasonable. Why? Because doing so will have a **deterrent effect** on those who seek to challenge the authority of the police. This is what the author refers to as the *dark side* of the police sub-culture.

NO JUSTICE NO PEACE

Protestors demonstrating against the use of force by police*

> In the wake of the very rare but dramatically publicized killings of unarmed men by police we hear protestors chant "No justice, no peace." What, exactly, do they mean?

It could be meant as a threat, as it most often is, the threat being that if there is a lack of justice, in the eyes of protestors, then they will attack. In the wake of the Michael Brown killing in Ferguson Missouri protestors were unwilling to allow the investigation to run its course, instead they took to the streets chanting in a highly charged emotional environment.

A former Congressman writing in the Washington Times interpreted this chant as a threat, stating:

> *Instead of waiting out the investigation, they're chanting, "No justice; No peace!" as a politically correct slogan that actually means, "We want revenge!" That attitude makes bad things become worse.*

---

* Image labeled for unrestricted use.

> *"No justice; No peace!" isn't simply a slogan; it's actually a threat . . . that will be extracted against anyone who doesn't bow to the protestors' demands.*[6]

A threat to engage in violence strikes at the essence of what the police exist to prevent. Yet, in this case it is actually the behavior of the police, the killing of Michael Brown, that is perceived as the injustice that provoked the threat leaving the police throughout the nation in an untenable crisis with regard to police community relations. The mission of the police is to maintain law and order, the peace that is being breached as the result of perceived injustice. The fact is that justice, in any objective sense, can never exist without peace. The police exist to provide the very condition that enables justice to emerge. Any initiative aimed at furthering social justice, however that is defined, needs a peaceful, thoughtful and rational setting to grow and develop. That is why the police are needed, to provide the peace so that rational minds can prevail and build a better sense of justice.

> *There can be no justice without peace and there can be no peace without justice.*
>
> —*Martin Luther King Jr.*

The chant "No Justice No Peace!" presents a fundamental conflict for our society. Without the rule of law enforced by the police justice erodes. Yet the very actions of the police to maintain law and order are viewed as unjust and illegitimate by emerging actors on a mission to bring about radical change. How can the police manage this conflict?

Chapter Summary

Enlightened thinkers such as Rousseau, Locke and Hobbes provided lengthy works on what is now referred to as the *social contract,* the idea that all members of society agree and surrender certain natural rights to the government in return for security. In order to provide that security, the government is invested with limited powers, such as the use of force and coercion to maintain social stability and protect the individual interests of societal members. Individuals, in turn, give up the right to use physical force in their own defense and in their efforts to secure the necessities for survival. The government, finally, is expected to provide an effective system for regulating conduct and to create forums for resolving conflict.

The term "state of nature" refers to the hypothetical conditions experienced by people before societies came into existence. In such a hypothetical condition, all people would have been subject to what is observable in nature, to natural conditions such as the supremacy of the physically and mentally strong and the subjugation of the weak. Conversely, Rousseau believed that the nobility of the

---

6 http://bigthink.com/praxis/what-does-no-justice-no-peace-really-mean.

state of nature was corrupted by the unnatural limitations of civilization. He believed in the nobility of the state of nature and that man, free from the unjust societal institutions, would pursue the social good as the highest virtue.

The police exist to provide a sense of security. The idea that people may go about their normal lives without fear of being attacked, without fear of having their property taken from them, and, in the Unites States, the ability to enjoy constitutionally protected rights from governmental intervention has been a fundamental characteristic of American life since the colonial period.

At the heart of the policing function is the capacity to use force and coercion, albeit as a last resort, to fulfill this basic mission. Civilized society in the United States, and in the western world generally, has rejected the idea of individuals using force with the exception of self-defense and has legitimized the use of repressive force by the police out of necessity.

Problems arise in the police community relationship when the actions of the police are not generally viewed as fair, just or reasonable. Perception is not the actual sensory input we receive from our eyes, ears, hands, etc. It is the process of creating meaning from those sensory inputs. Police officers can generate anxiety through their mere presence and the wise police officer understands how to mitigate, or enhance this affect. The best cops know how to manipulate emotion to their own advantage and emotion is often based on perception. The problem is that what is in the advantage of a typical police officer may not be conducive to great police community relationships; they may, in fact, cause conflict.

The police function is in a world governed by the law; the law in-turn is governed by the world of fact and objective reason. Subjective information is based on personal opinions, interpretations, points of view, emotions and judgment, whereas objective information or analysis is fact-based, measurable and observable.

Culture is the way of life shared by members of a society. It includes language, values, symbolic meanings, technology, and material objects. Policing has a unique sub-culture characterized with symbols that include the uniform, badge, gun, and squad car as well as the unique language (such as, coded communications, acronyms, euphemisms) that are rarely understood by those outside of the police subculture. Deeply embedded in the police subculture is the idea that effective cops control their assigned territories. This idea takes the form of a moral imperative in the socialization of a police officer: cops do what they must to control their turf in face-to-face encounters with the public. A shared sense of morality is built upon territorial control. To not exert complete and total control of the physical wellbeing of their territory is to fail as a police officer. Maintaining territorial control justifies the use of what can easily be perceived as excessive force.

The chant "No Justice No Peace!" presents a fundamental conflict for our society. The mission of the police is to maintain law and order and the rule of law, without which justice erodes. Yet the very action of the police to maintain law and order are viewed as unjust and illegitimate by emerging actors on a mission to bring about radical change. How can the police manage this conflict?

Bibliography

ABC News. (2016, October). Chicago Police Officer Says She Feared Using Gun While Being Beaten. *http://abc7chicago.com/news/chicago-cop-says-she-feared-using-gun-while-being-beaten/1543015/*.

Bitner, E. (1970). *The Functions of the Police in Modern Society as cited in Crank 2004*. Washington, DC: National Institute of Mental Health.

Breitman, G. (1965). *Malcom X Speaks*. New York: Grove Press.

Brogan, D. (2016, June). "It Looks Like Excessive Force Was Used". *Isthmus*.

Clark, D. (1998). The Many Meanings of the Rule of Law. In J. Kanishka, *Law, Capitalism and Power in Asia*. New York: Routledge.

Couper, D. (2016, August). A Different Way to Look at the Genele Laird Incident. *The CAP Times, Madison Wisconsin*.

Crank, J.P. (2015). *Understanding Police Culture*. Routledge.

Dobbin, F.K. (2016, July). Why Diversity Programs Fail. *Harvard Business Review*, 52–60.

FBI, Office of Partner Engagement. (2017). *The Assailant Study—Mindsets and Behaviors*. Washington, DC: Federal Bureau of Investigation.

Final Report of the President's Task Force on 21st Century Policing. (2015). *President's Task Force on 21st Century Policing*. Washington, DC: Office of Community Oriented Policing Services.

Gaines, L., Kappeler, V. (2011). *Policing in America, 7th ed.* Waltham, MA: Anderson.

Hunter, R.D. (2011). *Police Community Relations and the Administration of Justice, 8th ed.* Saddle River, NJ: Pearson.

Leibowitz, M. (2016, June). Forced Diversity Training Backfires, Claims Harvard Study. *Fox News U.S.*

Locke, J. (1680). *Two Treatises on Government.*

Loftus, E. (1996). *Eyewitness Testimony*. Cambridge: Harvard University Press.

Martin, J. (2014, December). Policing Is a Dirty Job, But Nobody's Gotta Do It. 6 Ideas for a Cop Free World. *Rolling Stone.*

Putnam, R.D. (2007, June). E Pluribus Unum: Diversity and Community in the Twenty-First Century. *Scandinavian Political Studies, 30(2)*, 137–299.

Roy, J.S. (2016, October 1). What Is the Ferguson Effect? *US Daily Review.*

Skolnik, J.H. (2011). *Justice Without Trial: Law Enforcement in Democratic Society*. New Orleans: Quid Pro Books.

Solar, P. (2016). Police Culture and the Use of Force. *Academy of Criminal Justice Sciences-Police Forum*, 9–18.

Wilson, J.Q. (1968). *Varieties of Police Behavior.* Cambridge: Harvard University Press.

Wilson, J.Q. (2007, October). Bowling with Others. *Culture & Civilization, Commentary Magazine.*

Zalman, M.S. (1999). Psychology of Perception, Eyewitness Identification, and the Lineup. In S.A. D'Alessio, *Criminal Courts for the 21st Century*. Upper Saddle River, NJ: Prentice Hall.

CHAPTER 2

The History of the Police Function

■ ■ ■

It is difficult to judge where we are if we know nothing about where we have been. This chapter provides an overview of the various eras of policing history as well as thoughts on what drove change, e.g., conflict.

Early police officers*

Learning Outcomes

Upon successful completion of this chapter the student will be able to:

- Identify the various eras of policing and what drove change.
- Understand the historical significance of the treatment of marginalized groups by the police.
- Describe the concept of justice and identify the conflicting perspectives, i.e., Social Justice vs. Criminal justice.

---

* Courtesy https://pxhere.com.

- Describe the *Graham v. Connor* legal standard for the police use of force.
- Describe the characteristics of the police subculture.

Important Concepts

- Hue and Cry
- Justice of the Peace
- Homogeneous vs. Heterogeneous
- Sir Robert Peel
- Dark Side of Policing
- Marginalized Group
- Progressivism
- Professionalism
- Exchange Relationship
- Legal Traditions

Questions for Discussion

- What is the historical difference between our American culture and the English culture? Are Americans more or less willing to accept governmental authority than the English? How does this impact the role of the police?
- Describe a few of the common attributes of the American police sub-culture.
- Discuss the legal standard for the use of force and speculate as to how that would place the police in conflict with particular groups and types of individuals.
- What is Community Oriented Policing and how does it compare to the professional policing model. Is the community oriented policing movement a throwback to the political era? Why or why not?
- Why are traditional measures, like crime rates, a poor measure of policing effectiveness? Speculate on better ways to measure policing effectiveness.

INTRODUCTION

This chapter discusses how the police have developed over time, the origins of basic concepts such as crime prevention, authority as vested in the police, professionalism and discretion. Police today confront a demand that they employ a "new" reform known as community oriented policing. This concept holds promise, in theory, for improving police community relations but there is a trade-off with regard to the fundamental mission of the police, that being the control of crime and disorder.

Conflicting views of justice have created new levels of ambiguity for the police function. Traditional measures of police effectiveness, such as crime and arrest rates, have come under fire and are often cited as the harbingers of injustice in our diverse society. Community oriented policing itself has been attacked as an excuse to perpetuate classic, unjust, and biased practices against poor people, leading to what may become a new reform effort, humanistic policing.

THE BASIC MISSION OF THE POLICE

The police are needed to maintain a civilized society. Their basic mission is to ensure safety: to protect citizens from harm when they cannot do this themselves or when members agree to give-up their right to do so as part of the *social contract.* What would life be like without the police? According to Thomas Hobbes (1651) in *Leviathan:*

> Hereby it is manifest, that during the time men live without a common power to keep them all in awe, they are in that condition which is called war . . . where every man is enemy to every man . . . in such condition, there is no place for industry: because the fruit thereof is uncertain: and consequently no agriculture . . . no society; and which is worst of all, continual fear, and danger of violent death; and the life of man, solitary, poor, nasty, brutish, and short (Hobbes, 1651).

In these words Hobbes paints an explicit picture of life without some mechanism to serve as a check against the basic nature of mankind, what is commonly referred to as the *state of nature*[1] where the strong prey upon the weak. He also states the societal implications: without a restraining force there can be no industry or agriculture in organized society, leaving man to live in a continual state of fear.

---

[1] The state of nature generally refers to the real or hypothetical condition of human beings before or without political association. In the political realm, the term refers to the absence of state sovereignty.

From this we can discern the basic mission of the police: **to control fear**. When people believe that they are relatively safe from crime, their quality of life will be enhanced allowing them to pursue "Happiness" as Jefferson put it. In such an environment agriculture, industry, and economic development can thrive leading to a higher standard of living for all those who choose to participate.

Early Beginnings, the Power of Coercive Social Control

In order to instill a basic sense of security, the predecessors of what became known as the police established a system by which people looked out for each other. The concept of "kin police" was one of the first policing models that had, "I am my brother's keeper," as its underlying philosophy. Form this philosophy grew the concept of the "communitarian" or community-based police system (Reith, 1956). This community-based system was formalized by the Normans into what was called the English frankpledge system where every male was charged with the responsibility of "keeping watch." A group of nine such citizens was referred to as a tything and these individuals, known as watchmen, were sworn to apprehend anyone who committed a crime. They were also charged with the responsibility of reporting and dealing with any problems that they might encounter such as fires, floods and other threats to persons and property. The protection of one's fellow citizens was considered a collective societal obligation, a failure to do so being considered a failure to perform one's duty to one's fellow citizens.

> What do you see as the weakness of this early non-professional police function? Does it have any appeal over todays "professional" policing practices?

Here we see the beginnings of a policing culture in that an unanticipated duty was also owed to one's fellow watchmen because if any one member failed or neglected their duty *all members* of the watch group were severely fined. Clearly, this practice created the inclination that one owed a duty to their fellow watchman as well as to the community generally. The idea that the watchman role was somehow special began to emerge in the twelfth century (Klockars, 1985). The conflict here can be defined in terms of the competing loyalties that were created by the incentive to not fail in one's duty to one's fellow watchmen as opposed to one's duty to the community generally.

Ten groups of nine watchmen were organized into a hundred and each hundred was directed by a constable, the first police official who had responsibility above that of the mere watchman. In the same way we view county law enforcement today, the hundreds were grouped in to a shire and the shire was headed by a shire reeve giving us the original organizational concept, the office of the sheriff that was eventually adopted in the United States.

Old English sheriff*

The typical watchman was not a professional; this was originally an unpaid but obligatory duty consisting of wandering the streets of the town late at night. Watchmen worked at their craft or out in the fields every day and likely found it difficult to focus their attention, in the same way that moonlighting cops experience fatigue today. They may have even found a quiet corner somewhere to grab some sleep, a practice that is not unheard of even today on midnight shift.

The voluntary and unpaid frankpledge system deteriorated in the 13th century and more power was shifted into the hands of the local parish constable. The death of this original form of community policing where every man had the obligation to serve can be attributed to basic incentives and disincentives. If one were a wealthy individual with influence, participating in the menial duties of the night watch was not likely viewed as fitting for one's advanced societal position. Wouldn't one's time be better spent at rest so that they could arise early in the morning and head off to their commercial enterprise, which, after all, is of much more benefit to the whole community? Individuals of means would pay others to perform their night watch duty, the unpleasant task now serving as a source of

* Courtesy https://commons.wikimedia.org/wiki/File:Sheriff_of_Nottingham.PNG. Image labeled for unrestricted use.

income to those without means. Over time the obligatory nature of this function was relegated to those who could hardly be considered the "best and brightest."

Beggar*

As power shifted to the parish constable, watchmen were relegated to the most basic functions such as guarding the gates at night. If a serious disturbance occurred, the constable had the option of raising the *"hue and cry,"* an alarm summoning all males to provide aid, what we now call "back-up." Before the days of police radios, the hue and cry consisted of the beating of the baton on the pavement, the police whistle, or even discharging a firearm all of which were intended to summon aid for the constable.

> To raise the "hue and cry" was to shout-out danger with the intent of calling forth voluntary assistance to the watchman.

An addition to the early criminal justice system was the position of *justice of the peace*. The town constable and sheriff assisted the justice of the peace by supervising the night watch, serving warrants, and housing prisoners to be brought before the justice of the peace court (Uchida, 2015). It is interesting to note that the local justice of the peace was typically not a lawyer and they seldom had any legal training at all, even when this concept was brought to the United Sates. Under the English common law, to which we owe our legal traditions here in the U.S., the law was assumed to be commonly understood, in most cases it was not even written down. Everyone shared a common idea of what correct and

* Courtesy http://etc.usf.edu.

lawful behavior was. These **homogeneous** communities not only shared these common ideas, but there was consistency across shires (counties) and other political divisions, so no formal legal training was required for the justice of the peace to sit in judgement of his fellow citizens.

> The Justice of the Peace is a judicial officer, not at the level of an actual judge, elected or appointed by local government officials.

Policing Comes to the United States

The colonial period of early America was a time of **informal social control**. There were no formal criminal justice institutions and little need for a codified system of laws. If one was wronged they handled it themselves. This spirit of self-reliance was reinforced by a high level of sameness, *homogeneity* that existed among the early settlers. There was a firm consensus about proper conduct reinforced by a strong sense of community and a clear line of authority, first to God, then to the religious leaders or clergy, and then to the male head of the household (Walker S., Popular Justice, 1998). The central principle was that people needed each other and they banded together for security against the unknown horrors of the wilderness.

> Homogeneity is a state of being the same. Of a similar kind, of a uniform structure. Heterogeneity is a state of being dissimilar, diverse in characteristics and thought. www.merriam-webster.com/

Early American settler*

The main source of social interaction and social organization in those days was the church. The small rural towns were highly influenced by religious affiliation and nearly everyone belonged to the same congregation; those that did

* Courtesy https://www.nps.gov.

not were outsiders. These foundational values drove growth and development and eventually caused conflict such as between the Quakers of Pennsylvania and the Puritans of Massachusetts. These were moral conflicts that still resonate today.

Public shaming was the informal tool used to reinforce values and behavior standards. Public humiliation was the motivating force creating a powerful incentive for correct behavior in these collectivist communities. The formal mechanism of a criminal justice system was absent with the exception of a judge, commonly known as the justice of the peace in the larger communities. These community leaders possessed little or no knowledge of proper procedure, but they had legitimacy by virtue of their standing among their peers. They were trusted to dispense punishments that ranged from whipping to death. The necessity to do so, however, was rare due to social pressure to conform (Walker S., Popular Justice, 1998).

> What do you think is more effective in controlling behavior, the law or informal mechanisms such as group pressure and shaming? Why?

Institutionalizing the Policing Function

With the growth and development of the new world came the need for more formal institutions of justice. The colonies naturally looked to the English system for guidance and established similar early institutions. In rural counties a sheriff was appointed by the governor and charged with the duties of apprehending criminals, serving subpoenas, testifying in court and collecting taxes. Cities employed constables and adopted the same night watch system used in Great Britain, but invested watchmen with a broader array of tasks that included reporting fires, maintaining street lamps, and detaining suspected criminals as well as just watching.

The activities of all of these actors were reactive in nature. Something had to happen before a duty to intervene was created; they did not respond unless summoned by a victim or witness. They did not normally engage in preventative activity such as confronting individuals on the street, seeking out criminal perpetrators who avoided any observation or detection of their activity, and they certainly did not engage in any kind of innovative problem solving activities. A return to such a passive role for the police has been advocated by those who are concerned with the impact of **pro-active policing** on poor communities of color, claiming that any pro-active policing activity is simply undemocratic (Way, 2013).

Urban poor*

The fundamental mechanism of colonial social control was private justice, usually within a family setting. The expectation in this male dominated, patriarchal system was that the male head would control misbehavior, employing public shaming if necessary. The ultimate punishment was expelling those who simply would not conform. Undesirables, including vagrants, religious dissenters and lazy individuals were simply kicked-out and left to fend for themselves in the indifferent, cruel and dangerous wilderness. The colonial era stressed the importance of community out of necessity and this translated into a preference for order over individual liberty. People did not have a right to exist in the community, that privilege could be denied based on a demonstrated unwillingness to conform. In stark contrast to our modern values, colonial communities were not tolerant, liberal or inclusive. Individual rights are a modern concept, having their foundation as recently as the eighteenth century and their practical application only in the twentieth century (Walker S., 1998).

The reactive nature of the constable's role met a challenge in the form of the industrial revolution. People flocked to the cities for the promise of economic prosperity and this created a breakdown in social control in the form of crime, violence, riots, and even health problems that overwhelmed the constables and watchmen of that time. Society was migrating off the farms to the industrial centers and the result was fear and insecurity. The urban centers were not homogeneous as were the rural towns. America was a draw for all kinds of different peoples seeking opportunity for a better life. The established majority sought shelter from these different people who came here. They supported the development of formal laws and institutions that would keep "those" people in

* Courtesy https://en.wikipedia.org.

line and perpetuate the *status-quo*. The result was the growth of **ethnocentrism**,[2] what we now call racist laws and blatantly discriminatory practices. What was the underlying incentive for what we not recognize as unjust practices? Fear.

The "Status Quo" refers to existing power and status arrangements. Maintaining current practices over the pressure to change.

Early police officers*

THE EVOLUTION OF MODERN POLICING

In order to combat the escalating rate of crime in our urban centers, the idea of a preventative police force emerged. It was, and still is, thought that highly visible constables roaming the streets randomly would provide a visible **deterrence** to crime and disorder. This concept reflects the influence of basic economics as applied to human behavior in the form of incentives and disincentives. The police may appear at any moment so if an individual was intent on crime and disorder the availability of beat officers raises the risk of apprehension, creating a disincentive for crime. Of course one can never know how much crime is discouraged or prevented this way, but the whole idea seems to just make sense and is still widely employed today despite our inability to empirically prove the effectiveness of routine preventative patrol.[3] The idea that a criminal perpetrator, intent on committing a crime, who observes a police officer drive-by is not deterred from committing a crime just seems counterintuitive. In order to combat the increasing fear of crime through preventative means, Americans again turned toward Great Britain for a model.

---

2 Ethnocentrism is the belief in the inherent superiority of one's own ethnic group or culture. Someone holding ethnocentrist ideas tends to view the actions of others from their own point-of-view, judging behavior that does not conform to this viewpoint as wrong, evil and immoral. We now simply call this racism.

* Courtesy https://en.wikipedia.org.

3 The Kansas City Preventative patrol experiment found that traditional routine patrol in marked police vehicles does not appear to affect the level of crime or the publics' sense of security.

> What motivates you? Are there incentives for reading this book? If so, what are they? Conversely, are their costs, or disincentives, for taking the time to read this book? For example, is their competition for your time in this regard? If so, how do you make the choice?

Preventative Policing

The establishment of a uniformed police service in London did not sit well with those who were very suspicions of a uniformed force that put them in mind of a military occupation and a standing army. Individuals, such as philosopher **Jeremy Bentham**, advocated the creation of a preventative force claiming that it would be in the best interests of society and rising rates of crime and disorder seemed to prove the need to do something more than the constable-watchman system. The conflict over the risk of despotic governmental control and fear of crime was settled as the result of public pressure brought to bear due to the growing crime problem. The Metropolitan Police Act of 1829 was the result. This act established a full-time, uniformed police force whose primary purpose was patrolling the city and preventing crime.

The task of creating the first urban police force fell to **Sir Robert Peel** and his commissioners, Charles Rowan and Richard Mayne. From the start, Peel was concerned with the legitimacy of the new force. He understood that the new police had to act in a certain manner or the public would reject them. Toward that end, officers were dressed in an unassuming uniform, distinct from the military red color. Men were recruited who were even-tempered, reserved, restrained, and polite. He did not allow these officers to carry firearms.

London Bobbies*

The legitimacy of the London Metropolitan police was vested in their authority, which was grounded in the English constitution, an officer's behavior

* Courtesy https://www.flickr.com.

was to be governed by strict national standards and the *rule of law* (Uchida, 2015). Here we see the beginnings of police professionalism as standards were developed for the selection of officers and for the behavior of those officers.

With their status as representatives of government their allegiance was clearly defined, the first principle being that their behavior as public servants was to be governed by the rule of law. This creates confusion today as many policing scholars consider Peel to be the founder of community oriented policing and advocate that the officer's first duty should be to the needs of the community. The implication being that officers should be free to *innovate* and employ extra-legal[4] solutions to crime problems.

This is inconsistent with Peel's original intent that the legitimacy of the police be based upon their institutional authority, as opposed to the wishes of the people with their diversity of ideas and priorities. This makes the Peelian form of policing much less democratic and removed from local control when compared to the American system, a distinction lost on the advocates of community oriented policing who beg for a return to Peel's principles. *It is likely that Peel correctly assumed English citizens naturally accepted institutional authority, an assumption that did not then, or now, translate to America given its pluralistic society.*[5]

> Sir Robert Peel made it clear that the legitimacy of the police is based upon their institutional authority, not the wishes of the people. Peel's police were removed and insulated from local control.

In the United States the establishment of municipal police departments was in response to the same urbanization issues. Conflict between ethnic and racial groups were common in the major cities such as New York and Philadelphia where crime rates were drastically rising, and riots were common. The constable and night watch system were inadequate in dealing with the problems of a rapidly urbanizing and diverse population. The influx of different immigrant groups and the diversity of values that they brought threatened the status-quo; established citizens were fearful and demanded a better system of maintaining order.

Initially American cities looked to London for a model of how to set up a preventative policing system, but soon it became apparent, through political discourse, that America held a very different political/cultural perspective about the police than did Great Britain. The American culture saw any centralized national force as **a threat to liberty**, one could say that they were also paranoid

---

[4] The term "extra-legal" implies action that is beyond the authority of the law or not regulated by law.

[5] Pluralism refers to a state of society in which members of diverse ethnic, racial, religious or social groups maintain and develop their traditional culture or special interest within the confines of a common civilization. From Merriam-Webster. https://www.merriam-webster.com/dictionary/pluralism.

and fearful of the power of despotic regimes but with good reason. They had just thrown off the repressive yoke of English tyranny; investing such authority in a centralized police force was simply unthinkable.

> Americans are highly suspicious of centralized authority preferring local control of their police.

Even though Peel avoided the appearance of the police as that of the military, the new endeavor was organized along the military model with highly centralized command and control. As a result, political influence over the police in London was minimal with officers owing their allegiance to the central authority. The standards for police officer selection were also centralized as originally established by the Home Secretary. He wanted officers to fit a certain mold and to be trained according to strict guidelines targeting their preventative role, that being to provide a uniformed, continuous, highly visible presence throughout the community. Officers were also encouraged to think of their employment in the police service, not as a mere job, but as a lifelong professional career (Uchida, 2015, p. 17). This was very different from how the police emerged in the United States.

The strategy Peel pursued was intended to deter crime through a highly visible police presence. He organized the force along military lines that included a hieratical rank structure and an authoritarian chain of command. Clearly, the focus was on **command and control**, as opposed to community engagement and local responsiveness as is advocated for American policing today (Walker S., 1998). When one considers that the police officer, then and now, wields the power to deprive our citizens of their liberty, and even lives, such control mechanisms should be the very first consideration, and the primary emphasis, for police leaders.

The political culture in the United States was quite different. Suspicion of centralized authority[6] systems meant that the new police organizations that were cropping up very quickly in the late nineteenth century stressed **democratic responsiveness to local authority**. Police officers were appointed on the recommendation of various politically connected individuals where professional standards and personal character were much less important than local allegiances and political affiliations. Police officers were selected based on whom they knew or whose election campaign they supported rather than merit as defined by a central authority such as a state commission, as is the case today. Early police

[6] The term "American policing" is intended to describe policing in the United States and of the American policing culture. Countries other than the United States that occupy the American continent may employ policing systems that are very different than that of the United States of America.

officers owed their jobs to their **political patron** as opposed to their personal merit as defined by selection standards or civil service exams. Peel's idea of a police officer being even-tempered, restrained, polite and unassuming did not translate to America. Political actors of the time were more interested in the ability of "their" police to resolve conflict and put down dissent, in the most effective way possible, generally through the employment of certain, prompt and overwhelming force. Democratic reforms have crushed the power of the political boss, but the tradition of deterring dissent and unlawful behavior with the display, and sometime use, of overwhelming force is still with us in the form of the "warrior" cop.

> The Political era of policing stressed local control of the police through the influence of local political actors. In contrast, Peels Metropolitan police owed their allegiance to national "professional" standards.

In the absence of centralized authority as the legitimizing factor for the police as in London, police officers in the United States were on their own. As with respect, true legitimacy rests in the willingness of people to grant it. The effectiveness of force and coercion only gets one so far, as the American revolution demonstrated. Ultimately, a wise police officer, in either London or New York, understands that respect and legitimacy must be earned; it cannot be demanded as a condition of one's position or dictated by a central authority. This is why Peel insisted that his officers be even-tempered and unassuming. This served as a huge advantage for those officers, with a legacy that still resonates today.

In the United State, however, early officers could not rely on formal institutional power, they relied on themselves. They did not have a "back-up" in the form of institutional legitimacy, so each officer had to establish personal authority among the citizens that they policed. What made this even more difficult is that these citizens were, and still are, of very different viewpoints in terms of what they expect from the police, what is acceptable and not acceptable in terms of behavior, and how law violators are to be dealt with, i.e., rule of law or compassion.

A police officer could then, and now, earn the respect of the citizens and enjoy acceptance as a legitimate authority simply by becoming knowledgeable about these local standards and expectations and then crafting his or her *discretion* accordingly. Neighborhoods sometimes become attached to individual police officers and commanders making it difficult when organizational changes occur as is the case today when a publicly popular district commander is promoted and/or re-assigned. People in that community protest at the loss of "their" police commander.

If the basis of police legitimacy, trust and respect rests in the ability of police officers to understand the unique local standards and expectations, what might be the implications for police training? How do you train a police officer to build a foundation of respect and trust? We have known the answer for decades. *Training is not the answer, education is.* The virtue of a liberal arts education was first put forth in the 1967 President's Commission on law Enforcement and the Administration of Justice report.[7] More recently, Chief Theron Bowman of the Arlington, Texas, police department made a plea for educated police:

> "A college degree promotes a culture of constant learning, where change is accepted and managed, and where creativity in solving problems is sparked by exposure to diverse ideas and alternative explanations. As the nature and function of police work changes, adaptability, fostered by a culture of continuous learning, will become an essential need in the police profession. Education must be ongoing; and better policing a constant pursuit" (Bowman, 2006).

History tells us that what needs to be cultivated in police officers today, as it was in the early years, is **wisdom**. A thorough understanding of the limits of legal authority combined with the knowledge that in the United States legal authority is of little value when people do not respect the individual wielding it. That level of wisdom is a product of education, not just training.

> What is the difference between education and training? We can train a police officer on how to make an arrest, educated officers know when to arrest and when to employ alternatives to arrest based on sound judgement.

Another profound aspect of American law enforcement emerged during the nineteenth century. Because there was no central authority upon which to base the legitimacy of the police, as was the case in London, police activity varied with the wishes of local officials as did selection standards, training procedures, rules, policies and the underlying policing philosophy. This is still the case today, with the exception of statutory minimum basic standards for selection and training. More than 17,000 police agencies exist in the United States, each owning their existence and allegiance to a local governmental body. As a result, the basic

[7] It is nonsense to state or assume that the enforcement of the law is so simple that it can be done best by those unencumbered by the study of liberal arts. Police agencies need personnel in their ranks who have the characteristics which a college education seeks to foster; a capacity to relate the events of the day to the social, political, and historical context in which they occur. **President's Commission on Law Enforcement and the Administration of Justice. Task Force Report: The Police. Washington, DC: U.S. Government Printing Office, 1967.**

culture, norms of behavior and common understandings of one police agency at the local level can be very different in another police agency, even when they are neighbors sharing a common border. This diversity of policing standards and practices is not the case in most other nations, such as Great Britain and Canada, who adhere to a centralized and coordinated policing system.

A police officer of the political era*

The United States does not have a centralized police authority nor a National police force. The American culture stresses local control of government and this has been particularly important with regard to the police. The **uncoordinated and decentralized** nature of policing in the U.S. means that each and every Mayor of every incorporated town, village or special district may create their own police agency, answerable to that local authority and owing no allegiance to any other unit of government be it at the County, township, state or federal level. Cooperation between police agencies at the local level and between law enforcement agencies existing at different governmental levels is strictly voluntary. For example, the Federal Bureau of Investigation (FBI) has jurisdiction at the federal level only. Unless an incident has been classified as a federal crime or has recognized implications that cross state lines, the FBI has no authority to investigate nor apprehend perpetrators.

* Courtesy Library of Congress.

The Political Era—The Police as Agents of the "Status Quo"

The American police officer of the nineteenth century owed his allegiance to the political "**powers that be**;" in the urban centers that would be the ward-boss. New officers were handed a badge and sent out on patrol. They wore a standard uniform that they purchased themselves, and were armed, or not, depending upon if they owned a firearm. They received little training beyond advice provided by veteran officers and a rule-book but the wise officer soon learned that his survival on the street depended greatly on his ability to integrate with the citizens with whom he interacted. There was no effective supervision, communication, or back-up so these officers, working alone, depended upon the good-will of community members to assist them should the need arise. In contrast, the London constable was selected for his even-temper, politeness, and reserved, professional demeanor; and subjected to a rigorous training program and was properly equipped for the job. Even though they were armed with the legitimate power of accepted centralized authority, the need to cultivate good-will in the community was equally important to these officers as it was to their American counterpart.

Wise police officers of the political era quickly learned of the need to generate cooperation and good will out in the community. Why? Self-preservation.

The absence of professional standards for selection and training, the lack of quality supervision, and the need to cultivate strong ties with certain members of the community in order to retain the job took its toll on the reputation of the American police in the late nineteenth century. Opportunities for **graft and corruption** were abundant in America and the *dark side* of policing emerged as a dominant force. Subcultural pressures were strong not only for those new officers who wished to be accepted into the police subculture but also pressure to conform with even unlawful behavioral norms under the threat of being ostracized from the group were and still are powerful motivators in American policing. There were countless opportunities to extort money, protect unlawful enterprises, and peddle the power and authority of the police to the highest bidder. Not all officers were corrupt, but the freedom of the job and the lure of easy money provided them with powerful incentives.

The "dark-side" of policing refers to the impact of corrupting influences on officer behavior. Examples include, brutality, police crime, corruption and misconduct.

Political considerations played an important role as there was no centralized policing authority or mandates. Police officers were called upon to enforce laws that reflected the norms of the majority, leaving marginalized groups such as immigrant communities struggling for assimilation into a culture that they did not understand. These marginalized groups were the targets of enforcement action and in some cases police officers themselves were members of these minority communities making them particularly susceptible to bribes and other minor forms of corruption. Corruption and even extortion became traditions in some agencies rather than professionalism and discipline. Police officers were part of the political machinery, reinforcing the will of the dominant political actors as opposed to impartial criminal justice actors (Cox S. M., 2017).

A "Marginalized" group is any group that is relegated to a lower status within society.

The 19th century American nation had a sad history of conflict between the police and minority community members. At one point, laws were in-place that made racial discrimination legal and it was the police who were charged with enforcing those laws. The police were also used to apprehend run-a-way slaves, restrict access to "whites only" public facilities, and to provide a sometimes frightening deterring presence aimed at keeping "those people" in line. As objectionable as we now find these practices, police officers were legally obligated to enforce them, some police officers doing so with pleasure because they approved. The police subculture has been slow to change and, because of its importance to the police community relationship, an entire chapter will be devoted to this ongoing source of conflict (Cox S. M., 2017).

In an era dominated by the legal marginalization and enslavement of Blacks, i.e., the Jim Crow South, the police had a duty to return run-away slaves and to enforce segregation, it was not a choice that the police made.

The social welfare role of the police during the political era provided the means by which certain individuals and groups were able to corrupt the political process. These social services included electioneering, rounding up loyal voters and harassing opponents. Walker also points out that the police enforced the narrow prejudices of their constituents and harassed "undesirables," discouraging any kind of unwelcome behavior (Walker S., 2015). The implications are clear for marginalized groups in that the "good ole days" were not so good.

Many of those intent on reforming the police today, under the banner of Community Oriented Policing, advocate for the same local control that led to some of the worst examples of governmental corruption, graft and abuse. They attack the professional model of policing as the enemy of the kind of policing promoted by Peel, but the two policing models are not incompatible; they can be integrated and made complimentary.

At the heart of efforts to raise the police above the arbitrary whims of politics and political considerations is the issue of accountability. Controlling the police was a driving force for the need to change yet controlling the police in a democratic society is an elusive enterprise. Those who led the effort to reform the political era sought means by which the police could be made more accountable to the concerns of citizens that they are employed to serve rather than the interests of politicians and the rich and powerful.

> The political era of policing resulted in a vision of the police as amateurish, incompetent, brutish, and corrupt. An overall need to "professionalize" government generally, known as the Progressive movement, provided a window of opportunity to reform the police along the same lines.

Reform Era—The Emergence of Professional Policing

In the late nineteenth century, good government advocates began a reform effort driven by progressive ideas of **professionalism** in policing as well as in government administration generally. These progressives of that era began a push toward the kind of policing Peel advocated, professional as opposed to the amateurish practices then in existence. Principles such as centralization of authority, merit-based selection, uniform training standards and an overall narrowing of the police function were advocated as necessary steps to professionalize the police. The era's progressives advocated for a power shift away from political actors and into the hands of trained and educated administrators, and removing politics from the day-to-day decision-making, deployment and enforcement practices. They sought legislation that required merit based civil service exams to weed out those who owed allegiance to political patrons as opposed to professional standards, police commissions were to serve as independent promotional and disciplinary bodies, but, most importantly, they attempted to redefine the role of policing in a way that divorced policing from the sources of corruption. The focus was to establish the police as an autonomous crime fighting entity without ties to political groups or powerful political actors. *This reform era sought to divest the police from their social service orientation and focus the attention solely on crime prevention and crime fighting.*

The reformers of the late twentieth century advocated for a police service governed by professional standards for selection, training, and management that took control away from local political actors. The reform agenda included:

- Defining policing as a profession
- Eliminating political influence from policing

- Appointing qualified chief executives (City Managers and professionally trained police chiefs)
- Raising personnel standards
- Introducing principles of modern management
- Creating specialized units (Walker S.K., 2018, p. 41).

Through civil service practices, the reformers sought to wrestle control of the police away from powerful political actors, but these reforms were resisted, in many cases, by the police themselves. For a police officer of the nineteenth century, **patronage** was the ticket to success. Officers owed allegiance to those who advocated for them as individuals, their patron. When the patron lost power the standing of the officer was similarly diminished, often to the extent of losing the job. Such employment was part of the *spoils system* whereby the political victor rewarded those who worked on their behalf.

The mission for an officer in those days was to merely serve the needs of their patron and, to the extent that the patron owed his success to the respect and legitimacy they held in the community, officers engaged in supporting activities such as running ambulances, housing the homeless and feeding the poor. The progressives sought to eliminate these kinds of patronage duties, insisting that officers adhere to what were often viewed as arbitrary, rigid and inflexible procedures.

The civil service exams did not measure what it took to be a good cop and were therefore viewed as an illegitimate by the police themselves. For the typical police officer of that day, the progressive reforms were contrary to the respect and legitimacy that they enjoyed in the neighborhood. They made the job of crime fighting and crime prevention more difficult because these reforms separated the police officer from the community they served and their new status as professionals contributed to a sense that the police are different, detached from the community and somehow elite.

The dramatic separation of politics from policing did not take place however, but a few of the reforms stuck and the most drastic instances of graft and corruption were curtailed. Police chiefs still owed their allegiance to political patrons, as most still do to this day, but there was enormous pressure to improve and professionalize routine practices. The idea of completely separating political concerns from police decision-making was impractical and ill-advised in America. The culture expects a certain level of local control and accountability of their police, unlike Great Britain where the culture more readily accepts centralized authority and accountability to professional standards. Still, the movement toward a more professional police service did not end with the reformers; a drive toward professionalism continued led by police leaders themselves.

The 1902 convention of the International Association of Chiefs of Police was held in Louisville, Kentucky, in May of 1902. This group of police reformers represented the heads of police agencies at that time and their keynote speaker was Francis O'Neil, then General Superintendent of the Chicago Police Department, who spoke on the subject of anarchy, a topic as important to American society then as terrorism is today. With regard to taking the politics out of policing, O'Neil had this to say about how political patronage actually worked in a large city police agency (Skerret, 2008):

> In every mayoral campaign no assurance of reform is so emphasized as the promise to take the police force out of politics, and this they invariably do, to the extent of taking the other fellows out and putting in their own. A new administration, like a new manager in a commercial house, loses no time before taking stock. The appointment of a new chief of police or general superintendent is inevitable. Then all ranks from the chief down to and including sergeants are classified and listed. After each name in appropriate columns are remarks; rank-when promoted-by whom-attitude last election-advancement-retains rank-reduction-discharge. Occasionally a few slated for discharge or reduction in rank are saved by powerful influences, thereby reducing the vacancies to be filled by friends of the elect. I remember an occasion when the slate was ready for a general order; some lieutenant had to be sacrificed to create a vacancy for the friend of an insistent politician. The method of selecting a victim is similar to that of a steer seeking a weak spot in a fence between him and a clover field. When found, power will force an opening. In this instance, lieutenant Anson S. Backus, a well-educated American with a clear record and no pronounced politics, was the victim. Ineligible for pension on account of age and length of service, Lieutenant Backus peddled cigars for a living until he was reinstated by the next administration (p. 106).

Such personnel practices were a common feature of American policing and were justified under the spoils system where political patronage was rewarded in an effort to sustain local control of the police. Those who supported the incoming mayor replaced experienced officers and managers, the priority was local control over professional competency. These practices reflect the nature of political (community) control and are now considered offensive to good government practices and *due-process*-fundamental fairness-for those affected.

Michael "Hinky Dink" Kenna, 1858–1946

Kenna is widely acknowledged as the quintessential political boss. As a saloon keeper in Chicago called the Workingman's Exchange, he doled out meals to the indigent in exchange for political support as first ward alderman. He and his partner "Bathhouse" John Coughlin hosted an annual Ball that raised thousands of dollars for the two men and was attended by known gangsters, career criminals, prostitutes, gamblers, corrupt politicians and other unsavory characters who supported the infamous duo in exchange for "favors."

At the end of his career as general superintendent of police in Chicago, O'Neil reflected on his idea of good police administration in another address to the International Association of Chiefs of Police, at New Orleans in 1903.

> The official life of a Chief of Police of a large city is mainly an unremitting effort to say "No," and to say it with the least possible offense to those whose requests and demands are denied. If the chief is an experienced and forceful man, who enters his office with a determination to give a good and efficient police administration, he must be prepared to resist the powerful pressure of political and other influences the moment he assumes the duties of his office (Skerret, 2008, pp. 122–123).

He went on to offer his definition of good police administration based on his own experiences through the years, beginning in 1873.

> First—the suppression of public gambling to a point where the police force does not know of its existence, and where honest and valiant effort is constantly put forth to discover its out-croppings and to punish its appearance. Second—the suppression of vice to a point where it can not affect those who do not, of their own choice, seek its haunts.
>
> Third—the placing of the saloon thoroughly under the control of the law. Fourth-the reduction of crime and disorder to that minimum which results from knowledge, on the part of the potential lawbreakers, that punishment shall be imparted and exempt from the influence of political "pull" or other form of official corruption, as far as the police are concerned (pp. 128–129).

From this brief summary, offered over a century ago, we may derive a few common themes that can guide police officers even today.

Policing should be guided by attention to those concerns that are most important to the community. In O'Neil's day, those concerns were alcohol, today those concerns could be alcohol, drugs, petty crime and even traffic complaints. Law enforcement should be directed at creating the perception, on the part of potential law breakers, that they will be held accountable for their behavior regardless of their personal affiliations.

The reform era of policing sought to inject modern management practices into the policing function. Good management practices aimed at ending the corrupt influences of self-interested politicians, the development of professional standards for selection, promotion and training beginning with merit based civil-service exams, and a growing sense that social service should be removed from routine police operations. The police officer was a **professional crime fighter** who should not be burdened with the arbitrary, petty and arduous demands of needy citizens.

The National Commission on Law Observance and Enforcement
The Wickersham Commission 1929*

The commission was established by Herbert Hoover to survey the U.S. Criminal Justice system and make recommendations for public policy initiatives in the wake of prohibition and dramatically increasing crime rates. This was the first national effort to observe police practices at the local level. Corruption, including the use of pain to extract confessions, was found to be widespread as the result of prohibition and the lack of professional standards for law enforcement. The commission shed light on the misconduct of criminal justice actors from judges to local police officers and reveled acts of corruption throughout the system.

The Professional Era & the Rise of the Police Subculture

A new reform effort emerged in the early 20th century led by police chiefs that was directed at professionalizing the police service. Because of the nature of police work, external reform efforts are usually ineffective, changing the police is most effectively accomplished when support for needed change is recognized and accepted by those who are actually engaged in the work. The idea of professionalization was attractive to officers and police leaders due to the prestige the term implies even though the commitment to such a concept was not likely to have been well understood at the time.[8]

---

* Courtesy Library of Congress.

[8] A professional is characterized as someone who is engaged in the practice of conforming to the technical and ethical standards of a recognized "profession." This involves a commitment to education, life-long learning, behaviors that are in compliance with commonly accepted standards and the practice of contributing to the body of knowledge, among others. Police officers who view themselves as professionals are likely to put forth a more limited behavioral definition such as exhibiting a courteous, conscientious and generally businesslike demeanor in the workplace and in interactions with the client(s). https://www.merriam-webster.com/dictionary/professional.

The idea that officers needed to evolve from amateur status, lacking selection standards and training, would have been hard to dispute. Still, local government officials such as Mayors argue about the need for mandatory officer training. Even today local government officials resist state action that increases the number of basic academy hours claiming that this is an undue financial hardship for the municipality. They ignore the potential risk in favor of short term budgetary concerns. Here we see a conflict between professionalism and basic democratic principles such as local control. Robert Peel did not have this conflict as he set the national standards and managed the policing enterprise free of local concerns and priorities. However, he did have the wisdom and forethought to invest the need for his officers to place a high priority on community relationships and priorities within the professional framework, something that was clearly missed as policing reform moved forward in America.

August Vollmer, 1876–1955*

August Vollmer is widely recognized as the father of professional policing. He began his career as town Marshall in Berkley California. He instituted reforms that included mandatory college education for police officers, the establishment of the first crime laboratory and a commitment to building a body of knowledge that could guide the future of policing.

* Courtesy Library of Congress

Under the leadership of progressive police chiefs, most notably August Vollmer,[9] the characteristics of the professional police agency began to take shape. These characteristics included first, the recognition of police officers as experts in the detection, investigation and prevention of crime. The ability to bring their knowledge and training to bear on crime problems was critical. Second, the agency was insulated from politics; political influence over the discretion of officers was minimized or eliminated. Chiefs were appointed based on **merit** and were given employment contracts that extended beyond the tenure of the elected chief executive of the municipality. Third, the rules that governed police operations were based on best practices and generally accepted norms for the function. They were not crafted with regard to the priorities and wishes of local elected officials. Fourth, efficiency of operation governed management practices. Officer deployment and work priorities were not based upon arbitrary standards or past practices, rather data drove decisions on where to assign officers and what cases to work (Uchida, 2015, p. 22).

> The professional police agency is comprised of experts in the detection and prevention of crime, insulated from politics through civil service protections, governed by clear rules and procedures based on the "best practices" as they are currently known, organized with an eye toward efficiency of operation brought about through bureaucratic organizational systems, officers are deployed based upon data, not arbitrary whims or political demands.

[9] August Volmer was Chief of the Berkley California police department in the 1920s. He stressed the need for professionalism based on credentials such as a college education. He was the first chief to institute intelligence, psychiatric and neurological testing for police applicants as well as vehicle patrol and forensic investigation.

The professional police officer*

Vollmer articulated a new vision for the police as a **craft** free of political influence committed to the betterment of society, not just the prevention of crime. The agenda included organizational reform to eliminate patronage, raising selection standards and adopting modern management technology. The modern *professional police organization* is a centralized, authoritarian, bureaucracy focused on crime control (Walker S., 1998, p. 131).

Nowhere were these reforms more in evidence than in Chicago where O.W. Wilson, a protégé of Vollmer, was called in to "modernize" the operation of the Chicago police department. Eight police officers were indicted in 1960 for operating a burglary ring resulting in a biting school yard taunt of "burglars in blue." The Summerdale scandal signaled the need to end politics as usual in the Chicago P.D. and the Mayor of Chicago decided to bring in an outsider to restore confidence in his department. An unassuming, agonizingly polite and wholly professional police reformer, Wilson was then Dean of the criminology school at the University of California, Berkley. He was known for works such as "Police Records: their Installation and Use," "Police Administration" and "Police Planning" (Benzkofer, 2013).

> The Summerdale Scandal (Chicago 1959) was not an ordinary example of police corruption common to the period, it was a throwback to the incompetence and amateurish practices of the political era. Police officer plotted and carried out burglaries in cooperation with known felon by the name of Richard Morrison.

* Courtesy Library of Congress.

Collecting bribes, expecting "presents" from merchants at Christmas-time and other examples of graft and corruption were accepted practices in Chicago. Police officers engaging in actual crimes was not and prompted then Mayor Richard J. Daley, the unquestioned political boss of the Chicago era, to take dramatic steps that were in effect symbolic, to bring about reform to *his* police department. The most important lesson was that the police star could no longer be considered as a badge of immunity or a license to steal.

Orlando Winfield Wilson, 1900–1972*

O.W. Wilson was an experienced, professional police chief prior to his appointment as Superintendent of Police for the City of Chicago in 1960. He furthered the reforms of August Vollmer including the need for college education for police recruits and the use of modern technology. He advanced innovations such as the use of motorized vehicle patrol, the police radio and modern centralized record keeping for the police.

This second reform movement enjoyed success in a number of areas. Even though the call for college educated applicants was only mildly successful, the era of the un-educated officer was largely over, education was established as a desired characteristic for police service with a high school diploma being mandated in many cases. The influence of political actors was greatly diminished in favor of more professional standards. Politics was not removed but the days of paying homage to political patrons was over, such influence being labeled as "unprofessional." Chiefs were given more power and the position of chief was

* U.S. Justice Department photograph.

established as the executive head of the police agency, the criteria for selection moved from political allegiance to professional credentials. Efficiency of operation gained importance with past practices, judged to be ineffective and inefficient, being cast aside. These reforms met with the acceptance and support of actual police officers and although it fell short of the "professionalization" goal, these efforts most certainly improved the quality of police officers and the service that they provided (Walker S., 1977).

The move toward policing professionalism in America also had an unexpected side-effect. As more and more officers began to view themselves as "professionals" they drew back into themselves. Engaging with the community became an "**unprofessional**" endeavor as the trained police officers were viewed as the experts in crime control and the citizen has no role other than prompt reporting. The reformers insistence on limiting the police function to crime and disorder gave officers the impression that calls for service that did not involve crime or a violation of the law were not their job. At the same time, the public was expecting more from its police as the result of technical innovations such as more efficient administrative practices, motorized patrol, rapid response to calls for service leading to more arrests and less crime. Conflict arose over the role of the police, with the police viewing themselves as crime fighters and the public demanding not only crime reduction but social services. This became an excuse for the police to hunker down into their crime-fighting image and to disengage from the communities they served, even into the 1980s police chiefs could be heard to say "Stop trying to counsel those kids. Find something to arrest them for. We are not social workers!"[10]

> What does it mean to be a "professional" as opposed to an amateur? How does a professional police officer treat people compared to an amateur?

THE POLICE SUBCULTURE

Within the dark confines of the police subculture rests profound insight into what drives many of our law enforcement officers today. At the foundation of this *dark-side* of policing rests a troubling vision of certain kinds of citizens. In the words of John Van Maanen, "The Asshole[11]" (1978):

> One of the biggest problems facing police today is the relationship they have with the people they must police. Understanding this relationship

10 A statement made by the author's first chief.

11 This derogatory term, contained in the title of this article, refers to those who consistently challenge the authority of the police, are disrespectful to the police, are antagonistic and are generally viewed as trouble-makers by the police and others.

> is important. Police rely on citizens to report crimes and to cooperate in the investigation and apprehension of criminals. Citizens rely on the police to provide services, to maintain order in their community, and to keep them safe. Thus, a cooperative and trusting relationship between the police and citizens is a key component in effective policing (p. 221).

Police officers tend to classify the individuals that they come into contact with. These *typologies* define at least the initial approach officers will take with particular individuals and they are based on learned stereotypes that have been reinforced throughout an officer's time on the job. The typologies take the form of a *cognitive shorthand* developed to enable the officer to cope with his or her surroundings and the inherent uncertainties of the job. They are a survival mechanism that officers develop in response to the perceived constant threat of danger but these stereotypical points-of-view, implicit and occasionally explicit, are particularly problematic for police agencies struggling with the need to improve police community relations.

Professional police officers have a tendency to view themselves as primarily law enforcers engaged in a struggle-war-with those who threaten peace and safety. They look to the law to define the standards that they are charged with upholding and those who violate the law, or those who are predisposed to violate the law in the officers' opinion, are viewed as in need of correcting. The ambiguity and complexity of the work, as discussed at length by Goldstein (1977), tends to make officers concentrate their attention on actual law violations and the need to respond in a manner as dictated by the law, department policy and as demanded by professional standards. Situations that do not involve actual law violations tend to be handled in a hap-hazard manner that can easily be perceived as insensitive, condescending and arbitrary to those affected (Goldstein, 1977).

For the police, common distinctions of individuals as normal and respectable or threatening or suspicious are much too general. Van Maanen (1974) outlined the following ideal types, through which he theorized that the police view their occupational world:

> **"Suspicions" persons**—When the police have or gain information that leads them to believe that an individual is responsible for a crime those individuals are categorized by the officer as *suspicions* persons. In most cases this level of suspicion may not reach the level of *reasonable suspicion* defined in the law that gives the officer the legal authority to seize, it is most often merely a hunch.

"Assholes"—these are individual who clearly communicate to the officer that they do not agree or accept the police perspective regarding the situation or event in question.

"Know nothings"—these are individual who are neither suspicious persons nor assholes but are uninformed regarding the police. Their ignorance means that they cannot know what the police are about. Their indifference toward the police makes them undeserving of police attention or consideration (Van Maanen, 1978).

These typologies provide a basis for understanding the expectations of officers when they interact with individuals who, based on the point-of-view of the officer, fall into each of these categories. When an officer encounters a *suspicious person* the officer's demeanor is likely to be thoroughly, and even agonizingly, professional. The goal is to ensure that the procedural guidelines are carefully followed. The first order of business is officer safety with officers displaying a demeanor that clearly communicates the concern for their personal well-being, this is not behavior likely to engender cooperation and trust in the eyes of the targeted individual. It is much more likely to create apprehension and fear.

Those individuals categorized as *assholes* are branded by the police as the result of their lack of willingness to accept the police point-of-view. They will be treated harshly and without the respect normally resulting from adherence to proper procedure or the deference afforded the know-nothing. It is this category of individual who offends the moral sentiments of the police officer in that their behavior is viewed as indicative of a corrupt, stained and morally flawed individual in need of correction. That correction sometime taking to form of insolent and disrespectful behavior sometimes culminating in malevolent acts. To the cop, the asshole is something less than human and viewing human beings as something less than human provides a moral justification for police action ranging from disrespect to physical brutality.

The *know-nothing* is the largest and broadest category of individuals who are generally indifferent to the police, they just don't care or haven't given much thought to the police function to be of concern. They neither like nor dislike the police but are most likely to come into contact with officers as the result of being victimized by crime, witnessing crime, requesting some kind of police service or being caught engaging in some minor infraction such as speeding. It is through the interactions police have with this category of individual that holds the most promise for building better police community relations or tearing those relations down. It is the behavior of the officer in this context that tends to paint a deep and lasting picture of all the police, through the perceptual process of generalization. These perceptions, on the part of the officer, can move the know-nothing from his or her position of indifference into the *asshole* category, this also creates a slippery-slope with regard to future police interactions. Conversely, the behavior of the officer in this context can also help to build trust and legitimacy provided that the officer is inclined to do so. It is much more difficult for the police to climb back up the slippery-slope than to slide down it with an individual possessing a negative generalization of the police based on previous encounters, gravity does not favor the police nor does it favor good police community relations.

Is classifying people in this way a kind of racism? Why or why not?

These typologies represent how police officers initially categorize individuals in order to relieve at least some of the ambiguity inherent to the police function. They are not precise, unchanging and absolute, they are merely a perceptual and cognitive shorthand that evolves and changes with the situation and course of events surrounding the interaction. A police officer can begin an interaction with what he or she determines to be a suspicious person and learn, through the course of the interaction, that the individual is a mere know-nothing. An example may be someone who is stopped by the police due to the officer's suspicion that they are driving intoxicated. The officer will be procedure focused and may learn that the individual is merely tired from a long drive, suggesting that they pull-over in a nearby rest area and take a nap. Conversely, the motorist my transform from a suspicious person to an asshole due to their refusal to follow the procedures outlined for the investigation of driving while impaired.

The professional era of policing ignored the human relations aspects inherent to the policing function because to be sensitive and compassionate was considered contrary to the professional standards of objective rationality. The goal was to administer justice, with regard to policing, in a fair and equal, if not equitable, manner. Subjective considerations were not viewed as rational and therefore things to be avoided. To act with feeling was deemed "unprofessional." The implications for police community relations was a vision of the police as coercive and authoritative societal actors to be avoided in the same way we avoid the gaze of the overly strict teacher.

The Kerner Commission, 1968*

> The 1968 Presidents National Advisory Commission on Civil Disorders sought to uncover the causes of urban riots that plagued the United States in the summer of 1967. The report famously stated "Our nation is moving toward two societies, one black and one white-separate and unequal. The report condemned racism as the primary cause of urban conflict. Expanded aid to African American communities was put forth as a remedy that would circumvent the polarization.

The era of professional policing was most clearly articulated in the **Kerner Commission report.**[12] The work of the commission uncovered compelling justification to elevate policing to the status of a true profession. Despite some valiant efforts and substantial public funding efforts this has not yet occurred. The racially charged violence of the late 1960s offered a clue to what was being overlooked by the professional policing model. The ability of the police to ignore the routine and varied concerns of the community in light of overriding "professional" concerns, especially in minority communities. This led to indifference on the part of officers who took shelter in their role as crime fighters-warriors-rather than guardians and true public servants.

> In response to the perceived shortcomings of the professional era, the community oriented policing era emerged as a new way to define the relationship between the police and the community.

* Courtesy Library of Congress

12 It is nonsense to state or assume that the enforcement of the law is so simple that it can be done best by those unencumbered by the study of liberal arts. Police agencies need personnel in their ranks who have the characteristics which a college education seeks to foster; a capacity to relate the events of the day to the social, political, and historical context in which they occur. **President's Commission on Law Enforcement and the Administration of Justice. Task Force Report: The Police. Washington, DC: U.S. Government Printing Office, 1967.**

COMMUNITY ORIENTED POLICING (COP)

The professional model of policing had limitations that undermined the primary mission of the police. In the wake of the riots of the 1960s and 1970s and the drastically increasing crime rates of the early 1990s another reform movement emerged, the goal was to bring the police back to their roots in terms of community engagement. This was a philosophic idea that led to a new paradigm that put forth the idea that the police cannot and should not be separate from the communities that they serve. The professional model allowed officers to drive into work from the suburbs, work their shift and then leave, maintaining "professional" separation from their customers and clients. In contrast, the community oriented philosophy promoted community linkages. If officers were not required to live where they worked then they were to be assigned fixed geographical areas or beats where they worked every day in the hope that positive interaction and relationships would develop. In general, it was thought that returning to an earlier era of community partnership and engagement would be effective in combating a growing crime problem.

Community oriented policing also called for organizational reforms such as flattening the bureaucracy and allowing officers to engage in creative practices to combat crime problems, i.e., Problem Oriented Policing (Goldstein, 1990). The idea that the police should be more pro-active in response to potential crime problems was supported by the theory of *broken-windows* whereby the police could head-off serious crime problems by paying more attention to the little things such as nuisance violations, pan-handling, loitering and broken windows, that create the conditions that lead to more serious crime (Wilson, 1982).

> Community Oriented Poling and Problem Oriented Policing are not the same thing. Community Oriented Policing is a philosophy, Problem Oriented Policing is a technology usually incorporated into the overall philosophy of Community Oriented Policing.

New and innovative ideas and programs developed as a result of this wave of reform. Putting officers back on foot walking beats in primarily downtown areas was thought to bring them closer to the community. Bike patrols got the cops out of the cars, walk-and-talk, cops in the schools, neighborhood sub-stations, youth athletic programs and a host of other innovations were aimed at building better relationships with the community. Bayley outlined three primary dimensions of this effort:

- Engaging and interacting with the community
- Solving community problems

- Adapting internal elements of the organization to support these new strategies, i.e., organizational re-design (Bayley, 1994).

The problem with this "new" philosophy is that it used the same old professionally minded cops to employ it, most of whom signed-up as crime fighters not social workers with badges.

Many of the fundamental beliefs about how to combat crime such as rapid response and preventative patrol were cast in doubt by the community oriented model due to their reactive nature. What was needed was a more pro-active approach that targets potential crime problems and attacks them at their source. The idea that the police should be more pro-active did not set well with those concerned about fundamental democratic principles such as Lori Beth Way (2013) who attacked pro-active policing as blatantly undemocratic due to its disproportionate impact on poor African Americans.

> The major findings of this book document how proactive police work, or specifically hunting, occurs in a large urban context. Officers do not hunt equally in all areas of the city. There are particular places that officers would not even consider hunting, however, there are also certain areas, mainly those where lower class people either reside or frequent, in which most of the proactive work is occurring. Officers even leave their assigned districts to hunt in areas that are deemed better to find "dirt-bags." If we take equal protection issues seriously, there is a cause for concern that lower class residents are subjected to a greater level of police surveillance than are their middle and upper class counterparts. Equal protection guarantees extend to privacy rights, meaning the level of surveillance should also be ruled by equal protection principles (Way, 2013, p. 136).

The argument here is that crime data should be ignored in both police officer deployment decisions and in the decisions officers make concerning where to hunt for the most serious criminals. To aggressively pursue drug violators disproportionately impacts people of color thus undermining the democratic value of equality under the law.

The outcomes of the war on drugs that corresponded to the advent of community oriented policing has clearly been mass incarceration of low income African American citizens. However, it was not the community oriented policing philosophy that was to blame for these outcomes; rather, it was the manner these proactive strategies, most notably drug interdiction, were employed.

The impact of basic economic factors need to be understood and anticipated. Incentives such as government grants to aid in proactive efforts provided incentives that caused a conflict between the *means* and *ends* of COP. When police officers are directed and rewarded for their aggressive arrest practices who are the targets of those actions likely to be? What area of a given community is most likely to garner more enforcement attention, the high-rent district or the ghetto?

The federal government threw billions of dollars at police agencies, to promote both pro-active programs, the hiring of 100,000 more cops in the 1990s and the war on drugs. Who did the proponents of these federal programs think was going to be arrested? Would it have really mattered given the crime problems they faced? *It was these very efforts directed at combatting a growing crime problem by pro-active policing, the hall-mark of Community Oriented Policing, that has driven a huge wedge between the police and those who most need their services. The problem was not a lack of wisdom in this new philosophy but a lack of wisdom in its application.*

As responsible managers of public resources, police chiefs deploy their personnel into areas where they are most needed. Not only has the quantity of calls for service been considered but also the quality-severity-of the calls. Equality is a defining concept for our American democracy but does this mean that police resources should be equally distributed among the neighborhoods, beats or districts? Deploying disproportionate numbers of police officers into low-income areas is justified based on the number and severity of calls for service in those areas.

When police officers are met with jeers, disrespect and threats they are going to demand protective apparatus and advanced weaponry, this leads to complaints about the militarization of the police (Filkins, 2016). Conversely, the police response to low crime areas or areas where they are much less likely to be met with jeers, disrespect and threats will be very different. It is the behavior of individuals within those areas, the character of the neighborhood that determines how any individual or group of police officers will respond, act and interact with the citizens that they encounter. This fact is often overlooked by those who voice criticism, they claim the police attention is a self-fulfilling prophecy.[13] However, the fact remains that the most serious and tragic incidents overwhelmingly come from the areas where those higher numbers of police resources are deployed, regardless of whether or not those who live there actually call the police.

---

[13] Predicting that a higher number of police officers are needed in low-income areas is self-fulfilling because those higher number of police are going to make more arrests thus justifying the need for all those police officers in those areas.

> The implementation of Community Oriented Policing has resulted in a number of serious unanticipated results such as mass incarceration. Now comes a new reform era called Community Guardianship where the primary focus is not to arrest criminal perpetrators, but to provide services thought to benefit communities and reduce crime.

COMMUNITY GUARDIANSHIP

The separation of the police from the community and the dysfunctional aspects of the professional policing era resulted in a new wave of reform. The advocates of Community Oriented Policing cite Peel and his principles as their source of inspiration in defining the idea, and hidden within this philosophy is the concept of *guardianship*. The fact is that community oriented policing is nothing new, it is what the best police officers have always done and understood as what was needed even when "professionalism" was the objective. A police agency, and individual police officers, who establish and maintain good relations with individuals in the neighborhoods know who to go to when crime problems occur. They know who the actors are; they know where they hang-out; they know who they hang-out with; they know how to approach them but most importantly people are willing to tell them these things. This is how the police solve and prevent crime and this is the legacy of Peel's original priorities for the selection of professional police officers, low-key, unassuming, even tempered, friendly and, as the author would add, "wise."

The most basic mission of the police as agents of the law can be summarized in the following points:

- To provide legitimacy to the existing social order and structure.
- To regulate social behavior.
- To restrict and define freedom.
- To provide a system of dispute resolution (Gaines, 2011, p. 10).

In addition to the order maintenance function of the police there is a much less formal expectation for the police to function as mediators, arbitrators and even judges yet we lack a common framework for understanding these roles. In order for society to exist there must be some common framework for predicting the behavior of others. Throughout history the law has provided that predictability by enforcing and guiding the **exchange relationships** that exist among people. When we speak of *exchange relationships* we are referring to the services or benefit we may offer to another individual with the expectation of receiving a comparable service or benefit from them in the future. We can compare exchange relationships with communal relationships in that the expectation of receiving something of value does not exist in the latter (Clark, 1993). The rule of law and formal police practices have their basis in the former while the virtue of the guardian is based on a more communal, altruistic and arbitrary vision that is difficult for the law enforcement officer to understand and accept.

Exchange relationships are the expected results, services, or benefits that will accrue to individuals as the result of social interaction. The expected result or benefit of cooperation and the anticipated result of a lack of cooperation or defection. Exchange relationships are violated when an individual refuses to behave as expected.

The police function within the legal framework but are often called upon to engage in extra-legal functions. Demands are made of the police that can change with the ever changing winds of politics, making the function appear arbitrary, capricious and unjust from the standpoint of societal actors and groups of actors who seek to use the police to promote a particular agenda or argue against the "status-quo." For example, those who advocate that the police should be agents of social justice argue that police discretion should be based upon compassion for specific groups and that the lack of compassion has resulted in an enormous injustice, i.e., mass incarceration (Alexander, 2011).

The police, therefore, are expected to take on the role of societal ombudsman who are sought out by those seeking an advocate to represent their interests against the interests of other individuals, individuals against the government and government against individuals and groups. This is a role for which the police officer is ill equipped yet failure to perform to everyone's satisfaction has resulted in the tendency to scapegoat the police.

> "In Plato's vision of a perfect society—in a republic that honors the core of democracy—the greatest amount of power is given to those called the Guardians. Only those with the most impeccable character are chosen to bear the responsibility of protecting the democracy" (Nila, 2007).

The idea of guardianship is rapidly gaining popularity by those intent on a new wave of police reform. This concept adheres to the premise that the fundamental goal of the police is to protect constitutional rights, it is a humanistic approach that appears to be somewhat in conflict with the more traditional goal of upholding the rule of law. In the wake of 911 the police were called upon to defend the nation from what was perceived as an imminent threat. The response was militarization of the police, a process that undermined the progress in community oriented practices that were prevalent just before that tragedy. The rise of the warrior cop in response to this threat illustrated the willingness of our citizens to give up certain freedoms, constitutional protections, in exchange for personal security. The guardianship mindset is a move back and away from the warrior mentality (Rahr, 2015).

JUDGING POLICING EFFECTIVENESS

The fundamental goal of the police is the prevention of crime, therefore, the absence of crime and disorder provides a basis upon which to judge policing effectiveness. This implies that low rates of crime and disorder should be found where great policing practitioners practice their craft and high rates of crime and disorder indicate the need for improvement. The problem with this reasoning is that there is no single accepted system upon which to measure crime, and this is due to the nature of policing in the United States.

The system of law enforcement in the United States is one best described as decentralized and uncoordinated. The Police Chief does not report to the County Sheriff who then reports to the Director of the state police who then reports to the head of the Federal police, rather, the Police Chief, Sheriff, and Director are autonomous, reporting to their respective oversight bodies such as the city council, county board and state legislature and/or Governor's office. This means that the activity of each of the 18,000 different municipal, county and state agencies are not linked in any formal way. Each agency is free to pursue sometimes very different goals and objectives even when the crime problems they share are similar.

In the same way that police agencies are decentralized and uncoordinated the criminal justice systems that they function within are not coordinated. Each state in the union has its own statutes, courts and independent agencies of justice. This creates a profound difficulty in crime reporting in that each police agency reports crime within their jurisdiction as they see fit, only broad guidelines are provided by the Uniform Crime Reporting system, reporting is voluntary and there is no audit provision (Beattie, 1955).

Using crime statistics to judge the effectiveness of a police agency, and using these statistics to compare one police agency to another is inherently problematic yet this is exactly how these figures are used. This creates an incentive, on the part of Chiefs and elected officials, to attack the crime rate with vigorous and sometimes socially unjust tactics.

CONFLICTING VIEWS ON JUSTICE

Most of us tend to view the concept of justice as fundamental fairness but what is fair to one person may constitute a profound injustice to others. There is a great deal of confusion regarding the concept of social justice and how it relates to criminal justice. Some try to make the case that the police should be social justice advocates even though this function would place a police officer in direct opposition to their sworn duty and the rule of law. If the police take on the role of advocates for a historically marginalized group they abandon impartiality. This may endear them to that group but alienate others who depend on the police as neutral fact finders and arbitrators.

Social justice speaks to how the resources of a society are distributed. With regard to the rule of law the emphasis is on equity in the application of the law. Therefore, law enforcement practices that have a disproportionate impact upon members of a particular group, i.e., non-causation individuals, or the poor, can be viewed as unjust. Social justice mechanisms include public policy, progressive tax laws, business regulation and the various governmental social intervention mechanisms. The goal is fairness in terms of how the rewards and punishments are distributed among citizens and equality whereby no one group of citizens is advanced by another group's loss.

Criminal justice speaks to a process of adjudication. It is process focused, not outcome focused as is social justice. Society sets-up a system by which we determine the guilt or innocence of an individual, and where the rights of private parties are upheld. Criminal justice is also concerned with the protection of legal rights of individuals and is charged with following a fair process for adjudication commonly referred to as due process.

Social justice is outcome focused. If the result is unfair then injustice must be present. Criminal justice is process focused, if correct procedures were not followed then the result or outcome is unjust.

Under the concept of social justice an action can be considered wrong or unjust if its impact adversely affects the distribution of wealth, opportunity or **fairness** within society. Under the concept of criminal justice an action can be considered unfair or unjust if it did not follow **correct procedure**. Social justice speaks to the impact of policies and practices on groups with particular attention to those groups that have earned particular attention due to their current or prior status as "marginalized" or disadvantaged. Criminal justice is concerned with the individual, holding them accountable for conduct viewed as wrong by the larger society regardless of group membership. Conflict results when we confuse these two principles.

Social justice is group focused. Criminal justice focuses on the individual.

These two perspectives are also at odds with regard to how criminal justice is to be administered. The *crime control perspective* speaks to the primacy of the rights of citizens to be free from crime. The crime control perspective places the rights of the accused **subordinate** to the right of society to be free of crime. In determining guilt or innocence this perspective relies on an inquisitorial process to get at the truth. The inquisitorial system, also known as non-adversarial, is one in which the court is actively engaged in asking questions of witnesses and the accused to ascertain the facts or the truth. Such a system has its foundation in the **civil law legal tradition** that exists in France, Italy and many European nations; this is not to be confused with the civil law system here in the United States that is used to adjudicate disputes between individuals.

> There are 4 broad legal traditions that exist today, the Common Law tradition that exists in the United States and Great Britain, the Civil Law legal tradition that exists in Italy, France and most of Europe, the Socialist legal tradition that exists in China, and the Islamic legal tradition that is based upon the Quran or law of God.

In contrast with the crime control model, the *due process perspective* places an emphasis upon the rights of the accused. The underlying principle of **due process** is that it is better for ten guilty persons escape justice than that one innocent to suffer.[14] The mechanism that prevents this is known as the **adversarial system** where procedure is followed meticulously with any perceived procedural violations vigorously attacked by the defense council. Under the common-law legal tradition, used in the United States, the truth is learned through a type of legal combat, the argument of each side being attacked by the opposition with reason and precedence in order to determine which is stronger. The judge does not question the accused or the witnesses, rather he or she serves as a referee. These two vastly differing perspectives, crime control versus due process, are continual sources of conflict for those preoccupied with the concept of justice.

A NEW REFORM ERA

We now find ourselves on the verge of a new reform era that has yet to be defined. The current criminal justice system that focuses on processes and procedures is under attack for its outcomes that can widely be perceived as unjust. The policing function has been stretched and pulled in many directions, some of these paths come into direct conflict with the primary mission of controlling crime and disorder. "Warrior" cops are attacked as undemocratic forerunners of a totalitarian state, enemies of the effort to build trust and legitimacy. Some of the best community oriented policing efforts are criticized as ineffective in combating crime and disorder and beyond the capabilities of police agencies strained by staffing shortages and dramatically increasing service demands. Community

[14] Sir William Blackstone. Commentaries on the Laws of England. 1766.

guardianship is being proposed as a new guiding philosophy for police agencies and police leaders, yet potential measures of the effectiveness of this new reform effort have yet to be considered or proposed leaving the focus for building better police community relationship right where it has always been, in the hands of individual police officers themselves.

Chapter Summary

The police function developed as human beings began to group together for protection against the law of nature, survival of the fittest (strongest). For human beings to develop as social animals there had to be a common mechanism to protect the group, living in constant fear hindered the ability to develop exchange relationships that are necessary for cooperative endeavors and economic development. The protective function began as a shared responsibility among the male population but soon evolved into a watchman system where certain members were compensated for taking on this responsibility for those who were not well suited, or inclined, to this function. Constables emerged as quasi-professionals devoted to the protective function as their full-time responsibility. The homogeneous nature of early settlement made life easy for these constables as everyone shared a sense of what was acceptable conduct. Strong ties to social mechanisms such as the church provided powerful incentives for compliance. Mechanisms such as public shaming were common with being ostracized from the protective group being the ultimate punishment as it meant going it alone out in the cruel wilderness.

With the advent of the industrial revolution came urbanization and the clustering of heterogeneous groups to the cities in pursuit of economic advantage. Crime and disorder exploded in both England and the United States as different groups struggled for acceptance and pursued assimilation. Robert Peel set forth the standard he felt would be acceptable for a professional body of men charged with the maintenance of law and order. He also specified the first selection criteria for police officers with a mind toward what would be acceptable (legitimate) in a democratic political system, even-tempered, self-controlled and unassuming. Low key individuals who would provide a calming presence representative of governmental authority.

In the United States the political culture, and the development of the police, was very different. Americans, by their very nature, are highly resistive to governmental authority, unlike the English. Local, rather than national, control of the police was viewed as preferable. The United States did not allow any armed National policing function, with the exceptions of the U.S. Marshals, until the

1930s. As a result the police owed their allegiance to local patrons and were used as a corrupting authority to suppress dissent and enforce the will and power of the "status quo" often engaging in unjust practices at the direction of the "powers-that-be." Reform efforts emerged in the late 1890s with a second wave beginning in the 1920s that endeavored to establish the police as a professional crime fighting force that owed their allegiance to the rule of law and developing professional standards of conduct. Efforts to remove political influence were widespread as the linkage between the police and the communities they served were severed in an effort to insulate law enforcement from corrupting influences. It was learned that because the police in the United States are creatures of local government, as opposed to the National government as in Great Britain, local control and politics can never be completely removed as a dominating influence on the police despite efforts at police professionalization. The police in America will always be a product of local direction, priorities and influence depending on the nature of the communities they serve.

The concept of Community Oriented Policing developed and continues to be heralded as a cure for the evils of the professional policing era. Civil unrest in the 1960s, 1970s and a growing crime problem in the 1980s resulted in an ill-conceived effort to re-build the vary linkages that precipitated some of the worst abuse of the rule of law. Armed with a shallow understanding of history, advocates preach the need for the police to embark upon "relationship building" in an effort to build trust and legitimacy. The wise individual police officer is fully aware of the value of their own credibility and the need to hold public trust as a crime fighting tool, none-the-less advocates have embarked upon an incredible array of outlandish programs and public expense that has not resulted in what Peel envisioned as the ultimate indicator of effective policing, lower levels of crime and disorder. A new reform effort is on the horizon that seeks to change the paradigm of policing from crime suppression to community guardianship. Managing the resulting conflict of visions is likely to be a huge challenge for both police leaders and police officers.

Bibliography

Alexander, M. (2011). *The New Jim Crow: Mass Incarceration in the Age of Colorblindness.* New York: The New Press.

Bayley, D. (1994). *Police for the Future.* New York: Oxford University Press.

Beattie, R.H. (1955). Problems of Criminal Statistics in the United States. *Journal of Criminal Law and Criminology, 46(2)*, 178–186.

Benzkofer, S. (2013, July 7). Legendary Lawman. *Chicago Tribune.*

Bowman, T. (2006, July). College Degree. *The Police Chief.*

Clark, M.M. (1993). The Difference Between Communal and Exchange Relationships: What It Is and Is Not. *Personality and Social Psychology Bulletin, 19*, 684–691.

Cox, S.M. (2017). *Introduction to Policing.* Thousand Oaks, CA: Sage.

Filkins, D. (2016, May 13). "Do Not Resist" and the Crisis of Police Militarization. *The New Yorker.*

Gaines, L., Kappeler, V. (2011). *Policing in America, 7th ed.* Waltham, MA: Anderson.

Goldstein, H. (1977). *Policing a Free Society.* Cambridge, MA: Ballinger.

Goldstein, H. (1990). *Problem Oriented Policing.* New York: McGraw-Hill.

Hobbes, T. (1651). *Leviathan, or the Matter, Form and Power of a Commonwealth, Ecclesiastical and Civil.*

Klockars, C. (1985). *The Idea of Police.* Beverly Hills: Sage.

Nila, M.A. (2007). *The Nobility of Policing.* West Valley City, UT: Franklin Covey Publishing.

Rahr, S.A. (2015). From Warriors to Guardians: Recommitting American Police Culture to Democratic Ideals. *New Perspectives in Policing, NIJ.*

Reith, C. (1956). *A New Study of Police History.* London: Edinburgh.

Skerret, E.A. (2008). *Chief O'Neill's Sketchy Recollections of an Eventful Life in Chicago.* Chicago: Northwestern University Press.

Uchida, G.D. (2015). The Development of the American Police. In R. Dunham and G. Alpert, *Critical Issues in Policing, 7th ed.* (pp. 11–30). Long Grove, IL: Waveland Press.

Van Maanen, J. (1978). "The Asshole". In P. Manning and J. Van Maanen (eds), *Policing: A View from the Street.* Santa Monica, CA: Goodyear Publishing.

Walker, S. (1977). *A Critical History of Police Reform: The Emergence of Professionalism.* Lexington: D.C. Heath.

Walker, S. (1998). *Popular Justice.* New York: Oxford University Press.

Walker, S. (2015). "Broken Windows" and Fractured History. The Use and Misuse of History in Recent Police Patrol Analysis. In R. Dunham and G. Alpert,

Critical Issues in Policing, 7th ed. (pp. 468–479). Long Grove, IL: Waveland Press.

Walker, S.K. (2018). *The Police in America.* New York: McGraw-Hill Education.

Way, L.B. (2013). *Hunting for Dirtbags: Why Cops Over-Police the Poor and Racial Minorities.* Boston: Northeastern University Press.

Wilson, J.Q., Kelling, G. (1982). "Broken Windows: The Police and Neighborhood Safety." *Atlantic Monthly*, 29–38.

CHAPTER 3

Historical Approaches to Police Community Relations

■ ■ ■

"Police in China can do whatever they want. There is no negotiation, no discussion, no rule of law to appeal to; there is only the power of the State whose agents, the police, can crush you at any time." —Anonymous author

Police in China resolving conflict*

Learning Outcomes

Upon successful completion of this chapter the student will be able to:

- Explain why the police need to develop good community relations.
- Describe the different approaches to police community relations.
- Describe the difference between the programs-approach and the community-relations approach.
- Discuss the value of community oriented policing as a community relations program.

---

* Image labeled for unrestricted use.

- Explain the significance of the police warrior mentality and its impact on police community relations.

Important Concepts

- Role Model, Mentor
- Public Relations
- Programs Approach
- Community Oriented Policing Approach
- Problem-Oriented Policing
- Agency Focused
- Community Focused
- Stakeholders
- Human Relations Approach
- Total Person
- Rapport
- Emotional Intelligence

Questions for Discussion

- Why is police community relations an important topic for police officers and police administrators?
- What is the difference between the public relations and the programs approach to police community relations?
- Discuss whether police work is actually social work, provide examples.
- Discuss whether community oriented policing should be considered as part of the community relations approach. Why is it different?
- What is the new reality that threatens the relationship between the police and communities?
- Discuss the problem of police deviance and how it impacts police community relations.

INTRODUCTION

The above quote helps clarify the unique nature of American law enforcement. Our culture places the citizen in charge, unlike most other nations throughout history where the ruling class and/or government were supreme. This distinction places the importance of police-community relations in clear perspective: the legitimacy of the police is not based upon the "God-given" right to rule rather; "God-given" inalienable rights to "life, liberty, and property (happiness)" are the basis of our political and criminal justice systems, as well as our American culture. In other systems the people serve the government or ruler, whereas in the American[1] system, the government is servant to the people. This new concept is difficult to reconcile with the police function, making the need for good police-community relations critical.

The importance of police-community relations is also based on a simple truth: law enforcement duties and policing are much easier to accomplish if police cultivate relationships, maintain legitimacy within various communities, and anticipate threats to those relationships. Building these relationships is simply a matter of good leadership and management. This chapter will also make the case that establishing and maintaining great police-community relationships is not just the job of the agency head or chief; that building relationships is more effectively accomplished at the line level; and that each and every police officer working the street has this responsibility.

"The police must be part of the community. They cannot be viewed as mercenaries or as an army of occupation" (Dempsey, 2016, p. 329).

In this chapter, we will explore the history of police-community relations, what police agencies have done to enhance their image, and how departments build better relationships with the communities they serve.

What Is Police-Community Relations?

The concept of police-community relations relates to the non-crime related interactions between members of the police organization and the stakeholders[2]. *Exchange relationships*[3] create expectations for both normal individuals and the

---

1 The term "American" refers to the United States and our unique legal tradition that may or may be prevalent in other nations of the American continent.

2 A stakeholder is any individual or group who has an interest in, or is impacted by, what the police do.

3 In exchange relationships, benefits are given with the expectation of receiving or having received a comparable benefit in return.

police. When these expectations are not met, the relationship breaks down and the cooperation necessary to control crime and maintain order dissipates.

> Consider a relationship you currently enjoy with your instructor, boss, work colleague or friend. What expectations do you have as it relates to this relationship? Discuss.

An example may include the police killing an unarmed man. The expectation is that the police have the capability to handle a violent encounter with an unarmed individual without having to resort to deadly force. When they are unable to do so, the exchange relationship (expectation) is violated and the relationship breaks down. In the absence of a foundation of understanding (e.g., trust), anger can result because one party feels violated, abused, or used. A breakdown in trust can occur when discriminatory beliefs gain traction within an individual, group, organization, or institution, e.g., racism[4], homophobia, transphobia, and sexism. When agencies take the time and effort to build better relationships the impact of these beliefs can be mitigated.

THE IMPORTANCE OF POLICE COMMUNITY RELATIONS

The police are the most visible representatives of government, and as such, they represent the most fundamental concept of our democratic tradition—all legitimate authority rests in the consent of the governed. This has been a hard lesson; throughout history, the powerful have exercised control over the weak, basing their legitimacy in their ability to imprison, coerce, and destroy the opposition. In the United States, drawing on the wisdom of our English traditions, police base legitimacy upon the will of the people to accept the government, and by extension, the authority of the police.

When it comes to the police, this means acting in a manner that reflects a sense of **subordination** to the will of the people. The problem for the police is that they are often called to incidents and situations that demand quick and certain action on their part; there is no time or opportunity for discussion, negotiation, and compromise, only the swift and certain application of the rule of law. The purely reactive nature of law enforcement requires that the police build a foundation of respect and legitimacy in advance of demanding situations because the application of coercion and force necessary to promote and preserve law and order can disrupt trust between the community and its police officers.

---

[4] Racism generally refers to the belief in the superiority of one race over another. It manifests itself in the belief that members of each race possess characteristics or abilities specific to that race that distinguish it as inferior or superior to another race.

> What kinds of actions on the part of the police can easily lead to a breakdown in the exchange relationship between the police and the community?

According to Ross (2012) when there is a good police-community relationship, police have a better understanding of the public's concerns. When there are poor police-community relations, the police typically lack a basic understanding of community's problems, goals, and desires. In many cases, the police are viewed as an occupying force that does more harm than good (Ross, 2012, p. 117). When the police are viewed as the enemy, cooperation is rare and a "don't snitch" mentality leads to further alienation in high crime areas. Numerous conditions that can lead to poor police-community relations include but are not limited to:

- Children being told to fear the police by parents and others.
- General hostility toward the police.
- Loss of confidence in the police.
- Few or no positive police contacts.
- Cops who are rude, corrupt, and violent (or at least perceived to be).
- Police distancing themselves from the community out of fear or even disgust.
- Poor police communication skills.
- Different perceptions between the police and community groups on the causes and control of crime (Ross, 2012, p. 118).

Police-community relations is a critical aspect of police work because all wise police work has its foundation in **social interaction**. The willingness and ability to cultivate good relationships with people is something that every great cop possesses. Too many police officers today view themselves as crime fighters waging war against the criminal element on behalf of society. They craft their own behavior around the assumption that they represent something special (i.e., the "thin blue line," the "sheepdog," the "warrior" cop), and they find comfort in the police subculture that accepts and glorifies this role. Retiring officers tell stories of high speed chases, shoot-outs, and fights that portray unrealistic but glamorous impressions for new officers, who long for the chance to prove themselves as worthy of respect among their peers. They view service calls as a nuisance and social service with disdain because such work is not what "real cops do" (Trautman, 2002).

However, the "wise" police officers, regardless of whether they are street officers, detectives, sergeants, lieutenants, or chiefs, understand that their success rests in their ability and willingness to seek out, build, and maintain **relationships** with people—all people—including the wealthy who typically hold power and influence in the community, the middle class who provide the foundation for social interaction, and the poor who are the most prevalent victims and perpetrators of crime. Even when dealing with hardened criminals, the epitome of real police work, the wise officer understands that the path to reliable information—be it a confession, witness statement, or investigative lead—rest in their ability to build a relationship, earn trust, and even develop a friendship with these individuals—community members, witnesses, and criminals alike.

A detective displaying sympathy for a criminal suspect*

Human relation skills are now and have always been at the heart of effective policing. Peel's principles of law enforcement eluded to those characteristics necessary to build legitimacy and trust:

> The police seek and preserve public favor, not by catering to public opinion, but by constantly demonstrating absolutely impartial service to the law, in complete independence of policy, and without regard to the justice or injustice of the substance of individual laws; by ready offering of individual service and friendship to all members of society without regard to their race or social standing, by ready exercise of courtesy and friendly good humor; and by ready offering of individual sacrifice in protecting and preserving life (Peel, 1829).

The author would add that in addition to friendship, good humor, and courtesy, police officers should exercise **compassion and understanding**. This

* Image labeled for unrestricted use.

raises the question of how police demonstrate these qualities and what limits their ability to do so. The presence and use of these qualities is developed in, or limited by, the following.

Selection

No national standards exist for the selection of police officers in the United States. Unlike Great Britain and most other developed countries, local authorities oversee the hiring of police officers based on local standards and priorities. A "get tough on crime" attitude at the local level is not likely to result in the selection of officers who are courteous, friendly, or compassionate. Local jurisdictions may hire anyone as a police officer who meets the minimum state mandated qualifications, e.g., United States' citizenship and a high school diploma.

Training

Most states now mandate officer basic training with a curriculum designed to inform recruited officers about the law and legal procedure. As the initial actors in the criminal justice system, police recruits become thoroughly skilled in criminal procedure and the rules of law enforcement. There is no room or capacity in these programs to teach friendliness, good humor, and courtesy, much less compassion and understanding. The objective is to teach these recruits how to properly apply the rule of law in various situations and how to minimize risk to themselves and their police agency.

> Following correct procedure is the foundation of justice under the rule of law.

Supervision

Unlike work that lends itself to direct and close supervision (e.g., assembly, manufacturing, packaging, and other very routine and repetitive endeavors), police work is largely autonomous. The police officer performs his or her duties relatively free from supervisory oversight. The routine aspects of police work, such as reporting and investigatory work, are subject to policy and procedural guidelines that can be verified by supervisors; however, interactions with the public, especially when these interactions do not generate a report, are very difficult to assess because there is not a strict rubric for assessing courtesy, professionalism, and responsiveness. Supervision in policing often depends on the willingness of officers to accept, understand, and emulate suggestions, actions, and behaviors of supervisors and peers. Formal supervisory activity is limited to periodic performance appraisal practices, or it may be the result of a citizen complaint. The best supervisors will actively engage their officers through direct observation and counseling to ensure their development, but the demands on supervisors' time often make this exceedingly difficult.

A Sergeant congratulates a new police academy graduate

THE JOB

Armed with a certificate of training, new uniform, and various other accouterments of the job, the probationary officer is thrust into a new and strange world for which few are prepared. Their training and initial socialization stresses the dangers of the job, and that sense of danger causes them to seek shelter within a tight fraternity of fellow officers. They are taught and rewarded within the police subculture to see first to their own safety; second, to see to the safety of their fellow officers, and then finally to the safety and concerns of everyday citizens. The compelling logic, even to those unfamiliar with policing, is that officers cannot help anyone as cops if they do not take care of themselves first.

In the new struggle for acceptance, the rookie officer seeks out a role model, someone to emulate on their road to acceptance into the police subculture. These individuals too often have not, historically, been the ones who have exhibited the friendly, courteous, and compassionate demeanor indicative of great police officers; rather, they have been those of whom "stories" are told. The embellishment of fights, chases, and other feats of courage garner admiration within a warrior culture. They sometimes speak of valor and high ideals, but most often, these legends result from ill-considered and uninhibited stupidity from which the officer prevailed due to sheer luck. Nevertheless, they easily become the feats that define "real cops" in the mind of the new officer.

A role model is someone who is looked to by others as an example to be imitated. A Mentor is an experienced and trusted adviser

Interactions with the public teach the new officer to categorize individuals. Van Maanen (1978) provides insight into how police officers cope with the incredible uncertainly of their interpersonal dealings with the public. One can easily imagine how Peel would view these typologies.

- The *know nothing* is an individual who is largely ignorant of the police perspective. They are generally indifferent to the police and can be viewed as a mere nuisance.

  It is this category of *citizen* that offers the most opportunity for engaging in a positive encounter, but the officer rejects such opportunity as an encumbrance on their crime fighting mission and is likely to be dismissed.

- The *suspicious person* is someone that the officer has reason to believe may be involved in a crime. The behavior of the officer in this case is motivated by the strict observance of their training. Their goal is to ensure that the formal procedures are observed for building a solid case against a criminal suspect.

- The *asshole*[5] is the third and most troubling category of individual from a police-community relation's perspective. These individuals do not accept the perspective of the police and tend to be argumentative, disrespectful and arrogant in asserting their rights. Their actions are viewed as stupid, senseless, and despicable, and in the mind of the police officer, they are not granted the status of human beings, the very label speaking to the need of the cops to de-humanize these individuals.

Assholes, by way of contrast to the other categories, are stigmatized by the police and treated harshly on the basis of their failure to meet police expectations arising from the interactive situation itself. Of course, street interactions can quickly transform *suspicious persons* into *know nothings* and *know nothings* in to *assholes*, or any combination thereof. It is the *asshole* category, which is most imbued with moral meaning for the patrolman-establishing for him a strained or flawed identity to attribute to the citizen upon which he can justify his sometimes malevolent acts. Consequently, the *asshole* may well be the recipient of what the police call "street justice"—a physical attack designed to rectify what police take as a personal insult (Van Maanen, 1978).

---

[5] This derogatory term was used by Van Maanen to describe an individual whom, in the eyes of the police, is viewed as a trouble-maker, someone who makes the job of the police difficult and does so as a matter of habit.

> Uncooperative persons are more likely to find themselves on the receiving side of disrespect, discourtesy and abuse by the police. Taken to an extreme, uncooperative and resistive behavior may result in extra-legal violence commonly referred to as "street justice." Officers may then decide not to formally charge an individual reasoning that their extra legal action has taught the individual a needed lesson. Ironically, many individuals subjected to "street justice" often accept it, even preferring it to formal legal sanction.

The following example, again from Van Maanen, provides an illustration of how a typical policemen may view a typical transaction, including the officer's subjective view of the citizen. The officer's point-of-view and socialization causes an attitude toward the citizen that is very likely to undermine the police-community relationship. The conflict between the officer's subjective views and the objective reality of the encounter is profound. Take this example between an officer and a motorist stopped for speeding:

Policeman: "May I see your driver's license please?"

Motorist: "Why the hell are you picking on me and not somewhere else looking for some real criminals?"

Policeman: *"Cause you're an asshole. That's why . . . but I didn't know that until you opened your mouth"* (Van Maanen, 1978).

HISTORY OF POLICE-COMMUNITY RELATIONS

The battle for better police-community relations has a long history, but it is important to point out that even the greatest efforts of the very best police agencies with the highest moral standards for officers can be completely undermined by the point-of-view, attitude, and behavior of just one officer:

> Strong relationships of mutual trust between police agencies and the communities they serve are critical to maintaining public safety and effective policing. Police officials rely on the cooperation of community members to provide information about crime in their neighborhoods, and to work with the police to devise solutions to crime and disorder problems. Similarly, community members' willingness to trust the police depends on whether they believe that police actions reflect community values and incorporate the principles of procedural justice and legitimacy (Community Relations Service, 2016).

> Discuss how in many urban environments the concept of street justice may be accepted as part of the police community exchange relationship.

Police Recognition of the Need for a Better Image

The history of police-community relations begins with the recognition that the police should always work in cooperation with the people. This can be accomplished with a strong emphasis upon the duty of the police, in a democratic society, to protect the rights of all individuals. The oath of office for every police officer stresses this duty, but the realities of the job, the police subculture, and the relentless focus on crime fighting undermine it. In far too many instances, the behavior of individuals and groups can convince the police officer that certain individuals are not deserving of protection and that their rights can be ignored in light of a greater good (i.e., the suppression of crime).

An example of "street justice" taken to the extreme*

Among the fundamental aspects of police work is the concept that the police should dedicate themselves to service, in addition to crime suppression, and in this way, earn the trust of the community they serve. While the absence of crime serves as proof of the efficiency of the police, there is no qualification more indispensable to a police officer than a perfect command of temper, never suffering himself or herself to be moved in the slightest degree by any language or threats that may be used (Lee, 1971).

* Image labeled for unrestricted use.

The Public Relations Approach

Within police agencies, public relations programs have been used to manipulate perceptions on the part of governmental authorities responsible for the allocation of police resources and in the public generally (Ross, 2012, p. 63). This approach is **internally focused** and aimed at creating a more favorable environment for the police to operate and pursue their crime suppression goals. The reform era of policing recognized that law enforcement was viewed as corrupt, primarily serving the needs of powerful political actors.

Public relations refers to the professional maintenance of a favorable public image.

The movement to "professionalize" the police had, as its underlying theme, the need to establish policing as a legitimate enterprise acting in everyone's interests. The first order of business was to establish selection and training standards that removed the police from the corrupt influence of political patrons. This was followed by the development of scientific forensic techniques to aid in the accurate identification of criminal perpetrators. It wasn't until the 1950s that the first programs emerged that were intended to "sell" the police:

> The reformers of the 1950s felt that it was necessary to overcome the attitudes of contempt that middle-class citizens held toward police and, literally, to sell the police to the people. This was done by sending speakers to high schools, to business luncheons, to meetings of civil organizations, and so on. These speakers argued that the police are the "thin blue line," the last bulwark of defense against the dark forces of crime and disorder (Hunter, 2011, p. 57).

Image Enhancements

This sales effort made no attempt to argue the efficacy of any given activity or program; it was merely an effort to **improve the police image** in the minds of the emerging middle class. These efforts ignored the upper classes, who were largely indifferent to the police, and the poor whose relationship with the police was defined by their status as targets rather than citizens deserving of the police's respect.

One of the best examples of these kinds of public relations programs was undertaken by the Federal Bureau of Investigation in the 1930s. Not only did the FBI seek to establish itself as the premiere law enforcement agency in the world, but it also embarked upon programs intended to endear local law enforcement to the bureau through cooperative programs, such as the FBI National Academy, a rigorous training program offered to local law enforcement officers. Even Hoover recognized the value of establishing and maintaining a cooperative relationship with local law enforcement; after all, the ability of the bureau to acquire informants and information was limited due to the lack of day-to-day contact. Local law enforcement was much closer to the community and was likely viewed as a resource by Hoover that could be brought to bear when needed. Training programs such as the National Academy facilitated these relationships.

J. Edgar Hoover, legendary head of the FBI*

The FBI National Academy is a professional course of study for U.S. and international law enforcement managers nominated by their agency heads because of demonstrated leadership qualities. The 10-week program—which provides coursework in intelligence theory, terrorism and terrorist mindsets, management science, law, behavioral science, law enforcement communication, and forensic science—serves to improve the administration of justice in police departments and agencies at home and abroad and to raise law enforcement standards, knowledge, and cooperation worldwide.

Leaders and managers of state, local, county, tribal, military, federal, and international law enforcement agencies attend the FBI National Academy. Participation is by invitation only, through a nomination process. Participants are drawn from every U.S. state and territory and from international partner nations. Sessions of approximately 220 officers take undergraduate and/or graduate

* Image labeled for unrestricted use.

courses at the FBI campus in Quantico, Virginia. Classes are offered in the following areas: law, behavioral science, forensic science, understanding terrorism/terrorist mindsets, leadership, communication, and health/fitness. Officers participate in a wide range of leadership and specialized training, where they share ideas, techniques, and experiences with each other, creating lifelong partnerships that transcend state and national borders.

> The Public Relations approach to police community relations seeks to build public confidence in the police and in police capabilities as professional crime fighters.

FBI National Academy participants*

The Programs Approach

The initial attempt to improve police-community relations took the form of public relations campaigns patterned after private sector branding attempts. The idea was to generate a **better image** for the police, raising them from the lower status reminiscent of what has been referred to as the corrupt *political era*. Programs were created with the intention to inform the public on the best attributes of professional policing in an effort to gain public support and allow the police to pursue their function in a more cooperative environment. The *programs approach* was, and still is, characterized as a "one-way street," where communication flows from the police to the community. The police tell the community about how great they are and seldom listen for feedback. This approach fails to acknowledge that the community is anything but homogeneous; there are multiple communities with very different attitudes, expectations, experiences and expectations of the

* Image labeled for unrestricted use.

police. Hunter and Barker (2011) outline some of the basic characteristics of the "programs" approach:

- At their best, the police employed highly sophisticated techniques of advertising, selling, and, of course, improving public relation perceptions.
- To police the "public" in a public relations sense, meant, essentially, policing middle-class adults and youth ("sold citizens" and their offspring).
- No attempt was made to improve the "product," the programs were designed solely to improve the police "image," there was little or no provision to recommend or effect needed changes in departmental policy (p. 57).

> The Programs approach to police community relations offers opportunities for citizens to engage with law enforcement in various crime prevention and educational endeavors. Citizen feedback is rarely a priority.

Examples of specific programs include the *Community Relations Unit* that engaged in various activities, such as speaking to civic organizations and groups, newsletters, equipment demonstrations, school education programs, and crime prevention talks. Initially these kinds of programs were caned and replicated in agencies that wanted to do something to promote themselves in the increasingly hostile environment of the 1960s. A few of the best endeavors broke free of the one-sided "selling" attitude and actually reached out and provided needed non-crime related services that illustrated a new kind of thinking that would later be called "Problem Oriented Policing."

In San Francisco, the commander of the community relations unit decided to take a different approach that involved working with the disadvantaged and aggrieved members of that community. Officers were deployed in under-served areas, including "skid-row" and the ghetto, to work with youth and previous offenders to help them find work and housing. These officers sought to assist people who lacked skills and resources, and these actions set an example that the police could actually engage in social service without sacrificing their professionalism. Other community relations programs that were born in this era and that can still be found today include:

Neighborhood Crime Watch

Residents are asked to serve as additional "eyes and ears" for the police, watching their neighborhood and reporting suspicious activity. These programs take on particular importance when there is a demand from citizens in response to a rash of crimes, typically burglary. They can also create enormous problems for the police if not carefully managed, as in the George Zimmerman case.[6]

Police Volunteers

Non-sworn citizens are recruited and trained to perform low risk police activities and services, such as crime scene security, weather watching, traffic direction and parking related duties.

Crime Prevention Programs

This category includes programs such as operation identification where valuable property is uniquely marked to facilitate its return if stolen; security surveys where officers give advice on how residents can make their property less attractive to thieves and burglars; and personal defense and awareness training where officers provide tips on how residents can keep themselves safe from violence and attacks.

Crime Stoppers

This program is a cooperative endeavor where individuals and businesses provide reward funding for information leading to arrests in serious or notorious cases.

These programs can be valuable in promoting the police function and engaging the public in a quasi-law enforcement role that is sometimes attractive. The case of George Zimmerman, however, illustrates how involving the public in the policing function can go terribly wrong. This makes these kinds of programs risky for the police. On the one hand, communities and officers, alike, want to do everything possible to maintain order, even to the extent of enlisting citizens in that role, but these programs are not without risk.

The other problem that these programs face is that they generally involve middle and upper-class citizens. Demands for protective services usually follow a horrific string of neighborhood incidents that generate fear and a demand that the police do something. A local resident may offer to host and organize a neighborhood watch group, but when the police arrive to help train and organize the group, they are met by only a few people who are somewhat interested in what they can do to help. The crime prevention officer, in some cases the police chief,

[6] George Zimmerman was a neighborhood watch captain in Sanford Florida in 2012 when he encountered and followed a "suspicious" black teenager, Travon Martin, in an apartment complex. An altercation resulted where Martin was shot to death by Zimmerman, who was not initially charged with a crime.

discusses the incident(s) and outlines exactly what citizens can do in terms of observing and reporting. These meetings often degenerate into petty complaints about speeding, loud music, junk vehicles (with broken windows)[7] as the officer actively solicits input (Wilson, 1982). After an initial "organizational" meeting, the police rarely hear from the new neighborhood watch group again. What is particularly problematic about these programs is that those who are most directly impacted by crime as victims, the poor and marginalized, rarely attend or become involved. This is a particular challenge for the police when pursuing a programs approach to police community relations.

Recognizing Police Work as Social Work

The general belief on the part of individual police officers has been that establishing and maintaining community relations is not "real" police work. Some believe that law enforcement activity unrelated to a crime is a nuisance and that time spent in crime prevention is time better spent investigating and seeking-out criminal perpetrators.

The prevalence of this kind of thinking has resulted in the general neglect of programs aimed at crime prevention and community relations. Thirty years ago there actually were agencies where an officer could make referrals for social problems, such as family counseling, substance abuse counseling and mental health—dumping grounds, if you will, for crime fighters looking to unburden themselves from these social problems. Today, most of those agencies no longer exist due to structural and budgetary changes.

A commitment to police-community relations means that the police accept their role as social workers dedicated to community service. Even if they don't feel that they possess the expertise to provide counseling services, they can take steps to better understand and mitigate the conflicts that drive the need for more competent social services.

Traditional police officers have not thought of themselves as social workers yet this is the kind of work that officers face most of the time. Inherent to social work is the need to develop solid conflict management skills.

The disadvantaged and marginalized members of society, largely ignored, have found their voice and are making new demands of the police. Minorities, recent immigrants, activists, as well as the poor, have voiced grievances that resonate today as demands for social justice. The police, helpless with regard to

7 The famous theory put forth by Wilson and Kelling that says serious crime can be prevented if the police would pay more attention to the small stuff.

these larger societal issues, are now being called upon to suppress the dissent and manage the inevitable conflicts.

As representatives of the status quo, the police were, and are today, vilified and met with open hostility. Public relations programs that are intended to create an environment in which the police can better operate are ineffective in dealing with these disadvantaged members of society. The professional policing model attempted to ignore the fact that police officers are largely social workers in uniform, a role looked on with disdain by many veteran cops that see social work as an unprofessional extension of the law enforcement role (Ross, 2012).

Evidence shows with certainty that the clear majority of police calls do not involve crime. If we accept the role of police officers as social workers, the concept of police community relations becomes much easier to accept and understand. A wise view of policing recognizes that there are underlying problems that lead to conflicts that can ultimately result in crime and disorder. The basic tenants of *Problem Oriented Policing* recognize the role of officers in identifying these underlying problems (conflicts) and taking proactive steps to mitigate them as a key part of policing effectiveness (Goldstein, 1990).

However, the use of the "special unit" approach to police community relations is problematic and not recommended for a number of reasons outlined by Hunter and Barker (2011):

1. By isolating the function in a special unit, the unit becomes vulnerable to organizational ridicule. The community relations unit become known as the "grin and wave" or "rubber gun" squads.
2. After a special unit is formed, everyone else in the department is seemingly relieved of responsibility for enhancing community relations.
3. If the community relations unit should obtain important information about community concerns or ways in which the community might be able to help the department, it is difficult to make those observations heard in the department. Department members are not receptive to bad news or unwelcome demands; after all, that is the responsibility of the unit to stamp out dissent in the community.
4. The organization no longer looks for other ways to improve community relations (p. 61).

Hunter and Barker have done an excellent job outlining not only the underlying problems with community police relations, but they have also hit upon the fundamental reasons why Community Oriented Policing remains a weak and ambiguous concept. It is the image and self-concept of the law enforcement officer perpetuated by popular media and ingrained within the police subculture that undermines officers' abilities to build trust and maintain legitimacy.

Police officers taking the time to engage with their "customers"*

The Community Relations Approach

The success of community police relations requires a "people's police" attitude. Internalizing the need, desire, and importance of good community relations should be the goal of the modern police agency, beginning with the officer selection process. Some agencies do this quite well, as we will discuss later on, but given the autonomous nature of police work, the practice of relegating police community relations to a "special unit" that promotes "special programs" and activities has not proven to be effective.

> The effectiveness of the public relations and Programs approaches to police community relations has been retarded because these strategies are internally or agency focused. An external or community focus is driving the best efforts today.

At the heart of great police-community relations is a police self-concept that stresses service rather than crime fighting. Viewing citizens—no matter rich, middle-class, and poor—as customers of the police or clients, as in the private sector, is useful in developing an underlying vision of what behaviors are desired. Feedback and citizen input is a key to improvement, and each individual officer

* Image labeled for unrestricted use.

must understand that they have a personal responsibility for how their behavior impacts citizen satisfaction with police service.

In the same way a private company does market research, the police agency should actively engage in an ongoing effort to monitor and analyze various indicators of community support and satisfaction. Individual officers should feel comfortable engaging with community members in non-crime related discussions about conditions, problems, and issues present in the neighborhood; this kind of "intelligence gathering" not only supports great police community relations but it also provides perhaps the most valuable intelligence on criminal activity.

Differences Between Programs Approach and Community Relations Approach

Police agencies that seek to improve their image engage in programs that promote the agency, its officers, and the special programs that they employ. In many cases, these agencies will segregate these activities by creating special units to manage various programs. The creation of these special units clearly demonstrates a commitment on the part of the chief to improving the police-community relationship and demonstrates a firm desire to build trust and legitimacy. These agencies, and this philosophy, can be characterized as being *agency focused.* These programs primarily serve the needs of the agency, provide benefits to agency personnel, and enhance the image of the agency in the eyes of the community.

Representatives of a typical police agency on public display*

In contrast to the agency focused perspective, the *community focused* (oriented) agency provides services that are important to the community. The legacy of the professional era of policing relates to a concept that the police should adhere to

* Image labeled for unrestricted use.

professional standards, best practices in crime fighting, and policing practices that are uncovered through a developed body of knowledge. Many police agencies submit themselves to the *Accreditation*[8] process, whereby their status as a professional law enforcement agency is affirmed. Even though the accreditation process is agency-focused, this does not imply that the agency is internally focused. One of the most risky endeavors a municipality engages in is law enforcement. The daily activities of police officers is inherently dangerous to themselves and others and is, therefore, the source of tremendous concern and liability from a legal standpoint. Accreditation seeks to minimize this risk through standardization and risk avoidance. Accreditation certainly serves the best interests of the community because it is the community that ultimately pays the price in money, reputation, and quality of life when things go wrong and tragedies occur.

Community Oriented Policing and Police-Community Relations

Community Oriented Policing emerged in the 1990s as a major philosophical shift in how the police are conceptualized. Originally put forth as a new and innovative crime suppression strategy, community oriented policing sought to enlist community organizations in the fight against crime and violence. Today, community oriented policing advocates point to the professional model of policing as a hindrance to the development of this new philosophy.

The modern police agency needs to adhere to professional standards, but the "hue and cry" has gone out clearly and loudly that the police need to listen and draw their priorities from the community, not from police leaders within the agency itself.

> In general terms, community policing is not a program; it is not a set of activities; it is not a personnel designation. Rather, community policing is a law enforcement philosophy, a way of thinking about improving public safety (Lawrence, 2013).

The professional police agency can and should be community-focused. In this way, it can pursue the goals of the community oriented policing philosophy without the risk of returning to the pre-reform era problems of owing allegiance

[8] Police Agency accreditation is a process by which an agency will submit itself for review by representatives of a professional organization, such as CALEA (Commission on Accreditation for Law Enforcement Agencies). Whereby the policies, procedures, and practices of the agency are compared to recognized standards and best practices of law enforcement. An agency that is deemed in compliance with these standards is awarded with "professional" status and deemed to be professionally managed.

to political patrons and the resulting corruption and lack of legitimacy. Police leaders from the chief down to the neighborhood police officer walking the beat can adhere to professional standards, while, at the same time, listening to community members about their issues and concerns. Such practices have utility and importance to both the crime fighting role and the community relations concept.

Community Oriented Policing is a philosophy that forces the police agency to step outside of its "professional" comfort zone and seek input and cooperation from the community.

Community Oriented Policing Background

Policing in the United States has been driven by a number of reform eras. The primitive town marshal or constable was the first incarnation of the desire to have men employed in a full-time capacity controlling crime and disorder. These were not professionals, as was the case in Great Britain, rather, they were individuals entrusted with this responsibility due to their reputation or "political" connections in the community.

As municipal police agencies grew due to the impact of urbanization, the selection of new police officers was based on political allegiance, rather than demonstrated merit or competency. Any comparison between law enforcement in the United States and the policing system set-up by Robert Peel, which was governed by his "people's police" perspective, needs to recognize the difference. Police in the United States were amateurs who owed allegiance to local authority, whereas police in Great Britain were professionals, selected for their merit, skills, and demeanor, who owed their allegiance to a national authority and professional standards that existed during that time.

The policing system in the United States has endured a number of reform efforts. First was the movement away from the corrupt influence of politicians who directed the police toward self-serving goals. The second was a move toward *progressive* ideals that valued efficiency in operation. The third reform, closely tied to the progressive movement, sought to professionalize the police. Professionalization recognized the need to identify *best practices* and grow a *body of knowledge* about policing that would result in a set of professional standards that trained and educated police managers could follow with regard to crime suppression and management practices.

The image of the professional crime fighter was attractive to the police themselves. The unintended side-effect was a tendency to isolate police agencies from the communities they served. Technology allowed officers to mobilize and deploy, so the primary measure of police effectiveness at that time—rapid response to calls for service—was achieved. Motorized vehicle patrol took officers away from the foot beat and further isolated them from the public.

Content to roam the city waiting for the dispatcher to assign a call, officers no longer had any incentive to stop their relentless patrolling and engage with people, especially the poor, marginalized, and disadvantaged members of the community. Because of their "professional" status, officers also felt free to live outside of the cities where they worked. To be a professional is to be wholly objective and remote from "those" people. Officers began to view themselves as somehow better than or superior to those who called for police assistance and certainly superior to those involved in crime and disorder. There was simply no **accountability** to the community, especially to that part of the community represented by the poor and marginalized who were most often the targets of repressive law enforcement practices.

Peaceful civil rights protestors*

Civil unrest of the 1960s was the first clear sign that something was going terribly wrong in urban areas. Large segments of the population were not being well served by the police, and the police response to these issues was to further withdraw from those areas where they were not likely to be well received. The incentives for ignoring crime and disorder in the ghetto were strong with police intervention being challenged with statements such as "the only reason you're arresting me is because I'm black." With no effective way to force officers to engage with those who most desperately needed the police, including poor people of color, police limited their contacts with the most vulnerable members and crime grew to epidemic proportions.

* Image labeled for unrestricted use.

To fight this new "War on Crime" and "War on Drugs," urban leaders who, ironically, were predominantly people of color themselves demanded action from the federal government. The president responded with a promise to put 100,000 more cops on the streets of our cities. The stated intent of this action was to deploy more officers into "Community Oriented Policing" activities, however, cops do what cops do, which resulted in a surge of drug arrests fueled by billions of federal dollars that incentivized aggressive enforcement practices and proactive policing. *This was not the kind of proactive, problem-solving policing intended by the community oriented policing movement, but rather a proactive policing that aggressively sought-out and hunted-down crime perpetrators.*

More proactive arrests led to more convictions and, when combined with mandatory sentencing guidelines, resulted in mass incarceration, which of course, disproportionately impacts poor people of color. The incentives were very clear: more arrests equal more funding. Where are officers going to go for these arrests? Would they target the high-rent district, where people of means engage in drug use but have the economic resources to fight an arrest? Or would the police concentrate their efforts in the ghetto where people have little to lose, where open drug use and drug dealing is easy to spot, and where people do not have the resources to challenge an arrest? The path of least resistance and incentives led cops to the ghetto and undermined exactly what community oriented policing was intended to develop—trust and legitimacy.

The professionalization of the police has led to increased isolation and created a whole new set of social justice issues. Community Oriented Policing is the latest reform effort that was initially put forth as a new and innovative way to reduce crime. Towards this goal, it has largely failed, but it does hold promise as a mechanism to build better police-community relationships.

As an overall philosophy, community oriented policing is vastly misunderstood and has resulted in confusion on the part of police officers and the public alike. From a conceptualization standpoint, it has a number of components.

> Community Oriented Policing has not been proven effective in reducing crime and disorder. It does however, correlate nicely with mass incarceration.

Organizational Transformation

Police agencies are traditionally structured as bureaucracies to facilitate efficiency of operations and control. Bringing about higher levels of innovation, which is seen as a key to the problem-solving approach to crime control, is thought to require decentralization of authority. Rather than having tall hierarchical arrangements with multiple levels of authority to facilitate accountability—command and control—community oriented policing stresses a flatter organizational structure with fewer levels of authority. This kind of organizational structure is intended to empower officers to make decisions on their own rather than seeking supervisory or management authority. In the typical bureaucratic police organization, officers are deployed with the goal of rapid response to calls for service and assigned to geographic areas based on call volume and crime severity. Community oriented policing seeks to re-deploy officers from random patrol to specific geographic areas with the goal of building better relationships with the people who live there. Revitalizing the old concept of having cops on the beat who are familiar with their territory and who are familiar to the residents is intended to facilitate a closeness that has been lost with the advent of motorized vehicle patrol tactics.

The past practice of only using sworn personnel in all policing roles is also challenged with community oriented policing:

> To deal with sworn-personnel shortfalls, some cities have expanded the civilianization of police services to include limited officer-level functions. For example, the City of San Francisco, faced with a slew of retiring officers for whom there was little funding to replace, began in 2010 a program to train 16 "civilian investigators." These paid, nonsworn, employees are trained to respond to service calls dealing with non-violent crimes such as car burglaries. They are tasked with performing basic work such as taking victim information, collecting evidence, and creating a report which is then referred to officers at the stations for further investigation (Lawrence, 2013).

Community Partnerships

The concept of community partnership means that, when deciding on operational priorities and programs, the police actively seek out community input. The question is not what is important to furthering department and professional goals—an internal focus, but it is rather what is important to the community—**an external focus**. The key is to focus on ways to make the department and its resources more accessible:

> Police had been dealing with an emerging gang and burglary problem that was centered around a set of high density, multi-family housing complexes. The Naperville Police Department in 2002 opened a neighborhood service center in the area with extended evening hours

> and a mix of sworn and civilian personnel. The center provided a number of basic civic and public safety services such as obtaining crime prevention information, filing police reports, paying utility bills, and obtaining parking permits. The center proved extremely popular, with hundreds of local residents utilizing a variety of services within the first three months of its opening (Lawrence, 2013).

Problem-Solving

Problem-solving involves a much closer analysis of crime problems. The traditional police agency is reactive in nature—a crime occurs and the police respond, investigate, and sometimes make an arrest. Problem Oriented Policing is a process, as opposed to Community Oriented Policing, which is a philosophy. Problem oriented policing involves grouping crime incidents and analyzing them in an effort to discover underlying conditions that can be addressed in a proactive manner by the police (Goldstein, 1990).

> Joint task forces made up of the police and one or more existing community groups were established to solve specific community problems. In the mid 1990s, the Anaheim Police Department successfully reduced blight and disorder in the Leatrice/Wakefield neighborhood by working with landlords, tenants, and the Office of Neighborhood Services to create a Neighborhood Advisory Committee tasked with removing problem tenants and reducing unit overcrowding. In the following years, the neighborhood saw marked improvements in building safety, vacancy rates, and reductions in incident reports (Lawrence, 2013).

EMERGENCE OF POLICE-COMMUNITY RELATIONS

According to Hunter and Barker (2011), police-community relations presents a new philosophical point-of-view, distinct from the professional model of policing. It is a higher-level concept than the programs approach; it is aimed at building trust and mutual understanding that identifies potential sources of conflict and seeks to mitigate them. To achieve its mission, a police agency needs the support and active participation of the citizens served. Such a mission requires that the agency seek to develop the following:

- A high level of police-community understanding and trust.
- Effective and meaningful two-way communication.

- Increased community awareness of crime problems and ways to reduce the probability of being victimized.
- Alternative resources for the agency that will increase productivity and more effective use of certified officers (Hunter, 2011, p. 77).

The common theme throughout the community oriented policing reform era and the philosophy of police community relations is community involvement. To what extent can and should the community be involved in policing? To what extent are individual citizens willing to partner with the police? To what extent are individual citizens willing to engage in the risky endeavors associated with law enforcement? Who in the community is willing to shoulder these burdens and why? These are critical questions to answer in an era of diversity and inclusion as those who are most likely to engage with the police may not be those with the greatest stake in the policing function. But it is important to recognize those who do feel a need for, or willingness to, engage with the police in community relations efforts. Such people are often called "stakeholders."

The Police Community Relations approach to police community relations recognizes the supremacy of community needs and desires. It requires that police agencies take affirmative steps to build and maintain cooperative relationships.

Recognizing Stakeholders

The concept of stakeholders relates to individuals who can affect and who are affected by the actions of the police. Examples of stakeholders include:

- The citizen who calls the police because they have been a victim of crime.
- A citizen who calls the police because they need emergency assistance or intervention.
- A citizen who enjoys economic prosperity reflected in the increasing property values of their home due to a higher quality of life than what is typical in a neighboring city.
- Those who are charged with a crime.
- The family of those who are arrested.
- The family of those victimized by crime.

By recognizing *the stakeholders* of police action, **compassion** on the part of the police can be employed to reduce resentment and build understanding for the police role. Identifying such people and utilizing them to help build bridges to the community can pay big dividends in improving police-community relations.

Community Oriented Policing as Community Relations

Community oriented policing has fallen short of its crime reduction goals, but it holds promise as one of the best externally oriented public relations programs. First, the effects include a focus on defending the police agency in times of crisis from relentless criticism and adverse media coverage. An agency that actively engages in community outreach is much better equipped to deal with an inevitable crisis because it has proactively engaged with important and significant community groups. Second, commitment to community oriented policing helps legitimize the law enforcement function and the need for social control. Third, less coercive and informal forms of social control can be fostered in order to paint the police as agents of social good rather than as a repressive force.

As a public relations program, community oriented policing also has a number of drawbacks. First, it consumes substantial police resources leaving the agency open to criticism for engaging in activities not directly related to its primary mission of crime suppression. Second, the idea that the police are, or can be, a one-stop shop for all manner of social services fosters an unrealistic image of their capabilities. Individuals and groups who are not well served, in their opinion, by the police are much more likely to withdraw their support. Third, community oriented policing efforts are not likely to engage those community members who are most affected by crime and disorder. Community outreach efforts and neighborhood meetings are seldom attended by poor people and others who are most directly impacted by crime. In most cases, police hear about concerns related to disorderly citizens, speeding cars, drug dealing and other quality of life issues. Armed with this information, the police may then engage in enforcement practices, such as directed patrol, hot-spot policing, and aggressive drug interdiction efforts that target low-income individuals in urban areas, including people of color. These efforts paint the police as a repressive force, an army of occupation, and further the perception that the police do not act in the best interests of the whole community, only those with means.

The problem with community oriented policing is the lack of active participation by the community, especially those individuals and groups who need the police the most because they don't have any other options. Conflict management between the police and communities of color is critical to effectively policing a democratic society. Managing these conflicts has its foundation in understanding the differing point-of-views, a consensus regarding the exchange relationships that govern communities of color may hold promise. It is in these areas of concern that stakeholders, once identified and utilized, can be most productive.

Police officers engaged in social work, the heart of police community relations*

RESPONDING TO TERRORISM: A NEW REALITY THREATENS EFFORTS TO BUILD BETTER RELATIONSHIPS

The threat of crime and criminal victimization allows the police to engage in practices that most would consider brutal and even barbaric. When directed at those who would harm society and cause us to live in fear, police behavior that is outside the bounds of acceptable conduct has been easily forgiven. In this type of climate, history teaches us that attention to police community relations can be set-aside. In the wake of the 911 attack, the threat of terrorism shifted priorities and led to police militarization, hardly the stuff of great police community relations. The following is the lead paragraph in a report from the International Association of Chiefs of Police:

> The September 11th attacks on the United States redirected priorities with a suddenness perhaps unprecedented in the American police experience. Homeland security, the constant threat of terrorism on our shores, concern with weapons of mass destruction, and security-related intelligence demands surged to the forefront of state and local policing. Requirements and implications of the Patriot Act, homeland security funding, and equipment and training distribution issues have penetrated the law enforcement enterprise at all levels. With no time for preparation, law enforcement repositioning to confront these demands and issues has been paralleled by 9-11 fallouts, including military (reserve) mobilizations that skim police manpower, material

* Image labeled for unrestricted use.

expenditures for overtime and color alert mobilization, and heightened concern for preservation of civil liberties (IACP, 2005).

> The terrorism threat promotes attitudes and behaviors on the part of the police that have a tremendous potential to undermine police community relations.

Militarized police officers*

Shifting the role of the police from domestic crime control to aggressive militarized defense of the homeland in the face of an eminent terrorist threat has had a transformative impact on how the police are viewed and perceived in many of urban areas. This is also a role that the police have largely embraced because it speaks to how they view their primary role as crime fighters, in this case the crime is terrorist-triggered mass destruction.

While some level of preparedness is certainly appropriate, an all-out focus on the assumed deterrence effect (a more military bearing) undermines the foundational principles of democratic policing. Officers are to be service-oriented, cooperative, friendly, even-tempered, and unassuming, but that doesn't happen when the police are hyper-militarized. The hallmark of effective policing, in both providing service and crime fighting, rests in the officer's ability to acquire information; the same thing is true in counter-terrorism investigations. The needed information comes from the people in the community, so essentially the officer needs to know who to talk to and community members need to be willing to share information with the police. Ironically, this is the mark of both effective policing and effective counter-terrorist efforts.

* Image labeled for unrestricted use.

Police Deviance as a Hindrance to Community Relations

The advocates of community oriented policing have pushed an attractive agenda for improving the police, yet the literature does not include any risk acknowledgment of increased police officer deviance that this philosophy offers. The professional policing reform movement sought to remove the police from the corrupting influence of local political control. It advocated a quasi-military organizational model to improve efficiency and accountability. These reform actors advocated for professional standards, training, and education to battle incompetency and brutality. The police function was limited to crime control rather than the myriad of social functions the police performed that took them away from their primary mission. The hallmark of the professional policing movement was that the police were encouraged to interact with citizens in a neutral and detached manner (Kappler, 1998).

Community oriented policing thus seeks to bring the police closer to the community, charging officers on the beat with establishing relationships with individuals and groups. It seeks to dismantle the quasi-military organizational systems in favor of decentralized control and administration but most importantly, community oriented policing seeks to expand the role of the police. Under the banner of problem-solving, the police are charged with undertaking the role of a community ombudsman, where literally nothing is beyond their reach (Goldstein, 1990).

> The Professional era of policing stressed accountability, command, control and a limited role for the police, i.e. crime control. Community Oriented Policing removes many accountability and control mechanisms and greatly expands the police role to include all kinds of "social work." At the same time it expands the opportunity for corruption reversing a fundamental priority of the professional policing era.

But the potential for deviance and corruption is profound in policing. History and basic economics show that people will take advantage of incentives where incentives exist. There are tremendous incentives for deviance in policing, and where the professional reform movement countered these incentives with firm dis-incentives in the form of discipline and other accountability mechanisms, community oriented policing inadvertently **weakens** them.

Police deviance, defined as any behavior that is perceived by members of a social group as violating their norms, generally takes the following forms as identified by Kappeler et al. (1998):

Police crime refers to violation of law by the police. A profound example was the Summerdale scandal in Chicago that led to professional reforms in the Chicago police department led by O.W. Wilson. In these cases, police officers are actively engaged in criminal acts for their own benefit. Modern examples include the lure of drugs and the money that can be extorted from drug dealers in exchange for protection or the active distribution of the illegal drugs by the police. This category of deviance refers to law enforcement officers committing traditional crime in their capacity as police officers (p. 21).

Occupational deviance refers to behavior both criminal and non-criminal that is committed under the guise of the police officers' authority. This kind of deviance is made possible because of the position that the law enforcement officer holds, such behavior would not be possible were it not for the position. This category of deviance is characterized as abuse of position; examples include taking property and equipment for personal gain, abusing prisoners, making false statements on police reports or in court, demanding sexual favors, etc.

Corruption refers to the acceptance of a reward, favor or money for engaging is behavior that the police have a duty to do anyway. It is the use of organizational or positional power for personal gain. Examples include accepting cash for ignoring gambling violations, liquor control laws or for intervening is personal (civil) disputes (p. 23).

Abuse of authority is any action by a police officer without regard to motive, intent, or malice that tends to injure, insult, tread on human dignity, manifest feelings of inferiority, and/or violate an inherent legal right of a member of the police constituency (stakeholder) (Carter, 1985). Examples include the physical abuse of others, such as excessive force, psychological abuse through the use of verbal assault, harassment, or ridicule, and legal abuse where the police violate an individual's legal or constitutional rights (Kappler, 1998).

It is ironic that much of the basis of criticism of the police today, what is commonly referred to as the "police problem," relates to isolated and exceedingly rare instances of police deviance. Advocates for change preach the philosophy of community oriented policing as the solution with its emphasis on "relationship building" combined with decentralization of control, de-militarization and empowerment of line officers. *This is exactly the opposite of what is needed to control police deviance and corruption.*

Human Relations Approach

What does it take to be a great police officer? All of them start out wanting to be successful, they prepare themselves for the chosen calling and seek out training and a mentor to help develop the necessary skills and competencies. Training and mentorship, however, can only get people so far, no matter what craft or profession they choose. Consider the individual who possesses extensive technical knowledge and training but cannot get along or relate to co-workers or the customer. Consider the physician who focuses purely on the disease and its symptoms or the cold and detached lawyer who focuses only on the legal arguments. Now consider the police officer who focuses only on the application of the law. What does this officer look like? What image do you have of an officer like this?

RoboCop: a police officer without humanity*

Technical skills are simply not enough. Demands for improving policing by mandating more training fail to recognize what is really needed, which, unfortunately, additional training hours will not produce. Reece (2014) puts it this way:

> A lack of technical skills is not the primary reason new hires fail to meet employer expectations and experienced workers falter on the road to career success. Today's best companies want new hires to be strong in two areas: technical skills and interpersonal skills. Interpersonal skills, sometimes described as soft or people skills, fall into two categories:

* Image labeled for unrestricted use.

> Personal qualities: Treating others with sensitivity, making the right ethical choices, emotional control, ability to work as a team member, etc.
>
> Thinking skills: Ability to engage in creative problem solving, make appropriate decisions, apply critical listening skills, etc. (p. 4).

What we have here is the difference between someone who is really smart in terms of training and education but can't seem to relate well with others. Some people refer to this person as the educated idiot, compare him or her to someone who may not have all the college degrees but who has the ability to make people feel welcome, valued, and appreciated. Once we recognize that policing is really a people business, the value of those people skills becomes clear. This section provides an overview of these skills, also referred to as the foundation of emotional intelligence. The importance of these skills in managing conflict cannot be overstated.

> This illustrates the concept of Emotional Intelligence, an individual attribute that is critical to the "wise" police officer today.

Human Relations

We can define human relations as the study of human behavior—why self-image, beliefs attitudes, prejudices, and bias sometimes cause problems in professional and personal contacts and relationships. For the police officer, competency rests in the understanding that all productive work is done through relationships. The very first relationship that needs to be cultivated is with **the self**, then the particular individual(s) we are relating to, and then the group(s) we associate with.

Police agencies hire individuals for particular competences that the agency feels are important to the organization. What many are coming to realize, however, is that effective policing depends on human relation skills; technical competency cannot be separated from the individual's particular characteristics or attributes. The **total person** concept relates to the understanding that an individual's characteristics, skills, attitudes, self-awareness, and values are interrelated and interdependent (Reece, 2014). When we hire someone, we hire the total package, or *total person* (Reece, 2014). Factors that influence an individual's human relations skills include communication, with self and others; self-awareness; self-acceptance (worth); motivation; trust; self-disclosure; and conflict resolution (management) (p. 14).

The ability to communicate effectively relates to both the words used and how words are used. Our choice of words not only facilitates understanding but also communicates to others how we view them, their relative importance to us, our self-concept and attitudes. We may, for example, use highly technical language when conversing with our college professor, but in a discussion with a significant other, we may use less technical language because we want them to understand what we have been learning in college. On the other hand, we may use a certain kind of language because we wish to communicate our superiority-feed our ego-or imply inferiority to others in order to facilitate rapport. The choice of communication strategy is always **situational**, dependent on the circumstance, location, surroundings, and the relationship between and among the individuals present.

Rapport

Rapport is the hallmark of great communicators that can be described as a harmonious and reciprocal mini-relationship between individuals or an individual and a group. It takes the form of a connection or linkage where the parties are in-sync with each other. We may all be familiar with the phrase "It's not what he said; it's how he said it." This is an indication of the lack of rapport and the lack of the acceptance of the message, or it can also be an indication that a specific message was made perfectly clear.

Non-Verbal Aspects of Communication

If we separate the words from the message, what is left is non-verbal. This term relates to the voice pitch, speed, tone, volume, and inflections used. It can also relate to body posture, proximity, facial expressions, eye movement, dress, physical contact, gestures, and even how people orient their feet. Everyone has their own **communication style**, and it is important for us to understand the signals we convey to others in both the verbal and non-verbal realm. The master communicator has the ability to flex their communication style based on the situation.

Self-Esteem and Self-Worth

Self-esteem is an element of human relations that greatly impacts our relationships with others. It can be described as our opinion or attitudes about ourselves that commonly takes the form of our confidence level, estimations of our own abilities, and our self-respect. **Self-esteem** defines who we are to ourselves and governs how we approach others, based on our perceptions, attitudes, prejudices, and bias toward them. **Self-worth** is the sense of our own value as an individual. Those with low sense of self-worth often engage in self-destructive behavior, including crime, and are likely to tolerate abusive treatment and situations. Self-esteem and self-worth are the starting point of our ability to relate to others.

Self-esteem and self-worth influence our behavior and are sensed, often at an unconscious level, by others. Those with low self-esteem tend to believe that their life is not within their own control. Outside forces or luck determine how successful or unsuccessful they will be, and they tend to blame others for their situation. These individuals are likely to engage in self-destructive behavior, such as smoking, drinking and drug use. They usually display antagonistic attitudes, fail to accept responsibility, and have generally poor people skills. They tend to rely on other people for validation and are hyper-sensitive to perceived slights. **Emotions drive behavior** in people with low self-esteem, and they are easy to anger. Police officers and others in authority can provide powerful sources of validation for those who continually seek support from sources outside of themselves.

People with high self-esteem are comfortable with themselves and believe that **they are responsible** for their own situation in life. When they make mistakes, they learn from them and are less likely to blame others, society, or bad-luck for negative outcomes. People with high self-esteem are in control of their emotions and can reason through problems more effectively. They are less sensitive to perceived slights and tend to not take things personally. They are more accepting of others, especially those who are different from themselves because they don't rely on others for their own validation. People with high self-esteem approach life in a positive way, are resilient, and are imaginative problem solvers. They are much less likely to come to the attention of the police, but when they do, they can make excellent partners in problem solving (Reece, 2014).

Human Relations and Managing Conflict

Conflict is not a bad thing. Recognizing the value of differing perspectives is the first step in developing solid conflict management skill. The ability to manage conflict is a characteristic of great police officers and can be the foundation of great police community relations. Conflict presents an opportunity for advancement, development, and change. Without it, humans stagnate and become complacent as individuals, and the same thing can be said for entire communities.

When police officers are summoned to intervene in conflict, it means that the conflict has risen beyond the capabilities of the parties to manage; this is likely dysfunctional conflict. Emotions are likely running high, and the situation is volatile. These situations present an opportunity to practice human relations skills with the goal of limiting the potential for deeper conflict or violence and enhancing the positive, relationship building.

Conflict has triggers, and these **triggers** vary depending on the characteristics of the individual, their self-esteem, self-worth and motivations. Recognizing potential triggers leads to the root causes of dysfunctional conflict. The root causes can be attributed to a history of dysfunctional conflict, unmet expectations of one party or both, self-perceptions, emotions or the lack of emotional control. Police officers are not equipped to engage in such analysis; however, they should always assume that dysfunctional conflict has deeper sources than what is being put forth in times of crisis.

Conflict is uncomfortable for people, even good conflict puts us on edge because we are hesitant to share insight or opinion out of fear of how it will be received by others. This causes us to engage in one of the most common conflict resolution strategies: **avoidance**. We tend to skirt around issues, situations, and people in an effort to avoid uncomfortable confrontations. People engage in non-assertive behavior just to avoid conflict, and this can make the inevitable conflict much worse. Police are not called upon to intervene unless the conflict has reached a critical point, and in these cases, emotions are running high. The passive nature of one party can actually lead to conflict as resentment builds over time until it explodes. Police officers with highly developed human relations skills can assist in helping the non-assertive party express their underlying resentment in terms of behaviors, not the characteristics, of the other party.

Negotiation in Policing

The police are often called in conflict situations when one party seeks to employ the coercive power of the police to intervene on their side of the issue. When the police understand this, they can employ human relations skills to convince the parties to think **win-win**. The battle for dominance needs to be replaced with a solution that provides benefit to both or all parties. A solution that advances on individuals interests at the expense of someone else is to be avoided. Win-Lose solutions are a "no deal"; each side must be willing to sacrifice something to maintain the relationship. The fundamental human relations skill required of the police officer here is *listening*.

Always seek "win, win" solutions. Don't accept "win-lose" where one party is diminished.

Human relations skill is a critical aspect of effective policing and when employed by individual police officers has a tremendous impact on the reputation of a police agency. Police officers who are sensitive and compassionate garner goodwill in the community and provide a foundation for great police community relations.

Chapter Summary

The job of policing is simply easier when the police enjoy good relations with the community they serve. People are more willing to report crime, cooperate with investigations, and offer support for the police when it is needed. The very nature of the policing function, however, generates resentment, and democratic societies are very leery of overreaching governmental control. Peel recognized this and was careful to create standards for selection and officer behavior that spoke to the need to mitigate that resentment, build trust, and maintain the legitimacy of his police.

The public relations approach to police community relations is intended to enhance the image of the police as professional crime fighters. These efforts are generally internally focused with the goal of creating a better environment for the police to engage in their policing and law enforcement activities. This approach is characterized by programs that often seek to engage and inform the public about police practices, capitalizing on the inherent fascination the police enjoy in the public eye.

The programs approach is characterized by efforts to promote the agency with activities that go beyond the routine basic mission. Officer Friendly, McGruff, DARE, and similar efforts seek to enhance the image of the agency in the eyes of the community. Crime prevention programs, such as operation ID and home/business security surveys, help to educate citizens on how to keep themselves safe. Other programs, such as neighborhood watch, encourage citizens to act as additional eyes and ears of the department. Some agencies have even offered citizens the opportunity to engage in low-risk policing functions, such as parking and traffic control. The citizen police academy seeks to educate citizens on the law enforcement function and further capitalize on the public fascination with policing to enhance the image of the agency. Overall, the programs approach seeks to educate citizens in the spirit of good public relations in order to build support for agency operations.

The community relations approach is characterized by a genuine effort on the part of the police to engage with the community. It is an externally focused effort to build cooperation that ranges from soliciting public feedback to the actual employment of citizens in low risk policing functions. The community relations concept seeks to advance the idea that the citizens are the police and the police are merely citizens who are paid to devote their full-time attention to crime control. Police agencies have allowed citizens to engage in what have been traditional law enforcement roles, even allowing citizens to engage in surveillance and low risk enforcement activities. Community relations programs, however, can be a risky endeavor if not managed and monitored adequately, as the George Zimmerman case illustrates. Overall, the goal of the community relations approach is to involve citizens in determining how and what police services will be provided. This approach used the programs approach as a foundation for educating citizens about policing and then seeks to draw support, involvement, and commitment from the community.

Community oriented policing is intended to replace the reactive professional policing model with a proactive strategy of community engagement to combat growing crime and disorder. Officers are tasked to identify problems and then engage in problem-solving to head off crime problems. Police agencies and individual officers are encouraged to build partnerships and relationships in the community. Police agencies are to abandon the traditional and impersonal organizational arrangements intended to control and direct police operations in favor of a decentralized organizational system that empowers officers to engage, problem-solve, and act on threats to citizen's quality of life.

The community oriented policing strategy has not proven effective in controlling crime but it does hold promise as one of the best police community relations strategies. The organizational culture of a police agency committed to community oriented policing recognizes a service orientation, as opposed to a crime fighting orientation. This becomes apparent when considering the difference between the warrior police mindset and the guardianship mindset that is most conducive to great police community relations.

Great police officers are always great people; they have a high level of human relations skill, sometimes referred to as emotional intelligence, and employ it regularly both within and outside the police agency. Developing and cultivating people skills is the next evolution in policing that has the potential to carry us beyond the limitations of community oriented policing.

Bibliography

Carter, D. (1985). Police Brutality: A Model for Definition, Perspective and Control. In A.S. Blumberg and E. Niederhoffer (eds), *The Ambivalent Force*. New York: Holt, Rinehart and Winston.

Community Relations Service. (2016). *Community Relations Toolkit for Police.* Washington: U.S. Department of Justice.

Dempsey, J.S. (2016). *An Introduction to Policing, 8th ed.* Boston: Cengage Learning.

Goldstein, H. (1977). *Policing a Free Society.* Cambridge, MA: Ballinger.

Goldstein, H. (1990). *Problem Oriented Policing.* New York: McGraw-Hill.

Hunter, R.D. (2011). *Police Community Relations and the Administration of Justice, 8th ed.* Saddle River, NJ: Pearson.

IACP. (2005). *Post 9-11 Policing. The Crime Control-Homeland Security Paradigm. Taking Command of New Realities.* Washington: BJA.

Kappler, V.E. (1998). *Forces of Deviance.* Prospect Heights, IL: Waveland.

Lawrence, S. (2013). *What Works in Community Policing.* Berkeley, CA: The Chief Justice Earl Warren Institute.

Lee, M. (1971). *A History of Police in England.* Montclair, NJ: Patterson Smith.

Peel, R. (1829). *Principles of Law Enforcement.*

Reece, B.L. (2014). *Effective Human Relations, 12th ed.* Mason, OH: South-Western Cengage Learning.

Ross, J. (2012). *Policing Issues.* Sudbury: Jones & Bartlett.

Trautman, N.E. (2002). *How to Be a Great Cop.* Upper Saddle River, NJ: Prentice Hall.

Van Maanen, J. (1978). "The Asshole". In P. Manning and J. Van Maanen (eds), *Policing: A View from the Street.* Santa Monica, CA: Goodyear Publishing.

Wilson, J.Q., Kelling, G. (1982). "Broken Windows: The Police and Neighborhood Safety." *Atlantic Monthly*, 29–38.

CHAPTER 4

The Nature of Conflict

■ ■ ■

The person who gets into an argument and his only resort is to take a gun or some offensive weapon and eliminate the other person. I understand that many of these persons do not have reasoning skills. They do not have the basic conflict management skills to resolve basic issues between themselves and others. So they resort to what they know best, which is violence, the animalistic instinct. —Mr. Hulan Hanna, Former Assistant Commissioner of Police, Royal Bahamas Police Force

Learning Outcomes

Upon successful completion of this chapter the student will be able to:

- Explain why conflict can be good.
- Describe the main sociological perspectives of social interaction.
- Describe the concept of the pristine self and how it comes into conflict with objective rationality.
- Compare and contrast the value of cooperation and competition.
- Argue why justice is seen differently from the distributive versus procedural perspectives.

Important Concepts

- Conflict Resolution vs. Conflict Management
- Subjective vs. Objective Meaning
- Symbolic Interactionism
- The Pristine Self

- Appropriate Honesty
- Distributive Justice
- Relative Deprivation
- Procedural Justice
- Restorative Justice
- Trust

Questions for Discussion

- Many individuals see conflict as a bad thing and seek to manage it by means that range from avoidance to coercion. Discuss the reasons why avoidance may be a good choice and a bad choice in particular situations.
- Discuss the difference between constructive and dysfunctional conflict. What are some strategies that can be used to encourage constructive conflict and avoid dysfunctional conflict?
- Identify the two types of conflict identified by Deutsch and discuss why most conflicts are merely disagreement related to how mutual goals are achieved.
- Identify and discuss the main sociological perspectives on conflict. Why is it important to differentiate between them?
- Identify and discuss each of the causes of conflict as well as the factors present in all conflict situations.
- Identify why the concept of justice is very often a basis for conflict. Why is this important for the police to understand?

> ***Conflict***
>
> *An active disagreement between people with opposing opinions or principles.*

INTRODUCTION

In this chapter, the basics of conflict will be explored, including where conflict originates and how differing perspectives often drive conflict. Not all conflict is bad; in fact, the greatest advancements in history have been driven by conflict. People, like animals, seek comfort in sameness—patterns of behavior, interaction, and associations. Differences cause stress, anxiety and, of course, conflict. Understanding the various perspectives upon which conflict is based offers the possibility of avoiding dysfunctional conflict and developing better conflict management strategies.

Conflict can be harmful and to avoid the harm that can result we need to understand what is referred to as the "Four Awful Truths:" Conflict will occur, it is inherent in human interaction; conflict always involves some risks and costs; the damage that occurs in conflict results not so much from the conflict itself but by the *dysfunctional strategies* that we use to deal with it; and some of the damage that occurs in conflict situations is irreversible (Dues, 2016).

SOCIAL CONFLICT

Conflict can take many forms. Differences of opinion, differing perspectives, and differing attitudes can lead to tension, where one party seeks to impose his or her views on another. Conflict can also occur within the individual, which is commonly referred to as cognitive dissonance. **Cognitive dissonance** occurs when an individual's attitudes are not consistent with his or her beliefs or behavior (McLeod, 2014).

Most conflict situations, whether between individuals or groups, are confrontations over power. The unequal distribution of power in society and between individuals can lead to either 1. cooperative arrangements as actors seek cooperation and order or 2. conflict as the actors struggle for a more equal distribution of power and resources in a zero-sum game where one party gains advantage by diminishing the other in some way.

> *A conflict is the moment of truth in a relationship-a test of its health, a crisis that can weaken or strengthen it, a critical event that may bring lasting resentment, smoldering hostility, psychological scars. . . . Few persons accept the fact that conflict is part of life and not necessarily bad.*[1]

Conflict can result from any situation in which one party's needs are not being met.

WHY CONFLICT MANAGEMENT AND NOT CONFLICT RESOLUTION

Conflict resolution seeks to eliminate all forms and types of conflict, whereas *conflict management* accepts that conflict is a natural and often a healthy endeavor. Conflict resolution assumes that conflict is a bad thing, something that needs to

[1] http://www.gordontraining.com/free-parenting-articles/the-nature-of-conflict.

be resolved so that the parties can move on. It ignores certain fundamental aspects of conflict that make it resilient. Assuming that we can resolve conflict situations to the satisfaction of all the parties involved is simply unrealistic.

> Conflict is going to happen: It's going to do damage. We surely have the reason to handle it as well as we can in order to minimize the damage (Dues, 2016).

When we view conflict as something evil, to be stamped out through a resolution process we ignore the positive side of conflict. It brings problems, hidden emotions and opportunities to the surface, it deepens understanding and improves relationships. When police officers engage in conflict management it provides deeper insight into the conditions existing in the community that a limited view of conflict can never provide.

> Conflict is natural and healthy to human endeavors and relationships. It should not be viewed as something to be avoided, but managed.

CONSTRUCTIVE VS. DYSFUNCTIONAL CONFLICT

Conflict situations can be either constructive or dysfunctional. Most people view conflict negatively and, because of this, tend to engage in one of the most dysfunctional forms of conflict resolution: avoidance. **Dysfunctional conflict** most often results from rigid competitive systems that pit individuals or groups against each other. The behaviors that follow can generate anger, resentment, and depression. These emotions can degenerate into behaviors that can lead the parties on a downward cycle that may result in violence.

Constructive conflict flows from wisdom and understanding. Constructive conflict recognizes others' value and contributions and creates a desire to treat others with dignity and respect, even in times of conflict. At its foundation, constructive conflict is self-interest at work as one person tries to understand the point-of-view of others in an effort to deepen his or her own base of knowledge and intellectual capacity.

Constructive conflict is **process-focused** as opposed to **outcome-focused**. The parties seek to build on the relationship rather than gain advantage by diminishing the other party in some way. All conflict has costs, including time, emotional commitment, and patience. We know that we have engaged in constructive conflict when benefits, understanding, cooperation, and potential future collaboration exceed the costs.

ELEMENTS OF CONFLICT

Conflict can be defined differently, from "discomforting differences" to a longer version offered by Wilmont and Hocker (2010) "An expressed struggle between as least two interdependent parties who perceive incompatible goals, scarce resources and interference from others in achieving their goals" (Wilmont, 2010).

The longer definition presents five distinct elements that are present in all conflict situations.

- Interdependence—Individuals involved in conflict situations have some degree of reliance on each other. A parent and child, a husband and wife, co-habitants, a supervisor and subordinate, co-workers or any pair or group of individuals who rely on each other in any way where the behavior of one party has an effect on the other(s).
- Difference—Individuals are dissimilar in their point-of-view, attitude, or goals regarding an event, relationship or other interdependent dynamic.
- Opposition—Expressed resistance or dissent as it relates to the other parties perspective, point of view, attitude, etc.
- Expression—The opposition has been made known to the other party(s).
- Emotion—The state of mind derived from circumstance, condition or the relationship with the other party(s) (Dues, 2016).

These elements of conflict provide a framework for understanding the context and developing strategies to aid people in better managing it.

CONFLICT AS COMPETITION

In western civilization we cannot escape the impact of the adversarial system on our relationships. It permeates everything we do despite noble efforts to build better mechanisms of cooperation. *The cultural assumption that conflict is a competitive event where we have a winner and a looser undermines our best efforts to achieve solutions that are beneficial to both parties.*

> Western civilization has its legal foundation in the "adversarial" system, as opposed to the inquisitional legal system that exists in much of Europe. This competitive instinct infects much of our economic and social thinking.

The element of interdependence, common to all conflict situations, suggests that competing parties have similar goals; this is often not readily apparent. According to Deutsch (2006) "a conflict situation exists when one party makes it harder for the other party to reach his goal." However, in many cases this conflict is actually a disagreement over how to achieve the goal. For example, a conflict between a parent and a teenager may initially appear to be a conflict over control, the parent sets boundaries and the adolescent resents those boundaries as an unreasonable infringement on their freedom. Both the parent and the adolescent have the same goal, for the child to grow-up and mature into a responsible adult they are merely at odds about how to achieve the goal (Deutsch, 2006).

The concept of *pure conflict* is based upon a situation that offers an opportunity for both parties to win, as opposed to conflict that requires one party to lose in order for the other party to win.

At the cornerstone of conflict management is the idea that most conflicts are of the pure type, meaning that the parties can negotiate and neither has to lose, a concept Deutsch refers to as a "win-win."

> Conflict resolution seeks to eliminate conflict, ignoring it's positive and growth producing aspects. Conflict management recognizes conflict as inevitable and natural.

SOCIOLOGICAL PERSPECTIVES ON SOCIETAL INTERACTION

Understanding conflict is the first step in learning how to manage it effectively. Toward that end, the field of sociology offers three primary perspectives through which we can frame our understanding of conflict as a part of social interaction.

Functionalist Perspective

This perspective sees society as a system of interconnected parts that work together in harmony to maintain a state of balance and social equilibrium for the whole. The functionalist perspective emphasizes the interconnectedness of society by focusing on how each part influences and is influenced by other parts. This perspective offers a distinction between functional and dysfunctional societal elements in that the former contributes to social stability and the latter disrupts it. An example offered by Mooney (2015) is crime. Crime, as a social element, is dysfunctional because it is associated with physical violence, property loss, and fear, but crime can also be functional because it leads to increased awareness of shared moral bonds and social cohesion (Mooney, 2015).

The functionalist perspective relates to a collectivist view of societal interaction and assumes that the interconnected societal elements will pursue cooperative arrangements in order to facilitate stability. Exchange relationships are key parts of this stability, where there is mutual understanding concerning the duties and responsibilities of these interdependent societal elements. Consider, for example, cooperative arrangements between units of local government.

> Recall that exchange relationships exist when the parties share a common understanding of mutual behavior. They break down, as does society generally, when that understanding breaks down, usually due to one party initially violating the behavioral expectations.

Both the local schools and the police have an interest in controlling crime; however, schools have a legal/moral responsibility to act in the best interest of the child. The concept is called *loco parentis* where an organization acts as a parent in some capacity. This manifests itself in our schools as administrators and teachers seek to restrict police activity in the schools in the interests of the children. The police have an interest in crime control and may see the school as a resource toward that end because many instances of crime and disorder involve young people. The police may wish to gather intelligence, conduct interviews, and maintain a presence in the schools, but this surveillance or interactions are viewed as contrary to the educational mission by school officials. These conflicting perspectives can lead to conflict. To manage this conflict, the police and school district officials have developed an exchange relationship, where information is shared and the functions of the police are defined and delineated when the police are present on school grounds.

This example demonstrates how conflict is managed with the goal of developing consensus regarding the interconnectedness of the police and the schools. The mutual need is public safety, but there will still be conflict as individual school officials, armed with subjective views of the police that may be negative or who take their *loco-parentis* duties too far, rebel against police presence in the school building. On the other hand, some police officers may abuse the cooperative relationship by pushing the limits of their authority and criticizing school officials who interfere with the crime control function. These conflicts can usually be handled informally because, under the functionalist perspective, each party seeks cooperation for the betterment of the whole, but the best practice is to have a document, memorandum of understanding, or policy that can be referenced when disputes arise.

> The functionalist perspective seeks cooperation of parties for the betterment of both. It does not typically allow for radical or even substantive change, change is incremental and the "status quo" is maintained. Can you think of a major governing body in the U.S. that fits this description?

This functionalist perspective has been criticized because it tends to perpetuate the status quo. It seeks to enable and strengthen the formal and informal exchange relationships that exist rather than facilitate radical or substantive change. It seems to prefer the path of least resistance, consisting of incremental adjustments that foster order and complacency rather than radical change.

Conflict Perspective

In contrast to the functionalist perspective, where society is viewed as having different parts working together, the conflict perspective views society as a collection of different parts engaged in a competition for power and resources. For example, a number of current activist groups argue that we live in a society dominated by white, heterosexual men. Social justice activists, including groups representing feminists, LGBTQ+ individuals, and blacks highlight ways in which society and society's institutions are set up in ways that benefit certain groups over others in a nuanced layering of privilege. As part of their advocacy, these social justice groups demand that the existing social arrangements be changed in order to achieve a more equal society.

The conflict perspective is often best understood through the work of Karl Marx, who suggested that society becomes divided into two distinct classes as the result of economic development. The owners of the means of production (i.e., capitalists;) are seen as separate from the workers who produce and earn wages. The capitalist uses the worker's capacity to earn profit, while the workers argue for higher wages as a reward for their efforts. This divides society into the "haves" and "have nots," a continuing source of conflict as the capitalists use their economic power to control and maintain the capitalist system, which exploits the workers. Under conflict theory, life is a competition that focuses on the distribution of power and resources.

> The conflict perspective is all about, well . . . conflict. Parties seek to dominate the other by putting forth arguments that label the other party as evil or morally corrupt. Marx used this to great effect to illustrate the evil of tyrannical economic hierarchies. The fact that most hierarchies of power today are based on competency and effort is conveniently ignored by those who still see value in Marxism.

The premise of conflict theory is that conflicts arise when the benefits of society are not evenly distributed. In regard to police service, there is the potential for conflict as the police, in pursuing a crime control agenda, target low income neighborhoods for aggressive arrest strategies. At the same time, preventative drug education programs and neighborhood outreach programs are focused in middle and upper-class neighborhoods. The conflict theorist would argue that it is the unequal distribution of wealth that determines where enforcement, surveillance, and arrests are higher. They would advocate for the elimination of aggressive enforcement tactics altogether due to the disparate impact on poor people. Even drug court, an alternative from the functionalist perspective, adversely impacts them due to the cost and time commitment. The conflict theorist ignores any deterrence value of pro-active policing and will even claim that aggressive and proactive law enforcement practices are un-democratic (Way, 2013).

Symbolic Interactionist Perspective

This perspective focuses not on societal groups and their interactions, but on the individual and his or her activity in small groups. The symbolic interactionist perspective relates to the meaning individuals attach to situations, rather than the objective situation itself. Here we have the problem of subjective vs. objective meaning. *Objective meaning* is based on fact and visible, measurable, concrete analysis and reasoning. *Subjective meaning* is based on personal feelings, attitudes, and emotion; it is a product of an individual point-of-view, past experiences, and the meaning that they attach to symbols, behavior, and situations. This perspective also suggests that individual identity and the sense of self is shaped by social interaction (Mooney, 2015).

> Objective meaning is based on fact and observable and measurable "empirical" data. Subjective meaning is based upon an individual's point-of-view, feelings and/or attitudes.

The term *symbolic interactionism* is attributed to Herbert Blumer who defined the term simply as the tendency for people to act toward things—behavior of others—based upon the meaning those things have for them. The core assumptions of this perspective include:

Meaning: human beings act toward people and things according to the meanings they, themselves, give to those people and things.

Language: the means by which human beings negotiate meaning through symbols. Meaning is identified through speech and interaction with others.

Thought: how individuals interpret symbols—an internal mental conversation involving different points-of-view.

Individuals use these assumptions to develop their own self-concept. They imagine how they look to another person by stepping out of themselves and viewing themselves as they believe others view them, also known as the "looking glass" self. The idea of self-concept and self-worth that defines relationships with others is framed by this process (Blumer, 1969).

> The symbolic interactionalist perspective recognizes that people draw meaning from what they perceive, see, hear, feel, based on their own unique and subjective interpretations.

The ability to see oneself as other see us is a fundamental aspect of the maturation process. *Those lacking maturity lack this capacity and are very likely to experience conflict in their adult interpersonal relationships.*

CAUSES OF CONFLICT

Conflict emerges in many different ways but the origin of conflict can be reduced to a few specific circumstances and conditions. When the cause of the conflict is understood and agreed upon by all parties, management of the conflict is more effective.

Personality Differences

People think and act in different ways. Some individuals like to be left alone to wrestle with a problem or situation while others crave the company of others. Obtaining a basic understanding of the needs of others and how they relate can provide insight into how potential conflicts can be avoided and how to manage them once they occur.

Communication

Many conflict situations result from misunderstanding in the way information is processed and transmitted. In many cases individuals make assumptions of the capabilities and shortcoming of others that have their basis in poor or inadequate communication habits.

Mutual Dependence

When we rely on others for task accomplishment, as in the case of group responsibilities and projects, it is common to make assumptions that may not hold true. When someone disappoints us with regard to their capabilities or task accomplishment, conflict can result. We are disappointed or may feel threatened or inadequate as a result of conditions out of our control or the task accomplishment of others, and conflict results.

Resource Limitations

The availability of time, money, equipment, and expertise is generally limited. This causes conflict as individuals and groups compete for those resources viewed as particularly scarce. The conflict often generates feelings and emotions that can range from anxiety to violence. Rarely are individuals and groups flush with all the resources that they view they need and this can lead to the use of enhanced competitive strategies that can make matters worse.

CONFLICT AND THE PRISTINE SELF

According to Deutsch (2006) the two kinds of conflict are pure and competitive. Pure conflict can be managed because the parties have the same goals, but are pursuing different strategies to achieve them. However, in some cases, this assumption is not true. **Managing conflict competently hinges on the ability to appeal to rationality**, but some conflicts are purely emotional, boarding on hysteria. Strong emotions cannot be reasoned with so conflict management strategies that rely upon observable, measurable facts, generally known as empirical information, are not useful in these kinds of conflicts. The concept of the *Pristine Self* provides an illustration of the problem, where the subjective views individuals hold about themselves come into conflict with reality.

> The Pristine self is a concept whereby individuals see themselves as entitled to unconditional love and respect for their feelings and attitudes, regardless as to whether those feelings and attitudes are known by others. They take immediate offence when their own world view is challenged and view those who would do this, such as parents, persons in authority, teachers and college professors, as evil.

Dysfunctional conflict results when situations and conditions are interpreted in such a way as to go against other individual narratives, including narratives unsupported by factual information, and the parties' reaction is to become angry and indignant. Many scholars have observed a growing trend today in that more and more people, typically young people, have a worldview that is often not supported by factual information, a view that is not empirically based. The concept of the *pristine self* refers to an individual who believes that the **world primarily revolves around them** and should offer them nothing but unconditional love and acceptance. They feel that they are entitled to live in a world that validates their own subjective world view, whatever that may be, and those who reject their world view are the enemy. When challenged with contradictory ideas or actual facts, they interpret them as wrong, insensitive, mean, and may respond negatively, even using acts of aggression:

> The "pristine self" is the fictionalized idea of a self touched by nothing but love. When "marginalized" students demand "safe spaces," trigger warnings, and protection from microaggressions, they work upon the assumption that they deserve a "pristine self," unchallenged by invading ideas or opinions (Schwartz, 2016).

The problem for police and those who encounter these individuals is that they feel that their identity should be obvious to all. Those who have never met them should gauge their behavior accordingly and relate to them in a way that is consistent with their worldview, emotional state, and self-perceived righteousness and importance (Lavender, 2016).

As an actual example, imagine a police officer who responds to a disturbance call involving a group of African American individuals. He pulls-up on the scene and says, "Ya'all need to calm down now." This behavior by the officer creates conflict and generates a complaint to the chief because, in using language reflective of the racist South, the officer has demonstrated that he is a racist himself. The fact that the officer is from the South and commonly uses that phrase is of no concern to the offended individual **who feels that a police officer should be more sensitive and aware of the legacy and implications of such word choice**.

Where does this extreme form of the symbolic interactionist perspective originate?

Lavender (2016) speculates that it is the result of a generation overindulged, entitled, and catered to by high schools, colleges, helicopter parents, those who have provided safe spaces or excessive accommodations. As a result of our collective efforts to insulate our children and adolescents from harm and build high self-esteem, we, as a society, have undermined their ability to develop, grow, and mature as responsible adults.

> Providing "safe spaces" can be viewed as a conflict resolution strategy, one that seeks to **avoid** conflict by isolating needy individuals from the anxiety resulting from being exposed to thoughts and ideas different from their own, an emotionally and intellectually crippling practice for adults, in the author's opinion.

A temper tantrum resulting from a triggering event that the individual cannot cope with*

Emotional hysteria often dominates these conflict situations. This is childish behavior even when the parties are adults. Seeking to manage these conflict situations requires the realization that an appeal to rationality is futile. These individuals are volatile, inconsistent, and unpredictable. They will fly of the handle at any perceived slight and **they are empowered** by making others uncomfortable and on-guard. These individuals should be treated in the same way that one should treat an adolescent having a temper tantrum; by respectfully listening to their concerns and not taking the bait that they toss out. Establishing cooperative relationships with such individuals presents a challenge unless incentives are made clear.

Emotionally immature individuals are empowered by making other individuals cautious and constantly on-guard. The best way to deal with these individuals is to remain perfectly calm and allow them to vent even probing them with reasonable questions until they become emotionally exhausted. Only then can they be reasoned with.

COOPERATION AND CONFLICT

Interdependence is a fundamental element of all conflict situations. When there is an expectation between individuals that defines the relationship as cooperative, the lack of cooperation by one party leads to conflict. Conflict can sometimes be used to the advantage of an interested third party as in the case of the prisoner's dilemma. However, the nature of cooperative relationships in the face of incentives and disincentives can provide clues to how interested third parties-negotiators and mediators-can and cannot manipulate incentives in an effort to manage conflict.

* Image labeled for unrestricted use.

A prisoner*

The prisoner's dilemma is a game studied in game theory that shows why two completely "rational" individuals might not cooperate with each other against a common foe, even if it appears that it is in their best interests to do so. It was originally framed by Merrill Flood and Melvin Dresher working at RAND corporation in 1950. The game illustrates that pursuing individual rewards logically leads both parties to not cooperate with each other but human beings display a systemic bias that overcomes the rationality in many cases.

> The prisoner's dilemma is a gaming strategy that challenges the limits of cooperation between individuals with a common interest.

Why do people engage in cooperative endeavors when doing so offers no actual benefit for them? Engaging in cooperation over and above selfish motivations has been referred to as "excess" cooperation (McAdams, 1995). The evidence of the existence of excess cooperation come to us from game theory, specifically a game that police officers should be intimately familiar with, the **prisoner's dilemma**.

This game has two mutually dependent parties each seeking release from police custody. The same bargain is offered to both, that being confess-don't cooperate with the other prisoner-and you will go free. The economic incentives are structured in this way, if both prisoners remain silent-cooperate with each other-the police will charge both with a lessor crime that they can support with existing evidence. If one of the prisoners' confesses-defects on the other, does not cooperate-he will be released and the testimony will be used to charge the other party with a serious crime. If both parties confess-defect on each other-then they will both be charged with an intermediately serious crime.

Each prisoner must make an irrevocable decision independent of the other and without knowledge as to whether the other party chose to cooperate with

* Image labeled for unrestricted use.

them or not. The dominant strategy that is best for each individual regardless of what the other party does is to confess, not cooperate with the other party. For example if prisoner A defects and prisoner B does not, prisoner A goes free. If prisoner A defects and prisoner B defects, prisoner A is charged with an intermediate crime. If prisoner A does not confess—cooperates with—B and B confesses A gets charged with a serious crime. The dilemma is that when each party seeks their own advantage by confessing the outcome is clearly inferior to remaining silent—cooperation with the other party (Axelrod, 1984).

In a world where everyone pursues their own *self-interest* we would expect each participant to pursue the ideal strategy, in this case confess, i.e., non-cooperation. This, however, is a collective action problem in which situations that demand an individually rational decision result in less than optimal outcomes for both. Mutual non-cooperation-confession is worse than mutual cooperation-no confession for each party, the question becomes why do many individuals, without knowledge of the other parties decision, choose not to confess-cooperate with each other-against the interests of the police?

The results of thousands of reiterations of the prisoner's dilemma under experimental conditions reveal that even when self-interest and incentives compel non-cooperation many subjects choose cooperation (Dawes R. A., 1990). What might explain the seemingly irrationality of this choice? Reciprocity or altruism.[2] However, reciprocity requires the possibility of future interactions, it does not explain the initial choices parties make.

Altruism is the intentional sacrificing of oneself, or one's own interest, for the benefit of others.

Individuals tend to segregate themselves into factions, in the case of an actual prisoner's dilemma, the parties have a common interest by way of the police. The police represent a repressive and coercive entity to the prisoner that pre-disposes the prisoners to cooperate with each other, i.e. to not confess.

> "Individuals have a propensity to divide into personal factions such that the smallest appearance of real difference (between their faction and another) will produce them" (McAdams, 1995, p. 1015).

There is a message here for those seeking to instill a sense of cooperation among parties in conflict, that being to **identify commonality** among them and frame that commonalty in such a way as to create a group identity that they share.

2 Altruism refers to the principle or practice of putting others need and concerns about our own. An unselfish devotion to the welfare of others.

> Often the first step in conflict management is to identify and articulate the common interests that the parties share.

For example; police agencies consist of multiple groups or communities. There is the community of street officers that may include groups defined by race, gender and age. Police officers working the streets may also develop a unique set of cultural norms that are distinct from those of detectives who may often view patrol officers as less competent, "Patrol idiots." Supervisors have a world view that is different from line officers either in patrol or detectives and also different from mid-management level officers. Lieutenants and watch commanders may be seen as working against the interests of line officers with supervisors being caught in the middle. Subgroups defined by race, gender and age may further complicate the mix.

Building a sense of commonality begins with identifying common goals, such as establishing a mission statement and specific department objectives that serve to unite all of these groups toward a common purpose, establishing a commonality of interest, and generating a sense that uncooperative behavior violates cultural norms.

Another profound aspect stimulating cooperation came out of the prisoners dilemma research, that being the value of discussion.

> "Repeated study shows that permitting communication between the subjects in a prisoner's dilemma situation dramatically increases the level of cooperation, indeed, discussion as much as doubles cooperation rates" (McAdams, 1995, p. 1016).

> Cooperation between prisoners is something to be avoided by the police when the police are seeking a confession by one or both parties. Cooperation is something to be encouraged, through communication, when the police are in a conflict management role.

Here we find the justification for the common law enforcement practice of separating the suspects. The police do not want criminal suspects to have a discussion as this produces cooperation between them, it gives them the opportunity to "get their stories straight," it enhances the perception that they owe loyalty to each other against the interests of the police and lowers the possibility of a confession. The law enforcement goal in these cases is non-cooperation. Conversely, communication and discussion within the police agency increases the level of cooperation among members and between levels facilitating better productive outputs and reinforcing organizational goals.

In the police function, where law enforcement and arrest is not the primary goal, the role for officers is that of a mediator. Separating the parties enhances the conflict because it prevents discussion. What the police want in these situations, after passions and emotions are brought under control, is discussion among parties because that increases cooperation. Managing conflict in these situations involves helping to cultivate a sense of commonality and group identification, even to the point of identifying some competing faction that the parties may perceive as a common enemy (Dawes R. M., 1977).

Consider a case where a police officer is called to intervene in a neighborhood dispute. The first step is not to launch into a list of nuisance laws that require citizens to keep their property maintained and orderly, pointing out obvious violations. A better course of action is to try and get the parties to understand that they have common interests or even a common enemy that they can better combat cooperatively.

INTRA-GROUP CONFLICT

Conflict among individuals often occurs within the context of some type of group affiliation. These groups can include the family, a social group, or a work group tasked with some responsibility for task completion. Jehn & Mannix (2001) provide a framework for categorizing conflict in groups.

> *Relationship conflict* involves interpersonal incompatibilities such as tension and friction resulting from feelings of annoyance, frustration, and irritation.
>
> *Task conflict* relates to difference in the point-of-view of the group members with regard to what is to be accomplished.
>
> *Process conflict* involves disagreement and controversy about how aspects of task accomplishment should proceed. Who should do what and how much responsibility each individual has dominate process conflicts (Jehn, 2001).

One of the most common calls for police service involves conflict in the form of the domestic dispute. In these cases, individuals within groups—husband-wife, parent-child, or other co-habitants—are in conflict. Conflict arises when one or more of the parties view the current situation, rules, or expectations as not in their own best interests or just not working anymore. It could be that **politeness norms**—seeking to avoid conflict—have prevailed up to this point but now at least one party is sufficiently dissatisfied to speak-up and seek a change. Feelings of annoyance, frustration, and irritation are at the foundation of these conflicts.

Politeness norms are conflict avoidance tools. Often, we avoid conflict by being polite to those who challenge us or our point-of-view. The phrase "With all due respect" is a good example of a politeness norm.

An example of a task conflict is the tenant-landlord dispute. In these cases it is the lack of a clear understanding of each person's responsibilities—tasks—that drive feelings of dissatisfaction. The landlord may expect the tenant to mow the lawn, shovel snow, or repair damage while the tenant may feel these are not reasonable expectations. The absence of clearly articulated expectations results in arbitrary decisions and opinions that create conflict.

An example of a process conflict arises in the relationship police officers maintain with prosecutors, school officials, and other representatives where interdependent relationships exist. Imagine that a detective has built what she believes is a solid case against a child predator. The mission was to support charges to the level of probable cause, but the prosecutor wants the detective to re-interview the suspect and firm up specific elements of the offense. The conflict arises about how that process should go: specifically who is responsible for follow-up interviews, the prosecutor's investigator or the detective.

Process conflicts are also common in the interdependent relationship the police have with school officials. School officials may feel the need to contact the parents of students and get their permission before allowing a police interview, police officers, especially when working a serious case investigation, are likely to view this as obstructing their investigation.

Intra-group conflicts often hold potential for what Deutsch calls the "win-win." The advantage is that the parties value and seek to maintain membership in the group. Managing these conflicts can be as simple as identifying the common goals and building consensus on how they are to be achieved, including exactly who is responsible for what activities.

Think "Win-Win" or "No Deal!"

Police officers come to conflict situations armed with the power of the state. They can resolve conflicts simply by invoking that power and this usually takes the form of an arrest, citation or some other coerced resolution. In these cases the officer has forced resolution where one party prevails and the other party is somehow diminished. This reinforces a "positional" arrangement between the parties where one party can be perceived as having more power in the relationship. In positional bargaining the parties lock themselves into positions where the ego is identified with a given position to the extent that any loss can be perceived as "loosing face." This is inefficient because it creates and builds on existing resentments.

> People will fight for their position, even physically, if giving in means a loss to their own self-esteem, what is commonly referred to as "loosing face."

One of the important requirements for effective conflict management is that both parties need to be committed to an ongoing relationship. **Positional bargaining** undermines the relationship because both parties engaged in a battle of wills. Anger and resentment build as the parties both seek to impose their views on the other, e.g., parent vs. child, landlord vs. tenant, husband vs. wife, etc. The role of a police officer is to first reinforce the importance of the relationship and secure a commitment to a managed solution where neither party is diminished, "Win-Win."

> Positional bargaining means holding fast to a point-of-view associated with the status one holds. Police Chief, Mayor, Union President, Parent, Boss, etc. These are power hierarchies that can easily be viewed as arbitrary and tyrannical, as Marx would put it. A better alternative is "principled" bargaining where the underlying basis for the conflict is explored.

This can be accomplished by abandoning the need to focus on positions and substitute **principles**. The first step is to separate the people from the problem.

Perceptions need to change; emotions need to be recognized, validated and acknowledged. The officer askes each party how the behavior of the other party makes them feel. In many cases the other party has no recognition of how their behavior effects the other. Once they become aware of it, a commitment to change the behavior may begin to emerge especially when the officer is wise enough to offer a "How would you feel if . . ." scenario that puts one party in the place of the other. Breaking the implicit bond between the position one party holds and the problem is the goal.

Step two—*Interests* need to be identified and legitimized, separate from the *positions*. For example, a parent is concerned about the adolescent's poor academic performance and is demanding a curfew. The parent is worried and concerned about the adolescent's future but this comes across as an overbearing effort to control the adolescent's life just as they are emerging into the adult world. The interest is how to build responsible adult behavior not parental control.

Step three—The next step is to brainstorm options in pursuit of the interests uncovered in step two. How can the interest(s) be facilitated without invoking the power of the position, in this case, parental authority? Getting this discussion going may be as simple as bargaining over the curfew time and reporting arrangements. What do both parties consider reasonable?

Step four—Determine an agreeable and practical way to measure results. Is there some objective standard that can be put in place to measure compliance and the resulting outcome? In this case a negotiated curfew time and criteria for reasonable action to be taken in the event of a violation of the standard, e.g., curfew violation.

The above process provides an example of a principled negotiation process that can be used in the case of conflicts that are driven by positional power imbalances such as parent and child, employer-employee, landlord tenant, etc. The exact principles and tactics to employ will, of course, be specific to the situation (Fisher, 1981).

COOPERATION VS. COMPETITION

Effectively managing conflict situations requires a level of interdependence, where both parties are dependent on the other for something in some way. When the needs of one party are not being met, the parties can seek a cooperative resolution, as in the functionalist perspective or they can engage in competition, where one party seeks to prevail at the expense of the other. The police can aid the former by seeking to manage the conflict. They can seek out and identify alternative courses of action where both parties prevail or where neither party is diminished; this is known as a "win-win" solution. When parties seek to resolve the conflict through competition, violence can occur; in these situations, the police take on a restrictive role in an attempt to restrain passions. *Cooperation* implies a positive attitude that we need the contributions of others; we are better-off working together. *Competition* implies that we are against each other; that one's advancement means the need to hold down, trample, and diminish someone else. In the extreme form, competition means that one person is out to harm someone else, justifying violence for self-defense.

> Inherent to conflict situations is power imbalance. Seldom are the parties on equal footing with regard to their actual or perceived power to control the other. Power relationships are always based upon dependency, there can be no power unless one party is dependent on the other in some significant way. The cure to dependency is competency.

Interdependence

Competing individuals arguing over power*

Ongoing conflicts result when parties engage in an overt struggle with one another. When one party can act unilaterally or independent of the other, conflict management cannot occur because the parties are not interdependent. In some cases the interdependence is real but not recognized, as in the case of a parent and teenage child. A parent may not choose to express the child's dependency on them through actions or words for the purpose of maintaining the emotional relationship, but without this realization the child may feel that he or she is free to act independently, leaving any attempt at managing the conflict lacking one of the interdependent parties. The teenager may believe that they have the option of just "doing their own thing" and that such an option is desirable. The question for both parties is how much influence are each of them willing to allow the other party to have over the choices that they make. How much influence do they want the other person to have over them? How they perceive their mutual dependency affects the choices that they make.

Dependence and interdependence are relationship factors that come and go depending on the situation and context of the interaction. At certain times there will be an emphasis on one party and their needs over the other, the "me" as in the case of a parent and child, husband and wife, employee and employer. At other times the interdependence will shift toward the "we" as in working together toward a common goal[3] (Galvin K. M., 1982) (Baxter, 1982).

Recognizing the interdependence is difficult in some cases. Police officers are routinely called upon to mediate disputes of a non-crime nature. For example,

* Image labeled for unrestricted use.

[3] Frentz, T., and J. Rushing. 1980. A communication perspective on closeness/distance and stability/change in intimate ongoing dyads. Unpublished manuscript, University of Colorado, Boulder.

a tenant may take issue with a landlord who refuses to repair a non-working water heater, an actual case. Managing this conflict requires the realization on the part of the landlord of the interdependence. Initially the landlord complains that the tenant has not paid the rent, he therefore feels justified in not making the needed repairs. He feels that he can act unilaterally in pursuit of his own interests at the expense of the tenant who refuses to pay the rent until the water heater is repaired. Both parties here are in the "me" mode seeking a competitive advantage, the tenant seeks to enlist the police, and the coercive power of the state as Bitner (1970) would put it, against the landlord. The landlord simply wants what he is due based upon the contract—lease—he has with the tenant. Managing the conflict effectively requires getting the parties to acknowledge their interdependence, the tenant is dependent on the landlord for hot water and the landlord is dependent on the tenant to pay the rent so that he can pay the property mortgage.

In many cases the interdependence is not recognized by one or both parties. In this case the principled negotiation approach as previously discussed may not be effective. It may be that one party digs in and refuses to negotiate, stating their position in certain and unbending terms. In this case the temptation may be to push-back by criticizing them or their position. In other cases an officer may face criticism for offering a proposal, this can be viewed as an attack and the temptation is to defend and counter attack. Both criticizing and defending locks people into a vicious cycle of attack and defense that is typical of positional bargaining. The better course of action is to not respond, rather, **deflect** their positional approach using the actual problem as an anchor.

> Typically their "attack" will consist of three maneuvers: asserting their position forcefully, attacking your ideas, and attacking you. Let's consider how a principled negotiator can deal with each of these. Fisher and Ury (1981) refer to this as negotiation jujitsu.
>
> Don't attack their position, look behind it. When the other side sets forth their position, neither reject it nor accept it. Treat it as one possible option. Look for the interests behind it, seek out the principles that it reflects, and think about ways to improve it (Fisher, 1981, p. 110).

Using the above scenario as an example, the landlord initially takes the position that he will not repair the water heater until the tenant pays the rent. This has always been his policy and he is not willing to deviate from it. Suggesting that he repair the heater first is stupid because that will destroy the tenant's incentive to "pay-up." The fact that the police officer is offering this as an option illustrates that cops know nothing about how business is conducted.

In this case we have the typical attack pattern, asserting a position, attacking the ideas, and then attacking the negotiator. The response is to treat that as one possible option and then seek out the interests behind it, those interests being purely economic with no realization for the hazard or potential harm such action causes. The goal is to bring the landlord to the realization that not repairing the heater threatens the health of the family and his reputation; what would he rather have, the late rent now or a sick child later? Would the sick child enhance or detract from his reputation and business interests?

Perhaps a better compromise is to repair the water heater now, he is going to have to do so anyway, with the tenant agreeing to pay the rent as soon as that is accomplished. This is a Win-win" solution that meets the needs of both parties. The position initially taken by the landlord has been deflected in favor of one addressing the actual problem.

The framework for principled negotiation is as follows:

Don't defend ideas, invite criticism and advice. In this case, asking the landlord and tenant how the proposed solution might be improved. What's wrong with it, exactly?

Reframe (Recast) an attack on an individual as an attack on the problem. The inclination to defend and attack needs to be resisted. The police officer may have actually run a successful business or may even be a landlord themselves but pointing that out in this situation will do nothing to address the real problem. The best course of action is to simply listen and let the landlord blow-off steam. When they have worn themselves out, reframe the problem by asking questions. "So, do you care more about the money or the health of the children?"

Ask questions and pause. Don't make statements that can prompt a new attack. **Statements generate resistance, questions generate answers.** The goal is to break down the competitive "Win-lose" atmosphere so that cooperation can prevail (Fisher, 1981).

EFFECTS OF COOPERATION AND COMPETITION

According to Deutsch (2006), the effects of cooperation include:

- **Effective communication** where individuals are attentive to one another, accepting of ideas and have few difficulties understanding each other.

- **Friendliness, helpfulness and lessened obstructiveness** where individuals affirmatively seek the acceptance and respect of others.
- **Coordination of effort** where cooperative arrangements are valued and seem to develop naturally.
- **Willingness to enhance the other's power** in the form of knowledge, skills and resources where mutual goal attainment is valued. There is a recognition that as the capabilities of others grow so do our own through the association we maintain with them.
- **Defining conflicting interests as a mutual problem** where individuals recognize the legitimacy of each other's interests and the necessity to search for a mutually satisfying solution, e.g., "win-win" or "no deal."

Competition, on the other hand, has the following effects:

- **Communication is impaired** because the competing parties seek to gain advantage through tactics such as misinformation, false promises, or positional power. They cannot trust each other's communication.
- **Obstructiveness and lack of helpfulness** where one party views the actions of the other with suspicion. One party's perception of the other focuses on the negative qualities as opposed to their positive qualities.
- The parties are **unable or unwilling to divide the work,** resulting in the duplication of effort or where one party continually checks on the work of the other.
- The **repeated and continual rejection of ideas** reduces confidence in both parties.
- **Concern over power and influence dominate**. Any increase in power of one party is viewed as a threat to the other party (Deutsch M., 2006, pp. 27–28).

When competitive effects go unchecked, hostility results where interaction and communication stops. There is no opportunity to address misconceptions and misunderstandings or to clear the air, so-to-speak. Hostile situations become self-fulfilling prophecies as parties engage in hostile behavior because one party believes the other party is out to do them harm. This behavior leads the other party to believe the same thing and provokes hostility, too, resulting in a downward spiral that can ultimately result in violence.

Research has shown that cooperative processes are more conductive to conflict resolution than competitive processes; however, not all competitive process are bad (Johnson, 1989). There is such a thing as **constructive competition**, whereby both groups see some gains towards their intended outcome and, in the end, are satisfied with the results.

The goal of constructive competition is for both parties to acquire a deeper understanding of the other's point-of-view, to value the different attitudes and perspectives, and to enrich mutual understanding. Cooperative competition is civilized, thought provoking, exhilarating. and even fun, but there needs to be a level of wisdom on the part of both parties that enables them to overcome the **passion** that often stands in the way of reason and civilized discourse.

> Competition and conflict over ideas can be fun and intellectually stimulating provided that parties recognize its value and keep their emotional baggage in check. What is required to do this??? **Emotional Intelligence.**

A cooperative orientation has certain indicators or norms that include:

- Disagreements are placed in perspective by identifying common ground and common interests.
- There are no verbal attacks on people, characteristics and personalities.
- Parties attempt to empathize with each other.
- When ideas are offered, they are not attacked; rather, the other party seeks to build upon them.
- Parties take responsibility for behavior and harmful consequences and are willing to apologize and forgive. They don't make excuses or blame the other party.
- Sincere officers of assistance are not viewed with suspicion; rather, they are accepted as a sign of a cooperative inclination.
- Both parties listen respectfully, asking clarifying questions and not interrupting.

> Complete honesty is problematic when such honesty triggers a negative emotional response in the other party. **Appropriate honesty** recognizes the impact of one's views, opinions and even facts are likely to have on the other party. Can you provide an example?

Honesty is the cornerstone of constructive competition. However, communicating every suspicion, doubt, fear, and anxiety is damaging to relationships. While being dishonest is a violation of cooperative norms, one should be *appropriately honest* by considering the likely consequences of what one says or does as it pertains to the current situation or context (Deutsch M., 2006). In many cases, silence communicates more than engaging in a critical diatribe that cites the other person's weaknesses or past misbehavior. **Appropriate honesty** means avoiding statements that may be offensive, thereby finding another way to communicate the message. **Radical honesty**—a careless disregard for the feelings of others—is a sign of dysfunctional conflict.

Conflict situations often generate intense emotions that are difficult to control. As a result, individuals are likely to engage in conduct that violates the norms of cooperation. A good example is when a clearly upset individual begins to push the other person's buttons. Each person has triggers that bring about strong emotions, such as anger, fear, self-doubt, and withdrawal. It is critical that each person knows his or her own triggers. By recognizing their own strong emotions as they emerge, people can develop a strategy to keep them from turning into regrettable behavior. This is the hall-mark of emotional intelligence that will be discussed at length. An enduring source of conflict in our society and our criminal justice system pertains to the concept of justice itself.

SOURCES OF INJUSTICE

Injustice can take the form of unfair treatment, such as discrimination, disparate impact, and other perceived collective wrongs. It can take the form of harassment, breach of contract, personal injury, and other forms of personal wrongs. These forms of injustice are often perpetrated by those who are insensitive to the feelings and perceptions of others, sometimes because they don't care and sometimes out of ignorance.

Wrongs perpetrated by the criminal justice system generally take the form of procedural errors that occur due to poor information, lack of knowledge, misinterpretation of procedures, and lack of information. When such errors rise to the level of negligence or willful conduct, they are actionable under the criminal and civil law. Managing conflict with regard to the various perspectives on justice requires a deeper understanding of where the sense of injustice comes from.

Justice as a Basis of Conflict

What is justice? Most of us understand this concept as fundamental fairness, but **what is considered fair is typically based upon one's point-of-view**. Without a solid foundation in the rule of law and its focus on objective rationality, people are free to pursue their own interpretation of justice based on subjective criteria. This is a profound source of conflict between individuals, between individuals and groups, and between groups that the police are often called on to mediate.

A sense of injustice generally leads to a sense of oppression—an individual or group is being oppressed by another individual or group in some way. The forms of oppression or injustice, include the following, according to Deutsch (2006).

Distributive Justice

Every type of system—from society to a family—distributes benefits, costs, and harms. *Benefits* includes such things as: income, education, health care, police protection, housing, and water supplies. *Harms* include accidents, rapes, physical attacks, sickness, imprisonment, death, and rat bites. Benefits and harms are often distributed differently among categories of people: males versus females, employers versus employees, whites versus blacks, heterosexuals versus homosexuals, police officers versus teachers, adults versus children. An examination of such distributions often reveals some gross disparities in the ways they are distributed (Deutsch, 2006, p. 59). Some disparities are intentional: employers often make more than employees within a business. Other distributions, whether intended or not, can generate severe hostilities: having separate facilities such as parks or bathrooms for people of different ethnic backgrounds has appropriately led to severe problems in the U.S.

> Distributive justice relates to how benefits are disbursed among societal members. It is understood based on the principles of equity, equality or need.

Distributive justice has a few basic principles: **equity, equality, and need**. The principle of equity asserts that people should be rewarded based on their contributions. How much they contribute to the whole should determine their level of reward (i.e., the more one produces the larger their pay check should be). This principle begs the question of what is the productive output desired. For a police officer, the economic commodity is time. We compensate police officers for the amount of time they spend utilizing their skills and abilities protecting and serving the community. The equity principle mandates that officers who dedicate the most time get a larger pay check. It can cause conflict because some officers may feel that the quality of their work is not rewarded because only the numbers matter or that their unique qualities are not valued.

> Equity means rewards are based upon relative contributions made to the group. Equality means that all group members hold an equivalent share of the benefits or have an equal opportunity to pursue their self-interest regardless of their individual contributions. Need means that those who are disadvantaged usually but not always through no fault of their own deserve more benefits than others who have less need.

The principle of equality states that all members of a group should share equally. In the case of a police officer, this means that everyone holding the same rank and time on the job gets paid the same. We often hear of unions demanding "across-the-board" wage adjustments; this supports this principle, but can cause conflict because some officers may feel that equal pay violates the equity principle because they choose to contribute more of what is desired in the organization than others.

The need principle states that members who need more of a particular benefit should receive more of that benefit than those who need it less. Some police officers need more time off to see to family needs as opposed to single officers without families who may seek additional time off for other, less noble reasons. The need principle can produce conflict over the distinction between needs and wants. It can also undermine basic understandings of duties and responsibilities to both the organization and to one's family.

These principles can easily come into conflict when distributive justice is considered. Each principle can hold different meaning and importance to individuals based upon their background, social class, beliefs, and values. Groups can also gravitate to specific principles when considering this aspect of justice. Scholarship committees frequently seek to award applicants based upon need—a lack of economic resources—but often gravitate to equality to avoid conflict over the relative need or equity principle. Deustch (2006) states that the situation, or mission, often dictates the dominant distributive principle. Equity is prominent where the goal is to increase productivity, equality is prominent when social harmony and good will are the goals, and need is most prominent when individual welfare is the goal.

> Conflict results when people differ on the principle that should be used to judge whether or not distributive justice exists, equity, equality or need.

> The judgment that you have received a fair outcome is determined not only by whether the appropriate distributive principles are employed, but also by whether your outcome is in comparative balance with the outcomes received by people like you in similar situations . . . The theory of *relative deprivation* indicates that the sense of **deprivation** or injustice arises if there is comparative imbalance: egotistical deprivation occurs if

an individual feels disadvantaged relative to other individuals; and fraternal deprivation occurs if a person feels her group is disadvantaged relative to other groups (Deutsch, 2006, pp. 46–47).

A comparative imbalance of outcomes or opportunity can create a sense of relative deprivation when some individuals perceive that they have less benefit or opportunity than other individuals.

Feelings of fraternal deprivation are clearly evident when the issue of racial bias and disparate impact arise. Different groups have certainly been treated differently by the police (both historically and currently); setting aside any justification for the variation, one can clearly see how a sense of injustice can emerge. The subjective nature of distributive justice makes it extremely difficult to mitigate. Those who feel victimized by this perspective often demand action that can easily cause a new type of injustice that impacts another group. Even if the action is judged to be reasonable given the impact of past injustice, **attempting to fix a past injustice with a new injustice is unwise**.

Social Justice

Closely related to the concept of distributive justice is *social justice*. It relates to how the resources of society are allocated among individuals and groups. Under the social justice concept, government has a responsibility to fairly allocate resources and distribute wealth. Redistribution of wealth practices like the progressive income tax demand that those with abundant wealth contribute more to society than those with less. Government regulation is used to curtail unfair business practices, and social intervention programs seek to support those in need; the goal is to treat all persons fairly. Conflict results as the quest for fair treatment of disadvantaged individuals and groups often necessitates a greater emphasis on the needs of individuals rather than their merit. Proponents argue that bias based on race, class, gender and ethnicity make capitalistic societies inherently unjust so greater efforts must be made to enhance life for these affected groups. These changes often necessitate diminishing other groups in some way, i.e., "win-lose" (Hunter, 2011).

Social justice applies a group identity to how resources and wealth are distributed in a society. It is an insidiously difficult concept to address and mitigate because groups consist of individuals who each have their own individual sense of perceived justice and injustice. Radicals often emerge who are allowed to speak for the group and if left unchecked will aspire to tyrannical rule, imposing their will on all others, i.e., Stalin, Mao, Hitler.

Procedural Justice

Procedural justice relates to how an outcome was achieved. Where distributive justice is related to outcomes, procedural justice focuses on the **process used**; the procedures used to determine guilt or innocence, in the case of criminal justice, must be fair. In addition, procedural justice asks whether all categories of people are treated the same, with politeness, respect, and dignity by those in authority. To be treated fairly, one must believe that the process by which a result or outcome was arrived at was reasonable, rational, consistent with past practices, and unbiased. Research indicates that when the procedures used for adjudicating grievances and finding fault are judged to be fair, people are much more willing to accept authority. People also feel affirmed if the procedures to which they are subjected treat them with respect and dignity. Often the perception of procedural fairness rests in the willingness to listen to the individual's point-of-view; even if the decision doesn't go his or her way, the individual feels affirmed and respected (Deutsch, 2006).

> Procedural justice is following fair and correct procedures, the essence of western legal tradition. Injustice results when mistakes in procedure are made.

Procedural justice is most intensely applied in matters of criminal law. Criminal justice rests on the principle that the process of adjudication must follow correct procedure; if the procedures are found to be in error with regard to past precedence or specific steps required by statute, court direction, or other proper authority, injustice results. One of the best examples of this is the requirement that evidence seized by police and held as proof of guilt must be obtained by means consistent with protections afforded by the Bill of Rights. When the rules of evidence or individual rights are violated by the police in the pursuit of prosecution, that evidence will not be admissible in court (i.e., the exclusionary rule).

Social Justice vs. Criminal Justice

Social justice and criminal justice principles regularly come into conflict. Social justice refers to a collective concern about the distribution of penalties and rewards in society and how the actions of societal actors impact groups. Arguments concerning the injustice of an action or outcome are based primarily on subjective interpretations relating to past experience, attitudes, and collective points-of-view. Criminal justice refers to the process that is followed in determining the guilt or innocence of a particular individual.

> Social justice is a universal concept that focuses on groups and how groups are treated in society. Criminal justice focuses on the individual and how the individual is treated by the criminal justice system.

Criminal justice largely ignores the outcome of procedures and processes with regard to the issues of concern to social justice advocates. These two concepts are in conflict because criminal justice is intended to be a wholly rational and objective analysis of the actions of actors within the criminal justice system. Conversely, social justice focuses on the unique points-of-view common to groups of people with regard to human rights and equality. Responding to social justice concerns is very likely to offend fundamental criminal justice concepts such as due process, and undermine the rule of law.

> Police officers cannot be social justice actors because doing so violates the equity principles that underlie the law enforcement function. They can, however, be sensitive to social justice issues when they are called upon to exercise their discretion.

Restorative Justice

The concept of restorative justice relates closely to conflict management as it seeks to mitigate adverse relationships between individuals. Punishment is set aside in favor of an attempt to resolve conflicts resulting from criminal behavior. Peacemaking practices, such as arbitration and just compensation for loss, are efforts to "make persons whole" in light of the trauma and loss they have suffered resulting from the behavior of another individual.

Restorative justice views crime as more than breaking the law; it also causes harm to people, relationships, and the community. So a just response must address those harms as well as the wrongdoing. If the parties are willing, the best way to do this is to help them meet to discuss those harms and how to bring about resolution. The principles invoked in this perspective include:

- Repair—crime causes harm and justice requires repairing that harm;
- Encounter—the best way to determine how to do that is to have the parties decide together; and
- Transformation—this can cause fundamental changes in people, relationships, and communities.[4]

[4] The Centre for Justice & Reconciliation website, http://www.restorativejustice.org.

> Restorative justice seeks to focus attention on the victims of crime, doing whatever can be done to mitigate the harm that they have suffered.

CIVIL JUSTICE

Distributive justice, social justice, and restorative justice perspectives speak to societal or collective aspects of fundamental fairness, whereas civil justice is a separate legal system that is governed by procedure, similar to criminal justice. The focus of civil justice is to regulate noncriminal behavior and provide relief to those who have been harmed due to the actions or lack of action by others. Individuals who have been harmed are entitled to monetary compensation for their injury or damages. For example, civil justice provides compensation to those whose property is taken by the government for public purposes (e.g. when land is taken from its owners to build a new road). The civil law system can also punish the wrongdoer by awarding punitive or restorative damages to help prevent further wrongdoing (Hunter, 2011).

> Civil justice seeks to repair private wrongs caused by negligence or willful conduct. It can be applied where no laws prohibiting injurious conduct exist.

The civil system can also regulate relationships between individuals through the issuance of court orders that are police-enforced. The system seeks to manage conflict between individuals in cases such as divorce, child custody, and other situations where the court weighs-in because the parties cannot or will not come to agreement. The police are often called to enforce provisions of civil decrees, and this places the officer in the difficult position of enforcing one individual's point-of-view at the expense of another person's rights. The court may provide that authority, but these situations are anything but a win-win proposition for the parties involved. The best police officers try to manage these conflicts, despite having no authority to do so, so that no one is actually diminished. In this way, the police act in a manner that seeks to restore a sense of justice. However, justice can be a very different when considered in light of the point-of-view of victims and perpetrators.

VICTIMS AND PERPETRATORS

The relationship between the victims and perpetrators of injustice is one that has its foundation in the human need to maintain self-esteem and self-image. It is difficult to see ourselves as the perpetrators of injustice if doing so undermines our sense of self. Similarly, the victim of injustice, in order to maintain self-esteem, may convince themselves that they did not deserve the treatment that they received. Take, for example, an assault case where one party confronts the other concerning how they are caring for a young child. A neighbor pounds on the door early in the morning and engages in a tirade with a mother, who worked all night, concerning the child who roams the neighborhood, causing mischief while the mother sleeps. The perpetrator, upset and worried about the welfare of the child, is merely "educating" the mother on proper parenting. The mother, tired and cranky as the result of holding down two jobs to support her family, feels attacked and undeserving of the treatment she is receiving from the neighbor. Regarding much larger issues, Deutsch (2006) states:

> Distributive as well as procedural injustice can advantage some people and groups and disadvantage others. Those who benefit from injustice are, wittingly or unwittingly, often its perpetrators, and they are usually not fully aware of their complicity. Awareness brings with it such unpleasant emotions as guilt, fear of revenge, and sometimes feelings of helplessness with regard to the ability to bring about social changes necessary to eliminate the injustice (Deutsch, 2006, p. 56).

In an effort to preserve one's sense of self, victims may turn away from acknowledging their complicity; they defend themselves from accusations and deny their advantage. At the same time, when they are being unfairly accused of wrongdoing, they may assert their good intentions and character:

> As one might expect, the disadvantaged are more apt to be aware of the injustice. Associated with this awareness are feelings such as anger, resentment, humiliation, depression and a sense of helplessness. Positive emotions related to self-esteem, sense of power, and pride are experienced by those who are engaged in effective actions to eliminate injustice, whether they are advantaged or disadvantaged (Deutsch, 2006, p. 48).

The apparently disruptive and even quasi-criminal actions of individuals and groups are often driven by the desire to preserve, protect, and defend a sense of personal or group self-worth and self-esteem. An ongoing sense of injustice; often accompanied by anger, resentment, and depression, drive people to engage in behavior that provides them with positive emotions and a sense of power and pride. For those wishing to be more effective in managing conflict, angry protests should not be viewed as an attack on them or the established social order; rather, they should be viewed as an effort to shake the powers-that-be out of a state of ambivalence.

A group seeking social justice for perceived wrongs against its members*

TRUST AND CONFLICT

The difference between constructive and destructive conflict is often a matter of trust. Advocates for police reform often point to the trust issue as a major impediment to police-community relations and charge the police with *trust building* in the community. The implication is that the police are responsible for the erosion of trust among poor people and people of color and, therefore, it is the police who need to fix the problem.

By definition, *trust* is an individual's belief in, and willingness to act on, the basis of, the words, actions, and decisions of another (McAllister, 1995). The factors that contribute to the level of trust one enjoys include 1. the individual disposition toward trusting others; 2. context or situational parameters; and 3. the history of the relationship.

Consider a typical police contact in which a citizen is stopped for speeding. The first factor in determining the level of trust, and the potential for conflict, relates to this particular individual's propensity to trust others. Is this an individual who willingly seeks out and engages in cooperative arrangements with others? Or is this an individual who is cautious, suspicious, or cynical when it comes to interactions with others. This range of predispositions is unique to each individual and is completely unknown to the police officer.

> Trust is the willingness of one individual to act on the basis of other individuals' words or actions. Trust is what holds exchange relationships together.

Next consider the situation. Traffic stops invoke anxiety in both the individual who is stopped and in the police officer who initiated the stop. Citizens

* Image labeled for unrestricted use.

feel much like a child who has been caught doing something wrong, even when they are unaware of the violation, and, like a child, do not do well with authoritative suggestion. The police officer has little or no information on the individual whom they stopped, including no information on their nature, history, or willingness to cooperate and submit to authority. Police officers are taught to always err on the side of caution and treat every unknown encounter as a potential threatening situation, hardly the stuff of great police community relations, but sometimes necessary for basic survival.

Finally, the level of trust depends on the history of the relationship. Sometimes police officers know the individual who they are stopping, but for some citizens, all cops are the same. People initially respond to the uniform as a symbol of authority. Individuals' history with police, what they have been told by others, including the media, and their perceptions concerning the officer's initial behavior may be the only information they have to use to form an initial attitude concerning this encounter. The downside of these kinds of encounters is enormous for the police, who are charged with the responsibility of "building trust and legitimacy" in the community. The rational choice would be to avoid such encounters as well as similar, proactive law enforcement endeavors.

Conversely, activities such as engaging in public relations programs are devoid of the negative situational implications for the police. This leaves the responsibility for the quality of these interactions to be determined by the individual's predisposition toward trust and their history with the police. Such encounters are much less risky for officers because they are devoid of the negative relational aspects of an enforcement encounter. Programs such as the citizen police academy, neighborhood watch, police athletic leagues, and similar endeavors can be powerful relationship and trust building activities, but they demand significant law enforcement resources and a special breed of law enforcement officer. When asked, those who are most severely impacted by crime and disorder generally prefer more police on the street (Maciag, 2015). Citizens want to *trust* the police to effectively handle crime and disorder.

> Trust is much easier to build and maintain when individuals are predisposed to trust the other individual or group, i.e., citizens who trust the police. Trust is difficult when the individuals of groups are not predisposed to trust the other group, i.e., those individuals and groups who do not like the police nor respect the police function.

When speaking of trust in the context of relationship building, society needs to recognize that there are two distinct kinds of relationships: the personal and the professional. **Personal relationships** imply an intimacy between parties based on emotional ties. This is inappropriate when it comes to police officers. The

professional relationship is characterized by task-based behaviors; trust emerges as individuals see their expectations met with regard to what they expect from the police. If individuals want bad people arrested, seeing proof of that builds professional trust. Conversely, if individuals want the police to be judicious in the use of force, videos showing police beating a citizen undermine that trust. This implies that there are different kinds of trust that need to be considered.

Behavioral expectations can be based on promises made either explicitly or implicitly, inferred or consistent with common expectations. Individuals do what they promise because they fear the consequences of not doing what they say. This kind of trust has been referred to as *calculus-based trust* (Lewicki, 1995). Police officers, for example, are expected to perform their duties in a competent and professional manner. Public trust is enhanced when they do so and trust is undermined when they do not, and there are tremendous consequences for police officers who violate professional standards in use of force cases—the threat of punishment is much greater than the reward for performing as expected. One of the reasons that public trust is eroded with regard to police use of force is that violating the expectations is such a rare event that it garners tremendous notoriety.

> Calculus-based trust exists when individuals fear the consequences of not doing what they are obligated to do.

The other side of this coin has to do with police expectations of citizens. The refusal to cooperate with a criminal investigation on the part of a witness or victim violates trust; there is an implicit expectation that citizens will offer information and testimony to aid in the prosecution of cases as part of their responsibility as good citizens. This expectation is routinely violated and undermines trust between the police and the public.

The police need to trust individuals to share information on criminal perpetrators*

The value of **calculus-based** trust is determined by the outcomes resulting from creating and sustaining the relationship relative to the costs of maintaining or severing it. For the citizen, especially a poor person of color, the possible outcomes of creating a trusting relationship with the police are dire when compared to the outcome of severing it. Conversely, severing, avoiding, and even developing an antagonistic relationship with the cops is generally rewarded in these communities.

Personal relationships are based on a different kind of trust referred to as *identification-based* (Lewicki, 1995). This develops among police officers who generally cultivate and maintain personal as well as professional relationships with each other due to the unique aspects of the job and shared experiences. The same is true for those who are the primary customers of the police, poor people, whose experience with the police lead to shared attitudes, views, and predispositions:

> **Identification-based** trust exists because the parties can effectively understand and appreciate one another's wants. This mutual understanding is developed to the point that each person can effectively act for the other. Identification-based trust thus permits a party to serve as the other's agent and substitute for the other in interpersonal transactions. They also come to understand more clearly what they must do to sustain each other's trust.

* Image labeled for unrestricted use.

> Certain kinds of activities strengthen identity-based trust such as developing a joint name (collective identity), co-location in the same neighborhood, and creating joint goals (Lewicki, 2006, p. 96).

> Identification-based trust exists when group cohesion creates a shared identity or subculture with commonly understood behavioral expectations.

Beginning with calculus-based trust, identification-based trust develops in police officers due to the appreciation of their shared duty, common training experiences, socialization into the police subculture, group membership, and collective goals. They know and understand consciously and unconsciously what each needs to do to earn and sustain trust among the group. Similarly, identification based trust emerges for the poor and marginalized due to their shared experience within their culture, common experiences (particularly with the police), and collective goals. These individuals know and understand, consciously and unconsciously, what needs to be done to earn and sustain trust within their group. Unfortunately, the stronger the trusting relationship with these two groups, the less realistic it is to expect them to work together, build a relationship, and even interact positively.

The Nature of Trust

The common rhetoric on trust and relationship building between the police and the communities they serve is devoid of a distinction between trust and distrust. One may assume that they are opposite ends of a continuum, ranging from trust on one end to distrust on the other. This is not the case because **trust and distrust are fundamentally different**. Trust has been previously defined as "confident positive expectations" regarding another's conduct; distrust can be defined as confident negative expectations regarding another's conduct:

> Just as trust implies belief in the other, a tendency to attribute virtuous intentions to the other, and willingness to act on the basis of the other's conduct, distrust implies fear of the other, a tendency to attribute sinister intentions to the other, and desire to protect oneself from the effects of another's conduct (Lewicki, 2006, p. 96).

> Trust and distrust do not exist along a continuum. They are different concepts. Police officers can avoid distrust by dealing with people fairly and with respect but this does not mean that these same individuals will ever trust the police.

Police officers come to know other individuals in a range of contexts and situations. In some of these situations, there may be trust; for example, individuals may and should trust a police officer to relay complete and accurate information when they ask for directions or procedural information. There are other situations, however, when individuals should not expect the police to act in their best interests as in the case of investigating possible involvement in a crime. Individuals should believe that the police are appropriately and accurately seeking to sanction or arrest those who break the law, which may have negative connotations for the criminals. Trust, therefore, has both positive and negative aspects regarding the police; to simply state the police need to work to earn everyone's trust implies that they should never reinforce negative expectations.

Individuals interact with others based on the level of trust, positive or negative expectations, and a number of other factors. According to Lewicki (2006) these factors include:

Personality predispositions. Some people are naturally trusting, and some are naturally suspicious. The higher an individual ranks in a predisposition to trust, the more that they expect trustworthy actions from the other. Distrust results when the individual's trust expectations are violated (Rotter, 1971).

Psychological orientation. People strive to maintain a consistent orientation between their own cognitive, motivational, and moral beliefs and those with whom they associate. They seek out relationships that are consistent with their own orientation—in other words, people who act and believe as they do (Deutsch, 1985). The opposite implication is that they avoid relationships with those who do not think like them or do not have similar motivational and moral beliefs.

Reputations and stereotypes. Expectations of others are shaped by what individuals hear and learn from sources that do not include their own direct knowledge. Casual associations, friends, co-workers, and the media shape our expectations of others. These expectations cause us to look for affirming or dis-affirming signs and predispose us to trust or distrust when relating to them (Glick, 2001).

Actual experience over time. While each person has a general predisposition to trust or distrust another individual based on the individual's personality, psychological orientation, or their reputation, these factors diminish in importance as the individual gains experience. Experience causes individuals to generalize their orientation to trust or distrust.

Conflict occurs when expectations, which may be based upon the above factors, is incongruent with an individual's experience. Understanding the impact of these factors can provide a significant advantage for individuals seeking to manipulate the trust/distrust orientation of others. Consider a case where a police officer engages in an interview/interrogation with a criminal suspect. The police officer's goal is to acquire an admission of guilt from the individual. One would expect that the suspect's orientation would be to distrust the police officer, and this is certainly reinforced by the legal requirement of reminding the suspect of their fifth-amendment rights, commonly known as Miranda Warning. Effective police interviewers understand that obtaining a statement from a suspect requires a high level of rapport built on trust. The police officer in such a case needs to work to overcome a likely distrustful predisposition towards the police. Skillful officers intuitively understand these factors and manipulate the interaction to overcome the predisposition to distrust.

Lewicki (2006) offers some general implications for this view of trust and distrust as independent predispositions:

> Relationships are multifaceted, and each factor represents an interaction that provides us with information about the other. The greater the variety of settings and contexts in which the parties interact, the more complex and multifaceted the relationship becomes.
>
> Within the same relationship, elements of trust and distrust may peacefully coexist, because they are related to different experiences with the other or knowledge of the other in varied contexts.
>
> Relationships balanced with trust and distrust are likely to be healthier that relationships grounded only in trust. . . Unquestioning trust, without distrust, is likely to create more problems than solutions. Unquestioning distrust can sometimes be healthy, but sometimes perverse.
>
> Facets of trust include calculus-based trust and distrust, identity-based trust and distrust. Relationships consist of transaction based considerations, i.e., rewards and sanctions related to violations of expectations and identification-based trust that is grounded in the perceived compatibility of values, goals and emotional attachments. Relationships begin with calculus based trust considerations with identification based trust developing with experience (Kramer, 2002, p. 100).

Calculus- and Identity-Based Trust in Policing

Police officers, and all individuals generally, experience calculus-based and identity-based trust considerations in most of their day-to-day interactions. A police officer may distrust the police chief and the commanding staff in matters related to wages, hours, terms, and conditions of employment. They will collectively seek-out representation for their interests in the form of a union and collective bargaining agreement. At the same time, they may trust the chief to fairly represent them in matters related to external politics—to "have-their-back" in matters where there is a shared understanding due to training, socialization into the police sub-culture, and experiences on the job. Trust/distrust are not two ends of a continuum; they are different and situational.

A citizen living in an impoverished inner-city neighborhood may value interpersonal relationships and socialization to the extent that they trust their neighbors in daily interactions and identify with them. The common predisposition to distrust the police is a unifying element in the solidarity of the group that prevents an individual from cooperating with the police in the event of a serious crime (i.e., "don't snitch.") At the same time, they may not trust their neighbors with basic considerations of communal life, such as respecting their property and intimate relationships. As with the police officer, trust and distrust are different and situational.

Because trust and distrust develop over time as people gain knowledge and experience with each other, certain actions can be identified as useful for managing conflicts. The key aspect of conflict management regarding trust and distrust is the quest for balance as this balance changes given the nature of repeated interactions.

Business and professional relationships are characterized by high levels of calculus-based trust or distrust. In these cases, predictability is the key to managing conflict. Calculus-based trust is enhanced if people behave the same, appropriate way consistently in each encounter and if they demonstrate mutual respect by honoring appointments and commitments and engage in activities as promised. In other words, they do what they say they are going to do. In the case of a police officer engaged with a criminal suspect, the officer may promise that the individual will not go to jail today and will be released to return to their family; when the officer releases the individual with the promise of calling them when an arrest warrant is issued, calculus-based trust is enhanced. The keys to enhancing calculus-based trust include:

- Agreeing explicitly on expectations.
- An upfront commitment to specific behaviors and consequences for violating the expectations reduces fear and apprehension.
- Agreement on the procedures used to monitor compliance.

- When moderate to high levels of distrust are present, agreement on practices used to ensure compliance by both parties is an indication of the desire to reduce the distrust and build good faith.
- Cultivating alternative ways to get needs met. Recall that the very basic element of any conflict situation generally involves unmet needs. In situations characterized by high levels of distrust, letting the other party know that alternatives exist that can be invoked, and that these alternatives will exclude them from future interaction can minimize future trust violations.
- Increase the other parties' awareness of how their behavior is perceived by others. People are not often aware of how they are perceived by others, especially in emotionally-charged situations. Behaviors that are typical within routine in-group social interactions can be perceived as rude and disrespectful to those who are not familiar with the in-group norms. Explaining how and why behaviors impact the perceptions of others can increase mutual understanding and minimize resentment. Being willing to listing and hear about behavioral norms can also decrease levels of distrust (Lewicki, 2006).

Identification-based trust can be enhanced if the parties spend time sharing personal values, perceptions, motives, and goals (Gabarro, 1978). The opportunity and desirability for police officers to engage in this kind of relationship building is highly questionable given the implications for corruption. Identification-based trust has a powerful emotional component that runs counter to the objective rationality foundation of the rule-of-law, yet the argument can be made that this is exactly what change advocates are currently demanding in the form of relationship building (Presidents Task Force Report, 2015). The risk for undermining the legitimacy of the policing function is considerable; however, there is room for highly competent officers to engage in non-enforcement related activities that can enhance identification based trust. Some of the most promising activities include common group memberships (common interests, goals, and objectives) and engaging in situations where each party stands for the same values and principles (Lewicki, 2006).

Engaging with community members in activities that take place outside of the policing and law enforcement context is a powerful way to build identification-based trust without undermining the standards of professional law enforcement; some specific examples will be covered in a later chapter. The key to effectiveness is to engender the belief that we share the values, beliefs and concerns of the other party.

Chapter Summary

In this chapter, we have explored conflict from a number of different perspectives. The idea that all conflict is bad was set aside in favor of various concepts illustrating the value of positive conflict. Most conflict situations are confrontations over power. The unequal distribution of power in society and between individuals can lead to either cooperative arrangements, as actors seek cooperation and order, or conflict, as the actors struggle for a more equal distribution of power and resources in a zero-sum game where one party gains advantage by diminishing the other in some way.

Conflict situations can be either constructive or dysfunctional. Most view conflict negatively and, because of this, tend to engage in one of the most dysfunctional forms of conflict resolution, which is avoidance. Dysfunctional conflict most often results from rigid competitive systems that pit individuals or groups against each other. The behaviors that follow can generate anger, resentment, and depression. Constructive conflict is process-focused as opposed to outcome-focused. The parties seek to build on the relationship rather than gain advantage by diminishing the other in some way.

The functionalist perspective sees society as a system of interconnected parts that work together in harmony to maintain a state of balance and social equilibrium for the whole. The functionalist perspective emphasizes the interconnectedness of society by focusing on how each part influences and is influenced by other parts. This perspective offers a distinction between functional and dysfunctional societal elements in that the former contributes to social stability and the latter disrupts it.

The conflict perspective views society as a collection of different parts engaged in a competition for power and resources. It is often best understood through the work of Karl Marx who suggested that society becomes divided into two distinct classes as the result of economic competition and power.

The symbolic interactionist perspective focuses not on societal groups and their interactions, but on the individual and his or her activity in small groups. The symbolic interactionist perspective relates to the meaning individuals attach to situations, rather than the objective situation itself. Individuals use these assumptions to develop their own self-concept. They imagine how they look to another person by stepping out of themselves and viewing themselves as they believe others view them (through the "looking glass" self).

Many scholars have observed a growing trend today in that more and more people, typically young people, have a worldview that is often not supported by factual information. Conflict results when offered facts go against their life narrative and their reaction is to become angry and indignant. The concept of the pristine self refers to an individual who believes that the world around them should offer them nothing but love and that they are entitled to live in a world that validates their own worldview. When challenged with contradictory ideas or actual facts, they interpret them as personally insulting and even acts of aggression.

Managing conflict situations effectively requires interdependence, where both parties are dependent on the other for something in some way. When the needs of one party are not being met, the parties can seek a cooperative resolution, as in the functionalist perspective, or they can engage in competition, where one party seeks to prevail at the expense of the other. The goal of constructive competition is for both parties to acquire a deeper understanding of the others point-of-view, to value the differences in attitudes and perspectives, and to enrich mutual understanding. Cooperative competition is civilized, thought provoking, exhilarating, and even fun, but there needs to be a level of wisdom on the part of both parties that enables them to overcome the passion that often stands in the way of reason and civilized discourse.

Most understand justice as fundamental fairness, but what is considered fair is typically based upon one's point-of-view. Without a solid foundation in the rule of law and its focus on objective rationality, we are free to pursue our own interpretation of justice based on subjective criteria. This is a profound source of conflict between individuals, between individuals and groups, and between groups that the police are often called on to mediate.

A sense of injustice generally takes the form of oppression. Injustice can take the form of unfair treatment such as discrimination, disparate impact, and other perceived collective wrongs. It can take the form of harassment, breach of contract, a personal injury, and other forms of personal wrongs. These forms of injustice are often perpetrated by those who are insensitive to the feelings and perceptions of others, sometimes because they don't care and sometimes out of ignorance. Managing conflict with regard to the various perspectives on justice requires a deeper understanding of where the sense of injustice originates.

The difference between constructive and destructive conflict is often a matter of trust. Advocates for police reform often point to the trust issue as a major impediment to police community relations and charge the police with *trust building* in the community. The glib implication is that the police are responsible for the erosion of trust among poor people and people of color and, therefore, it is the police who need to fix the problem. The factors that contribute to the level of trust one enjoys include: 1) the individual disposition toward trusting others; 2) the context or situational parameters; and 3) the history of the relationship.

Bibliography

Axelrod, R. (1984). *The Evolution of Cooperation.* New York: Basic Books.

Baxter, L. (1982). Conflict Management: An Episodic Approach. *Small Group Behavior, 13(1)*, 23–42.

Dawes, R.A. (1990). Cooperation for the Benefit of Us—Not Me, or My Conscience. In J.E. Mansbridge, *Beyond Self Interest* (pp. 97–110). Chicago: University of Chicago Press.

Dawes, R.M. (1977). Behavior, Communication, and Assumptions About Other People's Behavior in a Commons Dilemma Situation. *Personality & Social Psychology, I(5),* 35–47.

Deutsch, M. (2006). Cooperation and Conflict. In P.C. Morton Deutsch, *The Handbook of Conflict Resolution* (pp. 23–42). San Francisco: Jossey-Bass.

Dues, M. (2016). *The Art of Conflict Management.* The Great Courses.

Final Report of the President's Task Force on 21st Century Policing. (2015). *President's Task Force on 21st Century Policing.* Washington, DC: Office of Community Oriented Policing Services.

Fisher, R. (1981). *Getting to Yes.* New York: Penguin.

Galvin, K.M., Galvin, A.B. (1982). *Family Communication: Cohesion and Change.* Glenview, IL: Scott, Foresman & Co.

Jehn, K.M. (2001). The Dynamic Nature of Conflict: A Longitudinal Study of Intergroup Conflict and Group Performance. *Academy of Management Journal, 44(2)*, 238–251.

Lewicki, R. J. (2006). Trust, Trust Development and Trust Repair. In P.C. Morton Deutsch, *The Handbook of Conflict Resolution* (pp. 93–113). San Francisco: Jossey-Bass.

Maciag, M. (2015). What People Want from Police Departments. *Governing, The States and Localities.*

McAdams, R. (1995). Cooperation and Conflict: The Economics of Group Status Production and Race Discrimination. *Harvard Law Review, 108(5)*, 1003–1084.

McAllister, D.J. (1995). "Affect and Cognition Based Trust as Foundations for Interpersonal Cooperation in Organizations." *Academy of Management Journal*, 25.

McLeod, S. (2014). Cognitive Dissonance. *www.simplypsychology.org*.

Mooney, L.K. (2015). *Understanding Social Problems*. Stanford: Cengage Learning.

Rotter, J. (1971). Generalized Expectations for Interpersonal Trust. *American Psychologist*, 26, 443–452.

Schwartz, H. (2001). *The Revolt of the Primitive: An Inquiry into the Roots of Political Correctness*. Westport, CT: Praeger.

Schwartz, H. (2016). *Political Correctness and the Destruction of Social Order*. New York: Macmillan.

Wilmont, W. (2010). *Interpersonal Conflict, 8th ed.* Boston, MA: McGraw-Hill.

CHAPTER 5

The Nature of "Community"

■ ■ ■

"A community is the common life of beings who are guided essentially from within, actively, spontaneously, and freely . . . relating themselves to one another, weaving for themselves a complex web of social unity." —Robert MacIver

Community members united for a common purpose*

Learning Outcomes

Upon successful completion of this chapter the student will be able to:

- Describe the meaning of the term "community."
- Explain how social organization takes place.
- Identify a few common mechanisms of social control.
- Explain the difference between a primary and secondary social group.
- Identify various groups that exist in most communities.
- Describe the difference between the constrained and unconstrained visions.

* Image labeled for unrestricted use.

- Describe the difference between Community Oriented Policing and Problem-Oriented Policing.

Important Concepts

- Informal Social Control
- Social Organization
- Primary and Secondary Group Allegiances
- Diversity of Communities

Questions for Discussion

- What is meant by the term "community" and how does it relate to police community relations?
- What drives individuals to establish group affiliations?
- Compare and contrast the various methods of social control described in this chapter.
- Think of a group that is in conflict with the police. Analyze the source of the conflict based upon what has been discussed in this chapter.
- Compare and contrast Community Oriented Policing with Problem-Oriented Policing. Which one holds more value in actually reducing crime and disorder?

INTRODUCTION

The topic of police-community relations implies that the community can be defined in the same way the police are defined—as a particular entity—but this is not the case. A community is made up of groups of individuals who are often representing very different and diverse sets of concerns and issues. Examples include the religious community, the business community, the school community, the youth community, the elderly community, the LGBTQ community, the African American community, the Asian community, and the Hispanic community. In addition, each of these communities is likely to have sub-communities or groups with very different concerns and issues such as the Islamic community, the Catholic community and the Jewish community. Every community, therefore, is made up of a diverse set of sub-groups that differ from each other in terms of needs, desires, goals, and objectives. This multitude of communities also grows and dissipates, evolves, and matures over time.

Community membership and group affiliations can also overlap with individuals sharing and opposing concerns of the groups that they are a part of. This is the environment of municipal policing so to simply demand that the police become more "community oriented" begs the question as to which "communities" should the police orient to? Building better relationships with some will naturally alienate the police from others.

UNDERSTANDING "COMMUNITY"

The term "community" encompasses a plurality of concepts and meanings. To engage with the community often implies behavioral interactions where interpersonal relationships are developed, nurtured and maintained. The term often involves differentiating among groups with regard to unique habits, social norms, and roles of members; communities and groups can often be defined by a unique culture that separates and defines them as unique among other social groups and actors, e.g., the police subculture, the liberal-elite culture, the working class subculture, etc.

Communities provide support to individuals in times of crisis and celebration; they provided a cohesiveness and sense of belonging to members, and serve as the foundation of human society.[1]

People like people who are like themselves. Opposites do not attract!

SOCIAL ORGANIZATION—THE MICRO LEVEL

People engage in patterns of behavior that can be attributed to the circumstances and conditions in which they find themselves. They naturally seek comfort and security by seeking **relationships with others who are like themselves** in term of conditions, values and characteristics. Self-segregation has been the bane of government efforts to integrate schools, neighborhoods, and whole communities since the dawn of the civil rights era in the United States. The simple fact is that, by nature, people like people who are like themselves; they are simply more comfortable with sameness (Frankenberg, 2003).

Social organization can be understood as a function of the behavior of individuals. Common patterns of behavior emerge as a function of social interaction, when the actions of one individual affect another individual in some way. The behavior of an individual who is confronted by the police is facilitated or constrained by the expectations of other individuals. Because human beings are

---

1 From Basic Concepts to Understanding Community System by Jacqueline Ingrouille, Nov. 2004.

highly concerned about the expected or actual reactions of other people to our behavior we tend to conform to those expectations. For example, an individual who identifies with the business community—a local business owner—is going to react much differently to the presence of a police officer than an individual involved with a street gang, regardless of whether other people are present.

> Behavior can also be altered by the mere presence of other people. The way we behave (from the way we eat to what we think) is affected by whether we are alone or with other people. Even physical reactions such as crying, laughing, or passing gas are controlled by the individual because of the fear of embarrassment. It could even be argued that, except in the most extreme cases, people's actions are always oriented toward other human beings whether other people are physically present or not. We, as individuals, are constantly concerned about the expected or actual reactions of other people. Even when alone, an individual may not act in certain ways because of having been taught that such actions are wrong (Eitzen, 2013).

Interpersonal communication is the most basic level of social interaction; it can take the form of words, jesters or symbolic acts. Culture is the shared beliefs, attitudes and behavioral norms that unite members of a group and the culture is often reinforced through interpersonal communication.

> Through enduring social interaction, common expectations emerge about how people should act. These expectations are called norms. Criteria for judging what is appropriate, correct, moral, and important also emerge. These criteria are the values of the group. Also part of the shared beliefs are the expectations that group members have of individuals occupying the various positions within the group. These are social roles (Eitzen, 2013, pp. 26–27).

Common expectations or norms exist due to patterns of social interaction that begin in childhood. Violating these norms causes discomfort and stress not just for the actor but also for those around them.

Knowing and understanding these common expectations is extremely valuable for a police officer in managing conflict. It can be as simple as knowing who to interact with under certain circumstances. For example, it is generally unwise for an officer to approach a youthful individual concerning their possible involvement in a crime when that individual is interacting with his or her friends. Such action is not likely to be viewed as appropriate and may lead to hostility.

On the other hand, it may be useful in some situations for an officer to manipulate the social interaction in a way that bolsters the individual's standing with their group. Such action may actually engender a higher level of trust that can facilitate later cooperation. For example, a police officer may wish to minimize the negative group influence on an otherwise cooperative individual by refraining from approaching him when they are in close proximity; conversely, an officer may approach the group knowing full well that he or she will get an antagonistic response from the same individual that will bolster that individual's standing with the group, i.e., facing down the cop.

> The prevailing cultural standards and the structure of social relationships serve to organize human conduct in the collectivity. As people conform more or less closely to the expectations of their fellows, and as the degree of their conformity in turn influences their relations with others and their social status, and as their status in turn further affects the inclinations to adhere to social norms and their chances to achieve valued objectives, their patterns of behavior become socially organized (Blau, 1962, pp. 4–5).

Police officers hold a unique position in society that allows them to skillfully manipulate social conditions to their advantage.

Behavior is the primary focus of the police; understanding it provides a foundation for controlling it. Taking the time to understand the individual's place in the **social order**—status—of his or her group and the behavioral expectations of the individual as held by the other members of the group—role and hierarchy—provide a powerful tool for managing conflict and improving the police community relationship.

Social Control

A defining characteristic of all social groups is the demand for members to adhere to a common set of **behavioral expectations** or norms. Religious communities often specify these expectations in the form of commandments, rules, or covenants. To violate these standards of conduct is to be sanctioned in some way. Some of the most effective forms of social control are **informal** in nature.[2] Some examples of how groups and communities maintain order in informal ways include:

---

2 Informal social control drives conformity by interpersonal pressure rather than formal sanction.

The Use of Gossip

People care about what others think about them. Informal behavior control is often brought about simply due to fear. The individual fears what others will say about them or think about them if they engage in behavioral violations of group norms. In this way, strategic use of the "grape-vine" in organizational settings can serve as a social control method.

Folkways, Mores, Customs and Religion

Behavioral expectations are often communicated and reinforced through patterns of behavior repeated over time. These customs are internalized and in most cases "go without saying" as patterns of behavior that are expected from all members of the community. Violations of the mores or customs can often be viewed as immoral acts that invoke a sense of guilt on the part of the offender, accompanied by remorse and the need to repent or face ostracism from the group.

The practice of "shunning" is an example of how informal social control was used by some religious communities to maintain social control. The practice amounts to prohibiting other members of a community from recognizing or interacting with a deviant member, in effect, denying their very existence. Such a practice among devout members of religious communities is a devastating sanction; although informal, it strikes at a profound need for human beings to be socially connected and reinforces conformity to the dictates of the group (Eitzen, 2013).

THE POWER OF COMMUNITIES

A social group—community—is a type of human organization that is created by a **pattern of commonly accepted interactions**. It can be defined by a common culture, e.g., ethnic, religious, nationalistic; a way in which people within the group define themselves, e.g., gay, lesbian, outlaw; or it can be defined by what the group values or what they do, e.g., occupation, political allegiance. Primary and secondary groups are another group distinction separated by the level of intimacy and involvement individual group members enjoy.

Primary groups are those in which members partake in frequent, intimate interaction. These groups tend to be small and provide an emotional attachment for members along with a strong sense of **identification**. Groups such as family, sports teams and street gangs are examples of primary groups that provide a sense of belonging, identity, purpose and security.

Economic/Business Organizations

These groups often sit at the center of the power structures in most communities. Citizen advisory committees, police commissions, and other influential groups usually consist of successful business leaders, giving them undue influence over the police in many instances. This can be the source of conflict when the police allow the interests of big business to cloud more holistic decisions about what is in the best interests of the community.

Chamber of Commerce

The chamber of commerce works to actively promote local business members. The chamber will provide support, advertising and events that showcase their members within the geographic area. The chamber also provides linkages and networking to regional, state and national chamber organizations.

Small Business Advisory Council

These organizations serve business startups and generally have a mission to assist small business owners through education, political advocacy, networking, and development.

Religious Organizations

The police historically enjoy supportive relationships with religious organizations, but the advent of increased attention to radical Islamic terrorism has strained the relationship with the Muslim community. Backlash over foreign and domestic terrorist incidents creates a demand for increased surveillance and scrutiny of Muslim religious organizations and this, in turn, undermines the relationship that the police need to maintain with this community in order to acquire information to combat any potential threat.

Women

Women can constitute a unique community worthy of police attention whose members overlap many other groups depending on individual characteristics, needs, and interests. Women have been treated differently than men historically and can claim victimized status generally by the influence and behavior patterns of patriarchal[3] societal systems.

3 The term patriarchy refers to a male headed, dominated, and controlled social system.

Women are vulnerable to victimization in many ways with domestic violence as a primary concern for police. Most states now have strict state laws mandating arrest of those who commit violence against women. Human trafficking is now a national concern as women are deceived into willingly being smuggled into the country with a promise of improved economic opportunity only to be relegated into sexual slavery. Other issues that may demand police attention involve discriminatory practices and abuse. The following organizations illustrate the overlap of interests typical of multiple group affiliations.

The National Organization for Women

This organization is the largest organization of feminist activists in the United States. NOW has 500,000 contributing members and 550 chapters nationally with chapters in all 50 states and the District of Columbia. Since its founding in 1966, NOW's goal has been to take action to bring about equality for all women.

National Council of Negro Women

The National Council of Negro Women is a council of national African American women's organizations and community-based sections. NCNW's mission is to lead, develop and advocate for women of African descent as they support their families and communities. NCNW fulfills this purpose through research, advocacy, and national and community-based services and programs.

National Council of Jewish Women

The National Council of Jewish Women is a volunteer organization that has been at the forefront of social change through championing the needs of women, children, and families—while taking a progressive stance on such issues as child welfare, women's rights, and reproductive freedom.

The Elderly

The population of elderly people is rapidly increasing in the United States and these individuals are increasingly victimized by crime. People look forward to retirement and the "golden years," but they are finding this time in their life more and more challenging as changes in economic conditions impact where they can go, live, and maintain the quality of life to which they have become accustomed. The elderly are often targeted by criminals in many ways and have become increasingly vulnerable with age. The rate of elderly victimization is difficult to measure and predict because many of the elderly do not report crime, especially property related fraud scams, due to embarrassment and other concerns. Serving this population is often done most effectively through preventative education.

AARP

One of the best known organizations serving the needs of persons who have matured beyond middle age is the American Association of Retired Persons. This is a nonprofit organization working to improve the quality of life for those 50 and older. The organization also provides many benefits that appeal to mature persons.

National Council on Aging

The national Council on Aging is an organization for individuals aged 60 and above that partners with nonprofit and governmental organizations to provide programming, services and advocacy to assist individuals in meeting the challenges of aging.

Lesbian, Gay, Bisexual, Transgender, Queer (LGBTQ)

The relationship between law enforcement and the LGBTQ community has been troubled. Historically, homosexuals have experienced discriminatory treatment as well as indifference. Confrontations between the police and gay-rights activists and protestors has left a legacy of mistrust between these groups and the police that has also spread to other group affiliations that these individuals may have.

> Discrimination and harassment by law enforcement based on sexual orientation and gender identity is an ongoing and pervasive problem in LGBT communities. Such discrimination impedes effective policing in these communities by breaking down trust, inhibiting communication, and preventing officers from effectively protecting and serving the communities they police. While a patchwork of state, local, and federal laws provides some protection against certain forms of discrimination, there is no nationwide federal statute that comprehensively and consistently prohibits discrimination based on actual or perceived sexual orientation and gender identity (Mallory, 2015).

An organization that has been at the forefront of issues affecting the LGBTQ community is the American Civil Liberties Union.

ACLU

The American Civil Liberties Union is a nonpolitical organization dedicated to defending and preserving the individual rights and liberties guaranteed to every person by the Constitution of the United States. The ACLU also engages in lobbying activities specifically directed at opposing the death penalty, supporting same-sex marriage, supporting the right of LGBT people to adopt children and lobbying in support of other current issues that have constitutional implications.

The Poor

People living in generational poverty have a view of the police that is very different from those in the middle class or the rich. The poor tend to view the police as existing to protect the rich and privileged from themselves; not to keep them safe and protect their property, but to segregate them from those who feel threatened by them.

Poor people are most often the victims and perpetrators of crime and it is difficult for the police to relate to them because the police are generally representative of the middle class, holding middle class values that are very different from those living in poverty.

For example, a police officer who is called to investigate the theft of clothing and food is not likely to take the case as seriously as he or she would if they, themselves, understood the value of the property to someone living in poverty. When a full week's wages are needed to purchase Thanksgiving dinner, losing the food to theft is devastating; the police officer is likely to dismiss it as a minor matter unworthy of his/her time. This leaves the poor person reluctant to report crime as they don't believe that the police take their concerns seriously.

Youth

Young people often come into conflict with the police. Youth culture can appear strange and disorderly, prompting additional attention from the police, including stops and frisks. The problematic nature of the relationships between young people and the police is characterized by tension, mistrust, and conflict. In many cases, young people face adverse consequences including detention, arrests, and citations that are disproportionate to their representation in the population (Crime and Misconduct Commission, 2009).

Summarizing What Is Meant by "The Community"

The "community" consists of a wide variety of groups that are intertwined in complex ways. Individuals join with others in groups because they share characteristics, because they share common goals, or for countless other less precise reasons. Groups—**mini-communities**—join together for similar reasons and float together like a boat on the sea linking and splitting with other mini-communities depending on the tides and waves of opinions, points-of-view, and events that drive the need to cooperate or compete. For the police, relationship building requires intimate knowledge of the tides of public opinion along with a keen and practiced ability to anticipate events, conditions and trends that may drive intergroup activity.

However, even a sophisticated understanding of intergroup dynamics cannot explain why some individuals and groups hold such conflicting visions of reality that building relationships and engaging in cooperative endeavors becomes perilous and sometimes futile. The next section offers additional insight based on the concept of the constrained and unconstrained vision.

THE TWO CONFLICTING VISIONS: A PHILOSOPHICAL BASIS FOR COMMUNITY COOPERATION AND COMPETITION

The case for the necessity of the rule of law and the police may appear to be self-evident, yet there are those who argue against the "status quo" and the system of incentives and disincentives that exist to regulate human behavior in society. Managing the inevitable conflict that will arise between those who represent the existing social order (such as the police, prosecutors, and courts) and those who advocate for change requires an understanding of the opposing perspective.

> The impetus for change is generally directed at the "status quo," or the way things currently work or exist. The demand for change can be incremental—gradual small change—or universal—throw the whole system out and start over.

Vision is the sense of how the world works: visions set the agenda for both thought and action. We relate with others based on a set of **consistent premises** that we hold about ourselves, our standing (based upon our self-image) and our relationship with the outside world. An example of the first vision is the police officer who may believe implicitly—without conscious thought—that all people are pre-disposed toward compliance with the law and that those who violate the law are somehow evil and subject to sanction. He or she arrives at this premise as the result of their training and knowledge of the criminal justice system. This premise is just one of a set that flows from a vision of themselves and their place in society, one that reinforces the righteousness of behavior directed at controlling the unlawful acts of others.

A social activist, on the other hand, may have a different view; the activist may view the law as an unjust institution created by unjust societal actors for their own advantage. They point to instances of abuse as proof of their premise and advocate disobedience of the law as the only way to generate awareness and change. This vision is in conflict with that of the typical police officer who swears an oath to uphold the law.

People tend to view the world and events based upon grand visions of the world. For example, are people, by nature, basically good or basically evil?

Seeking to resolve conflict between these opposite visions of the law cannot be accomplished with facts. Facts and empirical evidence only have utility, in a logical sense, when used to test a theory. The vision an individual holds about how the world works is what their theory or premises are based upon. For example, a police officer attempting to convince a protestor that their argument or position is unreasonable based on facts is a futile endeavor because the protestor's vision of the world and their vision of the relationship between the police and the community is dramatically different.

Visions also tend to be very simplistic, e.g., people are basically good and seek to help each other; or people are basically evil and will relentlessly pursue their own self-interest at the expense of others. This can cause stress for individuals when observations and perception do not support their vision. They seek out other visions that help them resolve the internal conflict. For example, a criminal who commits a heinous act of inhumanity will shock the conscious of someone who holds a vision that says people are basically good. Reconciling the incongruity requires an explanation that maintains the belief that people are basically good. This is why some seek to blame societal conditions for crime rather than holding offenders accountable for their behavior directly. Those acts must be driven by a societal injustice, i.e., lack of opportunity, discrimination, racism, etc. Such explanations are likely to be dismissed by those who believe that people are basically animals—evil and self-serving by nature. These individuals are likely to demand accountability and punishment for the offender's behavior.

The difference between these two visions of reality can be understood as opposite ends of a continuum that ranges from constrained to unconstrained. People are rarely advocates of the pure visions these labels represent. Rather, an individual's point-of-view will fall along the continuum depending upon the issue or matter at hand. What is remarkable, however, is how these two opposite visions of reality have consistently endured over the centuries and how they structure debate and conflict today (Sowell, 2007).

The Nature of Man in the Constrained and Unconstrained Vision

The concepts of the constrained and unconstrained visions offer a framework for understanding a fundamental philosophical conflict that has endured for centuries regarding the nature of mankind and how to bring about societal change.

The Constrained Vision

In the constrained vision man is viewed as egocentric and self-centered. "By nature, men are self-deceptive, self-centered and when given a choice will always take the path of least resistance" (Enter, 2006). Adam Smith proposed that rather than trying to change the nature of man we simply accept it and seek out the most efficient way (least costly) to produce the desired social benefits within this vision.

Adam Smith, 1723–1790, Scottish economist*

Smith is widely recognized as the father of modern economics due to his book *The Wealth of Nations*. As a moral philosopher he focused upon the development of moral character in *The Theory of Moral Sentiments*, where he proposed that one's

* Image labeled for unrestricted use.

conscience develops due to the feedback received from our own judgements of how others see us. The act of observing others and seeing the judgements the form creates an *incentive* to achieve "mutual sympathy of sentiments."

Given this belief about the nature of man, the constrained vision relies on the importance of **incentives** and disincentives to encourage desirable behavior and to discourage undesirable behavior. Man is imperfect, in the words of Alexander Hamilton in the Federalist Papers, ". . . all human institutions have defects as well as excellences, good as well as bad propensities . . ." (Hamilton, 1985, p. 390). Given the imperfection of man and his natural inclination to act in his own best interests, there must be a system of mechanisms that **compel** man to sacrifice his own interests to that of the greater good. Through the action of artificial devices such as a devotion to moral principles, concepts of honor, and obedience to the law, man could be persuaded, for his own good, (self-image) to act in ways that serve the interests of his fellow man. A system of moral incentives and tradeoffs—the rule of law—was needed to restrict man from acting in self-interested ways that would diminish the standing of their fellow man. The constrained vision, therefore, focuses on trade-offs in the form of incentives and disincentives rather than ultimate solutions such as changing the nature of man (Smith, 1759).

> The constrained vision relies on incentives and disincentives to change behavior incrementally over time. Man is by nature defective and requires coercion, in the form of incentives and disincentives, to act in socially beneficial ways.

Regulating behavior toward the good of society is most efficiently accomplished when a system exists that encourages moral behavior and rewards it in ways that have a positive impact on one's self-esteem, i.e., doing good things makes you a good person. A shared vision of acceptable behavior makes one a bad person if they engage in behavior that is generally considered detrimental to the social good. The law is an extension of the shared system of morality that provides sanction and punishment for socially unacceptable, illegal, behavior. The constrained vision assumes that man is naturally defective and that socially beneficial behavior could only be evoked through a system of incentives.

The Nature of Man in the Unconstrained Vision

The unconstrained vision provides a contrast to Smith's philosophy in that it relies on man's ability to **reason** and to seek virtuous outcomes. William Godwin (1793) identified the intention to benefit others as the essence of virtue and virtue or a virtuous life as being the road to human happiness (Godwin, 1793). In this view of human nature, man is capable of feeling the needs of other people and viewing them as more important than his own. Godwin did not put this forth as a statement of what actually occurs, but rather as a statement of human potential.

> The unconstrained vision sees man as capable of feeling and responding to the needs of his fellow man. By nature, man is basically good and uses reason to arrive at morally virtuous outcomes that benefit society.

William Godwin, 1756–1836, English philosopher and novelist*

> Godwin was best known for his 1793 work *Enquiry concerning Political Justice and its influence on General virtue and Happiness.* His influence can be summarized by his view of the nature of mankind. "All control of man by man was intolerable. The day will come when each man, doing what seems right in his own eyes, would also be doing what is in fact best for the community because all will be governed by principles of pure reason.
>
> Men are capable, no doubt, of preferring an inferior interest of their own to a superior interest of others, but this preference arises from a combination of circumstances and is not the necessary and invariable law of our nature. Man is, in short, "perfectible"—meaning continually improvable rather than capable of actually reaching absolute perfection.[4]

In contrast to Godwin's unconstrained vision, we have Edmund Burke speaking to the constrained vision:

> We cannot change the nature of things and of men—but must act upon them the best we can.[5]

---

* Image labeled for unrestricted use.

4 Godwin (1793) as quoted by Sowell (2007) p. 18.

5 Burke (1789) as quoted by Sowell (2007) p. 18.

The unconstrained vision views socially contrived incentives, and disincentives such as the law as unnecessary **impediments** to the real solution identified as allowing people to do what is right because it is the right thing to do. The real goal is the long-run development of a higher sense of social duty, the immediacy of short term incentives provides only an illusionary benefit. The hope of reward and fear of punishment are wrong in themselves. The nature of man, governed by reason, empathy, and compassion is retarded by a system of rewards and punishments reflective of existing man corrupted by prejudice, passion, and existing social customs (Sowell, 2007).

The unconstrained vision claims that mans' moral goodness is retarded by a system of rewards and punishments (incentives and disincentives) because they reflect existing prejudice and social customs.

If it were not for the impact of socially derived customs and conditions based upon the expediency of incentives intended to bring about social good, such as law and order, man would be free to pursue his natural virtue identified by the unconstrained vision as the pursuit of socially beneficial outcomes.

The **unconstrained** vision seeks solutions resulting from a reasoned approach to the problems of mankind. If man were not limited (constrained) by socially contrived mechanisms, incentives and disincentives, he could rise to his full potential of goodness and virtue resulting in the continual improvement of the human condition. Human nature is essentially good and society should be guided and governed by the reason of those possessing **superior intellect**.

The **constrained** vision sees human nature as flawed. A system of incentives and disincentives, trade-offs, is necessary to make the best of the possibilities that exist. Given this view of human nature, it is assumed that there is a continual need to minimize the damage that could be done by individuals seeking their own self-interest at the expense of other individuals or society itself. An example of how we minimize the potential for harm is the law. Social good can only come about when the nature of man is efficiently governed by a **system of social controls** that evolve over time and through experience.

According to Sowell (2006):

> The *unconstrained* vision promotes pursuit of the highest ideals and the best solutions. By contrast, the *constrained* vision sees the best as the enemy of the good, a vain attempt to reach the unattainable being seen as not only futile but often counterproductive, while the same efforts could have produced a more viable and beneficial trade-off.

> The prudent reformer, according to Smith, will respect "the confirmed habits and prejudices of the people," and when he cannot establish what is right, "he will not distain to ameliorate the wrong. His goal is not to create the ideal, but to establish the best that the people can bear" (p. 27).

In the constrained vision human nature is viewed as remaining relatively constant over the ages and among different cultures, it cannot be changed by forceful intervention. The ideal state of being is weighed against the cost of achieving it in terms of regulation in a kind of cost benefit analysis resulting in good and expedient solutions that are acceptable *but not perfect.*

The unconstrained vision seeks to move human nature closer to the ideal regardless of costs, every closer approximation to the ideal state should be pursued, and costs are merely regrettable in consideration of the ultimate outcome.

Our system of justice reflects the ideal of the unconstrained vision when we state that it is better for a guilty man to go free rather than an innocent man be convicted. This statement is an illustration that the costs of allowing a guilty man to go free are of secondary importance when compared to the desired result. In contrast, the constrained vision stresses the importance of law and order even if it means that those suffering perceived injustice will continue to suffer. It focuses on the process with desired results constrained by the costs of bringing them about. Undesirable side effects are accepted and viewed as trade-offs.

> How are people made good? The constrained vision promotes self-discipline and hard work. The unconstrained vision promotes parental nurturing and taking care of others.

The problem for those engaged in the business of criminal justice under our legal tradition is the clash between our principles, reflected in the unconstrained vision, and having their foundation in the high ideals of Jefferson, Rousseau and Goodwin; and the economics of practical reality as put forth by Smith and Hamilton. One of the best modern illustrations of this conflict can be seen in the difference between conservatives and liberals today. Conservatives maintain that people are *made good* through self-discipline and hard work, everyone is taken care of by taking care of themselves. Conversely, modern liberals believe that people are *made good* through parental nurturing, everyone is taken care of by helping each other. Those who believe that the police are, and should be, a repressive entity held accountable to professional standards reflect the former; those who believe that the police should serve as social workers with badges reflect the latter (Lakoff, 1996).

Who rules? The constrained vision is governed by the rule of law and the guidance of past decisions-precedence-changed incrementally to meet new conditions. The unconstrained vision is governed by the intellectual elite, those who possess superior powers of reason in responding to existing problems without regard to what has been decided in the past.

Again, people do not fall neatly into these categories and generalizations. Individuals may be conservative on social issues and liberal on economic issues, vice-versa, and aspiring to varying degrees along a continuum that ranges between conservative and liberal. Understanding the nature of the community, and all of the sub-communities that exist within it, depends on the *ability to see the world as the other side sees it.* Building trust and relationships requires the ability to see the world through the eyes of those who are impacted by the actions of the police, i.e., individuals and groups that make-up the community.

COMMUNITY ORIENTED POLICING AS COLLABORATION

Traditional policing is reactive in nature; a crime occurs, someone calls the police, officers arrive, investigate the crime, and make an arrest. Traditional policing also employed pro-active enforcement techniques where officers don't wait for a crime to occur, but initiate action when violations are observed or suspected. The measure of law enforcement effectiveness in the traditional, also known as the professional, policing era was rapid response to calls for service; how quickly the police arrived. This was the impetus for 911 systems that assumed that arriving quickly increased the ability for police to make an on-scene arrest; it doesn't. What this relentless focus on rapid response to calls for service did do was force officers to respond and handle calls as quickly as possible; the demand from supervisors took the form of "Clear that call ASAP. There are jobs waiting." Officers learned to behave like automated machines, collecting the facts, conducting perfunctory interviews, treating citizens with callous indifference, documenting information, and getting back on patrol as quickly as possible in order to be ready to respond quickly to the next call for service.

What was learned is that increasing officer professionalism, sophisticated 911 systems, and computer aided dispatch technology could not keep up with dramatically increasing rates of violent crime and the "super-predators" emerging in urban communities. The level of fear was increasing and the police, constrained by the professional policing model, seemed helpless.

What was needed was a new way to view the police function, a more pro-active rather that the old re-active model. George Kelling and James Wilson responded with "Broken Windows" policing, (1982) making the case that the way to deal with big crime problems was to deal with the small disorder problems, those things that sent the signal that nobody cared. This was combined with Problem Oriented Policing, Goldstein (1990), to expound the value of pro-active policing, attacking disorder and crime problems before people become victimized and neighborhoods become crime havens (Wilson, 1982) (Goldstein, 1990).

This new mandate changed the nature of the policing function and laid the foundation for the Violent Crime Control and Law Enforcement Act of 1994. President Clinton vowed to put 100,000 new cops on the streets, mainly in urban areas plagued by drug and gang driven violence. This new reiteration of the "War on Drugs" shook the police out of their reactive mode and created powerful incentives to seek-out criminal prey and lock them up before they caused harm.

The pro-active or "preventive interventionist model," as put forth by Kelling (1999), was a part of a new overreaching policing philosophy called Community Oriented Policing. The incentives for the police to engage in pro-active enforcement was hidden under the umbrella of this new philosophy with federal grant money thrown at police agencies that promised to re-deploy officers from routine patrol into programs directed at developing it.

Community oriented policing is a proactive rather than reactive way to address underlying problems that cause crime.

The foundation of the community oriented policing philosophy is based on the idea of community collaboration with the police in pursuit of crime prevention. The police and the "community" work together to identify and solve crime problems, the community becomes a co-producer of public safety according to Skolnick and Bayley (1988). Community oriented policing was defined not as a single program but "it can encompass a variety of programs or strategies that rest on the assumption that policing must involve the community" (Skolnick, 1988). Because of this *profound ambiguity*, programs authorized under the community oriented policing banner ranged from police involvement in midnight basketball leagues hosted by the police department for underprivileged youth, to the give-a-way of sophisticated military equipment—urban tanks—to police agencies for their drug interdiction efforts.

The theoretical foundation for community oriented policing stressed the importance of shifting the focus from police practices that concentrated on process and procedure in favor of focusing on end results. Focusing on process, it was argued, made the police blind to the problems they were meant to solve Weisburd (2008) and Goldstein (1987) argued that the police needed to shift away from the reactive model by adopting community oriented policing as an organizing principle and fundamental philosophy. Rather than simply responding to calls for service, the police needed to concentrate on solving problems of crime and disorder in the neighborhoods, a focus that significantly expanded the scope of policing activities (Greene, 2000) (Weisburd, 2008).

> Community oriented policing with its emphasis on problem solving is outcome focused rather than process focused.

The context of Community Oriented Policing was provided by the argument that crime and disorder were the result of neighborhood decline.

> Another important context for COP was provided by Wilson and Kelling's (1982) argument that disorder in the local community when it reaches a critical mass creates a potential for more serious crime and urban decay. Their "broken windows" theory predicts that small signs of disorder—such as a broken window—communicates the **lack of social control** and thus invites increasingly larger acts of disorder and crime. Untended property becomes fair game for people out for fun or plunder, and even for people who ordinarily would not dream of doing such things. Such an area is vulnerable to criminal invasion. In response, the police—to protect the community and establish control—must engage in **order maintenance** and make *proactive arrests*. Four elements of the broken window's strategy explain its impact on crime reduction (Kelling and Coles 1996). First, dealing with disorder puts police in contact with those who commit more serious crimes. Second, *the high visibility of police causes a deterrent effect for potential perpetrators of crime*. Third, citizens assert control over neighborhoods, thereby preventing crime. And finally, as problems of disorder and crime become the responsibility of both the community and the police, crime is attacked in an integrated fashion (Development Services Group, Inc., 2010).

More specific guidance was offered with regard to the following elements of Community Oriented Policing:

1. The empowerment of the community
2. A belief in a broad police function
3. The reliance of police on citizens for authority, information, and collaboration
4. The application of general knowledge and skill
5. Specific tactics targeted at particular problems rather than general tactics such as preventive patrol and rapid response

6. Decentralized authority to better respond to neighborhood needs (Development Services Group, Inc., 2010).

Successful policing under the professional-reactive-model included numbers of arrests and number of crimes reported. Judging the success of the Community Oriented model includes assessing the safety of a community, perceptions of fear, and calls for service. Linking these measures with any of the above elements of Community Oriented Policing has been particularly problematic.

PROBLEM-ORIENTED POLICING—TARGETING COMMUNITY RESOURCES AND BRINGING PEOPLE TOGETHER

When compared to Community Oriented Policing, Problem Oriented Policing is much more focused. This strategy is aimed at solving persistent community problems rather than at an ambiguous goal of community involvement and by-in. Armed with this technology, officers can more clearly focus on crime reduction results rather than on policing processes and procedures.

> Police identify, analyze, and respond to the underlying circumstances that create incidents. The theory behind it is that underlying conditions create problems (Goldstein 1979). Thus officers use the information gathered in their responses to incidents, together with information obtained from other sources, to get a clearer picture of the problem (Eck, 1987).

Based on a problem solving analysis-known as SARA,[6] officers are empowered to employ alternative and innovative responses and solutions to crime problems. Examples of problem responses can include, but are not limited to:

1. Target hardening (i.e., reducing opportunities)
2. Changes in government services
3. Provision of reliable information to residents
4. Specialized training for police officers
5. Use of community resources
6. Increased regulation

---

[6] **Scan**—Identify problems and prioritize them with community input. **Analyze**—Study information about offenders, victims and crime locations. **Respond**—Implement strategies that address the chronic character of the priority problems. **Assess**—Evaluate the effectiveness of the strategies employed.

7. Changes in city ordinances or zoning (Development Services Group, Inc., 2010).

Research supports the increased effectiveness of the problem oriented approach over traditional policing in reducing crime (Eck, 1987) (Kennedy, 1996) (Sherman, 1995). One of the best and most successful examples employed a multi-agency approach to the problem of gun violence in Boston.

> A more recent example of the problem-solving approach is Operation Ceasefire, which was designed to reduce illegal gun possession and gun violence in the community. Operation Ceasefire is one element of a collaborative, comprehensive strategy (which also includes the Boston Gun Project and Operation Night Light) implemented in Boston, Mass., to address escalating violent crime rates. It consists of a combination of aggressive law enforcement and prosecution efforts aimed at recovering illegal handguns, prosecuting dangerous felons, increasing public awareness, and promoting public safety and antiviolence campaigns. The goals of the program are to implement a comprehensive strategy to target, apprehend, and prosecute offenders who carry firearms, to put others on notice that offenders face certain and serious punishment for carrying illegal firearms, and to prevent youth from following the same criminal path. The program has two main elements: 1) a direct law enforcement attack on illicit firearms traffickers supplying youth with guns and 2) an attempt to generate a strong deterrent to gang violence (known as pulling levers) (Development Services Group, Inc., 2010).

The Operation Ceasefire program, as evaluated by a careful analysis of a serious crime problem and a genuine commitment from the police, prosecutors and *social service providers* to stop young people from killing each other, was associated with a significant decrease (63%) in the monthly number of youth homicides in Boston (Braga, 2001).

Community Oriented Policing places community involvement at the forefront of policing, a noble endeavor but one that is incredibly difficult to achieve. Any community is incredibly diverse and building better relationships with individuals and groups that make-up the "community" inevitably will alienate the police from other equally important groups. Any veteran police officer knows that community oriented policing is nothing new, it is what the best cops have always endeavored to accomplish even during the peak of traditional-professional era-policing. However, the reality of the law enforcement and policing function leaves little room for such ill-defined priorities as empowering the community; a broader police function; reliance of police on citizens for authority, information, and collaboration; the application of general knowledge and skill; tactics targeted at particular problems rather than general tactics such as preventive patrol and rapid response; and decentralized authority to better respond to neighborhood needs. *The majority of citizens in the community—who are rarely represented on or in advisory councils, neighborhoods meetings, and community oriented policing activities—simply want to feel safe, they want to be able to let their children play in the front yard and walk to school without fear, they just want the police to do their job, controlling crime.*

The Problem-Oriented approach is a proven strategy that targets community resources on specific crime problems. Police should always be engaged with, and oriented toward, the communities that they serve, but this means looking to the community for operational priorities and listening; not engaging in "feel-good" activities that have no bearing on actual crime problems.

Chapter Summary

The term "community" encompasses a plurality of concepts and meanings. To engage with the community often implies behavioral interactions where interpersonal relationships are developed, nurtured and maintained.

People engage in patterns of behavior that can be attributed to the circumstances and conditions that they find themselves in. They naturally seek comfort and security by seeking relationships with others who are like themselves in term of conditions, values, and characteristics.

Social organization can be understood as a function of the behavior of individuals. Common patterns of behavior emerge as a function of social interaction, when the actions of one individual affect another individual in some way.

A social group—a kind of community—is a type of human organization that is created by a pattern of commonly accepted interactions. It can be defined by a common culture, e.g., ethnic, religious, nationalistic, etc.; a way in which people within the group define themselves, e.g., gay, lesbian, outlaw, etc.; or it can be defined by what the group values or what they do, e.g., occupation, political allegiance, etc. Primary and secondary groups are another group distinction separated by the level of intimacy and involvement group members enjoy.

Primary groups are those in which members partake in frequent, intimate interaction. These groups tend to be small and provide an emotional attachment for members along with a strong sense of identification. Groups such as family, sports teams, and street gangs provide a sense of belonging, identity, purpose, and security.

Secondary groups are large and impersonal, they are governed by organizational rules, organizational mechanisms, and formal procedures. Members within secondary groups may be diverse with regard to their primary group membership, but they are brought together for a larger purpose, condition, or circumstance. Families that share residency in a building, neighborhood, or city are members of that secondary group.

The term "community" encompasses a plurality of concepts and meanings. To engage with the community often implies behavioral interactions where interpersonal relationships are developed, nurtured and maintained. The term often involves differentiating among groups with regard to unique habits, social norms, and roles of members; communities and groups can often be defined by a unique culture that separates and defines them as unique among other social groups and actors, e.g., the police subculture, the liberal-elite culture, the working class subculture, etc.

A defining characteristic of all social groups is the demand for members to adhere to a common set of behavioral expectations or norms. Religious communities often specify these expectations in the form of commandments, rules, or covenants. To violate these standards of conduct is to be sanctioned in some way. Some of the most effective forms of social control are informal in nature. Some examples of how groups and communities maintain order in informal ways include the use of gossip, folkways, mores, custom, and religion.

Primary and secondary groups exist within a larger, community-wide setting. This larger social setting is also structured with specific norms and behavioral standards such as the need to respect the police, teachers and others in authority positions; to do "one's part" in advancing the needs or security of the society; and to support its members. The macro-level of social organization refers to society itself when the society can be defined by a common culture, people who live in a defined geographic region, and who may be autonomous from other societies.

When the term "community" is used it usually means the society at large, making this term of little use for a police chief or police officer seeking a better relationship with his or her customers. The community consists of many groupings of individuals who are brought together by way of culture, geography, or common interest. These subgroupings may join together in cooperation or they may compete with each other for attention and resources. The key to success rests in the ability to facilitate a balance between the interests of competing groups, and to build cooperation among groups with common interests.

The Nature of Man is usefully described as a continuum between what is called the Constrained Vision and the Unconstrained Vision. In the constrained vision man is viewed as egocentric and self-centered. "By nature, men are self-deceptive, self-centered and when given a choice will always take the path of least resistance" (Enter, 2006). Adam Smith proposed that rather than trying to change the nature of man we simply accept it and seek out the most efficient way (least costly) to produce the desired social benefits within this vision.

The Unconstrained Vision provides a contrast to Smith's philosophy in that it relies on man's ability to reason and to seek virtuous outcomes. William Godwin (1793) identified the intention to benefit others as the essence of virtue and virtue or a virtuous life as being the road to human happiness (Godwin, 1793). In this view of human nature, man is capable of feeling the needs of other people and viewing them as more important than their own. Godwin did not put this forth as a statement of what actually occurs but rather as a statement of human potential.

Traditional policing has been reactive in nature. The measure of law enforcement effectiveness in the professional policing era was rapid response to calls for service: how quickly the police arrived. Officers learned to behave like automated machines, collecting the facts, conducting perfunctory interviews, treating citizens with often callous indifference, documenting information and getting back on patrol as quickly as possible in order to be ready to quickly respond to the next call for.

The foundation of the Community Oriented Policing philosophy is based on the idea of community collaboration with the police in pursuit of crime prevention. The police and the "community" work together to identify and solve crime problems. In this scheme, the community becomes a co-producer of public safety.

The theoretical foundation for Community Oriented Policing stresses the importance of shifting the focus from police practices that concentrated on process—procedure—in favor of focusing on end results. Focusing on process, it was argued, made the police blind to the problems they were meant to solve.

When compared to Community Oriented Policing, Problem Oriented Policing is much more focused. This strategy is aimed at solving persistent community problems rather than at an ambiguous goal of community involvement and by-in. Armed with this technology officers can more clearly focus on crime reduction results rather than on policing processes and procedures.

Bibliography

Asch, S.E. (1958). Effects of Group Pressure upon the Modification and Distortion of Judgments. In E.N. Maccoby, *Readings in Social Psychology, 3rd ed.* (pp. 174–83). New York: Holt, Rinehart and Winston.

Blau, P.M. (1962). *Formal Organizations: A Comparative Approach.* San Francisco: Chandler.

Braga, A., Kennedy, D., Waring, E., Piehl-Morrison, A. (2001). Problem-Oriented Policing, Deterrence, and Youth Violence: An Evaluation of Boston's Operation Ceasefire. *Journal of Research in Crime and Delinquency, 23(3)*, 195–225.

Burke, E. (1789). *The Correspondence of Edmund Burke, Vol. VI,* 392. Chicago: Reprint University of Chicago Press 1978.

Crime and Misconduct Commission. (2009). *Interactions Between Police and Young People.* Brisbane: Crime and Misconduct Commission.

Development Services Group, Inc. (2010). *Community- and Problem-Oriented Policing.* Washington: Office of Juvenile Justice and Delinquency Prevention.

Eck, J.E. (1987). *Problem Solving: Problem-Oriented Policing in Newport News.* Washington, DC: Police Executive Research Forum.

Eitzen, D.S. (2013). *In Conflict and Order: Understanding Society, 13th ed.* New York: Pearson.

Enter, J.E. (2006). *Challenging the Law Enforcement Organization.* Dacula, GA: Narrow Road Press.

Festinger, L.R. (1956). *When Prophecy Fails.* Minneapolis, MN: University of Minnesota Press.

Frankenberg, E.L. (2003). *A Multiracial Society with Segregated Schools.* Cambridge, MA: Harvard University.

Godwin, W. (1793). *Enquiry Concerning Political Justice.* Toronto: Reprint by University of Toronto Press 1969.

Goldstein, H. (1990). *Problem Oriented Policing.* New York: McGraw-Hill.

Greene, J. (2000). Community Policing in America: Changing the Nature, Structure, and Function of the Police. *Policies, Processes, and Decisions of the Criminal Justice System, Vol. 3.*

Hamilton, A. (1985). *Selected Writings and Speeches of Alexander Hamilton, Morton J. Frisch ed.* Washington: American Enterprise Institute.

Kelling, G. (1999). *Broken Windows and Police Discretion*. Washington: DOJ.

Kennedy, D.P. (1996). Youth Gun Violence in Boston: Gun Markets, Serious Youth Offenders, and a Use Reduction Strategy. *Law and Contemporary Problems, 59(1)*, 147–83.

Lakoff, G. (1996). *Moral Politics: What Conservatives Know That Liberals Don't.* Chicago: University of Chicago Press.

Mallory, C.H. (2015). *Discrimination and Harassment by Law Enforcement Officers in the LGBT Community*. Los Angeles: The Williams Institute.

Rowlingson, K. (2011). *Does Income Inequality Cause Health and Social Problems?* London, UK: Joseph Rowntree Foundation.

Sherman, L.S. (1995). The Kansas City Gun Experiment. *Research in Brief:* DOJ.

Skolnick, J. (1988). Theme and Variation in Community Policing. In M. Tonry, *Crime and Justice: A Review of Research*. Chicago: University of Chicago Press.

Smith, A. (1759). *The Theory of Moral Sentiments*. London: Reprint by Pantianos Classics.

Sowell, T. (2007). *A Conflict of Visions*. New York: Basic Books.

Weisburd, D.T. (2008). *The Effects of Problem-Oriented Policing on Crime and Disorder.* Campbell Systematic Reviews.

Wilson, J.Q., Kelling, G. (1982). "Broken Windows: The Police and Neighborhood Safety." *Atlantic Monthly*, 29–38.

PART 2

Managing Conflict, Understanding Differing Perspectives

■ ■ ■

Chapter 6: Police Discretion in the Context of Police Community Relations

Law enforcement and *policing* are not interchangeable terms. *Law enforcement* pertains to formal and informal actions taken in response to a clear law violation; *policing* refers to order maintenance, conflict management, mediation, and service functions that officers are routinely expected to do. Police officers, at the local level, engage in both functions on a daily basis, whereas law enforcement officers at the state and federal levels may only engage in enforcement activity. Individuals are trained to perform the law enforcement function adequately, but policing is a higher-level skill, one that more closely approximates a true profession.

Police agencies tend to be categorized as one of the following types; officer discretion generally reflects the type of agency that employs him or her.

The Legalistic Style

> A legalistic police department will issue traffic tickets at a high rate, detain and arrest a high proportion of juvenile offenders, act vigorously against illicit enterprises, and make a large number of misdemeanor arrests even when, as with petty larceny, the public order has not been breached (Wilson, 1968, p. 172).

Situations and problems that come to the attention of the police are handled as if they are law enforcement problems, as opposed to order maintenance issues. In such an agency, officers may deny service if a particular situation does not involve a violation of the law. The goal is for officers to follow the established legal process and apply the law equally because to not do so, in the face of an apparent violation, could be considered neglect of their duty.

The Watchman Style

> The police are watchman, not simply in emphasizing order over law enforcement but also in judging the seriousness of infractions less by what law says about them than by their immediate and personal consequences, which differ in importance depending on the standards of the relevant group-teenagers, Negros, prostitutes, motorists, families, and so forth (Wilson, 1968, p. 141).

The watchman style places priority on order maintenance, and to the extent that enforcing the law is likely to illicit anger, hardship, resentment, or future disorder, an officer may use his or her *discretion.* The obvious downside is that, when officers are compelled to exercise formal authority, those actions are likely to be viewed as arbitrary, inconsistent, and potentially biased.

The danger here is that officers overuse their discretion, choosing not to arrest when an arrest is necessary.

The Service Style

> In some communities, the police take seriously all requests for either law enforcement or order maintenance (unlike police with a watchman style) but are less likely to respond by making an arrest or otherwise imposing formal sanction (Wilson, 1968, p. 200).

The service style of policing functions most effectively when there is a "high-level of agreement among citizens on the need for and definition of public order" (Wilson, 1968). Maintaining this style of policing becomes much more complex in diverse communities.

In addition to the agency styles offered by Wilson, Brown outlines individual officer operational styles as follows:

- The Old Style Crime Fighter Style
- The Clean Beat Crime Fighter Style
- The Professional Style
- The Service Style

Chapter 7: Humanistic Policing: Human Relations, Emotional Intelligence, and the Power of Respect

Human relations is the study of human behavior—why self-image, beliefs, attitudes, prejudices, and bias sometimes cause problems in professional and personal contacts and relationships. For the police officer, competency rests in the understanding that all productive work is done through relationships. The very first relationship that needs to be cultivated is with the self, then the particular individual(s) to whom we are trying, and then to the group(s) with whom we associate.

Rapport is the hallmark of great communicators; it can be described as a harmonious and reciprocal mini-relationship between individuals or an individual and a group. It takes the form of a connection or linkage, where the parties are in-sync with each other.

Non-verbal communication relates to the voice pitch, speed, tone, volume, and inflections used. It can also relate to body posture, proximity, facial expressions, eye movement, dress, physical contact, gestures, and even how people orient their feet. Everyone has their own communication style, and it is important for us to understand the signals we convey to others in both the verbal and non-verbal realm. The master communicator has the ability to flex their communication style based on the situation.

The ability to manage conflict is a characteristic of great police officers and can be the foundation of great police-community relations. Conflict situations present an opportunity to practice human relations skills with the goal of limiting the potential for deeper conflict or violence and enhancing positive relationship building.

The professional, community oriented police agency strives to meet the expectations of the whole community in setting enforcement priorities; the professional but non-community oriented police agency sets its priorities according to what may be professional standards, but these standards may not be responsive to the specific community that it serves. The non-professional police agency does neither.

The law enforcement function can have the impact of de-humanizing officers. There are subtle, and not so subtle, pressures within this function and within the police subculture that sometimes allow officers to step beyond what would be considered acceptable moral boundaries. Compassionate policing simply means treating all people with dignity and respect.

Emotional Intelligence (EI) has been defined as the ability to recognize and monitor one's own emotions, to differentiate between emotional responses, and to use emotional information to manage thinking and behavior. Those who master these skills also have a noticeable ability to recognize, monitor, and manage the emotions of others. Emotional awareness is the ability of officers to know how they personally are feeling at any given point in time; they can express their feelings and beliefs to others easily. They know their own capabilities, skills, and limitations, and they get along well with others, having many friends and acquaintances.

To have a strong moral grounding based on sound principles, such as honesty, decency, fairness, and honor, is the hallmark of integrity. Conversely, those who draw their values from social norms—what is acceptable at the moment—lack integrity.

Emotionally intelligent individuals who practice human relations skills understand that they have a choice in how to respond to others. They can chose to be rude, condescending, and abusive, or they can choose unconditional respect. Thinking individuals recognize that the former will likely result in dysfunctional outcomes; the latter, those who choose to display respect for disrespectful or abrasive others, have the real power in any given situation.

Chapter 8: Managing Conflict in the Law Enforcement and Policing Roles

In this chapter we explored the basics of conflict management in the law enforcement and policing functions. The nature of law enforcement dictates that officers will face conflict situations regularly. It is incumbent upon them to mitigate these conflicts whenever possible by employing proactive interpersonal skills consistent with self-awareness and emotional intelligence. In the policing role, officers are frequently called upon to intervene in conflict situations, serving as mediators. In these cases finding a reason to arrest and resolving conflicts with arrest does not serve the needs of the parties nor does it do anything to enhance the police community relationship.

Some basic tactics to mitigate conflict in the law enforcement role include listening, asking great questions, making reflective statements, and shifting the focus of disputants. Police officers are often called upon to intervene in conflict situations that do not involve law violations. In these cases there is usually a breakdown in the exchange relationships that exist between people. There is a misunderstanding of the relationship, a disagreement about the roles individuals should play, or simply a violation of the rules (formal or informal) that the people expected to follow.

Considerations for the police officers when called on to intervene include having sufficient time to invest; officers running from call-to-call may not have this opportunity. Self-awareness as to whether the officer has the necessary communication skill—especially listening skill, and the absence of a selfish reason to get involved. Officers should never take advantage of a situations to feed their own ego or for other selfish purposes. Emotional control is necessary because emotions are contagious, and officers cannot succumb to these emotionally charged situations.

Self-awareness is the ability to see ourselves as others see us. Police officers are charged with the duty of maintaining order in society, in order to accomplish this mission a basic understanding of what drives human behavior is necessary. Of even greater importance to their ability to manage conflict is an understanding of what drives their own behavior.

Tactics for conflict management in the policing role include listening, asking great questions, making reflective statements and engaging in behavior that is likely to mitigate the impact of emotion. The steps of conflict management include:

1. Make the Offer—Expressing a willingness to engage.
2. Build Rapport—Establish a commonality with the parties, a basis for sameness.
3. Define the Problem (Conflict) as Behavior—Attitudes and character are not negotiable, behavior is.
4. Identify Specific Behavior and Negotiate—Identify what it will take for one or both parties to change their behavior and secure a commitment to do so for the sake of the relationship.

Managing moral conflicts where parties view their adversaries as evil are particularly challenging. These kinds of conflicts are very difficult to resolve and can easily escalate to violence. Understanding that the parties may view the world very differently is a critical first step. Framing the conflict in a manner that helps them agree on common goals can help mitigate the negative feelings.

Moral conflicts are always *intractable*, they take on a life of their own and draw the involvement of other parties. They grow and spread with time and become complicated, never ending well for either party. The parties identify with a particular group that is at odds with the out-group, they tend to view the out-group as evil and immoral, disparaging them whenever possible.

Intractable conflicts need to be identified in advance using a type of early warning system. The potential for these conflicts should be mitigated with efforts to build a better foundation for understanding between the groups. Once the tendency to see the other group as something less than human develops tragedy, including repression and violence, may result. Managing moral conflict demands that each party value the relationship and see the validity of the other group's needs. One effective way to bring this about is to reframe the problem in such a way as to make the problem mutual, something that both sides need to work on for their mutual benefit or for a higher purpose.

Chapter 9: Perspectives of the African American Community

African Americans today encounter difficulties due to race that white people do not. There are hurdles to equality of opportunity that simply do not exist for white people and taking a colorblind approach denies their negative racial experiences, rejects their cultural heritage, and invalidates their unique perspectives (Williams, 2011). Poor people—the principal victims and perpetrators of crime—are primarily people of color and building better relationships with them requires that competent police officers understand their unique point-of-view.

The elite class in the early United States recognized the threat from poor people, both whites and slaves. The concept of justice, as defined in law, was different depending on the color of one's skin. The slave codes emerged as a formal mechanism to promote and preserve slavery. To enforce the slave codes slaveholders enlisted the *slave patrol* to hunt down and return runaway Africans and to put down slave revolts. The police in America have their origin in the need for the wealthy to protect their property from the lower classes, in the north the threat came from poor immigrants; in the south the threat to the economic prosperity of the rich was the property itself, i.e., slaves. The mission of the slave patrol was to ensure that slaves were quickly captured and returned to face the wrath of their primarily White masters.

When an end was finally put to slavery in the United States the lingering impact of the psychology of slavery was reinforced through "Black Codes," laws that targeted poor Whites and African Americans. The impact on institutionalizing the concept of White supremacy was profound and this was accomplished through a system of oppression that came to be known as "Jim Crow." Blacks who violated the law, in many cases for minor crimes such as vagrancy, were sentenced to serve time in prison camps where their labor was cheaply sold by state officials through the convict lease system that essentially returned blacks to their former status as slaves.

Blacks in America first encountered the police in the form of the slave patrol. Slaves were unprotected by the law especially as victims of crimes perpetrated by their owners and White people generally. Black people were arbitrarily stopped by these white patterrollers[1] and questioned about their absence from the plantation,

---

[1] Patterollers were organized groups of white men who hunted down runaways and disciplined slaves in the antebellum south.

they were routinely searched and the slave patrols also administered whippings (Websdale, 2001). Even free blacks were treated like slaves as in Virginia where blacks had to be employed in order to remain in the state, if not employed within 12 months there were threatened with the loss of their freedom (Taylor Green, 2000).

Blacks did not begin to join the ranks of the police in significant numbers until the 1960s. What kept blacks out of policing was an unwelcoming atmosphere perpetrated by white officers, supervisors and the majority white population generally. The face of law enforcement was unmistakably a *White* one.

The direct forces of discrimination have been recognized, outlawed and are now widely considered morally reprehensible. However, the residual effects remain in the form of stereotypes, prejudice and bias. Wise policing requires that officers seek a deeper understanding of what can be perceived as black animosity toward the institution of policing as a structural force in American society.

The argument has been made that there exists a number of structural, cultural and ideological forces arrayed against black Americans in the United States, see Wilson (2009), Alexander (2011), Tonry (1995) and others. These forces have relegated them to secondary status behind whites and the origin, development, and institutionalization of policing has been instrumental in this process. The legacy of past discrimination lives on in the subjective perceptions of black Americans regarding the police.

The behaviors, attitudes and points-of-view reflected in the police are a function of the same attitudes and points-of-view that exists in the community at-large. Each law enforcement agency is unique as a function of our uncoordinated and decentralized system of policing here in the United States.

The race based problems that are occurring in urban areas are the result of *social structures* and *culture forces* that dominate these areas. Social structures are the ways in which social relationships are arranged and exist in our institutions such as schools, commercial enterprises, the economy generally, markets, governmental organizations, political organizations and any other organization or institution that provides order to social interaction.

Cultural forces are the shared points-of-view among those individuals who occupy common places such as poor inner-city neighborhoods and schools; or who have shared experiences and circumstances such as generational poverty, perceived victimizations, advantages, or personal associations.

The law enforcement function is one that generates conflict, especially in those who have a negative impression of the police. The reasons for this negative impression on the part of black Americans relates to the history of black Americans, the structural and cultural factors that divide white from black, and the legacy of discrimination that persists in the form of residual discrimination.

The wise police officer knows how to mitigate conflict in the law enforcement role, but the policing role offers abundant opportunities to bridge the divide between the police-regardless of whether the officer is white or black- and the African American Community. It is in this role where the techniques of conflict management can be employed to fulfil the policing mission of order maintenance. However, there are unique characteristics of "Men of Color" that should also be considered in any genuine effort to support and build trust in these communities.

Chapter 10: Perspectives of the Police: Why the Police Do What They Do
(by Danny McGuire, Ed.D.)

In the face of dramatic criticism of the police function, the perspectives of everyday police officers is often missed. In this chapter, Danny McGuire presents information on the most common crime control strategies as a back drop to a discussion of how police officers are deployed in Chicago, Illinois. He explains how various calls for service are prioritized and how officers make decisions on who to stop and question. Regardless of the arguably unjust outcomes of police investigative and arrest activity, the decisions officers make are based upon valid and sound criteria as they seek to combat crime and disorder.

CHAPTER 6

Police Discretion in the Context of Police Community Relations

■ ■ ■

The new face of policing*

Learning Outcomes

Upon successful completion of this chapter the student will be able to:

- Describe the difference between the law enforcement and policing roles.
- Define police discretion.
- Compare and contrast the styles of policing.
- Compare and contrast the operational styles of officers.
- Define racial profiling and bias-based policing in the context of officer discretion.
- Discuss the history of the racial profiling controversy.

---

* Image labeled for unrestricted use.

- Identify actions and strategies that officers and police agencies can use to manage conflict related to racial profiling.
- Discuss how agencies can engage in "broken windows" policing without undermining public trust and legitimacy.

Important Concepts

- Law Enforcement vs. Policing
- Police Discretion
- Policing Styles
- Officer Operational Styles
- Racial Profiling
- Bias-Based Policing
- "Rational" Profiling

Questions for Discussion

- Why is the use of wise judgement critical to a police officer?
- Why would President Obama state that the police acted "Stupidly" in arresting Professor Henry Louis Gates?
- Describe the three styles of policing. What determines which style is used?
- Under what conditions should the discretion and judgement of officers be restricted?
- Compare and contrast the two type of service style police officers identified by Brown.
- According to Alpert's unpublished 2006 study, what actually drives a police officer's decision to stop individuals?

INTRODUCTION

Police discretion is a critical, but largely overlooked part of our justice system. The police-community relationship is often impacted by the decisions individual officers make when they act within (and especially when outside) the boundaries of department policy. The use of discretion is the mark of a highly competent and wise police officer. In this chapter, we will explore this aspect of policing, along with the implications for improving police-community relations beginning with identifying two distinct contexts of police-citizen interaction that guide officer discretion.

The "choice" to make an arrest*

POLICE DISCRETION

"The police function is incredibly complex" (Goldstein, 1977).

Inherent to the policing function is the idea of judgment or discretion. Herman Goldstein famously pointed out the complexity of the law enforcement function as the result of his research in the 1960s. The layman may, and often does, assume that if there is a law and a police officer becomes aware of a violation, then the perpetrator should be arrested or cited. This is a common expectation for the police; however,

> As one delves more deeply into the various factors that shape police functioning, one finds that laws, public expectations, and the realities of the tasks in which the police are engaged require all kinds of compromises and often place the police in a no-win situation (Goldstein, 1977, p. 9).

A police officer armed with a high school education, basic training, and just a few weeks on the job has complete authority to decide which crimes to investigate, who to arrest, and who to cite. Department administrators seek to guide officer discretion through the rule and policy making process, but these are less than ideal mechanisms for controlling what an officer does and does not do.

This is important to understand because in our system, it is the actions of the police officer that determines whether justice prevails in the multitude of

* Image labeled for unrestricted use.

situations officers are called upon to handle. Only when the officer makes an arrest do the other elements of our criminal justice system get the chance to weigh-in (Terrill, 2007).

The assumption that a police officer will make an arrest when factual, supporting evidence is present has been shattered by a wealth of research addressing this decision-making process. The American Bar Foundation study of the mid-1950s highlighted the extensiveness of non-arrest decisions (Walker, 1992). Joseph Goldstein (1960) was one of the first to address the options available to officers, such as enforcing all the laws without regard to procedure; enforcing all the laws within the boundaries of procedure; not enforcing the law because the police do not have the authority to do so; and actual enforcement practices. In a command and control hierarchy, one may assume that such discretion can be controlled, but Goldstein also pointed out that these decisions are not open to examination, much less control, due to their low-visibility.

Alternatives to arrest include: releasing the offender; arresting or citing the offender for a lesser offense; releasing the offender to a responsible third party who will take responsibility for them; extricating the offender from the scene; remanding the offender to the custody of a third party, such as a mental health facility; mediating or arbitrating the conflict; or giving a verbal warning. The option an officer chooses among these possible actions is a topic of interest for anyone seeking a deeper understanding of the police function.

ROLE DEFINITION

In the law enforcement role officers have, as their primary responsibility, the duty to apply the rule of law to the various situations they encounter. Pro-active law enforcement involves actively seeking out criminal perpetrators, building criminal cases and addressing potential crime problems in an effort to head them off. In this role officers use their own initiative to promote compliance with the law and public safety through apprehension and deterrence. The fear of arrest, fear of the police, and the apprehension resulting from highly visible police presence and activities, as well as the mysterious nature of covert police activity, increases the risk of criminal activity to the potential perpetrator resulting in less crime and disorder. Law Enforcement officers often view arrest as the preferred solution, the one tool, that they can employ to maintain order and control.

> Police officers who view themselves as primarily law enforcers see arrest as the foremost option to maintain law and order. Police officers see arrest as only one option among many with the necessity to use force being viewed as a failure.

In the policing role officers tend to view the application of the law, especially when force is required, as a failure. Police officers view themselves first and foremost as peace officers who will employ innovative and creative solutions to problems, mediate situations and use conflict management techniques to avoid having to resort to their formal authority. Police officers view arrest as only one option, in many cases as the last resort, because arrest brings the power of the state to bear on problems that are better managed with less intrusive means.

A Case Study Illustrating the Difference

Consider, for example, the 2009 arrest of Henry Louis Gates by the Cambridge, Massachusetts police for disorderly conduct. Gates, a black man, was observed forcing the front door of his home, resulting in a 9-1-1 call from a neighbor.

Sergeant James Crowley arrived and confronted Gates, demanding proof that Gates lived in the home, which had been the scene of a previous break-in. Gates was clearly upset and uncooperative with the officer; he was likely fatigued from a long trip and may have also held stereotypical attitudes about the police. He used the occasion to express himself and his deeply held prejudices. He called the officer a racist, a term that reinforces stereotypical views of black men that are often held by law enforcement officers, and continued to demean the officer even while Crowley was trying to disengage from the situation (Cambridge Police Incident Report #9005127).

Gates continued his tirade outside the home, and Crowley finally arrested Gates for behavior that, in Crowley's judgment, was alarming and disturbing. This would be an expected law enforcement response to a disorderly subject. Crowley had the ability to exercise discretion and not arrest Gates, but he chose to do so. We'll explore the dynamics of that decision later, but there is no indication that Crowley would have acted any differently had Gates been white. This action, however, prompted a public relations nightmare for the Cambridge police and an unprecedented response by the President of the United States, who initially stated that the police acted "stupidly" in arresting the prominent black scholar; a better characterization of the officer's action in this case would be that he merely acted "predictably."

Sergeant Crowley, who just happened to be a police expert on racial bias, acted in accordance with department policy and his training in dealing with a law violator. Law enforcement officers do not back down when faced with threatening situations or resistance to arrest. Crowley simply performed his duty properly, using the tools of the trade, to maintain order in the face of a disorderly individual.

This is what the community and society expects from law enforcement personnel, but it may not be the wisest choice in some situations.

The police sub-culture promotes the idea that "to not make an arrest in this situation would be perceived as a weakness." When certain people see the police as weak, it makes the job more difficult and dangerous the next time the police are called to deal with a similar situation. This is a fundamental aspect of the police subculture (Crank, 2004).

Law enforcement officers argue that enforcement action is based solely on the reasonable belief that the person is involved in crime. Since crime is overwhelmingly present in poor communities, law enforcement officers are thereby justified in stopping members of those communities, who just happen to be primarily black and Hispanic (Carter, 2002). This view does nothing to assuage the ongoing resentment of past injustice, often spurred on by those who have a vested interest in keeping these wounds fresh, but this view is of no concern to the law enforcement officer whose primary goal is to enforce the law equally.

However, many African Americans view the world very differently than the average police officer. In emotionally-charged situations, bias rises to the surface. Some in the black community believe that police behavior is motivated by racial prejudice, arguing that the police stereotype all people of color as being involved in crime. Ample data supports this point-of-view, including the over representation of blacks in our prisons, which has led to an obvious conflict between African Americans and the police in general. The police are agents of the elite members of society—the "status-quo"—who use the police to maintain their positions of power. African Americans today are likely to view the status-quo as unjust and worthy of resistance. Wise police officers understand this conflicting point-of-view and should be sensitive to it, particularly if improving or maintaining good police-community relations is an important goal.

> Virtually any specific behavior gains meaning by the context in which it occurs. Most police officers intuitively understand this and make their decisions about whether and how to intervene on their assessment of an act, or series of acts, within a context (Kelling, 1999).

In this case Sergeant Crowley was faced with an extremely disrespectful, irate, black man who used the situation to express a stereotype of the police as racist bigots. Crowley had a duty to respond to the home and investigate the situation based on a valid complaint, but what became clear, early on, was that Gates was not a burglar. Crowley had no legal reason to detain him after confirming that he had a right to be present in the home. He recognized this and wisely tried to extricate himself from the situation, but Gates would not let it go. Passion and emotions had taken over, and bias was now driving the behavior of both actors with a predicable result, that being a public relations disaster for both the police and Gates.

The Law Enforcement Role

Law enforcement and *policing* mean different things and require different skills and abilities. In today's diverse environment, treating everyone equally without regard to potential outcomes will predictably result in crises, such as the arrest of Henry Louis Gates by Cambridge police in 2009 and the Travon Martin event in 2012. Both of these incidents provide clues to the weakness of a criminal justice system constrained by a focus on following correct procedure. If the police are to maintain the trust and respect of a pluralistic[1] society, they need to contemplate their discretion in light of situational factors and likely outcomes, which is the benchmark of wise policing.

> For the law enforcement officer promoting justice is simple, it means following correct procedure.

The terms *law enforcement* and *policing* are not interchangeable. These two terms imply different roles and require different kinds of people. Individuals can be trained to perform the law enforcement function adequately, but policing is a higher-level skill, one that more closely approximates a true profession. Those who excel in the policing function come to the job armed with skills, abilities, and competencies that transcend those required in mere law enforcement. Given the increasingly complex nature of our American society, we would do well to recognize the difference:

> The complexity of police work has two dimensions: the complexity of the situations or problems confronting police, and the complexity of police responses to those situations (Kelling, 1999).

The complexity of *policing* is, perhaps, most evident in the relationship between the police and the African American community today.

The Policing Role

People who tend to focus on extremes, including some law enforcement officers who categorize individuals as either law abiding or law violators, may not recognize the complexity of today's world. The real world is not black and white,

---

1 A pluralistic society is one where differing points-of-view, belief systems, and value systems exist as part of a collective whole; diversity is actively promoted, and multiculturalism is valued.

but is incredibly complex; a more astute-dichotomous-outlook is the realization that rarely do the police encounter situations and human behavior that does not require some level of deeper scrutiny and judgment, preferably *wise* judgment:

> Law enforcement officers know how to enforce the law; police officers know when to enforce the law, employing reasonable alternatives to arrest when they are justified (Author, 2014).

> Discretion or judgement is a key component of our system of justice. Discretionary authority rests in the hands of the wise police officer. To not exercise wise judgement often results in what many would consider injustice.

The enormous amount of discretion invested in our police out of necessity provides a framework for understanding the difference between *law enforcement* and *policing*. Law enforcement officers react to conditions, invoking their authority as their technical training dictates. Police officers understand that invoking authority in a democratic-pluralistic-society inevitably generates resentment and can undermine trust. They sometimes choose creative and innovative ways to generate voluntary compliance, relying on formal authority only as a last resort. These are the characteristics of wise and highly effective police officers.

THE THREE STYLES OF POLICING

Wilson (1968) identified three distinct styles of policing that define how the **police agency** views its function. These styles have profound implications for how officers view their role in the community and how they interact with the public.

The **legalistic style** stresses the application of the law, threats and coercion to maintain order. The implication is that any call for service that does not involve a violation of the law is not the business of the police. The **watchman style** is a laid back view of the police role where officers only intervene when called to do so, initiating enforcement activity-arrest-primarily when serious violations are indicated or as a last resort. The watchman maintains order by employing informal methods rather than arrest. The **service style** emphasizes public service. Officers are not focused primarily on enforcing the law and will employ alternatives to arrest, including conflict mediation, in an effort to control crime and disorder without invoking the coercive power of the state whenever possible (Wilson J. Q., 1968).

The Legalistic Style

When we consider the role of the police officer, law enforcement is typically what comes to mind. This implies a certain style of policing behavior, that being, legalistic:

> A legalistic police department will issue traffic tickets at a high rate, detain and arrest a high proportion of juvenile offenders, act vigorously against illicit enterprises, and make a large number of misdemeanor arrests even when, as with petty larceny, the public order has not been breached (Wilson, 1968, p. 172).

Situations and problems that come to the attention of the police are handled as if they are law enforcement problems, as opposed to order maintenance issues. In such an agency, officers may deny service if a particular situation does not involve a violation of the law. The goal is for officers to follow the established legal process and apply the law equally because not to do so, in the face of an apparent violation, could be considered neglect of their duty.

A legalistic department is likely to be viewed as *racist* in contemporary society as the sheer number of arrests will almost certainly have a disparate impact on minority populations. In a legalistic agency, racial bias is of no concern to police supervisors and administrators; as long as officers follow proper legal procedure, this mindset simply does not recognize that this presents a community relations problem. This is not due to inherent racism but rather to incentives. Police officers who are charged with making numerous numbers of arrests will seek them out in places where they are easiest to acquire, which is impoverished, rundown areas typically described as ghettos.

> Why would an agency that focuses their efforts on obtaining large numbers of arrest be considered racist? Because the pressure to make arrests will inevitably drive police officers to focus on areas of the community where arrests are easiest to make, poor minority neighborhoods. Why is this the case? Discuss.

The Watchman Style

The Watchman style of policing places priority on context (or outcomes of potential enforcement action):

> The police are watchman-like not simply in emphasizing order over law enforcement but also in judging the seriousness of infractions less by what law says about them than by their immediate and personal consequences, which differ in importance depending on the standards

> of the relevant group-teenagers; racial, neighborhood, or interest group; prostitutes; motorists; families; and so forth (Wilson, 1968, p. 141).

The watchman style places priority on order maintenance, and to the extent that enforcing the law is likely to illicit anger, hardship, resentment, or future disorder, an officer may use his or her *discretion*. The obvious downside is that when officers are compelled to exercise formal authority, those actions are likely to be viewed as arbitrary, inconsistent, and potentially biased.

> Officers who view themselves primarily as watchmen tend to understand discretion as making the choice not to arrest.

The danger here is that officers overuse their discretion, choosing not to arrest when an arrest is needed. A contemporary example would be the choice to issue warnings to black motorists rather than run the risk of being labeled a "racist cop."

Consider an actual case of an accident investigation where a white driver is proceeding along a residential thoroughfare driving a newer vehicle that he owns and is struck by a vehicle being driven by a black teenager who ran a stop sign. The black teenager is not the owner of the older vehicle that he was driving and cannot produce a driver's license or any proof of insurance.

The police officer has discretion to cite the driver for the stop sign violation, driving without a driver's license, driving without proof of insurance, not wearing a seatbelt, and unsafe vehicle equipment. A legalistic officer would be inclined to do so, knowing full well that the young man does not have the means to pay the fines or repair the damage to either vehicle. However, the law is the law and he or she will carry out his or her duty in compliance with department, as well as community, expectations. Conversely, a watchman style officer sees the issuance of multiple citations as futile. They may only cite the most serious violation and convey to the other driver that they are unlikely to see any restitution for the damage to their vehicle even though the black motorist was clearly at fault.

The Service Style

The service style of policing is distinct from those previously discussed and is perhaps most prevalent today given its consistency with the Community Oriented Policing philosophy.

> In some communities, the police take seriously all requests for either law enforcement or order maintenance (unlike police with a watchman style), but are less likely to respond by making an arrest or otherwise imposing formal sanction (Wilson, 1968, p. 200).

This style of policing, called the service style, functions most effectively when there is a "High-level of agreement among citizens on the need for and definition of public order" (Wilson J. Q., 1968). Maintaining this style of policing becomes much more complex in diverse communities.

> Should the police really treat everyone equally without regard for race, gender, or age? Discuss.

The reality of today's policing is that consensus on acceptable public behavior is elusive. Any man ranting and raving at the police may tend to violate community norms; the expectation then is that the police should make an arrest. Does a black man ranting about the "racist police" deserve patience and understanding, as opposed to a white man engaging in similar behavior? Does this not run contrary to the goal of equal enforcement? Or, should the police be more lenient with black offenders because of past discrimination and a recognition of the black community's subjective perception of current and past bias? Can or should past racist behavior by today's police officers justify biased behavior favoring blacks today? And, if it does so, how long should this new, reverse, form of discrimination be justified and used? In short, what should be the future, on-going nature of implicit bias on the part of the police?

Summary

Wilson's *Varieties of Police Behavior* (1968) was aimed at characterizing entire police agencies as falling into one of these categories/styles: 1. Legalistic; 2. Watchman; or 3. Service. It is common, however, that police officers working within the larger police organizations regularly adopt a given style depending on the situation. Law enforcement officers act **unwisely** when they insist on adhering to only one style in all cases. Police discretion should be tempered by a reasoned assessment of the situation and likely outcomes, but this is a much higher-level skill that is not supported by our criminal justice system; it is certainly beyond the capability of current police training institutions; and it is likely to elicit conflict even amongst police officers.

HOW OFFICERS VIEW THEIR ROLE

The typical "Cop on the Beat" views himself or herself as a law enforcer; the reality, however, is that they exist to maintain order, sometimes by enforcing the law:

> Police typically envision their role as enforcers, making arrests is paramount. They tend to view other activities as unimportant and a

hindrance on their crime fighting ability. They avoid tasks perceived as non-essential (Trojanowicz, 1990).

An example: Based upon the perceived relationship between neighborhood decay and the prevalence of crime and disorder, the strategy of the law enforcement officer may amount to a "sweep" of the neighborhood. The objective is to cite nuisance violations, such as inoperable vehicles, tall grass, or building maintenance violations (broken windows). The enforcing officers do this under the authority of law, and their justification is the perceived relationship between disorder and crime as outlined by the Broken Windows theory of crime control (Wilson, 1982). When confronting the citizen on an observed violation, the conversation may go like this:

> **Law Enforcement Officer:** I'm here because your property is in violation of the city code. This is a municipal citation that you can pay either by mail or by appearance at City hall. You are hereby commanded to remove this inoperable vehicle, mow the lawn and repair the building code violations or be subject to progressive daily fines for your lack of compliance.
>
> **Citizen:** Yes officer, I understand. I'll do my best.

The "wise" police officer, on the other hand, recognizes the potential for generating resentment when dealing with these minor infractions and takes behavioral steps to minimize resentment and to encourage compliance with community standards. The conversation goes like this:

> **Police Officer:** Excuse me, Sir. May I speak with you for a moment?
>
> **Citizen:** Certainly officer, is there a problem?
>
> **Police Officer:** As you may know, we are concerned about what most people consider to be minor issues related to the deterioration of our neighborhoods. This deterioration leads to crime and disorder. Are you concerned about crime and disorder in your neighborhood sir?
>
> **Citizen:** Well, yes, Officer, I certainly am.
>
> **Police Officer:** The way that you can help prevent it is to remove this inoperable vehicle, mow the lawn, and repair these broken windows. This sends a signal that people care about the neighborhood. Is that something that you are willing to do for us, Sir?
>
> **Citizen:** I am officer, but I just don't have the money right now. I was planning on fixing this car next week after I get paid. I can have my son come over and mow the lawn because my mower is broken. And

perhaps I can get the window repaired in a few weeks when I get my disability check. Would that be okay?

Police Officer: Yes, Sir. What we are asking for is voluntary compliance with the law, and if you are willing to bring your property into compliance, I am certainly willing to forgo enforcement action that will only cost you more money. Would it be alright if I check back with you in a couple of weeks to see how things are going?

Citizen: Yes officer that would be fine with me. Please stop by anytime. I would also like you to know about some suspicious activity down the street.

The above example serves to illustrate the difference between law enforcement and policing. At heart, both perspectives have the goal of compliance with the law, but they go about it in very different ways. One's approach is direct, efficient, and consistent with a general view of the role of the police; the other is less direct, less efficient, and more ambiguous, but it supports the recognition that *the best police officers go about their duty in a manner that seeks to assuage the resentment of authority common in a democratic society, especially a society that is sensitive to social justice issues.*

Even though the actions of Sergeant Crowley in the Gates case were consistent with proper police procedure, there was a missed opportunity and a substantial risk to the police-community relationship (i.e., the reputation of the agency) that was entirely overlooked. Rather than being wholly concerned with procedure and process, wise police officers need to consider the likely outcomes of law enforcement action, a view that is at the foundation of the concept of Problem Oriented Policing (Goldstein, 1990).

Herman Goldstein, the father of "Problem Oriented Policing"*

> Herman Goldstein's work has focused primarily on the challenge in trying to develop a form of policing that is effective but also committed to maintaining and extending democratic values. His earliest writings explored the discretion exercised by the police, the policy-making role of police administrators, and the political accountability of the police. His book *Problem-Oriented Policing* (1990) spells out a radically new way of conceptualizing the police function that is designed to increase police effectiveness, while at the same time refining the use of police authority. The concept has been adopted, in various forms, in a large number of police agencies in the United States and abroad.

Police are expected to enforce the law and maintain order, but how they do that is a matter of discretion. The law enforcement officer seeks to apply the law to the behavior of individuals and exercise his or her authority equally without regard to individual characteristics and circumstances, an entirely noble goal. Enforcement action primarily consists of arrest or citation.

The professional police officer exercises judgment, taking context into consideration. The goal is compliance and maintaining good relations with the public. Arrest is an acceptable course of action in many situations, but it is not the primary goal. Maintaining order is the desired outcome, and the wise police officer may seek to employ informal devices or strategies. Informal mechanisms are, in many cases, much more effective in controlling deviant behavior (Conkin, 2013).

* Reprinted with permission from Herman Goldstein.

POLICE DISCRETION & CONFLICT

Police discretion refers to the judgment officers use when deciding whether or not to exercise their formal authority to stop and to arrest. The exercise of individual officer discretion can initially be divided into discretion in the case of initiated and assigned activity. When officers develop suspicion and engage with persons, as in the case of most street and traffic stops, this is *officer-initiated* activity. When officers are called to the scene of a disturbance or crime and need to exercise discretion, this is *assigned* activity.

> Officer discretion is not only crafted based on the context of a given situation but by the type of activity the officer is engaged in. Decision criteria in Assigned activity-calls for service-is different from cases where the officer initiates the contact-officer initiated stops.

Officer Assigned Activity. One of the most powerful factors affecting officer discretion in assigned activity is the will of the complainant or victim. Officers routinely rely on the desire of the victims of crime in determining what to do with the offender. A statement like "I want him arrested" usually results in an arrest; whereas a statement like "just have a stern talk with him" usually does not.

There may be, however, policy and legal guidelines that restrict officer discretion, even in the face of the desire of the victim; domestic violence provides such an example. The victim of a minor domestic violence assault is generally reluctant to see the perpetrator arrested. These are complex situations when an arrest can threaten the victim's livelihood and welfare. The number of arrests for domestic violence cases have been historically low due to this reluctance.

Tremendous public pressure to do something about the problem of domestic violence has resulted in new laws that limit officer discretion. At the agency level, pro-arrest policies have been developed that mandate an arrest in most situations, thereby taking the judgment away from the officers on the scene. The need to get offenders into the system for treatment justifies the decision to take discretion away from police officers, who may feel that an arrest is not the best solution in a given case. As a result, the number of domestic violence cases has gone down dramatically; however there are indications that the underlying problem still exists (Garner, 1997).

Officer-Initiated Activity. A classic example of officer discretion is the traffic stop where a motorist is caught exceeding the speed limit. At what point does the officer decide to issue a citation as opposed to letting the motorist go with a warning? This decision may be influenced by department policy, whereby the *degree* of the law violation is to be considered such as 5, 10, 15, or more miles per hour over the posted limit. In a legalistic agency, based on Wilson's typologies, officers may be mandated to cite any violation in excess of a certain level such as 10 miles per hour over the limit. A watchman agency, on the other hand, may only dictate the need to cite a violation if it contributed to a hazard or a traffic collision.

The decision to issue a citation may also be influenced by the number of violations present and the motorist's past record. Speeding, cruising through a stop sign, and having bald tires may cause an officer to cite one or more violations as opposed to just the speeding violation. Similarly, a past record of citations, stops, and warnings may influence the officer's decision to cite due to the need to reinforce the importance of highway safety with a potentially indifferent motorist.

The degree of the law violation and past history are objective factors impacting officer discretion, but another aspect of this critical function of our justice system is the demeanor of the motorist (i.e., their willingness or unwillingness to accept responsibility for the violation). Beyond the emotional impact of being stopped, there comes a point where the offender's attitude becomes a factor in officer discretion. A legalistic department may give officers a *bright-line*[2] rule for decision-making, such as 10 miles per hour over the limit, but an apologetic motorist who expresses regret for the violation and promises to be more careful is much more likely to benefit with a warning, in the subjective view of a police officer. A belligerent motorist is likely to receive a costly citation and may even be subjected to additional investigative attention. In the absence of a bright-line rule, officers employed in a watchman style agency will have much more freedom to employ discretion, making subjective assessments concerning the need to invoke formal authority (i.e., citation or arrest) that are based on the perceived need to do so (i.e., the need to reinforce the rules through punishment and sanction based on the violator's attitude.)

OFFICER OPERATIONAL STYLES

The essence of discretion rests not so much on style of policing as dictated by the agency, as Wilson suggests, but rather on the operational style of the **individual officer** as described by Brown (1988).

> An operational style initially derives from the choices a patrolman must make about how to work the street. Our observations of crime fighting revealed that patrolman could be differentiated in terms of two characteristics: how aggressive they were in pursuit of the goal of crime

2 A bright-line rule is a clearly defined standard, generally composed of objective factors. The idea of a bright-line rule is to minimize variation in interpretation among actors (e.g., police officers).

control, and how selective they were in the enforcement of the law (Brown, 1988, p. 223).

The leadership and priorities of the administration have only a subtle influence on officer discretion because the exercise of discretion occurs outside of situations that lend themselves to observation, evaluation, or criticism by higher authority. Efforts to control officer discretion at the department level usually take the form of operational policies, special orders, and rules, which are looked upon with suspicion by veteran street officers. Even when policy guidelines are developed with an eye toward protecting officers from legal risk—civil liability—officers will be resistant, jealously guarding what they consider to be an area of professional entitlement from the overly controlling tendencies of a malevolent police administration.

Beyond the characteristics of police agencies rests the individual officer's attributes that define the essence of police discretion. It is not the political environment, police leadership, rules, and procedures that drive the decision whether to invoke legal authority, but rather the willingness to take action, *aggressiveness*, and the choice of what to prioritize (i.e., *selectivity*) that define the typologies of police officer operational styles offered by Brown. Each of these styles presents opportunities and challenges for the quality of police-community relationship.

Police officers providing a deterring presence*

* Image labeled for unrestricted use.

Old Style Crime Fighter

The old style crime fighter is highly **aggressive** in his or her approach to law enforcement, but highly **selective** in what they view as deserving of their attention. These officers pride themselves on their ability to judge people and situations quickly, reacting quickly and decisively to control people and situations that present a threat to law and order. They are meticulous in gathering information and cultivating sources that may prove useful in the future, and they display a no-nonsense and ruthless demeanor on the street. Minor violations are not generally worth their time, unless the perpetrator is known as someone who needs to be reminded of their place.

These individuals are comfortable with violence and use it with judicious proportionality; they do not shy away from the use of force, viewing it as a tool of informal social control related to the character and intention of the potential violator rather than as a tool of lawful authority.

This style of officer is likely to be perceived as abusive, rude, and condescending by those unfamiliar with this style. This is the kind of officer who may employ violence in the form of a push, forceful grasp, or even slap or punch as an informal sanction when disrespected and then back-off with a warning once he or she is satisfied that order and respect for authority has been restored. They tend to reserve the exercise of lawful authority (i.e., arrest) for what they feel are serious crime problems.

> The old style crime fighter views themselves as an enforcer, not a social worker. They avoid what they consider trivial matters not worthy of their crime fighting attention, they are highly selective in what deserves their attention.

This style of officer regards order and traffic enforcement duties as trivial matters, demands on their time to be avoided whenever possible. When left without a choice, these calls are handled in an obligatory and even callous manner, and resulting perception is likely one of indifference and even contempt for those who take up their valuable time. When actually dealing with crime problems, however, the old style crime fighter displays a high level of skill and subtlety. The skillful application of techniques learned on the street provides this style of officer with the ability to recruit informants, spot criminal violators, and acquire a wealth of knowledge about the people who exist on his or her beat. In short, they have the ability to use discretion and extra-legal solutions to exert control over their assigned territory without the use of formal coercive tactics, such as arrest and prosecution.

The demeanor of this officer style is likely to cause conflict both from those who perceive that they do not take their complaint seriously and from those who feel victimized by the officer's indifference and even abuse. However, the judicious wisdom that these officers display can engender a level of trust and legitimacy rarely attributed to other styles (Brown, 1988, pp. 225–229).

Clean Beat Crime Fighters

These officers are both **aggressive** and **non-selective** in their initiated enforcement activity. They view the world as consisting of those who violate the law and those who do not and will aggressively seek out even minor and nuisance violations. They share a dislike of order maintenance calls with the old school officers, but lack the skill and subtlety of the former. They believe in a rigid and unrelenting enforcement of the law through the aggressive prosecution of even minor offenses. The clean beat crime fighter believes in making as many stops as possible, and justifies this action as necessary for deterring other kinds of more serious crime. Establishing a consistent hard-nosed reputation for enforcement is the goal of this style.

> The clean beat crime fighter is aggressive but also shuns the social work role. They view the world as consisting of those who respect the law and those who do not, they are not selective in their enforcement activity and will make lots of arrests.

Order maintenance calls are viewed as a nuisance to the clean beat officer, but rather than trying to avoid them, this style of officer accepts them as part of the job and handles them as quickly as possible, so that they can get back to the business of fighting crime. Because of their disdain for minor calls, they are likely to seek out short term solutions that allow them to dispose of situations as quickly as possible. In many cases, this tends to be an arrest or citation.

Whereas an old school crime fighter may take the time to mediate a domestic situation where he or she feels that there is a high risk of violence, the clean beat crime fighter will simply arrest the aggressive party and move on. When called for a nuisance complaint, such as municipal code violation related to tall grass, the old school officer may counsel the offender, stating "Look, cut your grass tomorrow, or I'll be back. You don't want me to come back and start sniffing around here. There's no telling what else I may find." Conversely, the clean beat crime fighter is likely to just write the violator a ticket.

Conflict management is simply not part of this officer's tool-bag. These officers believe in conflict resolution and expedited solutions to crime problems. The law provides the ability for officers to resolve conflict, often through the use of citation, arrest, or assured and overwhelming force; they see these options as simply the most efficient course of action. Not only does it decisively settle the matter, but it also deters future problematic behavior. The actions of these officers breed the idea that all the laws should be enforced all the time, and this leads to conflict with those who are more discriminating about what should and should not demand the time and attention of the police (Brown, 1988, pp. 229–232).

The Professional Style

Both the old school and clean beat crime fighters are likely to play fast and loose with the law and department policy. The officers may "stretch" the facts a bit when aggressive tactics are needed, in their view, to maintain law and order. The professional police officer, on the other hand, respects the rule of law even to the extent that it may get in the way of holding criminals to account.

> The professional officer adheres to professional standards even when those standards may conflict with what is best in a given situation. They will honor the law even when doing so allows criminals to escape justice.

Professionalism requires a stern devotion to the standards and rules of one's profession. For the professional police officer, this begins with demonstrating respect for the constitutional rights of citizens, compliance with the law, and adherence to the rules and codes of conduct adopted for his or her profession. The professional style officer is active but **not aggressive**. They are not at all reluctant to stop people, but do so with much more solid, fact-based suspicion of criminal wrongdoing.

To the professional officer, each situation is unique and deserving of their attention. They would not, for example, adhere to the old crime fighters rule that one ought to make a decision to issue a citation based on the merit—severity—of the violation as opposed to the violator's excuse or attitude. The professional officer, on the other hand, **listens** to the driver. They believe that people have a right to be treated with courtesy by the police and that law enforcement should be tempered with judicious understanding—compassion—with regard to individual circumstance. According to Brown (1988),

> The professional police officer adheres as much as possible to department rules and policies. They are preoccupied with doing a good job as that is defined by their supervisors. As one of them said in the midst of issuing parking tickets, 'I'm out here for eight hours and I might as well give the city its money's worth.' They firmly enforce the law, but they believe they are flexible enough to know when not to; they vigorously pursue felons, but they are less likely to indulge themselves in the frequent and wanton use of illegal tactics; in short, *they believe that*

a policeman can enforce the law and cope with crime while maintaining rapport with the people in the community (p. 235).

Internal conflict is common between the professional police officer and the crime fighter types: the old school officers being viewed as lazy, and the clean beat types being viewed as unprofessional and "badge heavy." The inherent conflicts in these styles can be most apparent in the relationship between management—usually comprised of professional style officers—and labor, generally represented by those who may not generally be considered professional.

Professional Standards and Recognition Through CALEA

The Commission on Accreditation for Law Enforcement Agencies, Inc., (CALEA®) was created in 1979 as an organization offering various credentials to law enforcement agencies, correctional agencies, communication centers and other policing related organizations that meet the established standards for professional operations. The commission has representation from each of the major law enforcement executive organizations including:

- International Association of Chiefs of Police (IACP);
- National Organization of Black Law Enforcement Executives (NOBLE);
- National Sheriffs' Association (NSA); and the
- Police Executive Research Forum (PERF).

The Accreditation Process itself provides management guidance to law enforcement executives, a model that can be employed in any size law enforcement agency that speaks to the best practices of modern police management.

The Service Style

The service style of policing is **non-aggressive** and **highly selective** according to Brown (1988). He categorizes service style police officers into two sub-groups.

Service style officers come in two varieties; those who seek to only do as much as necessary to keep the supervisor off their backs and those who want to help people with their problems, whatever those problem may be.

The attitude of the first group is summed up by a patrol man, who said "I don't want to chase every asshole on the street. I'm just as happy if things don't come up."

> These patrolmen neither worked very hard to enforce the law nor paid much attention to people's problems; their actions were calculated to keep the sergeant happy and do the minimum amount of work necessary to get by. They were notorious for ignoring violations and treating disturbances in as perfunctory a manner as possible. Some of these individuals were merely using police work as a means to another occupation . . . Others were burnt out patrolmen, at one time in their career they may have been "hustlers," now they were coasting and hoping to make twenty years and retirement in one piece. Their code was to take problems as they occur and above all else to stay out of trouble (Brown, 1988, p. 235).

The second category of the service style is quite different, as described by Brown.

> Their belief is that crime suppression is not the most important goal of a police department. They argue that the police should take a positive role in assisting people to solve their problems. Consequently, impersonal and legalistic law enforcement is deemphasized, and one of the defining characteristics of this approach is the belief that the exercise of discretion ought to be based on a sensitivity to community values and needs (p. 236).

The conflict between this style and both the crime fighters and professionals is profound. If we discount the first category of service style officer as basically retired in place, the second category of service style officer rejects the utility of citation and arrest as the "go-to" technique for law enforcement. To be a suitable target for enforcement, violations need to point back to an identifiable problem that may be attacked more effectively by some vaguely identifiable arrest alternative. These officers push for diversionary programs that circumvent formal prosecution, such as peer mediation and what is now called restorative justice programs (as opposed to simply arresting violators as would the crime fighters and professionals).

> The service style, more than anything else, reflects submerged ideological conflicts which presently animate the practitioners of the police craft. This is partly a matter of the changing values among young policemen, but it is also indicative of the responses of policemen to the social and political turmoil of the late sixties. Be that as it may, what unites the few individuals who, to a greater or lesser degree, practice this style is a singular distaste for the doctrines of police professionalism and

many of the practices endemic to contemporary police (Brown, 1988, p. 237).

> Conflict regularly arises within the police agency itself between these categories of officers who all view their function very differently.

Summary

These ideological conflicts inherent to the service style of policing are difficult to resolve and cause conflict between those who adopt this style and the professionally-minded officers. The essence of this conflict can be attributed to the vision each type of officer holds regarding the basic nature of man. As with the constrained vision, professional police officers accept that man is flawed and their role as police is to mitigate harm within the constraints of the rule of law, using incentives to produce desired outcomes (i.e., law and order).

Service style officers of the second variety identified by Brown likely hold a different view of man's nature that is often in conflict with the nature of the job and certainly with what they see and deal with on a daily basis. The belief that man is capable of continual improvement if it were not for the burdens of societal injustices may lead these officers into a state of cognitive dissonance[3], where the demands of the job conflict with their underlying beliefs. In a world constrained by policy and procedure, the idea that the wise should lead by virtue of their advanced intellectual capacity to reason is likely to place them at odds with their supervisors as well as with the criminal justice system as a whole which would prefer that these officers merely follow correct procedure.

POLICE DISCRETION AND RACIAL PROFILING: CONFLICTING VISIONS

Selective enforcement is a practice common in policing. Officers cannot enforce the law equally with regard to all laws or all violators; this is the essence of police discretion and can be quite controversial as seen recently in regards to racial profiling. Perceived abuses of power may be alleged when individuals and groups feel that they are selected for unjust enforcement by police. To the police, however, profiling is commonly viewed as a powerful tool of efficient law enforcement. *Here we have a conflict between efficient operations in pursuing the law and unjust outcomes as reflected in dramatically disparate impact based on race.*

---

3 Cognitive dissonance is a state of mind where one has inconsistent thoughts, beliefs or attitudes as they relate to their own behavior. They behave in ways they don't believe in.

Racial profiling can be defined as using race as the sole factor in determining whom to stop. This is blatantly unlawful. Conversely, using race as only one factor among others in determining whom to stop is a legitimate law enforcement tactic. Discuss the difference.

Racial profiling is defined as "law enforcement activities such as stops, detentions, arrests and searches that are initiated solely on race"(Fridell, 2001). However, the Drug Courier Profile developed by the U.S. Drug Enforcement Administration (DEA) uses race as a profiling factor and it is widely taught as a tool of aggressive drug interdiction efforts as part of the War on Drugs (Fridell, 2001). The profile identifies race and ethnicity as one of the factors that officers should consider as part of their discretion. Even though it is **objectively reasonable**, in many situations, to include race as a factor in establishing reasonable suspicion to stop an individual suspected of a crime, such use is commonly considered to be racially biased. Racial bias occurs when police officers **inappropriately** consider race or ethnicity in deciding whom to stop and engage in the law enforcement capacity. Even though the use of race as a factor in deciding the legality of a seizure under the Fourth Amendment to the Constitution is lawful, it can, and is, viewed as inappropriate due to its adverse impact on members of protected groups.

Professionally-minded police officers look to the law, professional standards (e.g., CALEA), and department policy to resolve confusion and to avoid arbitrary decisions regarding their discretion. Because biased-based policing is such a divisive issue, all agencies seeking accreditation are required to address it in their written policies and procedures. These policy statements generally mandate that all stops of citizens be based upon objective facts amounting to reasonable suspicion of a crime. Race and ethnicity can only be considered when the officer possesses specific verifiable information related to race, such as a victim or witness statement indicating the suspect's race. In general, race can be a factor, but it cannot be the only factor, nor the primary factor, driving the officer's decision/discretion to stop or arrest.

HISTORY OF THE RACIAL PROFILING CONFLICT

Discrimination in the application of the law strikes at the heart of our democratic traditions. Targeting individuals solely because of their race is appalling to both those with the *unconstrained vision* (i.e., those who minimize the value of incentives in advancing society's interest) and to those with the *constrained vision* (i.e., those who view it as a blatant departure from the rule of law), including professional police officers.

The question as to whether dominant societal actors make use of social institutions, including the police, to advance their own interests is fundamental to *conflict theory*. Those who advocate for a more balanced allocation of power between socioeconomic classes claim that evidence exists to prove the relationship between *conflict theory* and *racial profiling*. That evidence takes the form of police traffic stop data (Petrocelli, 2003; Smith, 2001).

> Conflict theory, based upon Marxism, asserts that competing groups in society compete for dominance to further their own collective interests at the expense of other social groups. Power is the determining factor in group competition with unjust power arrangements-hierarchies-viewed as the enemy of justice.

According to conflict theory, society is molded and shaped by the competing interests of social groups who compete for dominance in order to enact or maintain a social structure most beneficial to them (Simmel, 1950; Petrocelli, 2003). Conflict theory asserts that the relative power of a given social group dictates social order in that powerful groups not only control the lawmakers, but also the law enforcement apparatus of the state. In essence, laws are made which serve the interests of the privileged and the police are used to suppress and control any segment of society that poses a threat to the status quo (Petrocelli, 2003, p. 2).

The police are seen as armies of occupation empowered to hold down the lower classes who are viewed as a threat to the privileged members of society. According to Blauner (1972), those privileged members are whites who oppress people of color in order to maintain their position of privilege. Proof of this assertion rests in an analysis of police traffic stop data that indicate that minorities are stopped, searched, and ticketed at rates that exceed those for whites when compared to a benchmark, such as the geographical racial make-up. In short, racial profiling exists when non-white persons are stopped and searched at a rate greater than their representation in the community (Harris, 1999; Lamberth, 1997).

Conflict theory assumes that police discretion—how police choose who to stop and arrest—is a function of the socioeconomic make-up of the community, and the privileged whites use the police to hold down the marginalized and underprivileged people of color. Petrocelli et al. (2002) put this to the test and concluded the following with respect to his study conducted in Richmond, Virginia:

> The total number of stops by police was determined solely by the crime rate of the neighborhood. Neighborhoods with higher crime rates were likely to evidence a higher number of stops by the police. In fact, none of the demographic and socioeconomic characteristics exerted direct

> effects on the number of police stops. At first glance these results appeared troubling for conflict theorists. Second, the percentage of stops that resulted in a search was determined by only one characteristic; the percentage of black population. This result suggested that in areas predominantly inhabited by Blacks, police stops were likely to result in a search. Third, when examining the percentage of stops that ended in an arrest/summons, the analysis revealed a slightly different pattern of substantive results; namely, both the percent Black population as well as the crime rate served to decrease the percentage of police stops that ended in an arrest/summons (p. 7).

These researchers concluded that a "hurdle" effect existed; the first hurdle (i.e., being stopped) was driven by the crime rate in the neighborhood rather than race or socioeconomic status. Searches, however, were more prevalent in black neighborhoods suggesting that police respond differently, depending on the type of neighborhood where they are assigned.

In an attempt to address racial profiling by police, a profound societal injustice, laws now require the police to record traffic stop data in each state, including location, observed violation, race of the driver, whether or not a search was conducted, and whether or not citation(s) were issued. These laws frustrate police officers who assert that a fundamental premise underlying these early studies is faulty, that faulty premise is that there is no difference in the rate of offending amongst races. In order to properly assess the existence of racial bias in traffic stops or arrests, one must know the rate at which the different racial groups violate the law.

> The racial profiling narrative has been based upon the premise that there is no significant difference in offending rates among the races. Is this true? Discuss.

The racial distribution of the general population as recorded in census data does not reflect rates of criminal participation, and using this kind of data as a benchmark in analyzing stop data has been widely discredited. A better benchmark is the racial distribution of individuals identified in crime/suspect descriptions. In other words, a better way to analyze the prevalence of racial bias in policing is to compare the racial make-up of suspect and witness descriptions to the racial make-up of persons stopped and arrested. Such a measure also has serious pitfalls but it is a much more promising benchmark than census data (Ridgeway, 2007).

The lawful authority to stop or seize an individual is governed by the Fourth Amendment to the U.S. Constitution. In order to exert their authority to stop (i.e., seize) an individual, the police need to have a level of suspicion that the individual has, was, or is about to be involved in a crime equal to a standard called *reasonable suspicion*. Reasonable suspicion is an objective and fact-based standard, as opposed to a subjective standard (i.e., based on one's point-of-view, attitude, experience, etc.).

> Police officers need factual justification at least equal to reasonable suspicion to stop an individual. Stopping people without this level of factual justification is unlawful, a violation of civil rights under the fourth amendment. Race may or may not be part of the factual justification.

How do officers choose who to focus their attention on with regard to collecting the facts, observations, and other justifications that make up reasonable suspicion to stop? A 2004 study by Alpert et al. provides insight. Officers formed suspicion when they observed something unusual or became curious or distrustful of an individual. Categories of unease included appearance, behavior, time, place, and other information:

> "Appearance" refers to the appearance of an individual and/or vehicle, and can refer to things such as distinctive dress, indicators of class, vehicle type, color, condition, and the like. "Behavior" refers to any overt action taken by an individual or vehicle that seemed inappropriate, illegal, or bizarre. "Time and place" refers to an officer's knowledge of a particular location (e.g., park, warehouse district) and what activities should or should not be expected there after a particular time (e.g., after hours). Finally, "Information" refers to information provided by either a dispatcher or fellow officer (e.g., BOLO) (Alpert, 2006, p. 4).

> Behavior forms the basis of the factual justification for a police stop, not appearance, i.e., race.

Behavior of the individuals that drew the attention of officers accounted for 66% of the reason for the stops. 18% of the stops were based on information received from fellow officers or dispatch. This would amount to information obtained by victims, witnesses, or other involved persons and relayed to the officers in some way. 10% of the reasons given for the stops related to time and place, such as an individual out roaming the street in the early morning hours or roaming an area not usually inhabited at the particular time, that drew officer suspicion. Only 6% of the reasons given for becoming suspicious were related to the appearance of the individual.

If one believed that police are inherently biased based on race, that would correspond to a belief that appearance would be a fundamental factor contributing to suspicion and police stops. Recall that racial profiling is defined as "Law enforcement activities such as stops, detentions, arrests and searches that are initiated solely on race" (Fridell, 2001). This research, based on direct observation and interviews with police officers, *indicated that appearance is the least important aspect of forming suspicion.* They went on to explain the role appearance actually plays in forming suspicion for officers who rated appearance as a medium or high priority in forming suspicion.

> Despite ethnicity, if someone is wearing all black clothing, this is an indication that they are up to no good. If an officer is well acquainted with people and places in his beat, he can tell based on appearance who "doesn't belong." Persons who look "different" raise suspicion (e.g., white person in black neighborhood). In contrast, officers who rated appearance to be of low priority typically provided one of two explanations: (1) that most people encountered looked similar enough to render appearance meaningless as a factor that might arouse suspicion, or, (2) that they did their best not to judge people based on their appearance (Alpert, 2006, p. 5).

> Appearance of suspects is only important when it draws the attention of officers because it is out of place or unusual.

Behavior, on the other hand, was described as significant, with nearly half of the officers reporting that it was a high priority in forming suspicion. The following comments about behavior were notable:

> A Police officer stated that he watches out for the "felony stare" (i.e., getting nervous when they see a police car, making every effort to avoid the police).
>
> A Police officer said that behavior is very important to him because he can tell when a person is lying to him. He can tell this by the way they act.
>
> A Police officer said he can tell if someone has done something just by how they respond to him. "It is very important to tell if they are fidgeting" (Alpert, 2006, p. 6).

Forming suspicion that an individual is involved in criminal conduct does not always result in a stop. Even though officers have a duty to stop those suspected of criminal conduct, many choose to merely continue to observe the individual until continued observation convinced him or her that a stop was warranted. This is a fundamental aspect of officer discretion addressed in this study:

> Once an officer became suspicious of an individual they were equally likely to stop the person whether or not the person was male or female,

> African American or white, young or old or perceived to be of low or high economic status (Alpert, 2006, p. 7).

This study, a comprehensive analysis of how officers form suspicion and make stops, lends little support to the premise that officers stop individuals because they are black or of low socioeconomic status; rather, *it is the behavior of individuals that drive these decisions:*

> Officers were significantly more likely to make stops when they had formed suspicion on the basis of a suspect's behavior, rather than on the basis of time and place, information or appearance. Suspect characteristics, such as gender, ethnicity, socioeconomic status, and age, did not significantly influence the likelihood of a stop after a suspicion was formed. However, non-behavioral suspicions were most common when a suspect and an officer were both Black, and least common when an officer and suspect were both white (Alpert, 2006).

The above study was federally funded under award number 2001-IJ-CX-0035 and was submitted in February of 2006, but the study has not been published by the U.S. Department of Justice (DOJ). The conclusion offered above, stating that behavior was of lesser importance when both the suspect and the officer were black as opposed to when the officer and suspect were white, is compelling.

POLICE VIEW OF RACIAL PROFILING

The existence of widespread perceptions of biased-based policing leads to the assumption that the police engage in systematic discrimination. This is very problematic for police as it affects the way many people of color interpret their interactions with police. Henry Louis Gates, Jr. (1997) observed that black men "swap their experiences of police encounters like war stories, and there are few who don't have more than one story to tell" (as quoted in Kennedy, 2011).

> Attitudes or predispositions are important to understanding why some people view the police positively or negatively. Those with positive predispositions toward the police will initially view police action as reasonable, those with negative predispositions toward the police will not.

A person who has a positive view of the police, positively predisposed, is likely to accept being stopped as the police just doing their job to keep the community safe. Most people who hold a positive predisposition toward the police will react, even in ambiguous situations, with deference to the officer, being polite and respectful. An individual who is not so favorably predisposed toward the police is likely to view the motives of the officer as evil, bad, or unjust and act accordingly. The resulting behavior of disrespect, antagonism, and sometimes violence challenges even the most professional police officer's patience. *Herein lies basis of the problem for anyone charged with the responsibility of improving police-community relations.*

To what extent is there racial discrimination in policing? *Racial profiling* is generally defined as "the scrutiny of a person based **solely** on his or her race." Based on this definition, one would be hard pressed to find any police officer or chief who would argue that this is appropriate; it is, in fact, unlawful under the U.S. Constitution.

An alternative, less restrictive definition, is that *racial profiling* is any practice that **takes race into account**. This less restrictive definition sets racial characteristics (i.e., appearance) aside in all determinations of suspicion and has been embraced by a number of agencies including the U.S. Department of Justice. To not consider race at all is a disservice to the fundamental mission of the police. Race is merely one factor that may, or may not, be considered in the overall decision to stop an individual in light of the situation depending on whether it is relevant to that situation.

The Narrow Definition. Under the narrow definition, racial profiling occurs when a police officer stops, questions, arrests, or searches someone solely on the basis of the person's race or ethnicity. Critics typically use this definition when condemning racial profiling, as do law enforcement agencies when denying the existence of racial profiling.

The Broader Definition. Under the broader definition, racial profiling occurs when a law enforcement officer uses race or ethnicity as one of several factors in deciding to stop, question, arrest, or search someone. An example of racial profiling under this broader definition would be a police stop based on the confluence of the following factors:

- age (young);
- dress (hooded sweatshirt, baggy pants, etc.);
- time of day (late evening);
- geography (in the "wrong" neighborhood); and
- race or ethnicity (white, black or Hispanic).

Under this broader definition, then, racial profiling occurs whenever police routinely use race as a factor that, along with an accumulation of other factors, causes an officer to react with suspicion and take action (Clearly, 2001).

Is racial profiling ever morally or legally justifiable?

Police may argue that racial profiling when intelligently deployed (as in the case of drug courier profiles and victim/witness descriptions) contributes to the effectiveness of law enforcement efforts. Are the police ever justified in stopping a black man when the suspect's description is of a white man absent any other factors? No. Similarly, it would be silly not to consider race in cases where race is put forth as an identifying characteristic. Criminal behavior sometimes does fall out along racial lines (Kinsley, 2001; Taylor, 2001).

> Not considering race as a legitimate factor in stop decisions when race is of importance in identifying a suspect is irresponsible, right? Discuss.

Conversely, some argue that what has been referred to as "rational" racial profiling tends to be a self-fulfilling prophecy. When race is used as a qualifier (or disqualifier) in establishing suspicion of criminal conduct, the police will naturally target certain racial groups, leading to more stops and arrests of persons within that group. If, for example, the Drug Courier Profile identified those of Hispanic origin as those most likely to transport drugs along the major drug corridors, the police will focus their attention on Hispanic drivers, stopping them more often, based on the profile, and finding more criminal activity among that group than they otherwise would if race were not considered.

> Many researchers believe that the War on Drugs fosters negative encounters with minorities. The basis of racial profiling is the premise that minorities commit most drug offenses. Although the premise is factually untrue, it has, nonetheless, become a self-fulfilling prophecy. Furthermore, because police look for drugs primarily among Blacks and Latinos, they find a disproportionate number of these individuals with contraband. This perception creates a profile that results in more stops of minority drivers (Ioimo, 2007, p. 272).

> When race is a consideration in stop decisions the police will gravitate toward those who are stopped and arrested most often. Agree or disagree?

A police officer who stops an individual because he is black, using race as the sole factor to stop the individual, is behaving as a racist. A police officer, who stops a black individual who is attempting to conceal themselves late at night in an industrial area known for a high rate of break-ins, is doing their job. The idea of "rational" profiling justifies the use of race as a qualifying factor of suspicion. In the same way that Affirmative Action uses racial profiling to promote the noble goal of advancing the standing of previously marginalized groups, rational profiling has the noble goal of advancing public safety in the wake of 9/11 and the scourge of drug trafficking. Unfortunately, innocent people will be affected. In the words of Michel Kinsley (2001),

> Both racial profiling and affirmative action are dangerous medicines that are sometimes appropriate. So, when is 'sometimes'? It seems obvious to me, though not to many others, that discrimination in favor of historically oppressed groups is less offensive than discrimination against them. Other than that, the considerations are practical. How much is at stake in forbidding a particular act of discrimination? How much is at stake in allowing it?

Rational profiling uses race as only one factor, when it is appropriate to do so, given the situation or context.

To what extent do police officers actually engage in bias-based policing? A 2007 study of policing in the Commonwealth of Virginia offered a new definition of biased policing: "practices by individual officers, supervisors, managerial practices, and departmental programs, both intentional and non-intentional, that incorporate prejudicial judgments based on sex, race, ethnicity, gender, sexual orientation, economic status, religious beliefs, or age that are inappropriately applied" (Ioimo, 2007).

Ioimo et al. surveyed a large group of officers in Virginia and found that 21% of responding officers believed that officers in their department practice biased-based policing and that 15% of the responding officers witnessed such behavior. It is important to note, however, that they did not provide the above definition of biased-based policing in their survey instrument:

> It is recognized that the failure to provide a definition of bias-based policing at the onset of this study could be viewed as a limitation for this study. However, it was determined that forcing respondents to apply a standard definition when completing the survey had the potential to skew the results. The entire premise of the survey was to assess the occurrence of bias-based policing using citizen and police perceptions. Therefore, it was important to this study that those perceptions be based on the following two factors: (a) conclusions drawn from the fact that bias-based policing is an issue that has been in the mainstream of the media for the past few years and (b) subjective factors such as experiences, opinions, views, and beliefs (Ioimo, 2007, p. 277).

They go on to state that "... in a culture that has sought to embrace tolerance, justice and communication, if just 1% of police officers reported the occurrence of bias-based policing in their departments, it should be enough to signal a problematic area in need of investigation and correction" (p. 285). Clearly, these researchers reject the concept of rational bias in the true spirit of the unconstrained vision.

A more realistic definition of racial profiling is offered by Ramirez (2000):

> We define 'racial profiling' as any police-initiated action that relies upon: (a) the race, ethnicity or national origin of an individual; rather than (b) the behavior of that individual, or (c) information that leads the police to a particular individual who has been identified as being engaged in or having been engaged in criminal activity (p. 5).

This definition offers much more specific guidance in defining whether or not an officer's actions constitute racial profiling in that:

1. Police may not use racial or ethnic stereotypes as factors in selecting whom to stop and search.
2. Police may use race or ethnicity to determine whether a person matches a specific description of a particular suspect (Clearly, 2000).

Using this definition, the concept of "rational" bias can now be articulated in a manner that distinguishes it from racial discrimination.

MANAGING THE CONFLICT & CONTROLLING OFFICER DISCRETION

When police officers engage in profiling based on a belief that certain groups (e.g., African Americans) violate the law more than others, arrest rates are used to justify this belief. For some, it only makes sense to focus law enforcement efforts on members of a group shown to violate the law more than other groups; to them, it's not racism but the byproduct of sound police practices. This reasoning, however, may not be sound. According to Harris (1999):

> The belief that blacks are disproportionately involved in drug crimes will become a self-fulfilling prophesy. Because police will look for drug crime among black drivers, they will find it disproportionately among black drivers. This will mean more blacks arrested, prosecuted, convicted, and jailed, which, of course, will reinforce the idea that blacks are disproportionately involved in drug crimes, resulting in a continuing motive and justification for stopping more black drivers as a rational way of using resources to catch the most criminals (Harris as cited in Cleary, 2000, p. 13).

Mitigating this problem begins with the understanding that bias-based policing aggravates the long held feelings of injustice and deepens the distrust and cynicism many have about the police. This cynicism leads to an unwillingness to cooperate with the police in more serious criminal investigations or to appear as witnesses in court. In short, bias-policing practices have created the "don't snitch" problem that makes the law enforcement job much more difficult (Harris, 1999).

LEVELS OF DISCRETION

Targeting efforts to control biased policing requires a distinction between levels of discretion officers possess in certain situations. A case where an officer has a report of crime or suspicious activity where a suspect is specifically described is categorized as low discretion. Race may be a factor in the suspect description among other behavioral or situational factors, amounting to reasonable suspicion. The officer has little choice other than to exercise their authority and stop the individual.

> Low discretion incidents are occurrences where an officer does not have a choice, the ability to exercise their professional judgement is restricted. High discretion incidents allow officers to employ their own judgement to a much greater extent. Examples?

On the other end of the discretionary continuum is the high discretion stop that most often involves minor infractions. The officer may have a hunch of more serious criminal wrongdoing, but has wide latitude as to whether or not to exercise their authority. They may legally stop the suspect for the minor infraction, or not. According to Ramerez (2000), high-discretion stops invite both intentional and unintentional abuse: "Police, obviously, are just as subject to [society's] racial and ethnic stereotypes . . . as any other citizen. Unless documented, such stops create an environment that allows the use of stereotypes to go undetected" (Ramirez, 2000, p. 14).

Broken windows policing, where the police concentrate enforcement efforts on minor infractions under the assumption that doing so deters more serious crime, is ripe for the kind of abuse Ramirez discusses and Harris identifies as the very kind of police action that undermines the trust and legitimacy of the police. How can police agencies and individual officers engage in effective law enforcement and "broken windows" policing without undermining trust and legitimacy? The following recommendations are worthy of consideration in managing this conflict.

Officers should clearly explain to individuals why they are being stopped. For the officer, this means arming themselves with the lawful justification for the stop in advance. Asking the questions "What do I know, see, and objectively sense regarding the behavior of this individual that gives me the lawful authority to stop them?"

> To mitigate the discomfort of such interactions and to bolster community trust, officers should explain the reason for the stop, discuss specifically the suspect's manner that generated the suspicion, and offer the contact information of a supervisor or appropriate complaint authority, so that the person stopped can convey any positive or negative comments about the interaction (Ridgeway, 2007, p. 44).

Explaining why a particular action is taken and the importance of this action in light of community safety and security is the essence of what is now called "procedural justice."

Whenever an officer employs the lawful authority to stop or to arrest, the factual justification for the action amounting to reasonable suspicion or probable cause must be articulated in an official agency report or stop card. Any use of force by officers requires documentation clearly articulating the reasonable suspicion or probable cause for the stop or arrest and the behavior of the subject that justified the level of force used.

Documentation pertaining to stops, arrests, and use of force should be reviewed on an annual basis. Ordinary stop patterns should be identified, and any officers outside of the ordinary stop patterns in regards to the race of those stopped should be identified. Extreme deviations from ordinary stop patterns is evidence that an officer's stop patterns differ substantially from their peers. It is not conclusive evidence of bias-policing, but it should prompt supervisory inquiry.

To effectively manage conflict in stop situations where racial bias may be an issue, officers should simply explain themselves and be nice. *There is simply no upside in being a nasty cop.*

Chapter Summary

Law enforcement and *policing* are not interchangeable terms. *Law enforcement* pertains to formal and informal actions taken in response to a clear law violation; *policing* refers to order maintenance, conflict management, mediation, and service functions that officers are routinely expected to do. Police officers, at the local level, engage in both functions on a daily basis, whereas law enforcement officers at the state and federal levels may only engage in enforcement activity. Individuals are trained to perform the law enforcement function adequately, but policing is a higher-level skill, one that more closely approximates a true profession.

Police agencies tend to be categorized as one of the following types; officer discretion generally reflects the type of agency that employs him or her.

The Legalistic Style

> A legalistic police department will issue traffic tickets at a high rate, detain and arrest a high proportion of juvenile offenders, act vigorously against illicit enterprises, and make a large number of misdemeanor arrests even when, as with petty larceny, the public order has not been breached (Wilson, 1968, p. 172).

Situations and problems that come to the attention of the police are handled as if they are law enforcement problems, as opposed to order maintenance issues. In such an agency, officers may deny service if a particular situation does not involve a violation of the law. The goal is for officers to follow the established legal process and apply the law equally because to not do so, in the face of an apparent violation, could be considered neglect of their duty.

The Watchman Style

> The police are watchman, not simply in emphasizing order over law enforcement but also in judging the seriousness of infractions less by what law says about them than by their immediate and personal consequences, which differ in importance depending on the standards of the relevant group-teenagers, Negros, prostitutes, motorists, families, and so forth (Wilson, 1968, p. 141).

The watchman style places priority on order maintenance, and to the extent that enforcing the law is likely to illicit anger, hardship, resentment, or future disorder, an officer may use his or her *discretion.* The obvious downside is that, when officers are compelled to exercise formal authority, those actions are likely to be viewed as arbitrary, inconsistent, and potentially biased. The danger here is that officers overuse their discretion, choosing not to arrest when an arrest is necessary.

The Service Style

> In some communities, the police take seriously all requests for either law enforcement or order maintenance (unlike police with a watchman style) but are less likely to respond by making an arrest or otherwise imposing formal sanction (Wilson, 1968, p. 200).

The service style of policing functions most effectively when there is a "high-level of agreement among citizens on the need for and definition of public order" (Wilson, 1968). Maintaining this style of policing becomes much more complex in diverse communities.

In addition to the agency styles offered by Wilson, Brown outlines individual officer operational styles as follows:

> An operational style initially derives from the choices a patrolman must make about how to work the street. Our observations of crime fighting revealed that patrolman could be differentiated in terms of two characteristics: how aggressive they were in pursuit of the goal of crime control, and how selective they were in the enforcement of the law (Brown, 1988, p. 223).

The Old Style Crime Fighter Style

The old style crime fighter is highly aggressive in his or her approach to law enforcement but highly selective in what they view as deserving of their attention. Minor violations are not generally worth their time, unless the perpetrator is known as someone who needs to be reminded of their place. These individuals are comfortable with violence and use it with judicious proportionality; they do not shy away from the use of force, viewing it as a tool of informal social control related to the character and intention of the potential violator, rather than as a tool of lawful authority.

The Clean Beat Crime Fighter Style

The clean beat crime fighters are both aggressive and non-selective in their initiated enforcement activity. They view the world as consisting of those who violate the law and those who do not and will aggressively seek out even minor and nuisance violations. They believe in a rigid and unrelenting enforcement of the law, through the aggressive prosecution of even minor offenses. The clean beat crime fighter believes in making as many stops as they can and justifies this action as necessary for deterring other kinds of more serious crime; establishing a consistent hard-nosed reputation for enforcement is the goal.

The Professional Style

> The professional police officer adheres as much as possible to department rules and policies. They are preoccupied with doing a good job as that is defined by their supervisors. As one of them said in the midst of issuing parking tickets, 'I'm out here for eight hours and I might as well give the city its money's worth.' They firmly enforce the law, but they believe they are flexible enough to know when not to; they vigorously pursue felons, but they are less likely to indulge themselves in the frequent and wanton use of illegal tactics; in short, they believe that a policeman can enforce the law and cope with crime while

> maintaining rapport with the people in the community (Brown, 1988, p. 235).

The professional police officer respects the rule of law even to the extent that it may get in the way of holding criminals to account. Professionalism requires a stern devotion to the standards and rules of one's profession. For the professional police officer, this begins with demonstrating respect for the constitutional rights of citizens, compliance with the law, and adherence to the rules and codes of conduct adopted for his or her profession. The professional officer is active, but not aggressive. They are not at all reluctant to stop people, but do so with much more solid, fact-based suspicion of criminal wrongdoing.

The Service Style

The service style of policing is non-aggressive and highly selective. Brown categorizes service style police officers into two sub-groups. The attitude of the first group is summed up by a patrol man who said, "I don't want to chase every asshole on the street. I'm just as happy if things don't come up." The second category of the service style are quite different, as described by Brown:

> Their belief is that crime suppression is not the most important goal of a police department. They argue that the police should take a positive role in assisting people to solve their problems. Consequently, impersonal and legalistic law enforcement is de-emphasized, and one of the defining characteristics of this approach is the belief that the exercise of discretion ought to be based on a sensitivity to community values and needs (Brown, 1988, p. 236).

The conflict between this style and the crime fighters and professionals is profound. To be a suitable target for enforcement action, violations need to point back to an identifiable problem that may be attacked more effectively by some vaguely identifiable arrest alternative. These officers push for diversionary programs that circumvent formal prosecution, such as peer mediation and restorative justice programs, as opposed to simply arresting violators.

> The service style, more than anything else, reflects submerged ideological conflicts which presently animate the practitioners of the police craft. This is partly a matter of the changing values among young policemen, but it is also indicative of the responses of policemen to the social and political turmoil of the late sixties. Be that as it may, what unites the few individuals who, to a greater or lesser degree, practice this style is a singular distaste for the doctrines of police professionalism and

many of the practices endemic to contemporary police (Brown, 1988, p. 237).

Selective enforcement is a practice common in policing. Officers cannot enforce the law equally with regard to all laws or all violators; this is the essence of police discretion and can be quite controversial as seen recently in regards to racial profiling. Perceived abuses of power may be alleged when individuals and groups feel that they are selected for unjust enforcement by police. To the police, however, profiling is commonly viewed as a powerful tool of efficient law enforcement. *Here we have a conflict between efficient operations in pursuing the law and unjust outcomes as reflected in dramatically disparate impact based on race.*

Conflict theory assumes that police discretion—how police choose who to stop and arrest—is a function of the socioeconomic make-up of the community. The existence of widespread perceptions of bias-based policing leads to the assumption that the police engage in systematic discrimination. This is very problematic for police as it affects the way many people of color interpret their interactions with police. Henry Louis Gates Jr. (1997) observed that black men "swap their experiences of police encounters like war stories, and there are few who don't have more than one story to tell" (as quoted in Kennedy, 2011).

A person who has a positive view of the police (i.e., positively predisposed) is likely to accept being stopped as the police just doing their job to keep the community safe. Most people who hold a positive predisposition toward the police will react, even in ambiguous situations, with deference to the officer, being polite and respectful. An individual who is not so favorably predisposed toward the police is likely to view the motives of the officer as evil, bad, or unjust and act accordingly.

Bibliography

Alpert, G.D. (2006). *Police Officers' Decision Making and Discretion: Forming Suspicion and Making a Stop*. Washington: NCJRS.

Blauner, R. (1972). *Racial Oppression in America*. New York: Harper and Row.

Brown, M.K. (1988). *Working the Street: Police Discretion and the Dilemmas of Reform*. New York: Russel Sage Foundation.

Carter, D. (2002). *The Police and the Community, 7th ed.* Upper Saddle River, NJ: Pearson/Prentice Hall.

Cleary, J. (2000). *Racial Profiling Studies in Law Enforcement: Issues and Methodology*. St. Paul: Minnesota House of Representatives.

Conkin, J.E. (2013). *Criminology, 11th ed.* Upper Saddle River, NJ: Pearson/Prentice Hall.

Crank, J.P. (2004). *Understanding Police Culture, 2nd ed.* Routledge.

Fridell, L.L. (2001). *Racially Biased Policing: A Principled Response.* Washington, DC: Police Executive Research Forum.

Garner, J. (1997). Evaluating the Effectiveness of Mandatory Arrest for Domestic Violence in Virginia. *William & Mary Journal of Women and the Law, 3(1),* 223–239.

Gates, H.L. (1997). *Thirteen Ways of Looking at a Black Man.* New York: Random House.

Goldstein, H. (1977). *Policing a Free Society.* Cambridge, MA: Ballinger.

Goldstein, H. (1990). *Problem Oriented Policing.* New York: McGraw-Hill.

Harris, D. (1999, December). The Stories, the Statistics and the Law: Why "Driving While Black" Matters. *Minnesota Law Review,* 265–326.

Harris, D. (2002). *Profiles in Injustice: Why Racial Profiling Cannot Work.* New York: New York Press.

Ioimo, R.T. (2007). The Police View of Bias-Based Policing. *Police Quarterly, 10(3).*

Kelling, G. (1999). *"Broken Windows" and Police Discretion.* Washington: National Institute of Justice 178259.

Kennedy, R. (2011). Race and the Administration of Criminal Justice in America. In J.Q. Wilson, *Crime and Public Policy* (pp. 237–255). New York: Oxford University Press.

Kinsley, M. (2001, September 30th). When Is Racial Profiling Okay? *Washington Post.*

Lamberth, J. (1997). *Report of John Lamberth, Ph.D.* American Civil Liberties Union website.

Petrocelli, M.P. (2003). Conflict Theory and Racial Profiling: An Empirical Analysis of Police Traffic Stop Data. *Journal of Criminal Justice, 31,* 1–11.

Ramirez, D. (2000). *A Resource Guide on Racial Profiling Data Collection Systems: Promising Practices and Lessons Learned.* Washington: U.S. Department of Justice.

Ridgeway, G. (2007). *Analysis of Racial Disparities in the New York Police Department's Stop, Question and Frisk Practices.* Santa Monica, CA: Rand Corporation.

Simmel, G. (1950). *The Sociology of Georg Simmel.* Glencoe, IL: Free Press.

Smith, M. (2001). Racial Profiling? A Multivariate Analysis of Police Traffic Stop Data. *Police Quarterly, 4*, 4–27.

Taylor, S.J. (2001, September). The Case for Using Racial Profiling at Airports. *National Journal.*

Trojanowicz, R.K. (1990). *Community Policing: A Contemporary Perspective, 3rd ed.* Cincinnati: Anderson Publishing.

Wilson, J.Q., Kelling, G. (1982). "Broken Windows: The Police and Neighborhood Safety." *Atlantic Monthly*, 29–38.

Wilson, J.Q. (1968). *Varieties of Police Behavior.* Cambridge, MA: Harvard University Press.

CHAPTER 7

Humanistic Policing: Human Relations, Emotional Intelligence, and the Power of Respect

■ ■ ■

You need laws to survive and you need law enforcement to have an intelligent, peaceful society; but we have to live in these places and suffer the type of conditions that exist from (police) officers who lack understanding and who lack any human feeling, or lack any feeling for their fellow human being . . . —Malcom X

Malcolm X*

* Courtesy, Library of Congress.

Learning Outcomes

Upon successful completion of this chapter the student will be able to:

- Explain the nature, purpose, and importance of human relations.
- Explain how human relations concepts can help police be more effective.
- Identify the major forces/themes that influence human behavior.
- Explore the concepts of self-esteem and self-awareness.
- Define *emotional intelligence* and explain how it can be developed and assessed.
- Describe the importance of empathy and how it can be used to improve relationships.
- Describe each of the economic cultures and their "hidden" rules.

Important Concepts

- Human Relations
- Economic Culture
- Emotional Intelligence
- Intelligence Quotient
- Sympathy vs. Empathy
- Rational Emotive Behavior Theory
- Working Memory
- Rapport
- Unconditional Respect

Questions for Discussion

- Discuss the human relations approach to policing. How is it different from the professional and community oriented perspectives?
- Compare the "hidden" rules of poverty to the "hidden" rules of the middle class. How are these rules communicated and passed down from generation to generation?

- What are the differences between someone raised in generational poverty and someone who has fallen into poverty due to a life-situation?
- Describe what is meant by compassionate law enforcement.
- What is meant by unconditional respect? What kinds of threats does it protect officers from?

INTRODUCTION

The business of policing is human relations. This has not always been the case; but today, the demands for police to be more accountable to the communities they serve necessitates that officers develop higher level skills. Intelligence and mastery of the law and its application is necessary, but skill in relating to people in a manner that builds a foundation of trust and respect is now required. This is not something that the typical police basic training curriculum can provide; rather, dedicated police officers must develop it on their own.

> Those who enter the work force today encounter a work/life landscape that is more complex and unpredictable than at any other time in history. The mastery of interpersonal relationship skills gives us the self-confidence needed to achieve success in our highly competitive work force. People who have effective interpersonal skills are more likely to be hired and more likely to receive promotions (Reece, 2014).

In recent years, the power of the intelligence quotient in predicting the success of individuals has been challenged by a new concept, *emotional intelligence*:

> A view of human nature that ignores the power of emotions is sadly shortsighted. The very name *Homo sapiens*, the thinking species, is misleading in light of the new appreciation and vision of the place of emotions in our lives that science now offers. As we all know from experience, when it comes to shaping our decisions and our actions, feeling counts every bit as much-and often more-than thought. We have gone too far in emphasizing the value and import of the purely rational—of what IQ measures—in human life. For better or worse, intelligence can come to nothing when the emotions hold sway (Goleman, 2005, p. 4).

The challenge for police officers is understanding the unique attitudes, values, and point-of view of those with whom they interact. Inherent to this goal is developing a framework for understanding the cultural diversity that permeates the urban landscape; such an understanding is a logical first step in building rapport, developing better police-community relationships, and managing conflicts.

HUMANISTIC POLICING

The law enforcement function can have the impact of de-humanizing police officers. There are subtle—and not so subtle—pressures within this function and within the police subculture that sometimes allows officers to step beyond what would be considered acceptable moral boundaries. Reports involving officers justifiably killing unarmed individuals are accepted under the law as reasonable; the law provides the rationalization for such action. Through training and socialization into the law enforcement culture, police officers accept the law as the primary source of moral guidance. Society invests police officers, out of necessity, with the discretion to use deadly force, and it collectively expects them to do so when it is legally justified. When officers are not charged with crimes for their actions, it is not a failure of the legal system. The fact that these kinds of events occur in the first place is an indication of a failure elsewhere, perhaps in the very fabric of our society, *because, as a source of moral guidance, the law is woefully inadequate.*

> Police work can be de-humanizing. Why is this? Can you provide some examples of what police officers do and see that might cause it?

Policing is a people business; finding clues to increasing the effectiveness of the modern police officer in terms of building better relationships and trust can be found in the field of human relations.

HUMAN RELATIONS

Human relations can be defined as the study of human behavior—it is a field of endeavor that studies why self-image, beliefs, attitudes, prejudices, and bias sometimes cause problems in professional and personal contacts and relationships. *For the police officer, competency rests in the understanding that all productive work is done through relationships. The very first relationship that needs to be cultivated is with the self, then the particular individual(s) one relates to, and then the group(s) that individuals associate with.*

> Policing is all about human relationships. When positive relationships exist, the job is easier and police community relations thrive, when officers view themselves primarily as enforcers and discount the value of relationships the job itself becomes much more difficult and police community relations suffer.

Police agencies hire individuals for particular competences that the agency feels are important to the organization. What many are realizing, however, is that

effective policing depends on human relation skills; technical competency cannot be separated from the individual's particular characteristics or attributes. The total person concept relates to the understanding that an individual's characteristics, skills, attitudes, self-awareness, and values are interrelated and interdependent (Reece, 2014). When a department hires someone, they hire the total package or *total person* (Reece, 2014). Factors that influence an individual's human relation skills include communication (internally and externally); self-awareness; self-acceptance (worth); motivation; trust; self-disclosure[1]; and conflict resolution (management) (p. 14).

> When we hire police officers we accept the total person into our organization. This includes their values, attitudes, education, training, maturity (of lack of maturity) communication skill, motivation, trust and human relations skills.

The ability to communicate effectively relates to both the *choice* of words used and *how* the words are used. Choice of words not only facilitates understanding, but it also communicates to others how they are viewed by us, their relative importance to us, and our individual self-concept and attitudes. For example, the use of highly technical language when conversing with a college professor may be expected, but in a discussion with a significant other, one may use less technical language as the goal is to help them understand what has been learned in college. On the other hand, one may make the choice to use a certain kind of language because of a wish to communicate superiority, or inferiority, to others in order to facilitate rapport. The choice of communication strategy is always situational, dependent upon location, surroundings, and the relationship between the individual(s). The goal of interpersonal communication is rapport, the linkage that develops between people that forms the basis of the relationship.

Rapport

Rapport is the hallmark of great communicators. It can be described as a **harmonious and reciprocal mini-relationship** between individuals or an individual and a group. It takes the form of a connection or link between parties who are in-sync with each other. Most individuals are familiar with the phrase "it's not what he said; it's how he said it." Such a statement may be an indication of the lack of rapport or the lack of acceptance of the message, or it may be an indication that a specific message was made perfectly clear.

---

[1] Self-disclosure refers to the willingness of individuals to revel information about themselves for the purpose of building better relationships.

Rapport is like a mini-relationship between people or between a person and a group. It is a kind of mental linkage that facilitates acceptance and understanding.

Gaining rapport with another person can be hard work. The goal is to establish commonality, to communicate likeness, and to minimize perceptions of dissimilarity. In a diverse society, this can mean a heightened level of awareness and complete control over one's bias, prejudice, and emotions. Since non-verbal communication is critical to interpersonal relations, one wrong move can destroy even the most skillful attempts to gain rapport. The goal for a police officer is to see similarity, people like people who are like themselves and police officers are automatically not like other people, anything that the officer can do to minimize this dis-similarity is a positive step toward rapport.

Non-Verbal Aspects of Communication

When the words are separated from the message, what is left is *non-verbal.* This term relates to the voice pitch, speed, tone, volume, and inflections used. It can also relate to body posture, proximity, facial expressions, eye movement, dress, physical contact, gestures, and even how people orient their feet. Consider how an individual unconsciously orients themselves when they have some place to go but are being held back by someone. They don't want to break off contact abruptly but their feet will point to the door as they try to disengage and move on to another appointment.

Non-verbal communication accounts for the majority of the message that is conveyed between individuals. "It's not what he said, it's how he said it."

Everyone has their own communication style, and it is important to recognize and understand the signals that are conveyed to others in both the verbal and non-verbal realm. The master communicator has the ability to flex their communication style based on the situation.

Police officers are taught always to be ready for physical attack. Body posture, known as the *ready stance*, is drilled into new recruits and often becomes the routine manner that officers use to engage with individuals, regular citizens and known criminals alike. Experience teaches officers the importance of non-verbal cues. When the ready stance sends the wrong signals and undermines rapport, officers who rise to higher levels of responsibility and authority (e.g., detectives) often abandon such habits. Higher levels of career success also aid in the development of higher levels of self-esteem and self-confidence, which also makes rapport and, in general, better interpersonal relationships easier to achieve and maintain.

Some things that police officers are taught to do inhibit good communication, e.g., the ready stance, taking command of the situation, command presence, etc. The wise officer understands how to adjust their habits when facilitating rapport is the goal.

Self-Esteem and Self-Worth

Self-esteem is an element of human relations that greatly impacts relationships with others. It can be described as opinions or attitudes about ourselves that commonly take the form of confidence, strong/meaningful estimations of personal abilities, and self-respect. Self-esteem defines self-image and governs how others are approached, based on perceptions, attitudes, prejudices, and bias toward them. *Self-worth* is the sense of value as an individual. Those with a low sense of self-worth often engage in self-destructive behavior, including crime, and are likely to tolerate abusive treatment and situations. Self-esteem and self-worth are the starting point of the ability to relate effectively to others.

Self-esteem is how we feel about ourselves. Self-worth is our own sense of value as an individual. Both of these concepts impact how well we get along with others and our ability to illicit cooperation and build relationships.

Self-esteem and self-worth influence behavior and can be sensed, often unconsciously, by others. Those with low self-esteem tend to believe that their life is not within their own control. They believe that outside forces or luck determine success, and they tend to blame others for their situation. These individuals are likely to engage in self-destructive behavior, such as smoking, excessive drinking, and drug use. They usually display antagonistic attitudes, fail to accept responsibility, and have generally poor people skills. They tend to rely on other individuals for personal validation and are hyper-sensitive to perceived slights. Emotions drive behavior in people with low self-esteem, and they are easy to anger. Police officers and others in authority positions can provide powerful sources of validation for those who continually seek support and validation from external sources.

People with high self-esteem are comfortable with themselves and believe that they are responsible for their own situation in life. When they make mistakes, they learn from them and are less likely to blame others, society, or bad luck for negative outcomes. People with high self-esteem are in control of their emotions and can reason through problems more effectively. They are less sensitive to perceived slights and tend not to take things personally. They are more accepting of others, especially those who are different from themselves, because they don't rely on others for their own validation. People with high self-esteem approach life in a positive way, are resilient, and are imaginative problem-solvers. They are much less likely to come to the attention of the police, but when they do, they can make excellent partners in problem-solving (Reece, 2014).

> Our own level of self-esteem enables us to effectively interact with others, low levels of self-esteem inhibits our ability to interact with others. Question for discussion: What causes high self-esteem?

Police officers who have great human relations skills are much better equipped to face the challenges of the job. They can read other people, and even their co-workers and supervisors, in terms of those messages that people send continuously without conscious thought. They pick-up on the subtle gestures that send meaning and convey feelings, thoughts and desires that aid in building better relationships as well as in improving conflict management efforts.

HUMAN RELATIONS AND MANAGING CONFLICT

Conflict is not a bad thing. Recognizing the value of differing perspectives is the first step in developing solid conflict management skills. The ability to manage conflict is a characteristic of great police officers and can be the foundation of great police-community relations. Conflict presents an opportunity for advancement, development, and change. Without it, humans stagnate and become complacent as individuals, and the same thing can be said for entire communities.

Police officers are not equipped to engage in conflict analysis; however, they should always assume that dysfunctional conflict has deeper sources than what is being put forth in times of crisis. When police officers are summoned to intervene in conflict, it means that the conflict has risen beyond the capabilities of the parties to manage; this is likely dysfunctional conflict. Emotions are running high, and the situation is volatile, these situations present an opportunity for the police officer to practice human relations skills with the goal of limiting the potential for deeper conflict or violence.

Conflict has **triggers**, and these triggers vary depending on the characteristics of the individuals involved, their self-esteem, self-worth, and motivations. Recognizing potential triggers leads to the root cause(s) of dysfunctional conflict. The root cause(s) can be attributed to a history of dysfunctional conflict, unmet expectations of one party or both, self-perceptions, emotions, or the lack of emotional control.

People sometimes engage in "triggering" behavior, that is behaviors that are intended, either consciously or unconsciously, to elicit an emotional response. Some people love to do this with the police. It is a power game, when you allow your emotions to emerge, they win and you lose.

Conflict is uncomfortable for people; even good conflict puts individuals on edge because they are hesitant to share insights or opinions because they fear how others will receive the information. This causes them to engage in one of the most common conflict resolution strategies: avoidance. People tend to skirt around issues, situations, and other individuals in an effort to avoid uncomfortable confrontations. People engage in non-assertive behavior just to avoid conflict, and this can make the inevitable conflict much worse. Police are not called upon to intervene unless the conflict has reached a critical point, and in these cases, emotions are running high. The passive nature of one party can actually lead to conflict as resentment builds until it explodes.

Police officers with highly developed human relations skills can assist in helping the non-assertive party describe behaviors (not characteristics) of the other party that has led to the feelings of resentment.

Negotiation

The police are often called in conflict situations when one party seeks to employ the coercive power of the police to intervene on their side. When the police understand this, they can employ human relations skills to convince the parties to think "**Win-Win**." *The battle for dominance needs to be replaced with a solution that provides benefits to all parties.* A solution that advances one individual's interests at the expense of someone else is to be avoided. "Win-Lose" solutions are a "no deal;" each side must be willing to sacrifice something to maintain the relationship. The fundamental human relations skill required of the police officer here is *listening.*

Calling the police in dispute situations means that one party is seeking to employ the coercive power of the state at the expense of someone else. They are seeking a "win-lose" outcome.

Human relations is a critical aspect of effective policing and when employed by individual police officers has a tremendous impact on the reputation of a police agency. Police officers who are sensitive and compassionate garner goodwill in the community and provide a foundation for great police community relations. *This begins with a concerted effort to understand the different facets of the community that can often be understood as cultural differences.*

UNDERSTANDING THE WHOLE COMMUNITY

The professional, community oriented police agency strives to meet the expectations of the whole community in setting enforcement priorities; the professional but non-community oriented police agency sets its priorities according to what may be professional standards, but these standards may not be responsive to the specific community that it serves. The non-professional police agency does neither. Nevertheless, police agency leaders can make the mistake of soliciting community input concerning its operations, assuming that those who choose to provide input adequately represent the community. Rarely do efforts, such as citizen advisory committees and review boards, adequately represent the views of those who are in the greatest need of law enforcement and policing services (i.e., the poor and disadvantaged). The following sections explore a framework for understanding the most vulnerable members of our communities.

> Formal mechanisms of community engagement such as citizen review boards or citizen councils seldom adequately represent the interests of the whole community. These groups typically pursue agendas that can be quite different than what is in the best interests of the community as a whole.

The Rich, the Middle-Class, and the Poor

There are distinct differences between groups of people in our communities; a *cultural differentiation or framework* enables us to understand how these three broad groups view the world, their own lives, and the police. However, generalizations, such as those offered below, can be precarious; generalizations should merely be used as a foundation because all generalizations have exceptions.

> Culture is the beliefs, values, characteristics and life habits that can be generalized to a particular group. This is merely a framework for better understanding group member behavior, but there are always individual exceptions.

Culture has been defined as the sum total of ways of living that are created and maintained by a group and transmitted from one generation to the next and includes the behaviors and beliefs characteristic of a particular group.[2]

Assumptions:

- Every community has individuals and families who are wealthy and poor; these are not absolute conditions. Wealth stratification exists along a continuum rather than a clear-cut distinction, known as the wealth-poverty continuum. Where one falls along this line can

[2] http://www.dictionary.com/browse/culture.

change, but it is initially based on generational or situational factors; people move along the line as their life conditions change.

- The amount of wealth one possesses is relative to their own expectations, in other words; individuals have a subjective view of what it means to be wealthy or poor. The perception of wealth or poverty one possesses predisposes them to certain behaviors.
- Each broad economic category—rich, middle-class, and poor—contains unique rules, perspectives, and norms that form an *economic culture*. The police operate from middle-class norms that can easily come into conflict with the norms of the wealthy and the norms of the poor. Individuals tend to retain the rules of the economic class in which they were raised.
- Relationships are critical to those in poverty; to move from poverty to middle-class requires that an individual sacrifice these relationships and form new ones based on middle-class norms.
- *The burden for developing relationships with those in any of the economic cultures rests with the police. Officers must understand the differences and adapt. Understanding and responding to these differences can be an effective way to build better police-community relationships.*
- Influencing a culture (ethnic, racial or economic) and building trust rests on the ability to provide an image worthy of respect and imitation (Payne, 1996).
- Poor people are overwhelmingly the "customers" of the police. They are most often the victims and perpetrators of crime.

Understanding the Poor

Poverty is a condition into which one can be born (i.e., *generational*) or into which one is thrust due to life circumstance (i.e., *situational*). Some people are born into working-class families, where one's parents, grandparents, and great-grandparents were poor. These individuals especially value relationships because they need them for survival:

> Generational poverty is defined as having been in poverty for at least two generations; however, the patterns begin to surface much sooner than two generations if the family lives with others who are from generational poverty. Situational poverty is defined as a lack of resources due to a particular event (i.e., a death, chronic illness, divorce, etc.).

> Generational poverty has its own culture, hidden rules, and belief systems. One of the key indicators of whether it is generational or situational poverty is the prevailing attitude. Often the attitude in generational poverty is that society owes a living. In situational poverty the attitude is often one of pride and a refusal to accept charity (Payne, 1996, p. 47).

Poverty can be either generational or situational. Those in generational poverty are more likely to have ingrained habits, values, attitudes and habits of behavior as opposed to those in situational-temporary-poverty due to life events.

An individual raised in generational poverty is likely able to employ violence on their own behalf or they have someone who is willing to employ violence for them as a way to resolve conflict (e.g., they know how to assert themselves and how to fight). This comes across as an attitude resembling the same *insolence of behavior* discussed by Skolnick (2011). The police are likely to interpret the behavior as threatening, based on their middle-class norms, and behave accordingly. *However, when the wise law enforcement officer understands the importance of showing physical prowess to the norms of poverty, they can circumvent their own behavioral response that may easily be considered disrespectful, intimidating, or even threatening.*

Poverty can be **generational** or **situational**. In situational poverty, life circumstance moved an individual or family from the middle-class into poverty. Job loss and divorce are the most common situations that can cause this shift along the poverty-wealth continuum. Individuals who find themselves in situational poverty retain the norms or **hidden rules** of the middle-class, even though their economic resources are diminished.

Hidden Rules of Economic and Social Culture

The rich, middle-class, and the poor all have rules that their members follow. These rules are not written down, but people internalize them based on their interaction with others. These are the unspoken cues and habits attributed to a particular economic or social group, notwithstanding race or ethnicity. Those within these groups assume that everyone knows and follows similar social rules.

Hidden rules exist for those in poverty that are very different from the hidden rules of the middle class. Wealthy people also have their own set of hidden rules, but wealthy people seldom call the police for assistance, unless they are having a problem with a poor person.

Police officers are predominantly middle-class; they may have been raised in poverty, but they aspire to middle-class norms. This makes it difficult for them to relate to generational poverty because they just do not see things the same way.

Typical differences between the life patterns of those in generational poverty and those who are middle class are portrayed in Table 1.

Table 7.1—Comparing Generational Poverty to Middle-Class

Generational Poverty	Middle-Class
I know which churches and sections of town have the best rummage sales.	I know how to properly set a table.
I know which grocery stores' garbage bins can be assessed for discarded food.	I know which stores are most likely to carry the clothing brands my family wears.
I know how to get someone out of jail.	I know how to order in a nice restaurant.
I know how to fight.	I know how to use a checking account, credit card and savings account.
I know how to live without a checking account.	I know the difference between term and whole life insurance.
I know how to live without electricity or a phone.	I talk to my children about going to college.
I can entertain my friends with stories.	I know where to get the best interest rates on a car loan.
I know how to move in half a day.	I know the difference between principal and interest.
I know where the free clinics are.	I know how to help and advocate for my children.
I'm very good at trading and bartering.	I know how to use tools and who to call if something needs repair.

Source: Ruby Payne, *A Framework for Understanding Poverty*. Highlands, TX: aha! Process, Inc., 1996.

The driving force for those in poverty is survival; the driving force for those in the middle class is the acquisition of "things." These are generalizations, so, of course, there are always exceptions. There are also differences between the middle-class and wealthy, but these are less important for the police as the police seldom interact with the wealthy. The wealthy are much less likely to call upon the police for assistance with problems, unless they are having a problem with someone in poverty. Typical differences between the middle class and the wealthy are characterized in Table 7.2.

Table 7.2—Comparing Wealth with Middle-Class

Middle Class	Wealthy
I know how to properly set a table.	I have favorite restaurants in different countries.
I know which stores are most likely to carry the clothing brands my family wears.	I know how to hire a decorator.
I know how to order in a nice restaurant.	I can read a menu written in another language.
I know how to use a checking account, credit card, and savings account.	I have at least two homes that are maintained and/or staffed.
I know the difference between term and whole life insurance.	I have "screens" to keep people away if I do not wish to associate with them.
I talk to my children about going to college.	I know how to enroll my children in private school.
I know where to get the best interest rates on a car loan.	I have a favorite financial adviser.
I know the difference between principal and interest.	I know how to read and interpret a financial statement.
I know how to help and advocate for my children.	I am on the board of at least two charities.
I know how to use tools and who to call if something needs repair.	I know how to host parties that "key" people attend.

Source: Ruby Payne, *A Framework for Understanding Poverty*. Highlands, TX: aha! Process, Inc., 1996.

The following table illustrates how each of the classes views and interprets a few key concepts. One should avoid cumulative generalizations as individuals may have a *social emphasis* common to those in poverty but a *view of time* more reflective of middle-class norms; again, there are always exceptions.

Table 7.3—Hidden Rules Among Classes

	POVERTY	MIDDLE-CLASS	WEALTH
POSSESSIONS	People.	Things.	One-of-a-kind objects, legacies, pedigrees.
MONEY	To be used, spent.	To be managed.	To be conserved, invested.
PERSONALITY	Is for entertainment. Sense of humor is highly valued.	Is for acquisition and stability. Achievement is highly valued.	Is for connections. Financial, political, social connections are highly valued.
SOCIAL EMPHASIS	Social inclusion of people he/she likes.	Emphasis is on self-governance and self-sufficiency.	Emphasis is on social exclusion.
FOOD	Key question: Did you have enough? Quantity important.	Key question: Did you like it? Quality important.	Key question: Was it presented well? Presentation important.
CLOTHING	Clothing valued for individual style and expression of personality.	Clothing valued for its quality and acceptance into norm of middle class. Label important.	Clothing valued for its artistic sense and expression. Designer important.
TIME	Present most important. Decisions made for moment based on feelings or survival.	Future most important. Decisions made against future ramifications.	Traditions and history are most important. Decisions made partially on basis of tradition and decorum.
EDUCATION	Valued and revered as abstract but not as reality.	Crucial for climbing success ladder and making money.	Necessary tradition for making and maintaining connections.
DESTINY	Believes in fate. Cannot do much to mitigate chance.	Believes in choice. Can change future with good choices now.	*Noblesse oblige.*
LANGUAGE	Casual register. Language is about survival.	Formal register. Language is about negotiation.	Formal register. Language is about networking.

	POVERTY	MIDDLE-CLASS	WEALTH
FAMILY STRUCTURE	Tends to be matriarchal.	Tends to be patriarchal.	Depends on who has money.
WORLD VIEW	Sees world in terms of local setting.	Sees world in terms of national setting.	Sees world in terms of international view.
LOVE	Love and acceptance conditional based upon whether individual is liked.	Love and acceptance conditional and based largely upon achievement.	Love and acceptance conditional and related to social standing and connections.
DRIVING FORCES	Survival, relationships, entertainment.	Work, achievement.	Financial, political, social connections.
HUMOR	About people and sex.	About situations.	About social *faux pas*.

Source: Ruby Payne, *A Framework for Understanding Poverty*. Highlands, TX: aha! Process, Inc., 1996, pp. 42–43.

Money

Money and money management is one of the most profound ways to distinguish between poverty and middle class. To those in generational poverty, money is to be used and spent immediately, its utility rests in the capacity to provide instant gratification. The poor also tend to spend money quickly on social occasions because money is a mechanism by which one can be included in the group. If someone from poverty receives a windfall of money, he or she is likely to use it immediately for pleasurable activity that includes their friends. For those in the middle-class, money is to be managed (i.e., budgeted) in anticipation of future needs; these individuals may also seek some kind of immediate gratification, using a portion of a windfall, but they consider their long-term dreams and their future needs and consider how they will be met. Rich people view money as something to be set aside and invested in terms of future utility. These individuals have the luxury of not worrying about where their next meal is coming from, so they save their money.

Money management is particularly problematic for those in poverty and it will inevitably be a cause of conflict among them. People in poverty have a hard time with money management because they don't have any money to manage and they don't see any value in saving it.

> One of the biggest difficulties in getting out of poverty is managing money and just the general information based around money. How can you manage something you've never had? Money is seen in poverty as an expression of personality and is used for entertainment and

> relationships. The notion of using money for security is truly grounded in the middle and wealthy classes (Payne, 1996, p. 44).

Poor people live for today; middle-class and wealthy people plan for the future. Appealing to those in poverty about the virtue of saving for the future or basic money management concepts will simply not resonate with them.

Education

Education and its value is also viewed very differently between these economic cultures. Those in poverty do not see becoming educated as realistically attainable. The poor revere education, but they set educational aspirations aside for immediate survival needs. Those in the middle-class view educations as essential for future success, and they will plan and save for it. The rich view education as a tradition; they wouldn't even think of not going to college as it is essential for networking and building connections and acquiring power.

Family Structure

The matriarchal family structure often, but not always, defines the family in generational poverty; the mother is the center of the organization with formal marital arrangements notably absent. Relationships are the most important aspirations in life, and for those in generational poverty, relationships are often informal; many couples enter common law relationships as opposed to legal marriages. There is a pattern of babies born out of wedlock to young teenagers; the infant is then raised by the teen-mother's mother as her own. The biological mother is viewed more like a sister to the infant. The role of the father is also very different in poverty; the male is sometimes present, but there is no predictable pattern for a father's involvement in generational poverty. Understanding the nature of these relationships is important for the police as internal feuds often define family life.

> Allegiances may change overnight; favoritism is a way of life. Who children go to stay with after school, who stays with whom when there is trouble, and who is available to deal with school issues (and police issues) are dependent on the current alliances and relationships at the moment (Payne, 1996, p. 57).

The male role is profoundly different in the culture of poverty. Men tend to be loaners, hang-out with other men, and orient themselves around work and bars. They strive to be viewed as "real men," who are not pushed around by anyone.

> In generational poverty, the primary role of a real man is to physically work hard, to be a fighter, and to be a lover. In the middle class, a real man is a provider. If one follows the implications of a male identity as one who is a fighter and a lover, then one can understand why the male who takes this identity (fighter and lover) as his own cannot have a stable life. Of the three responses to life—to flee, flow or fight—he can only fight or flee. So when the stress gets high, he fights, then flees from the law and the people closest to him, leaving his home. Either way he is gone. When the heat dies down, he returns to an initial welcome, then more fights. Then the cycle begins again (Payne, 1996, p. 60).

Escaping Poverty

How then do people escape from poverty? How can the police help? Education is the key, but recall that earning an education is revered but seen as an unrealistic goal. This is because one's thinking is limited to trying to find the next meal or avoiding a constantly evolving, chaotic, and often violent home situation.

> The police have an opportunity by virtue of their status to make an impact by providing a positive example of what is possible in life. There will be more on mentorship and youth engagement in a later chapter.

According to Payne (1996), individuals leave poverty for one of four reasons:

- A goal or vision of something they want to be or have;
- A situation that is so painful that anything would be better;
- Someone who "sponsors" them (i.e., an educator, spouse, mentor, or role model who shows them a different way or convinces them that they could live differently); or
- Having a specific talent or ability that provides an opportunity for them (p. 61).

More and more, in today's world, there are fewer individuals who serve as role models for young children. Authority figures, like the police, have a distinct advantage in that they are admired by nearly every young person until such time as they are disparaged by some influential adult or peer. Even then, the desire to be like the police officer is strong deep inside of the pre-adolescent. Better understanding the culture of poverty can help build trust and better police-community relations even when the law needs to be enforced.

> The economic traits which are most characteristic of the culture of poverty include the constant struggle for survival, unemployment and

underemployment, low wages, a miscellany of unskilled occupations, child labor, the absence of savings, a chronic shortage of cash, the absence of food reserves in the home, the pattern of frequent buying of small quantities of food many times a day as the need arises, the pawning of personal goods, borrowing from local money lenders at usurious rates of interest, spontaneous informal credit devices organized by neighbors, and the use of second-hand clothing and furniture (Lewis, 1971).

Building rapport, and better relationships, with the poor has its foundation in interpersonal communication, yet there is a **unique language** of poverty that is seldom understood and often misunderstood by the police.

THE LANGUAGE OF POVERTY

Communication skills are critical in nearly every human endeavor—law enforcement and policing are not exceptions. Police officers are overwhelmingly middle-class, aspiring to, or raised with, middle-class norms. Officers are sent to high crime ghetto neighborhoods with the mission of *relationship building,* but they quickly discover that they don't even speak the same language.

> Language registers refer to the way language is used in different cultures. Middle-class language is very different from how language is used by people in generational poverty.

In order to understand the role of language in relationship building between the police and people in generational poverty, Montano-Harmon (1991) describes the concept of the language register. There are five language registers or styles. Each level has an appropriate use that is determined by the varying situation. For example, it would be inappropriate to use language and vocabulary reserved for an intimate partner when speaking in the classroom. It would also be inappropriate to use formal language in conversing with a close personal or intimate acquaintance. Thus the appropriate language register depends upon the audience (who), the topic (what), purpose (why), and location (where) (Montano-Harmon, 1991).

Individuals must control the use of language registers in order to enjoy success in every aspect and situation encountered.

Static Register

This style of communications rarely changes. It is "frozen" in time and content. Examples include the Pledge of Allegiance, Lord's Prayer, Preamble to the US Constitution, the Alma Mater, a bibliographic reference, and laws.

Formal Register

This language is used in formal settings and is one-way in nature. This use of language usually follows a commonly accepted format. It is usually impersonal and precise. A common format for this register are speeches (e.g., sermons, rhetorical statements and questions, pronouncements made by judges, and announcements).

Consultative Register

This is a standard form of communication. Users engage in a mutually accepted structure of communication. The tone is typically formal and professional. Types of this discourse include strangers meeting, communication between a superior and a subordinate, doctor & patient, lawyer & client, lawyer & judge, teacher & student, and counselor & client.

Casual Register

This is informal language is used by peers and friends. Slang, vulgarities, and colloquialisms are normal. This is group language; that is, one must be a member to engage in this register (e.g., buddies, family members, or teammates) and the medium of communication is also informal (e.g., chats, Facebook posts, emails, blogs, and letters).

Intimate Register

This communications is private. It is reserved for close family members or intimate people (e.g., husband & wife, partners, siblings, and parents and children).

Rules of Language Use

One can usually transition from one language register to an adjacent one without encountering repercussions. However, skipping one or more levels is usually considered inappropriate and even offensive (Montano-Harmon, 1991). The use of the *formal register* is critical to both job success and education.

> . . . the majority of minority (poor) students do not have access to the formal register at home. As a matter of fact, these students cannot use the formal register. The problem is that all the state tests—SAT, ACT, etc.—are in formal register. It is further complicated by the fact that to get a well-paying job, it is expected that one will be able to use formal register. Ability to use formal register is a *hidden rule* of the middle class. The inability to use it will knock one out of an interview (job interview) in two or three minutes. The use of formal register, on the other hand,

> allows one to score well on tests and do well in school and higher education (Payne, 1996, p. 28).

> Using the casual language register, i.e., referring to someone by their first name, is not appropriate in formal settings such as the classroom when a student is interacting with the professor. Similarly, using the formal language register may not be appropriate when interacting with a neighbor in their own home.

Police officers, who are well versed in the formal register, are unsettled when they communicate with someone who does not know how to use it, does not understand the significance of it, and insists on using a casual register. *For someone from generational poverty, who exclusively utilizes the casual register, police officers appear strange, aloof, and arrogant.* Unlike the relationship that they find with their teachers, which is a comfortable/casual relationship, having a relationship with a police officer seems to be just not possible.

> This use of formal register is further complicated by the fact that those students do not have the vocabulary or the knowledge of sentence structure and syntax to use formal register. When student conversations in the casual register are observed, much of the meaning comes not from the word choices, but from the non-verbal assists (Payne, 1996, p. 28).

In addition to the registers, the pattern of discourse is important to understand. In the formal register, the pattern of discourse is to get straight to the point. Police officers are notorious for this, as in the case of the famous Jack Web quote "Just the facts please, Ma'am." However, in the casual register, the pattern of discourse is to **tell the story**, going around and around before finally getting to the point. Their story meanders, testing the endurance of even the easiest-going police officers. When the police officer is frustrated, impatient, or simply not at his or her best, listening wanes, resulting in exasperation and demands, such as "Please, get to the point!" This most certainly undermines rapport and cooperation.

> People in generational poverty converse with stories that can try the patience of the police who simply want them to "get to the point."

Payne (1991) speaks to teachers and educators, but the same principles apply to the police. What people from generational poverty lack in knowledge related to the formal register, they make-up for in non-verbal aspects of interpersonal communication. Given what is known about how poor people view the world, the hidden rules of poverty, the use of the casual register, and the pattern of discourse, it is clear why police lack legitimacy in poor communities and are often viewed with suspicion. Understanding and compassion hold promise for how this situation can be reversed.

> The police can use knowledge about language registers to strategically manipulate the context of their interactions. The use of the formal register conveys superiority to those who are not familiar with it. Is this always what we want? Conversely, the use of the casual register may convey equality or even subordination and this may be useful when the ultimate goal is rapport. Discuss.

COMPASSIONATE LAW ENFORCEMENT

In her bestselling book *The New Jim Crow,* Michelle Alexander (2011) presents a profound moral conflict. She makes the case that the War on Drugs and the resulting mass incarceration has perpetuated a system of racial control that is reminiscent of Jim Crow laws, relegating millions to a permanent second-class status. Cornel West (2011) characterized Alexander's work as "the secular bible for a new social movement." One of her recommendations is that the police need to become more compassionate as it is the police officer who is the gatekeeper of the criminal justice system. Understanding this perspective is valuable to any effort aimed at improving police-community relations and to mitigating conflict in the law enforcement role (Alexander, 2011).

What should guide law enforcement officers when engaging with the poor and disenfranchised? With regard to law enforcement, Alexander (2011) argues for a new premise/guidance, citing unjust incentives that drove police agencies in the War on Drugs:

> Equally important, there must be a change within the culture of law enforcement. Black and brown people in ghetto communities must no longer be viewed as the designated enemy, and ghetto communities must no longer be treated like occupied zones. Law Enforcement must adopt a compassionate, humane approach to the problems of the urban poor—an approach that goes beyond the rhetoric of "community policing" to a method of engagement that promotes trust, healing, and genuine partnership (Alexander, 2011, p. 233).

> Compassionate policing means treating all people with dignity and respect, as human beings.

Alexander does not argue that law enforcement officers should abandon their duties or treat disadvantaged and marginalized people with leniency; she argues that they treat such people with fairness and compassion. Compassionate policing, in her view, simply means men and women who treat all people with the dignity and respect that we are all owed as members of the human race; treat all people like human beings. This is not a new idea. Consider the following passage from Hermann Goldstein (1977):

> Perhaps more important than these administrative devices, however, is the need for aggressive advocacy by police leaders of a quality of police service that is more responsive to the diverse needs of the community, that is more sensitive to humanitarian concerns, and that reflects a full awareness of the delicate nature of the police function in a democracy (Goldstein, 1977, p. 105).

This is the hallmark of wise, *compassionate policing*, and it begins with a firm understanding of what the police are actually working to accomplish.

Law enforcement focuses on law and order; this is a place of comfort for those who find themselves overwhelmed by today's rhetoric and dissent. It gives them the ability to filter calls for service based on whether or not a law violation is indicated, labeling "service" as not the business of the police. Consider a typical response to a landlord tenant dispute, where an officer may say, "Those are civil problems. We deal with law violators." The law enforcement perspective is reflected in the recruiting and in-service training programs, where the indifferent application of the law and procedures describing how to arrest people properly are taught. The law enforcement perspective is intended to be color-blind with the decision to arrest based on the severity of the offense, the demeanor of the perpetrator, and the need to protect society from the criminal predator.

The danger here is that when the police aspire to "color-blindness," they give up faith in their own humanity and the ability to care and show concern for others. A relentless focus on the application of the law as well as the dysfunctional aspects of the police subculture creates a danger of embracing a belief that some people are *less than human* and can be treated as if they are undeserving of their God-given status as human beings and undeserving of respect (Alexander, 2011, p. 243).

> A relentless focus on procedure and the application of the rule of law can result in a tendency on the part of police officers to view some people as something less than human, undeserving of dignity and respect.

Today, officers are thrust into situations that routinely take them out of their comfort zone; examples of this can be found on "YouTube" nearly every day. Applying law enforcement tactics, particularly use of force, in situations that require expert "people skills" sometimes ends in disaster. Given the lack of education, training, and the current recruitment focus of most police agencies, it is actually amazing and a credit to the wisdom of the typical police officer that even more tragic events do not occur.

A Path Toward Compassionate Policing

Compassionate policing means that officers are sympathetic to the unique standing, attitudes, and point-of-view of the people they encounter. Compassionate police officers demonstrate concern for the suffering and misfortunes of others, and respond in a manner that communicates pity, empathy, and sensitivity. Chuck Wexler, Executive Director of the Police Executive Research Forum (PERF), provides additional targeted insight:

> This sense of ever-present danger has shaped police training, tactics and culture in ways that can lead to responses that are neither proportional nor necessary in situations that don't involve guns. We need to rethink our tactics in such circumstances.
>
> Perhaps the best example is the so-called 21-foot rule. In many police departments, officers are trained to be prepared to shoot if they are within 21 feet of someone with a knife. This can lead to what's known among the police as a "lawful but awful" response.
>
> This is because the legal standard used in police shootings allows prosecutors and grand juries to conclude that although an officer's shooting of a suspect may be questionable, it isn't criminal.

In developing what has becomes known as the 30 Guiding Principles, designed to take police use of force to a higher standard, PERF (2016) states:

> We looked at how officers are trained for situations in which a person is armed with an edged weapon like a knife. Although these confrontations can be extremely dangerous, the police should not automatically handle these people as they would a gunman. Often there are ways to defuse these confrontations without resorting to deadly force.
>
> The key for the police in such circumstances is to slow things down: to ask questions rather than bark orders, to speak in a normal tone, to summon additional resources if necessary. Pulling out a gun on an anxious person may unintentionally raise his level of stress. In "suicide by cop" confrontations, this can make a bad situation worse.
>
> We found that this approach works—not only in Britain, where police officials say it has increased the safety of officers and the public, but also in places like New York City and in Camden, N.J. (The Police Executive Research Forum, 2014).

This is what is meant by *compassionate law enforcement*—the ability to look beyond the law to a higher sense of moral authority and justice in consideration of the unique conditions that affect individuals and groups. The question is whether the American system of law, having equality as the foundational principle, will allow officers to make what can easily be considered arbitrary decisions when law violations are indicated. Additional illustrative guidelines are also offered in PERFs 30 principles, which includes the following statements:

1. The sanctity of human life should be at the heart of everything an agency does.
2. Adopt de-escalation as formal agency policy. De-escalation is the preferred, tactically sound approach in many critical incidents. De-escalation policy should also include discussion of proportionality—using distance and cover, using tactical re-positioning, slowing down situations that do not pose an immediate threat, calling for supervisory and other resources, etc. Officers must be trained in these principles, and their supervisors should hold them accountable for adhering to them.
3. Respect the sanctity of life by promptly rendering first aid. Officers should render first aid to subjects who have been injured as a result of police actions and should promptly request medical assistance.
4. Prohibit use of deadly force against individuals who pose a danger only to themselves. Agencies should prohibit the use of deadly force, and carefully consider the use of many less-lethal options against individuals who pose a danger only to themselves and not to other members of the public or to officers. Officers should be prepared to exercise considerable discretion in order to wait as long as necessary so that the situation can be resolved peacefully (Police Executive Research Forum, 2016).

Recognizing Compassion in Policing

A new understanding about what is needed in our law enforcement agencies today is that we need men and women of goodwill, armed with experience that consists of thoughtful contemplation about the role of the police, which is backed-up with a level of emotional maturity and wisdom that is reinforced and supported by supervisors and police leaders. "The trained law enforcement officer knows how to enforce the law. *The wise police officer not only knows how, but also when to enforce the law, employing sound alternatives to arrest when warranted based on wise judgment*"

(Author). The compassionate police officer can be recognized not by the number of arrests they make, but by the goodwill they generate, both within and outside of the police agency.

> The wise police officer not only know how to enforce the law but when, employing sound alternatives to enforcement in the quest for better police community relations.

Conflict management in the law enforcement role means recognizing the potential for resentment, distrust and animosity in advance and taking affirmative steps to mitigate it. In the policing role, officers can be effective as mediators without jeopardizing their fundamental mission.

EMOTIONAL INTELLIGENCE AND THE POWER OF RESPECT

Aristotle*

Anyone can become angry—that is easy.
But to be angry with the right person, to the right degree,
at the right time, for the right purpose,
and in the right way—this is not easy. —Aristotle

Emotional Intelligence **(EI)** has been defined as the ability to recognize and monitor one's own emotions, to differentiate between emotional responses, and to use emotional information to manage thinking and behavior. Those who master

* Image labeled for unrestricted use.

these skills also have a noticeable ability to recognize, monitor, and manage the emotions of others. One can easily see how important this skill can be in the law enforcement and policing functions.

> Emotional intelligence is the ability to recognize our own emotions, control them, and to recognize emotions in others. Ultimately, the goal is to control the emotions of others by being in complete command of our own.

When officers can sense the build-up of an emotional response in themselves, they can more effectively manage their own behavior and avoid unwise actions. When law enforcement officers develop the capacity to read the emotions of others, they will be much better equipped to interact with others in a productive and positive way; they will have the ability to build better relationships and enhance trust.

> Emotional Intelligence is emotional recognition and control. The Intelligence Quotient is a measure of reasoning ability. Both of these are necessary for "wise" policing.

Conversely, the *Intelligence Quotient* **(IQ)** is a measure of an individual's reasoning ability, which is determined through standardized tests.

Individuals who have high levels of emotional intelligence are easily recognized. They have a certain way of thinking, feeling and behaving. Some characteristics of these individuals include:

- Having the ability to successfully manage difficult situations.
- Expressing themselves clearly.
- Easily gaining respect from others.
- Having influence over other people.
- Keeping cool under pressure
- Recognizing their own emotional reactions to people, situations, and events.
- Knowing how to say the right thing to get great results.
- Knowing how to be positive even in difficult times.
- Motivating themselves and others (Stein, 2009).

In comparison, people who score high on standardized intelligence tests tend to be good problem-solvers, are adaptable, strive for perfection, and are comfortable being alone. Cognitive intelligence—what these standardized tests are designed to measure—focuses on the ability to think rationally and deal effectively with problems and the environment.

IQ and EI are not mutually exclusive as most successful people possess the characteristics of both. However, these are very different concepts. The fundamental difference is that emotionally intelligent people center their thoughts on the other person rather than themselves and their own needs.

Policing is a people business; as such, *officers are judged on their actions and behavior much more so than on what they know*. Actions and behavior that continually demonstrate care for others is much more important than the ability to memorize the vehicle code. The implication is that highly successful police officers may not know everything about law enforcement and policing, but they do know how to interact with people.

> A big part of wisdom and maturity is developing the capacity to view ourselves as others see us. Stepping outside of ourselves and observing how we interact and communicate with others.

Emotional intelligence has been conceptualized as a fundamental aspect of *wisdom*. As people mature, they develop the ability to see themselves as others see them, *as objects existing in an indifferent world*. When people develop the ability to see beyond their own circumstance, they recognize the value of cooperative relations with others and they focus less on themselves and more on the needs of others. In this way, they become more sensitive to how their words, actions, and behaviors impact those with whom they engage.

This maturity is not wholly a function of age, but rather of life experience. Interacting with others and being challenged by attitudes and points-of-view that are different from their own helps them develop this wisdom in much the same way as routine exercise builds physical strength. Conversely, those who are isolated from the outside world and prefer the company of those who only hold similar beliefs, attitudes, and points-of-view as themselves may find their emotional wisdom delayed. Rather than finding the potential for self-development in their interactions with people who are different than themselves, they find anxiety, stress, and frustration, reverting back to their comfort zone of sameness in order to avoid the exertion much in the same way as people give into the desire to remain in their comfortable beds rather than getting up in the morning and exercising.

> Individuals who are only comfortable with individuals, ideas, attitudes, and points of view similar to their own are not "wise." Facing view-point diversity head-on helps us develop understanding, tolerance and wisdom.

Emotional Awareness

Individuals cannot change or improve their behavior if they are unaware of their emotions. Individuals who are emotionally self-aware know how they, themselves, are feeling at any given point in time; they can express their feelings and beliefs to others easily; they know their own capabilities, skills, and limitations, and they get along well with others, having many friends and acquaintances. They also deal with stress well and rarely feel anxious; they are happy people and look at the bright side of things (Goleman, 2005).

Managing Emotions

Emotions are fundamental characteristics of human beings. They protect people and guide them in situations that present an immediate threat to safety. Before human beings have a chance to think things through (i.e., engage their intellect), there is an emotional-instinctive response to a threat (i.e., a challenge, an insult, or a sudden stimulus). This automatic reaction takes the form of the fight or flight response of the limbic system: when facing a threat, people will respond automatically. Consider the following true story:

> A new police officer is out on a late night patrol and is conducting a routine check at the high-school. He observes an open door at the rear of the building, so he calls it in as a possible burglary because there have been a number of break-ins recently. As he enters the building, he hears a strange noise, so his anticipation and fear engages. Based upon his training and the fact that this could be a forcible felony, he draws his side-arm and moves down the darkened hall carefully scanning the area with his flashlight. As he rounds a corner, the light falls onto a large dark figure just ahead, and before he can think, he discharges his sidearm in that direction, striking the statue of Abraham Lincoln, center mass.

In this case, fear took over his behavioral response and led to what could easily have been a tragedy. These are the kinds of situations officers face on a daily basis, situations where passion can overwhelm reason and lead to crisis.

Bad Emotions

Emotions have wisely guided humans throughout evolutionary history. The fact that humans have survived and prospered as a species is a testament to the value of these instinctive drives, mainly fight or flight. However, civilization has demanded that reason take on a guiding role in human affairs. *Bad emotions can lead to bad behavior.* The ability to recognize emotions and manage behavioral tendencies that do not serve individuals well is a critical aspect of interpersonal relations, especially in high-risk professions like law enforcement and policing.

The Two Brains

Thought and feeling are governed by two distinct aspects of mental and physiological processes, but both are required in a healthy human being. Thought is a function of cognitive ability, commonly measure by the intelligence quotient (IQ). This is where our ability to reason lies. The prefrontal cortex, one of the last parts of the brain to develop, contains our ability to think, reason, and analyze facts—what psychologists call *working memory*.

> **Our ability to think and reason is a function of "working memory." Intense emotion, especially fear, hinders working memory and our ability to think.**

Feelings and passion reside in a different part of the brain called the limbic area, which is one of the first areas of the brain to develop. Strong emotion has its origin in the limbic brain, and these automatic survival instincts short circuit the thinking part of the brain, disabling working memory. When human beings are in a highly passionate state, they simply cannot think straight, and the brain responds by placing individual survival above reason. It is the same primitive and instinctive process that causes a dog to attack when cornered and threatened (Selemon, 1995).

In studies of students who had above-average IQs but were having trouble in school (thus considered "At Risk"), it was found that they were anxious, impulsive, and disruptive. This suggested a problem in the functioning of the prefrontal cortex; likely, the thinking part of the brain was deficient in controlling the primitive or limbic emotional urges. These children were identified as at risk for drug abuse, criminal activity, and academic failure because of their overall behavior. However, the problem is not a deficiency in their cognitive ability, but in the ability to control their emotions (Damasio, 1994; Goleman, 1995).

Emotions Matter

Despite their sometimes debilitating effects, feelings are indispensable for rational decision making. Emotional learning is the meeting point between the rational brain and the emotional brain, both of which are needed. According to Damasio (1994), emotions point people in the right direction, where the rational brain's logic can then be best used.

> While the world often confronts us with an unwieldy array of choices (How should you invest your retirement savings? Whom should you

marry?), the emotional learning that life has given us (such as the memory of a disastrous investment or a painful breakup) sends signals that streamline the decision by eliminating some options and highlighting others at the onset. In this way, the emotional brain is as involved in reasoning as is the thinking brain (Goleman, 1995, p. 28).

The idea of a balance between the two brains, thinking and feeling, resonates more as harmony between the two. The initial fight or flight response and those signals that point individuals in the right direction lead to better problem-solving because the thinking part of the brain takes over (Goleman, 2005).

This is all part of what can be labeled *cognitive restructuring,* a process by which individuals grab hold of their irrational or distorted thoughts and replace them with healthier thoughts that enable them to avoid dysfunctional behaviors. Emotionally intelligent people know how to "change their own minds" as opposed to allowing others, events, or situations to take control. Wise individuals understand that "you are what you think" (Stein, 2009, p. 80; Beck, 1999).

EMPATHY AND POLICING

One of the hallmarks of emotional intelligence is knowing how others feel. This is a dangerous endeavor for police officers as it requires a high level of emotional control to avoid being drug down into someone else's emotional abyss. The law enforcement role has traditionally been governed by the requirement to be wholly objective, dispassionate, and even indifferent to the needs of individuals and groups before the law. To do otherwise invites criticism of acting in an arbitrary manner or, more simply, taking sides.

> Professional law enforcement requires that officers be wholly objective in their dealings with individuals, never appearing to take sides. Effective policing requires that officers avoid appearing indifferent. How can these be reconciled? Discuss.

Highly effective policing requires that the officer avoid appearing indifferent, while at the same time remaining objective and rational; accomplishing this requires a high level of emotional intelligence. Sympathy is defined as the awareness of how a person feels toward someone else and a recognition of how situations and events affect them. *Sympathy* shows that an officer cares about another person's situation. *Empathy* is a connection with another person, demonstrating that the officer understands how someone feels. Police officers who empathize with others run the risk of actually experiencing the same emotions—sorrow, anger, resentment, anxiety, apprehension and even fear. The risks for a police officer who has not mastered control of her or his own emotions are profound.

Sympathy means showing that we care about another person's problems or situation. Empathy is connecting with other people, attempting to actually experience what they are experiencing so that we can fully understand. Complete command of one's emotions is critical.

The goal is to help the individual out of his or her emotional abyss, and a good way to do this is to make a statement that acknowledges how the other person is feeling at that moment. For example, "I can see that you are having a rough day. To me it looks like you are very angry. Is this true? Would you like to tell me about it?"

When skillfully done, such a statement can effectively disarm an angry or upset person, it sends the message that their existence and pain has been acknowledged. The officer does not have to agree or descend into the emotional abyss with them, merely acknowledging the other person validates their existence as a fellow human being and can assuage their emotional crisis.

Social intelligence begins with the understanding that emotions are contagious.

MANAGING OTHER PEOPLE'S EMOTIONS

Social intelligence is reflective of a person's ability to understand how other people feel and to influence the emotions and behavior of those people. Those who seek to manage the emotions of others understand that being able to control their own emotions is key because *emotions are contagious.*

> We **transmit** and **catch** moods from each other in what amounts to a subterranean economy of the psyche in which some encounters are toxic, some nourishing. This emotional exchange is typically at a subtle, almost imperceptible level, the way a salesperson says "thank you" can leave us feeling ignored, resented, or genuinely welcomed and appreciated. We catch feelings from one another as though they were some kind of social virus (Goleman, 1995).

A police officer who is angry is very likely to spread that anger to those with whom they encounter and interact. Conversely, a police officer who is friendly, pleasant, and cooperative is likely to lessen the anger of those with whom they interact.

> We send emotional signals in every encounter, and those signals affect those we are with. The more adroit we are socially, the better we control the signals we send; the reserve of polite society is, after all, simply a means to ensure that no disturbing emotional leakage will unsettle the encounter (a social rule that, when brought into the domain of intimate

> relationships, is stifling). Emotional intelligence includes managing this exchange; "popular" and "charming" are terms we use for people whom we like to be with because their emotional skills make us feel good. People who are able to help others soothe their feelings have an especially valued social commodity; they are the souls others turn to when in greatest emotional need. We are all part of each other's tool kit for emotional change, for better or for worse (Goleman, 1995, p. 115).

> Managing other people's emotions is actually quite simple. Because emotions are contagious, simply display the emotional state you want in the other person. Be consistent and patient and they will eventually come around and adopt the same emotional state.

Managing emotions in others is accomplished simply by displaying the desired emotions, mood, attitude, and demeanor (mindset) that one wants to see in others. Individuals unconsciously imitate the emotions displayed by others. This begins with the outward signs of emotion and mood as indicated by behavior. Officers need to be in complete control of themselves, displaying the desired behavior that will be imitated by others. Once the other person begins behaving in the desired manner, their actual emotions, attitude, and demeanor will change to match their behavior.

> How does this magical transmission occur? The most likely answer is that we unconsciously imitate the emotions we see displayed by someone else through an out-of-awareness motor mimicry of their facial expression, gestures, tone of voice, and other nonverbal markers of emotion. Through this imitation people re-create in themselves the mood of the other person (a low-key version of the Stanislavsky method) in which actors recall gestures, movements, and other expressions of an emotion they have felt strongly in the past in order to evoke those feelings once again (Goleman, 1995).

Policing is a people business; officers who have the ability to soothe the exaggerated feelings of others are looked upon with envy by their fellow officers and sought out by those in the community who know them (or at least know of them). If officers continually try to dominate people they will fail in both the law enforcement and policing missions. Conversely, the wise officer understands that the path to cooperation, minimizing resentment, and building better relationships requires skill in recognizing, controlling, and redirecting the dysfunctional emotional responses that interfere with *rapport.*

BUILDING RELATIONSHIPS

Today, police officers are charged with the responsibility of *building better relationships* in the communities they serve (President's Task Force on 21st Century

Policing, 2015). Proponents of the professional model of policing may argue that police officers should maintain a professional distance from corrupting influences and political considerations. This attitude has led to the acceptance of police officer behavior characterized as a kind of aloofness that creates the perception that the police officer is superior, indifferent, and calloused. This behavior drives a wedge between officers and those they serve. However, the best police officers have always recognized the need to establish and maintain relationships in the community, despite professional reforms. They have understood that such arrogant behavior undermines relationships in the same way that uncaring behaviors destroy marriages.

> An early warning signal that a marriage is in danger is harsh criticism. In a healthy marriage, husband and wife feel free to voice a complaint. But too often in the heat of anger, complaints are expressed in a destructive fashion as an attack on the spouse's character (Gottman, 1994).

Building relationships in the community requires mutual respect. Criticism undermines respect between the police and the community in the same way that it does in a marriage. When police officers begin to characterize people who happen to live in certain areas, they are inadvertently attacking the character of those who live there. Taken to the extreme, such characterizations can lead to dehumanizing behavior on the part of officers, destroying any hope of reconciliation or a productive relationship. In the same way as a wife levels harsh criticism against her husband, calling him selfish and thoughtless, instead of simply stating that his tardiness made her feel unimportant, the police officer's harsh criticism of "those people" is a sign of a troubled relationship.

> Criticizing others leads to attitudes about their character, prejudice and bias. Professionals do not criticize other people's character, they identify inappropriate or problematic behavior, offering sound alternatives. Why do people seem to have a natural tendency to criticize others? Discuss.

Words can be a sure sign that the relationship is in trouble, but feelings conveyed non-verbally are much more common indicators. Contempt can be conveyed in tone-of-voice, body positioning, and gestures. In many cases, the positioning that officers are taught in the police academy conveys unintended meaning. The ready-stance, with one foot slightly back, weight evenly distributed and hands at the ready, means the officer is ready to fight. When the goal is cooperation and relationship building, officers need to be aware of the non-verbal messages that they send.

> Contempt comes easily with anger; it is usually expressed not just in words used, but also in tone of voice and as angry expression. It's most

> obvious form, of course, is mockery or insult—"jerk," "bitch," "wimp." But just as hurtful is the body language that conveys contempt, particularly the sneer or curled lip that are the universal facial signals for disgust, or a rolling of the eyes, as if to say, "Oh, brother!" (Goleman, 1995).

When faced with harsh criticism, contempt, angry words, intimidation, and even threats, many police officers have learned to back-off and refrain from lashing out physically. The harsh reality is that today people stand ready to record the officer's reaction to threats and upload any inappropriate response to YouTube. As an alternative to lashing out, officers may stonewall; this takes the form of withdrawing from the conversation, remaining silent and displaying a "stony expression;" "stonewalling sends a powerful, unnerving message, something like a combination of icy distance, superiority, and distaste" (Goleman, 1995, p. 198). A better alternative is to manage the apparent conflict, and this begins with understanding the point-of-view that is the basis for the criticism. A question such as "Why would you say that to me?" or "Why would you think that?" may cause the person to pause, think and reflect; perhaps providing additional clues to their point-of-view.

When police officers develop the ability to see the world as others do, their ability to manage other people's emotions and the conflicts that result will be significantly enhanced. The ability to step into someone else's world is an important facet of personal integrity.

INTEGRITY & UNCONDITIONAL RESPECT

Having a strong moral grounding based on sound principles, such as honesty, decency, fairness, and honor, are the hallmarks of integrity. Conversely, those who draw their values from social norms (what is acceptable at the moment) lack integrity (e.g., those who believe it's acceptable to join a gang and hate the police). These individuals will suffer from the following:

- They will automatically feel threatened by and have disdain toward others who draw their values from sources different from their own, such as a professional code of ethics, an oath, or religious beliefs.
- They will not possess the ability to have **unconditional respect** for others (i.e., seeing others and treating others as human beings), and they will blame others for the contempt that they feel toward them.

- They will automatically be blinded to the deteriorating social values in which they are immersed.
- They will lack the courage to stand on enduring principles—tested by time and circumstance—of right and wrong against the social tide (Colwell, 2010).

People who lack integrity *allow themselves to be deceived* into believing that their behavior is acceptable. They reason their way out of moral dilemmas by telling themselves that such behavior is common; that those who would criticize their behavior are old-fashioned or out-of-touch; and that their behavior is somehow justified in light of current social trends. This lack of integrity manifests itself in law enforcement when officers feel justified in being untruthful in case reports and activity logs; when officers speed through traffic without cause; and when officers break the law in order to enforce it (usually by abusing or violating an individual's constitutional rights). Conversely, integrity rests within the individual and is a product of wisdom and character strength—the character to stand against prevailing social thought. The concept of *unconditional respect* provides a framework for understanding the kind of personality this requires.

> When individuals have the integrity to identify right from wrong and not get swept up in a social tide of self-justification, self-righteousness, and contempt toward others, the desire to see and treat others as human beings surfaces in their character. This desire is expressed as unconditional respect for all people and the courage to confront those who treat others as with disdain (Colwell, 2010, p. 17).

> To have character means having the ability to stand on principle, against prevailing thought or pressure from others to conform.

Integrity assumes the courage to act in the face of potential social alienation. One of the most powerful motivating forces for police officers has been acceptance into the police subculture; all new officers strive for acceptance as it speaks to a very human need—that is a deep desire to develop, maintain, and protect one's standing in the social group. However, some officers fall victim to manipulation and pressure to conform to values that are the product of rationalization based on self-deception, self-centeredness, and the ease of taking the path of least resistance. Combating this tendency requires commitment to a set of ethical standards that are consistent with enduring moral principles, such as those found in the law enforcement officers' code of ethics and many other sources.

There are many historical examples of individuals who have acted with integrity in the face of a social tide that leads most down the path of least resistance. The names include Mahatma Gandhi, Nelson Mandela, and Dr. Martin Luther King, Jr. These individuals acted in a manner that provided constructive social influence and inspiration, which led to positive social change. Rather than taking the path of least resistance, they stood for **enduring principles** that transformed culture. Police officers can do the same thing by employing a simple principle in everything that they do; that principle is called *unconditional respect* (Colwell, 2010).

Building unconditional respect begins with self-awareness. This provides officers with the ability to not be influenced by the behavior of others. It arms them with the ability to demonstrate respect even in the face of extremely disrespectful behavior directed at themselves. It gives the officer *response-ability*[3], meaning that their response is *their* choice and not the product of someone else's behavior, bias or prejudice.

According to Colwell and Huth (2010) building the integrity and character necessary for unconditional respect involves understanding the following principles:

- I am a human being, endowed with the gift of self-examination (self-awareness). In other words, I have a conscience and am therefore responsible for my thoughts, words, actions, and inaction.
- I am not a simple stimulus-response mechanism. I cannot simply blame others for my reactions and responses.
- I must face the fact that I have prejudices, loyalties, desires, and fears that cloud my judgment and shroud me in self-deception. Said another way, when I am wrong I will most certainly deceive myself with self-justification (rationalization) and/or blame other people and circumstances. I will naturally assume I am right at my most wrong points (p. 5).

> Unconditional respect means respecting others as human beings without pre-condition. The ability to do this rests on a foundation of self-respect. One must have respect for themselves before they can have unconditional respect for others.

3 (Covey, 1989)

Unconditional respect should not be understood as a purely altruistic[4] concept; *one cannot effectively demonstrate respect for others if they do not first respect themselves.* In the same way that assertive, relevant, and respectful communication demonstrates respect for others, the practice of assertive, relevant, and respectful communication with one's self fine tunes the self-image. Greater self-awareness enables individuals to become cognizant of the fact that they alone are responsible for their own thoughts, words, and actions and that they alone are responsible for their own prejudices, loyalties, desires, fears, and rationalizations. Principles provide guidance to stand in opposition to contradictory social movements or fads; they give people the ability to display courage, integrity, and unconditional respect by providing a center. Steven Covey (1989) speaks about a personal center in this way:

> By centering our lives on correct principles, we create a solid foundation for development of the four life supporting factors.
>
> Our *security* comes from knowing that, unlike other centers based on people or things which are subject to frequent and immediate change, correct principles do not change. We can depend on them.
>
> Principles don't react to anything. They don't get mad and treat us differently. They won't divorce us or run away with our best friend. They aren't out to get us. They don't depend on the behavior of others, the environment, or the current fad for their validity. Principles don't die. They aren't here one day and gone the next. They can't be destroyed by fire, earthquake or theft.
>
> The *wisdom* and *guidance* that accompany principle-centered living come from correct maps, from the way things really are, have been, and will be. Correct maps enable us to clearly see where we want to go and how to get there. We can make our decisions using the correct data that will make their implementation possible and meaningful.
>
> The personal *power* that comes from principle-centered living is the power of a self-aware, knowledgeable, proactive individual, unrestricted by attitudes, behaviors, and actions of others or by many of the circumstances and environmental influences that limit other people (Covey, 1989).

Common themes run through the discussion of emotional intelligence, unconditional respect, and principle-centered living. Humanistic policing

[4] Altruism refers to the belief in, or practice of, displaying a selfless concern for others. Living for the sake of others and not for ourselves.

incorporates these themes as the foundation of the character and behavior of the very best police officers. The principle of unconditional respect provides a center that protects the police officer from physical, emotional, and career-ending threats; it is a tactic that the best officers learn to develop.

THE "TACTIC" OF RESPECT

Emotionally intelligent individuals who practice human relations skills understand that they have a choice in how to respond to others. They can choose to be rude, condescending, and abusive, or they can choose unconditional respect. Thinking individuals recognize that the former will likely result in dysfunctional outcomes, but the latter, choosing to display respect for themselves and others (even those acting rude, condescending, abusive, and even threatening), **have the real power** in any given situation.

Expecting others to respect the police automatically today is unrealistic; respect cannot be demanded because it has to be earned. Due to no fault of their own, individual police officers—thanks to the highly publicized actions of a few—should not expect deference or respect from many individuals that they will encounter. Knowing this, police officers may question whether they should respect the disrespectful people they may encounter. Do other people have to earn the respect of the police? "Chip" Huth (2010), who at the time of this writing was a SWAT team leader, put it this way:

> True respect is "earned" by virtue of our individual existence. In a very real sense, respect can be considered the realization of another's intrinsic value as a human being and the accompanying degree of unpredictability—and thus danger—that comes with being human; therefore, it is possible to respect someone without requiring any particular behavior on his part. It is a fundamental truth; one can choose to have regard for another, while still recognizing the presence of differing value systems and memory schema that render the other person potentially unpredictable (p. 25).

> How others view us and their attitudes toward us are most often a function of how we view ourselves and our role. If you wish to be respected, then act respectfully toward others. If you wish to be viewed as a professional, then look and act like a professional.

Sound, principle-centered living helps police officers protect themselves, not only from physical threats to their own safety, but from the perils of the job, including the dysfunctional aspects of the police subculture. Consider that the police are often viewed as an occupying force in inner city neighborhoods. It is not the people who live in those neighborhoods who created this perception; it was actually the police themselves because *that is how they, themselves, view their role.*

The beliefs, attitudes, and point-of view of the police became a self-fulling prophecy resulting in the "us vs. them" mentality that, in turn, allows officers to adopt an adversarial demeanor with the very people who need them the most.

In order to feel comfortable, too many officers seek to distance themselves, first, physically by eliminating officer residency requirements, then mentally, and finally emotionally. This distancing allows officers to dehumanize those who engage in abhorrent behavior, which then leads to the dehumanization of everyone who lives in the area or displays similar characteristics to those who live there (i.e., race, national origin, religious affiliation, or even gender identification). Dehumanization can then result in abuse, mistreatment, and other forms of police deviance that can ruin an officer's career, warrant that an officer be convicted of a crime, lead to successful lawsuits against the officer, and, of course, injure or kill the officer.

> It has become fashionable for officers to adopt an adversarial perspective toward the public, especially when they perceive the public as being unsupportive or overly critical of their actions. This distorted perception reinforces the idea that the police are a separate entity from the public, and this can result in a pattern of self-justification that can be used to legitimize rudeness, a lack of empathy, and, in some cases, illegal behavior. This kind of unconscious programming—reaffirmed over hundreds of interactions and years of typecasting—is the inevitable result of a police culture that has slowly drifted away from a service mentality. Having the ability to change the oil in your car does not make you a mechanic. Having the ability to use force effectively—as a soldier or police officer—does not make one a warrior. A warrior understands that the most important battle to be fought is an internal one. It is a battle against our own tendency to be self-deceived about ourselves and others that demands the warrior's attention, above all else. The key to understanding others—even our enemies—resides within us, and that knowledge and pursuit of the animal[5] that will facilitate it are what define a warrior (Colwell, 2010, p. 45).

Unconditional respect provides an additional layer of "body armor" for officers, protecting them, not only from physical attack, but from the other hazards endemic to police work.

---

5 Anima refers to the part of the psyche that is directed inward, toward the subconscious.

Chapter Summary

Human relations is the study of human behavior—why self-image, beliefs, attitudes, prejudices, and bias sometimes cause problems in professional and personal contacts and relationships. For the police officer, competency rests in the understanding that all productive work is done through relationships. The very first relationship that needs to be cultivated is with the self, then the particular individual(s) to whom we are trying, and then to the group(s) with whom we associate.

Rapport is the hallmark of great communicators; it can be described as a harmonious and reciprocal mini-relationship between individuals or an individual and a group. It takes the form of a connection or linkage, where the parties are in-sync with each other.

Non-verbal communication relates to the voice pitch, speed, tone, volume, and inflections used. It can also relate to body posture, proximity, facial expressions, eye movement, dress, physical contact, gestures, and even how people orient their feet. Everyone has their own communication style, and it is important for us to understand the signals we convey to others in both the verbal and non-verbal realm. The master communicator has the ability to flex their communication style based on the situation.

The ability to manage conflict is a characteristic of great police officers and can be the foundation of great police-community relations. Conflict situations present an opportunity to practice human relations skills with the goal of limiting the potential for deeper conflict or violence and enhancing positive relationship building. Conflict has triggers, and these triggers vary depending on the characteristics of the individual, their self-esteem, self-worth, and motivations. Recognizing potential triggers leads to the root causes of dysfunctional conflict. The root causes can be attributed to a history of dysfunctional conflict, unmet expectations of one party or both, self-perceptions, emotions, or the lack of emotional control. Police officers are not equipped to engage in such analysis; however, they should always assume that dysfunctional conflict has deeper sources than what is being put forth in times of crisis.

The professional, community oriented police agency strives to meet the expectations of the whole community in setting enforcement priorities; the professional but non-community oriented police agency sets its priorities according to what may be professional standards, but these standards may not be responsive to the specific community that it serves. The non-professional police agency does neither. There are distinct differences between groups of people in communities. Economic/cultural differentiation or frameworks enables us to understand how these broad groups view the world, their own lives, and the police. These different economic groups are: the rich, the middle class, and the poor. Each of these broad generalizations provide unique challenges for the police in terms of relationship building because each group has distinct points-of-view.

The law enforcement function can have the impact of de-humanizing others. There are subtle, and not so subtle, pressures within this function and within the police subculture that sometimes allow officers to step beyond what would be considered acceptable moral boundaries. Compassionate policing simply means treating all people with dignity and respect.

Emotional Intelligence (EI) has been defined as the ability to recognize and monitor one's own emotions, to differentiate between emotional responses, and to use emotional information to manage thinking and behavior. Those who master these skills also have a noticeable ability to recognize, monitor, and manage the emotions of others. Emotional awareness is the ability of officers to know how they personally are feeling at any given point in time; they can express their feelings and beliefs to others easily. They know their own capabilities, skills, and limitations, and they get along well with others, having many friends and acquaintances.

The law enforcement role has traditionally been governed by the requirement to be wholly objective, dispassionate, and even indifferent to the needs of individuals and groups before the law. To do otherwise invites criticism of acting in an arbitrary manner, or more simply, taking sides. Highly effective policing requires that the officer avoid appearing indifferent, while at the same time remaining objective and rational; accomplishing this requires a high level of emotional intelligence. *Sympathy* is defined as the awareness of how we feel toward someone else, a recognition of how situations and events affect them. Sympathy shows that an officer cares about another person's situation. *Empathy* is a connection with another person, demonstrating that the officer understands how someone feels.

To have a strong moral grounding based on sound principles, such as honesty, decency, fairness, and honor, is the hallmark of integrity. Conversely, those who draw their values from social norms—what is acceptable at the moment—lack integrity.

Emotionally intelligent individuals who practice human relations skills understand that they have a choice in how to respond to others. They can chose to be rude, condescending, and abusive, or they can choose unconditional respect.

Thinking individuals recognize that the former will likely result in dysfunctional outcomes; the latter, those who choose to display respect for disrespectful or abrasive others, have the real power in any given situation.

Sound principle-centered living helps police officers protect themselves, not only from physical threats to their own safety, but also from the perils of the job and the dysfunctional aspects of the police subculture. Unconditional respect provides an additional layer of "body armor" for officers, protecting them, not only from physical attack, but also from the other hazards endemic to police work.

Bibliography

Alexander, M. (2011). *The New Jim Crow: Mass Incarceration in the Age of Colorblindness.* New York: The New Press.

Beck, A. (1999). *Prisoners of Hate.* New York: Harper-Collins.

Colwell, J.L. (2010). *Unleashing the Power of Unconditional Respect.* New York: Taylor and Francis.

Covey, S. (1989). *The 7 Habits of Highly Effective People.* New York: Fireside.

Damasio, A. (1994). *Descartes' Error: Emotion, Reason and the Human Brain.* New York: Grosset/Putnam.

Ellis, A. (2004). *Rational Emotive Behavior Therapy.* Albert Ellis Institute.

Final Report of the President's Task Force on 21st Century Policing. (2015). *President's Task Force on 21st Century Policing.* Washington, DC: Office of Community Oriented Policing Services.

Goldstein, H. (1977). *Policing a Free Society.* Cambridge, MA: Ballinger.

Goleman, D. (2005). *Emotional Intelligence: Why It Can Matter More than IQ.* New York: Bantam Books.

Gottman, J. (1994). *Why Marriages Succeed or Fail.* New York: Simon and Schuster.

Knaus, W. (2008). *The Cognitive Behavioral Workbook for Anxiety.* Oakland: New Harbinger Publications, Inc.

Montano-Harmon, M. (1991). Discourse Features of Written Mexican Spanish: Current Research in Contrastive Rhetoric and Its Implications. *Hispania, 74(2)*, 417–425.

Payne, R. (1996). *A Framework for Understanding Poverty, 4th ed.* Highlands, TX: aha! Process, Inc.

Reece, B.L. (2014). *Effective Human Relations: Interpersonal and Organizational Applications, 12th ed.* Mason, OH: Cengage.

Selemon, L.E. (1995). Prefrontal Cortex. *American Journal of Psychology,* 152.

Stein, S.J. (2009). *Emotional Intelligence for Dummies.* Mississauga, ON: Wiley & Sons.

The Police Executive Research Forum. (2014). *Legitimacy and Procedural Justice: A New Element of Police Leadership.* U.S. Department of Justice, Bureau of Justice Assistance.

CHAPTER 8

Managing Conflict in the Law Enforcement and Policing Roles

■ ■ ■

The terms "Law Enforcement" and "Policing" are not interchangeable. They mean different things, imply different roles and require different kinds of people. We just can't arrest our way out of this.

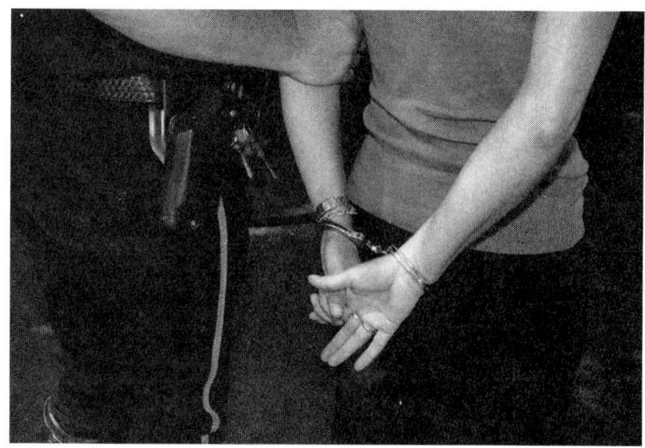

A criminal suspect under arrest*

Learning Outcomes

Upon successful completion of this chapter the student will be able to:

- Explain the difference between law enforcement and policing.
- Define Conflict.
- Explain why conflict management is preferable to conflict resolution.
- Explain why the police response to crime should not be limited to arrest.

* Image labeled for unrestricted use.

- Discuss how law enforcement officers can mitigate conflict and resentment.
- Identify basic mediation strategies police officers can use when called upon to intervene in non-crime related disputes.

Important Concepts

- Conflict Management vs. Conflict Resolution
- View-point Diversity
- Alternatives to Arrest
- Economic Culture
- Generational vs. Situational Poverty
- Mediation
- Self-awareness
- Post-modernist Point-of-view
- Tractable and Intractable Conflict
- In-group and Out-group Distinctions

Questions for Discussion

- What are the implications of police officer behavior in the law enforcement role versus the policing role when it comes to conflict?
- What is meant by view-point diversity and how does it relate to racial, gender, religious and the other commonly understood characteristics?
- What are the stages and characteristics of Freud's personality development model?
- Why do the police have trouble understanding the point-of-view of individuals who have been indoctrinated into post-modernist thought?
- What is in intractable conflict and how can they be best approached?

INTRODUCTION

At the municipal level, police officers are regularly called upon to manage conflict situations. Disputes between co-habitants, such as a husband and wife, domestic partners, parent and child, or other intimate relationships can account for a significant amount of a police officer's compensated time. In addition, significant potential for conflict exists when officers carry out their law enforcement duties. When law enforcement officers are aware of the potential for conflict they may be able to employ more effective mediation strategies. Such strategies may take the form of behavioral tactics normally associated with the concept of procedural justice.

In non-law enforcement situations, police officers are in a unique position to assist community members in managing interpersonal conflict, thereby fulfilling their peace-keeping role more effectively than simply resolving these conflicts by arresting one or both of the parties involved.

Self-awareness is a key aspect of conflict management as those who engage in these efforts are limited by their own perceptions, attitudes and point-of-view. Understanding how an individual's personality develops provides a framework for understanding how individuals become more self-aware.

Our emotions are part of our nature as human beings. They exist as a primitive survival mechanism that drives our behavior in stressful situations. Effectively managing conflict requires that individuals understand their own emotions as well as those with whom they interact.

Conflicts may be tractable or intractable. The former are manageable and may even lend themselves to resolution if a common framework and understanding exists. The parties may share mutual goals, even though they may not recognize those goals. Conversely, intractable conflicts take on a life of their own. They draw the involvement of other parties and in-group loyalties. Emotions often run high with one party accusing the other of immoral and evil behavior, attitudes and points-of-view. In-group and out-group rivalries encourage the disparagement of one group by the other to the point where the competing group is viewed as inhuman.

Managing intractable conflict, such as a prolonged marital dispute, is a challenge that goes beyond the normal capabilities of the police. Where no ongoing commitment to the relationship exists, and where one party refuses to acknowledge or accept the other party's needs, aspirations or point-of-view confrontation and violence may result. Once the conflict reaches the level of destructiveness and violence, the only course of action is to contain the damage and then begin the process of repairing the destruction.

CONFLICT RESOLUTION VS. CONFLICT MANAGEMENT

Conflict resolution seeks to eliminate all forms and types of conflict, whereas *conflict management* accepts that conflict is a natural and often a healthy human condition. If eliminating conflict is unrealistic, conflict management can seek to recognize and limit the negative aspects of conflict that can arise.

> Conflict resolution seeks to eliminate conflict. The assumption is that conflict is bad and something to be avoided. Conflict management recognizes that conflict is inevitable and natural to human interaction. The assumption is that conflict helps us grow and develop as human beings.

Without conflict, problems and opportunities can go unnoticed, creating tension and unnecessary competition that can undermine human relationships. The key is to strike a balance, having just enough conflict to challenge the *status quo* and move forward-progress-without undermining cooperative relationships. As an example, ongoing efforts to enhance view-point diversity[1] can be a source of "positive" conflict.

If all the viewpoints we hear come from people who are like us, we assume that we have the same information and the same perspective. We think we have the right answer and, since we don't hear otherwise, we have no reason to think otherwise. It's these beliefs, according to Phillips, that explain why creativity and innovation are more likely to spring from diverse rather than from identical groups (Phillips, 2014).

> Diversity helps us grow and develop only if it is a diversity of view-points, as opposed to race, gender, age, etc. It does us no good to have a gathering of people who look different, but who all think the same.

The ability to manage conflict arising from view-point diversity and other areas, as opposed to the futility of resolving it, is a critical skill necessary to the maintenance and advancement of social order. Without these skills and the orderly exchange relationships that they serve, life, in the words of Thomas Hobbs (1651), would be "solitary, poor, nasty, brutish and short."

Today many people reject the point of view of others when those viewpoints do not align with their own. Studies have consistently shown that individuals now

---

1 View-point diversity is the natural condition of holding beliefs, values and attitudes that are different from those around you.

are increasingly willing to show contempt for viewpoints other than their own. Opposing the viewpoint of others results in animosity, resentment and conflict (Pew Research Center, 2016).

This problem is not limited just to politics. Confusion over the very meaning, impact and value of diversity is driving a wedge between families, friends and co-workers. A shallow understanding of diversity, one that limits consideration to race, gender, religion, national origin, etc. ignores the real value. We strive to bring people of different backgrounds and experiences together so that all may benefit from the different point-of-view that these groups hold. It is through this understanding, discussed openly and freely, that we all grow and prosper.

Today we are seeing intense conflict that is based upon individuals' group affiliations. Ornstein (2016) outlines some profound implications for this kind of conflict.

> "What I really wanted to emphasize, especially with 'It's even worse than it looks' was that we've moved from partisanship to tribalism. And there's a real difference. You can be a strong partisan—view people on the other side of the aisle as worthy adversaries. And that's partisanship. If you view people on the other side as evil and trying to destroy your way of life, and the enemy, that's tribalism" (Mann, 2016).

Tribalism refers to "a way of being," and implies a strong sense of cultural belongingness or ethnic identity to the extent that the values of one's tribe become more important than intellectual discourse. Those with views that go against one's tribe, or culture, are viewed as the enemy. Tribalism provides intense pressure to conform to accepted ways of thinking and behaving, i.e., "if you are not with us, you are against us." Conflict management provides a way to circumvent the implications of this tribalism by mitigating the behaviors-on the part of law enforcement-that aggravate it and by offering tactics that police officers may use to help mitigate it.

THE TWO ROLES OF THE POLICE

Law enforcement officers spend relatively little time actually enforcing the law. When called upon to do so, the function is straightforward: follow correct procedure. To do otherwise creates injustice, undermines legitimacy, and creates conflict. Policing, however, is different from law enforcement, even though the very same individuals are frequently charged with both responsibilities.

The terms "Law Enforcement" and "Policing" are not interchangeable. They mean different things, imply different roles and require different kinds of people.

We can train individuals to perform the law enforcement function adequately, but policing is a higher-level skill, one that more closely approximates a true profession. Those who excel in the policing function come to the job armed with skills, abilities and competencies that transcend those required in mere law enforcement. Given the increasingly complex nature of our American society, we would do well to recognize the difference (Solar, 2015).

> Justice, in the law enforcement role, amounts to following correct procedure, i.e., the result is just because correct lawful procedures were followed. Justice in the policing role focuses upon outcomes, i.e., going beyond legal procedure to arrive at a fundamentally fair result.

Even when law enforcement activity is carried out according to correct procedures, conflict can still result. Specifically, conflict can occur when the law enforcement officer behaves in a manner that does not support a common view that the officer is acting in a procedurally just way (President's Task Force on 21st Century Policing, 2015).

The professional law enforcement officer understands that properly performing this role in a free and democratic society will likely result in conflict, resistance and resentment. This is simply the nature of the craft. However, the best officers understand how to mitigate these consequences.

CONFLICT MANAGEMENT IN THE LAW ENFORCEMENT ROLE

In the law enforcement role, officers can use behavioral tactics to mitigate and manage conflict. These tactics are intended to generate respect for authority, minimize resentment, and reinforce the legitimacy of the police; *they serve as a foundation for "procedural justice."*[2]

People are more likely to obey the law when they believe that those who are enforcing it have the legitimate authority to tell them what to do . . . the public confers legitimacy only on those they believe are acting in procedurally just ways (President's Task Force on 21st Century Policing, 2015).

This quote, however, uncovers the problem of **perception**. People have different views, attitudes, and opinions concerning what the police should and should not do as well as how they carry out these actions. Some even believe that they possess a legitimate right to disobey the law or resist the police because of their status as members of a marginalized, victimized, or disadvantaged class (tribalism). However, it is inherently unreasonable for society, either society as a

2 Procedural justice refers to the manner in which the police and other legal actors interact with the public. Interactions should affirmatively promote the willingness to listen, respect for the individuals' point-of-view, objective neutrality, and understanding.

whole or individual ethnic, racial, or neighborhood/community groups, to expect a law enforcement officer to be subordinate to these subjective views. However, society can expect cognoscente or "wise" law enforcement officers to be sensitive to them. Indications of this wisdom can be found in the behavior that is displayed by these officers.

> Wise police officers are aware and sensitive to the subjective views that make individuals believe that they have a legitimate right to disobey the law and resist the authority of the police.

For example, one of the most conflict-laden activities for any law enforcement officer is traffic enforcement. Traffic violations are a major source of frustration for citizens and they consistently voice their complaints about poor driving behavior to the chief, who in turn makes this activity a priority in most agencies. Traffic enforcement is a stressful endeavor for officers as well as motorists who are stopped by the police. In recognition of this inherent conflict an agency may establish a specific procedure for the interaction that requires, for example, officers to state their name, identify the agency that employs them, and clearly state the reason for the stop—naming the specific statutory violation.

> Police officers routinely must deal with individuals who are in a state of emotional crisis, the "emotional hijack" where emotions circumvent the ability to think and reason. How should a police officer behave in these situations? Discuss.

This is a good start, but the wise officer will go further by then asking the violator if they were aware of the violation or have any justification for it, such as rushing an injured person to the hospital or other emergency situation. This tactic provides a number of benefits for the police. First, it gives the violator a chance to explain themselves, which is the hallmark of due-process and procedural justice. Second, it neutralizes the emotional hijack[3] common in these situations and encourages the violator to engage the thinking part of their brain. Third, it allows the violator to provide additional information to help guide the officer's discretion; this also aids in prosecution should the violator choose to contest a citation. Following this procedure reinforces the corrective aspect of the law enforcement function and can minimize resentment on the part of the motorist.

At the completion of the transaction (a citation, warning, or arrest), the officer has another opportunity to manage conflict and build legitimacy by asking if the violator has any questions. Rather than simply stating, "Here is your ticket. Follow the instructions. Have a nice day!" the officer askes, "Do you have any

---

[3] An emotional hijack is a condition where an individual's ability to think is overcome by strong emotion or passion.

questions for me?" The *wise* officer actually *listens* to the citizen and responds appropriately.

It is these basic human relations skills that, when appropriately and sincerely employed, can have the impact of minimizing resentment and increasing legitimacy for the law enforcement function on the part of even the most self-absorbed individuals. These behavioral tactics are effective forms of conflict management in the law enforcement role.

RESOLVING CONFLICT WITH ARREST

Law Enforcement officers have always known how to settle conflict situations: arrest. The law provides the authority to arrest persons suspected of crime(s), and to not arrest in situations where an arrest is legally justified has been commonly viewed as neglect of duty. However, what has become painfully obvious is that arrest is often an unwise response to the *problems* officers confront. Conflict management and problem solving focuses on working with the community to uncover areas where arrest may not be the wisest choice in light of the more important goal of improving and maintaining legitimacy as well as police community relations.

When the goal is to maintain an orderly community, arrest may appear to be the best choice for those who choose to violate community norms and laws. However, in an increasingly diverse society, where viewpoints concerning acceptable and unacceptable conduct vary widely, arrest becomes merely the **easiest** rather than the best choice. The hallmark of community based policing places arrest as only one option among other choices. Officer discretion is encouraged when based on an objective analysis of law enforcement priorities as they relate to the needs, tolerances and expectations of the community.

> Arrest is often viewed by the police as the best way to resolve conflict, in reality it is merely the easiest choice.

The primary concerns of the police agency should be the concerns and priorities of the community in both the legal and social context. This implies the need to establish and maintain a partnership between the police and the community, all aspects of the community, where the police acquire an intimate knowledge of the community and its problems. Police managers must continually fight the idea that officers maintain what has been referred to as "professional" distance from the community. The best officers are *part of*, and not *apart from* the community that they serve (Hunter, 2011, p. 316).

The professional police agency recognizes the need to maintain "professional' distance from the community. Why was this needed? Discuss.

Police agencies recognized as "professional" by the Commission on Accreditation for Law Enforcement Agencies (CALEA) or their own State accreditation entity[4] provide guidance to their officers pertaining to *alternatives to arrest.* The professionally minded police agency recognizes that it *cannot arrest its way out* of the problems that it faces today concerning legitimacy, trust and police community relations.

The modern police agency recognizes that the police should be part of the community. Does this undermine professionalism? Discuss.

CONFLICT MANAGEMENT IN THE POLICING ROLE

The vast majority of services that the police provide do not involve crime. The police, as the one-stop-shop for social services, are called whenever a citizen feels the need to employ the coercive authority of the state (Bitner, 1970). Police chiefs have yet to learn how to "just say no" to calls for police service where the coercive power of the police, intimidation, or use of force have absolutely no place, such as in the case of an out-of-control eight-year-old at an elementary school, an actual example. The lack of any reasonable alternatives to police involvement means that police officers need to develop solid conflict management strategies—strategies that will also aid the police in maintaining a positive relationship with the communities they serve.

The "wise" police officer quickly learns some rudimentary conflict management techniques, usually after painful experiences marked by the acquisition of a few injuries and scars. Other officers generally drift from call to call, relying on conflict resolution techniques consisting of determining the primary aggressor (aka, the problem individual) and finding a reason to arrest them, thus ending the conflict. The "path of least resistance" is often the path chosen by officers facing pressure to dispose of calls quickly and move on. Any resistance offered is of no consequence as the police enjoy a monopoly on the use of force when it is legally justified (Crank, 2004). Clearly, this path of least

[4] Law Enforcement Accreditation is offered by many State entities as well as through CALEA. For example, ILEAP stands for the Illinois Law Enforcement Accreditation Program.

resistance goes a long way toward undermining police legitimacy as well as the police community relationship.[5]

Conflict Management Framework: Challenges and Opportunities

Police officers are often called upon to intervene in conflict situations. Disputes between co-habitants, parents and children, neighbors, property owners and tenants, and many other situations represent a breakdown in the exchange relationships that exist between people. There is a misunderstanding of the relationship, a disagreement about the roles individuals should play, or simply a violation of the rules (formal or informal) that the people involved are expected to follow. *The key thing that the police officer needs to bear in mind is that someone has called the police for the purpose of bringing the coercive force of the state to bear on their side of the conflict* (Bitner, 1970). The person calling seeks a resolution in their favor, so they are seeking the assistance of the police in getting their way by resolving the conflict in their favor. Navigating this expectation requires that the officer remains objectively neutral in the face of demands resonating from people who are often caught in the grip of an emotional crisis or an emotional hijack.

> When someone calls the police concerning a non-crime related dispute they are seeking to bring the coercive power of the police (the state) to bear on their side.

The first step for the officer—after the emotional crisis has abated and any potential for violence has passed—is to try and get the parties to commit, even in some small way, to the value of their relationship. Both parties must recognize value in maintaining the relationship, and this can be quite difficult when one party tries to dominate the other. In the words of Deutsch (2006), they are trying to force a win-lose conflict resolution. Getting the parties to realize the value of the relationship between them can be accomplished by discovering their common interests and then re-framing the conflict as a challenge that the two parties can, and should, work on together (Deutsch, 2006).

Sometimes people just don't want the help of the police. They don't recognize the value of the relationship or one of the parties is just not interested in finding a mutually satisfactory solution. If this is the case, the police should respect this decision to the extent that the law allows it. "If people don't want to be helped, leave them alone" (Sirolli, 1999, p. 103). The officer's role shifts from a mediator to a coach where only one person can be helped. The officer can

---

5 "The degree of cooperation of the public that can be secured diminishes proportionally to the necessity of the use of physical force." Robert Peel.

express understanding, validate the disputant's feelings, and empathize *as long as he or she is careful not to take sides.*

> People will seek advantage with the police by appealing to an officer's bias. Discuss.

CONSIDERATIONS FOR THE POLICE OFFICER

The role of the police officer in conflict management is that of a neutral third party. Both sides will try and win the officer over by appealing to commonalities that may speak to the officer's own bias. Being effective at conflict management means having the ability to recognize the competing perspectives from the point-of-view of the disputants. *The question to ask is whether the officer has clear authorization from both parties to intervene.* If this is the case and both parties are committed to a negotiated solution, then the following questions need to be asked:

Is sufficient time available?

Conflict management is a time consuming process: officers need the freedom to engage no matter how much time it may take. If an officer is under pressure from his or her supervisor to clear the call and move on to the next job then they need to re-schedule the conflict management session.

Does the officer have the necessary communication skills (primarily listening skills)?

> Some officers are not well suited for conflict management; advanced interpersonal skills are required.

Some officers are well suited to engage in conflict management; some are not. There must be a clear commitment on the part of an officer to this process—the willingness to take a shot at managing the conflict, as opposed to simply using threat and coercion to resolve it for the moment. This cannot be dictated by management; it has to come from the officer himself or herself.

Is there a selfish reason to get involved?

Having the right motives is critical for success, so self-centered reasons for getting involved will doom the effort to failure as these reasons will emerge as bias. The officer must be viewed as honest, trustworthy, and open minded, just like a professional mediator (Dues, 2010).

CONTROLLING EMOTIONS: A GUIDE FOR POLICE OFFICERS

Exerting control of emotions is the foundation of *emotional intelligence.* Emotions and passion are part of the natural make-up of human beings and, as long as police officers continue to be recruited from the human race, emotional competency—the ability to control emotions in ourselves and recognize them in others—will be a critical skill.

> The foundation of emotional intelligence is self-awareness and self-control.

Emotional intelligence, like the intelligence quotient, can grow and develop over time. It begins with self-awareness—awareness of our own feelings as they occur. Self-awareness means being aware of both our mood and how our thoughts are affected by that mood (Goleman, 1995, p. 47). Police officers will be confronted with heated emotions so the ability to control their own is a critical first step in the conflict management endeavor.

Self-Awareness

In today's policing environment officers are being called upon to build better relationships in the community. One of the most important ways to accomplish this is for officers to first know themselves. "Self-awareness enables us to stand apart and examine the way we 'see' ourselves as well as to see other people" (Covey S. R., 1989).

The ability to see ourselves as others see us is a key aspect of our personal development and maturity. Police officers are charged with the duty of maintaining order in society; in order to accomplish this mission, a basic understanding of what drives human behavior is necessary. Of even greater importance to their ability to manage conflict is an understanding of what drives their own behavior.

> Freud 's work provides insight into the human personality that is useful for the modern police officer in relating to individuals and groups.

Freud's Contributions

Sigmund Freud (1859–1939) *

An Austrian neurologist known best for his work in the development of psychoanalysis. He pioneered techniques such as transference, free association, and dream interpretation to study the human personality. His concept of psychoanalysis dominated the development of psychology and are influential even today despite controversy. His framework for understanding the human personality, and the behavior that flows from it, included concepts such as the Id, Ego and Super Ego.

The Id

From birth we all have unconscious motivations, Freud referred to these as the *id*: instinctive drives that lead to primitive behavior. The Id is driven to seek pleasure and avoid pain. It strives for immediate gratification of wants, needs and desires and when, those things are not met or satisfied, anxiety and tension results.

When an infant is hungry he or she cries until they are fed. When the baby is entertained it smiles and laughs. When something is unpleasant they demand immediate relief, there is no reasoning with them as they have not yet developed the capacity to defer immediate gratification in consideration of social norms. Observing the Id is as simple as walking a child down the toy isle, they will grab things that they see and want to have. Say no and watch the hysteria[6] that results. The pleasure principle is foremost for the Id; that being the idea that impulses need to be fulfilled immediately.

* Image labeled for unrestricted reuse.

6 The term hysteria refers to ungovernable emotional excess, irrationally upset.

The Id remains with us as we grow and mature. Most individuals learn how to control it often with the help of others-parents-who teach us how to behave through the use of incentives and disincentives. However, for some the pursuit of pleasure and **immediate gratification** remains strong, leaving them vulnerable to situations and persons who "trigger" a hysterical response.

The Ego

As human beings grow and mature they begin a process of developing the capacity to deal with the real world-objective reality. No longer completely sheltered by a loving parent-mother, the child ventures forth and begins to interact with other human beings. These other human beings are indifferent to them; they neither like nor dislike them.

Reality and the world outside of the loving maternal world of the home make demands on the individual. These demands require that the desires of the Id are satisfied only in socially appropriate ways.

Reality forces the individual to consider risks, incentives, and possible outcomes related to their behavior. The immediate gratification of the Id is halted by the Ego, with desires being deferred in consideration of what is considered appropriate behavior in a given time and place. This is what is referred to as **deferred gratification.**[7]

The Ego provides the capacity to relieve the anxiety and tension caused by unmet desires. Freud refers to a secondary process that develops with the Ego that helps the individual defer the energy caused by the Id's demands for immediate satisfaction. The ability to control impulses increases as the individual grows and develops a **relationship** with the outside world.

The ego represents what we call reason and sanity, in contrast to the id which contains the passions (Freud, 1923).

The Superego

Concepts related to right and wrong conduct, our moral base, rests in the development of the Superego. This aspect of our personality provides the guidelines for making **judgements**. As the superego develops individuals begin to see themselves as other see them. They gain the capacity to see themselves as mere objects existing in an indifferent world or reality. They step away from the sheltered maternal world where they are surrounded by unconditional love and

---

[7] Deferred or delayed gratification means the ability to put-off immediate satisfaction of needs, wants and desires. It implies the ability to wait for a later reward or incentive.

acceptance and face the challenges of interacting with reality. Freud identified two components of the superego:

The **ego ideal** promotes rules for good behavior, standards that are approved of by parents, teachers, relatives and others in authority. Obeying these rules creates self-esteem in the individual, feelings of pride, value and accomplishment. We being to acknowledge our place in the real world and seek the approval of others by engaging in behavior that others see as noble and worthy of praise.

The **conscience** provides information about what is deemed bad by parents, teachers, relatives and others in society. Such behavior leads to harsh consequences, punishment and guilt things to be avoided. Violating the standards leads to remorse and guilt unless such behavior can be rationalized.

The superego is the aspect of our personality that civilizes us. It helps us craft our behavior in accordance with the acceptable rules of society and achieve high levels of self-esteem. Most importantly, it helps us relate to the outside world by building the understanding that **it's not all about us**. The concept of the pristine self provides additional insight.

> The concept of the pristine self provides additional insight based upon Freud's original framework.

The Concept of the Pristine Self

The term "pristine self" refers to an individual who believes that the world around them should offer nothing but love, a world where their every need is met by an omnipotent mother. These individuals feel that they are entitled to live in a fictionalized world which consistently validates their world view. When faced with contradictory ideas and facts, they interpret them not only as incorrect, they actually interpret them as acts of aggression (Lavender, 2016). The pristine self must never be challenged; even by factual information.

> The 'pristine self' is the fictionalized idea of a self touched by nothing but love. When 'marginalized' students demand 'safe spaces,' trigger warnings, and protection from micro-aggressions, they work upon the assumption that they deserve a 'pristine self,' unchallenged by invalidating ideas or opinions (Schwartz, 2016).

When development of the superego is hindered for any of a number of reasons, individuals lack the capacity to see themselves as others see them. Their behavior is driven by the Ego and, when under stress, reverts to that of the Id launching them into fits of **hysteria** and emotional hijack.

This is a particular problem for the police because these individuals cannot be reasoned with. They are threatened by facts and data that are contrary to their world view; they also feel that individuals who have never met them should know just who they are ahead of time and modify their behavior accordingly, responding emotionally in a way that is consistent with their self-perceived righteousness and importance (Schwartz, 2016).

Self-awareness is the ability to have a clear and accurate perception of one's own personality, strengths, weaknesses, thoughts, beliefs and motivations. Of primary important to the professional police officer is knowledge about one's "triggers." Emotional control is critical to improving our relations with others. Our own behavior provides clues to others about our emotions, especially our non-verbal behavior. In order to control these behaviors, we need the ability to recognize those situations, events or actions that cause an emotional response in us.

For example, consider an adolescent who is constantly in trouble. Their behavior is defiant and oppositional and they go to great lengths to show that they are in control and "in-charge." These individuals are usually expelled from school, don't have any friends and are excluded from most cooperative activities, they are anything but "in charge" of their lives. The need for immediate gratification has taken over and they are allowing their emotions to be "in-charge," a slave rather than the master of their own destiny (Stein, 2009).

Paying attention to other people helps us understand and better relate to our own emotions. Observing and studying the body language of others who are caught-in-the-grip of strong emotions enables us to better understand the impact of an emotional response in ourselves. Once we master this ability we can better control our own behavior in an effort to avoid sending the wrong signals or displaying body language that is likely to be interpreted in a manner that is not conducive to gaining their cooperation, respect and trust.

The police are in the problem-solving business. People don't call the police when everyone is at their best. They call for help when someone is hostile, angry, frustrated, aggressive, intoxicated, under the influence of drugs or emotionally or psychologically disturbed. In other words, people request law enforcement's assistance only when someone is at his worst, when he has lost the ability to think logically. The best cops are able to gain compliance by demonstrating command presence, building rapport and communicating effectively (Fitch, 2010, p. 4).

What Fitch is speaking to here is command over one's own emotions and behavior. Being emotional with someone who is already in the midst of an emotional hijack is unwise. Self-awareness and self-control are the characteristics of the best police officers.

Managing the emotions of others begins with managing our own response. Responding emotionally to someone who is already irate, frustrated, or angry will almost certainly make a bad situation worse. Everything that we do and say is potentially important. To make the right impression, we must send the right message. This means controlling our verbal and nonverbal behaviors to ensure that we communicate appropriate levels of professionalism, interest, sensitivity, and objectivity.

Carefully monitoring our actions also allows us to influence the behavior of others by demonstrating the kinds of conduct that we want the others to model. If we appear anxious, nervous, or emotional, they will respond in kind. On the other hand, if we appear calm, professional, and interested, they are more likely to respond in ways that facilitate, rather than inhibit, successful communication and problem solving (Fitch, 2010, p. 32).

Having a foundation of Self-awareness *empowers* officers to more effectively craft their interactions with others in conflict situations. There are situations in which individual traits, personality and points-of view will clash, these are situations that knowledgeable police officers should avoid, if possible. Conversely, there are situations where there will be a basis of rapport that can advance the efforts toward great police community relations.

THE ROLE OF EMOTIONS IN CONFLICT

Our emotions are part of our nature as human beings. They exist as a primitive survival mechanism. Emotions are transmitted among us just as they were in the primitive human tribes; the purpose is to focus the group on a threat (Goleman, 1998, p. 165). This phenomenon is particularly acute in police officers who are socialized into a group that is hyper-vigilant to a perceived constant threat of danger (Crank, 2004). Falling victim to toxic emotions is a danger to the effectiveness of any conflict management effort. Police officers must walk a fine line between sensitivity and indifference so that they are perceived as someone who is objective and unbiased, a high level skill.

TACTICS OF CONFLICT MANAGEMENT FOR POLICE OFFICERS

The role of the law enforcement officer is straightforward. Officers swear a duty to enforce the law and are expected to seek out violators, through the observation or investigative process, and arrest them. The potential for conflict in the law enforcement role rests with the law enforcement officer himself or herself as the instigator. In other words, the conflict begins with the actions of the officer. Wise officers recognize this, they do not shy away from it, and they employ tactics to minimize it.

Policing, on the other hand, is everything else the police do. The role of the police officer is inarguably ambiguous (Goldstein, Policing a Free Society, 1976), but it nearly always involves conflict management. Police officers are called to intervene in conflict situations generally by one individual who is seeking the assistance of the police (coercion) to resolve the conflict in his or her own favor, what has been referred to as the "win-lose" focus (Dues, 2010). The wise officer views his or her role as that of a negotiator who seeks opportunities to create "win-win" situations (Deutsch, 2006, pp. 33–34).

> Conflict results when someone's needs are not being met. Discuss.

Conflict can be understood as a disagreement arising between individuals or groups that can be related to differing opinions, principles, values, and meanings, or it can simply be an issue regarding differing points-of-view. More simply, *conflict means that someone's needs are not being met.* Discovering the bases of the disagreement is the logical first step. The path of least resistance, employing coercion or force, may expedite resolution, *but it will most certainly not resolve the conflict* (Deutsch, 2006).

The first principle to understand is that the police officer will not be effective in managing conflict if both parties are not committed to the relationship. In the absence of this commitment, the job of the police is simply to separate the parties until passion (emotional crisis) has abated to a point where violence is no longer imminent as is the case with interactions between strangers. Most police training programs stop here, as this is the limit of what basic training programs can accomplish. However, some officers develop the capacity to do more. This often begins with the ability to make both parties realize that maintaining the relationship is important, that they have a common interest. Without this realization, efforts at conflict management will not be effective. The following sections describe how to do this.

Listen

The socialization and training of the modern police officer rarely addresses this skill and the police culture does not rewarded an officer who employs such advanced interpersonal skills; rather, the judicious use of force and territorial control have been stressed as indicators of what it takes to become "a cop's cop"

(Crank, 2004, p. 104). The wise police officer today recognizes the importance of great interpersonal skills, not only to keep themselves safe from attack, but also as a tool to engage the community and manage various conflict situations. Nevertheless, emotions get in the way of good listening. People don't call the police when everything is fine; they call when they are in crisis, so a police officer who has little or no control over his or her own emotions is of little value.

The simple act of listening can go a long way toward reducing emotional distress. Listening provides people with important opportunities to express their feelings, attitudes, and concerns. Listening, however, is not as easy as it might appear. To listen effectively, we must do more than simply process information. Good listeners pay attention not only to people's choice of words, but also to their paralanguage[8] and other nonverbal cues. This means that we must listen with our eyes as well as with our ears. It also requires that we take an interest in others. We must learn to listen to people with the same concern and respect that we expect from others, regardless of our personal feelings (Fitch, 2016, p. 32).

Ask Great Questions

What questions to ask is a function of the situation, but the first rule is "Do Not Argue." Instead, officers should ask questions with the goal of draining the emotional energy. They should start with the primary aggressor and ask for the cooperation of the other parties, assuring them that they will get their turn. Time is the officers' ally here, and officers need to allocate enough time to allow strong emotions to dissipate. There can be no pressure to dispose of the call and "move on."

- Officers should adopt a positive, calm, but firm tone and make sure the non-verbal's project confidence, not condescension.
- Officers cannot judge because the tendency to do so is a signal that the emotions are trying to re-engage.
- Officers need to understand that aggressive personalities will use hostility and intimidation to win. This means that they are seeking assistance in resolving the conflict in their favor. The mission is to reduce the negative aspects of conflict, not to advocate for one side. An officer who falls into this trap will lose credibility with the other party and the respect of the primary aggressor.

[8] Paralanguage refers to the features that accompany speech such as tone of voice, pitch, volume, speed, gestures, and the use of inflection.

- Officers need to display understanding and empathy as tools for building rapport. Any effort of conflict management is doomed without rapport.[9]

Strong emotions are products of the emotional brain. One way of reengaging the rational brain is to ask questions. Because answering questions requires the person to process the request, search for information, and formulate a response, questions naturally engage the rational brain. This is especially true of open-ended questions that require as extended search for information and a narrative response, such as "Tell me more about that" or "What happened next?" Unlike binary questions, narrative questions cannot be answered with a simple yes or no. The more we can engage the person in answering narrative questions, the greater our chances of reengaging with the rational brain (Fitch, 2016).

Make a Reflective Statement-Paraphrase

The goal here is to get the person to see themselves as the officer sees them. Examples of reflective statements include "I can see that you are upset because . . ." or "You seem down about this situation, perhaps I can help." Statements like these validate the person. They send a signal that the officers cares, i.e., that there is a heart behind the badge.

Paraphrasing involves the restatement of a person's message in another form. It can be used to clarify, summarize, or expand on the original message. Paraphrasing also offers a number of advantages for managing highly emotional people. To begin with, it allows us to interrupt someone without making things worse. For example, after listening long enough to grasp the crux of a person's complaint, an officer can politely interrupt by stating "I want to be sure that I understand what you have told me so far" or "Okay, if I understand you correctly . . ." One of the reasons that paraphrasing is so effective is that it requires the other party to stop talking and listen to discover if the officer has, in fact, gotten the story right. Further, similar to active listening, paraphrasing provides a way of modeling appropriate behaviors and reducing tension (Fitch, 2016, pp. 32–33).

Let's Take a Walk

Putting the body to work can defuse emotions because it forces the brain to change its focus. The officer wants to shift that focus away from supporting the

---

[9] Rapport is a close and harmonious interpersonal relationship recognized by a sub-conscious connection where individuals understand and recognize each other's feelings and enjoy great communication.

dysfunctional emotional state, and exercise—making the body do physical work—is a great tool for accomplishing this.

Let the Person Vent

People just like to talk. Complaints, even crime related complaints, are driven by the human need to express anger, frustration, and dissatisfaction in others. In many cases an individual will complain to help make themselves feel better, as if expressing the short-comings of others can enhance one's own self-esteem. Letting people talk demonstrates our respect for them and our willingness to invest the time it takes to do so.

One of the most effective ways of dealing with someone who is angry or frustrated is to allow the person to blow off steam. Rather than arguing, debating, or disagreeing, our best course of action is to let the person vent. The simple act of venting provides people with a form of psychological release. Our job is not to react to emotional outbursts or to personal attacks. Rather, we should listen quietly, acknowledge the person's concerns, and demonstrate interest. This includes allowing the person to have the last word. If she stops talking, we should prompt her to continue. Not only does letting someone vent allow that person to blow off steam, but it also demonstrates our patience, empathy, and genuine desire to listen (Fitch, 2016).

Conflict Management Steps

When police officers are called to intervene in a conflict or dispute, the following framework should guide the process:

1) Make the Offer

A police officer needs the ability and willingness to engage the parties in conflict management. This begins by introducing himself or herself as a neutral third party with no hidden agenda. This sets the stage for securing a commitment from both parties to the relationship and the conflict management process.

2) Build Rapport

Rapport is a tool used by the best police officers to engage with people. It can be described as a sympathetic connection between people that enables highly effective interpersonal communication. A great way to build rapport is to establish commonality with the parties. Empathetic police officers have a huge advantage here in that few conflict situations are unique. Officers can call upon their past experiences to provide insight to which both parties can relate.

> Never frame a conflict in terms of individual characteristics, i.e., stubborn, angry, uncooperative, etc. Frame conflict as individual behavior(s) and behavior patterns that have been observed and are troubling.

3) Define the Problem (Conflict) as Behavior

Conflicts are always charged with emotion, and discussing feelings is likely to invoke an emotional response. Rather than discussing how one party is feeling, *officers should focus on specific behaviors.* The goal is to attack the conflict by identifying a voluntary behavior that invokes an emotional response in the other person. *Officers should not focus on attitudes or the character of the other person as these attributes* ***are not*** *negotiable, behavior is.* However, the perception may be that the source of the conflict is the feelings, character, or personality of the other person. This perception needs to be changed because feelings are always reflected in behavior, but it is the specific behavior that needs to be identified and controlled. If the officer cannot define the conflict as voluntary behavior then they *cannot* help these people. The options left to officers in this case are, first, the parties need to accept the *status quo;* second, one or both parties may impose sanctions and this may escalate the conflict; or third, the parties can agree to end the relationship (Dues, 2010, p. 39).

> Character, personality, feelings and attitudes are NOT negotiable, behavior is.

4) Identify Specific Behavior and Negotiate

If both parties agree that they wish to manage the conflict, the next step is to identify the behavior(s) that are causing the bad feelings. Officers should begin with one party and challenge them to cite a specific behavior. Then ask them how that behavior, on the part of the other party, makes them feel. In many cases the other party is completely unaware of the impact of their own behavior. *If they are truly committed to the relationship, they will acknowledge their responsibility for generating those feelings.*

The next thing is to ask each party what would be a fair resolution in their view. Now the negotiation process can begin. The key is to focus on one party and one behavior before switching and giving the other party their turn.

Following a standard interview protocol will be useful here:

1. **Introduction/Orientation**—Identify yourself and give each party a business card. Ask permission from each party to engage them in a process of managing the conflict, specifically state what is to be accomplished, how long it is likely to take, and the desired outcome.
2. **Rapport**—Establish rapport with each individual by seeking commonalities, asking for assistance or offering a sincere compliment. The goal is a connection where great communication can take place.
3. **Questioning**—Ask direct questions as objectively as possible. Do not show bias or take on a condescending or patronizing tone. Discover and articulate the common interests/goals of the parties. Conflict arises over the means to achieve goals, not the interests and goals themselves.
4. **Start Broad/Be Specific**—Ask open ended questions and then drill-down on specifics. With reluctant interviewees, such as teenagers, it may be necessary to start with specific "yes" or "no" questions just to get them started. Identify specific behaviors, negotiate those behaviors, and identify indicated behavior changes.
5. **Summarize**—Recap what each party says as it relates to the behaviors and ignore the emotional appeals and the "hidden agendas."
6. **Close**—Ask for agreement and offer to return if things do not go well. Establish a follow-up date.

This step-by-step process, addressing one behavior at a time with each party in turn, is likely to result in negotiated agreement between parties that are committed to the relationship.

5) Secure a Commitment

For each behavior officers uncover in the interview and negotiation process, they should identify specific new behaviors or actions that the other party can commit to. For example, one party in a domestic situation may identify yelling and a raised voice as specific behaviors that generate anger and fear. The negotiated remedy may be to allow that party to simply walk away when yelling occurs and when he or she starts to feel angry. The agreement is that this person is allowed to do so by the other party.

Officers should commit the parties to agreement in writing. Identify each of the behaviors discussed by each party, the feelings and emotions that these behaviors generate in the other party, and the negotiated remedy. This should be done for each behavior identified by each party. Then both parties sign the document. A great place to store this document is on the front of the refrigerator or some other place regularly visited by both parties.

With this process accomplished and an agreement in place, future conflicts can be mitigated by simply referring back to the agreement, or adding to it.

> Moral conflicts confound even the best efforts to manage them. They require a different strategy.

MORAL CONFLICT

Conflicts in which the parties do not share a common understanding about what is proper and improper action or behavior can be framed as moral conflict. *Moral conflicts are intractable, meaning that they are resilient, tend to develop a life of their own, and appear impossible to resolve.* They attract the attention and involvement of other parties and groups, become increasingly complicated over time, and tend to result in negative outcomes for everyone involved. Examples include prolonged marital disputes, ongoing employer-employee labor disputes, and ideological disputes over such fundamental concepts as the proper role of government.

Conflicts between the police generally and particular interest groups usually take the form of moral conflicts. These kinds of conflicts are very difficult to resolve and can easily escalate to violence. A framework for understanding the moral conflict between the police and various interest groups may rest in the belief in the sanctity of the rule of law vs. *postmodernism.*

Objective reality has its basis in reason where claims to knowledge and truth are products of unique social, historical or political discourses and interpretations. Postmodern thought, characterized as consistent with moral relativism, is the absence of absolute standards of morality and conduct, as specified in the rule of law (Duignan, 2010).

The following comparison provides a framework for understanding the source of conflict between the police and various groups.

> Modernism recognizes the value of facts and empirical objective data in defining reality. Post-modernism contends that all facts and empirical data is relative, dependent on subjective interpretation by individuals and groups.

Rational Objectivity vs. Postmodernism

Modernist[10] thought places *objective reason* as the fundamental way to understand reality. What we can see, hear, feel and measure-facts-define our world. Postmodernist thought challenges our ability to reason by asserting that *all facts are relative*, subject to interpretation based on subjective[11] factors such as race, gender, national origin, etc. The following sections apply this distinction to the police officers role in conflict management.

Police officers are educated and trained in the defense of the rule of law[12]. The rule of law, in Western civilization, has its foundation in the concept of objective rationality[13]. These concepts are part of the fabric of modern society, they define the exchange relationships[14] necessary for any cooperative endeavor among people.

In a free society individuals and groups may challenge the legitimacy of existing standards of behavior, a common understanding of correct behavior may not exist. The exchange relationships become ambiguous and the rule of law breaks down.

The rejection of the law, rules or even the tenants of common decency leads to conflict and sometimes violence, as in the case of an individual resisting the efforts of a police officer to arrest them. To those indoctrinated into the rule of law such actions are viewed as *immoral* and a violation of the rules necessary to the maintenance of society, but to those who reject the legitimacy of the law, due to their personal feelings, attitudes or point-of-view, such action may be considered morally righteous. *"Moral conflicts are those in which the issues are framed as matters of what is morally right and morally wrong"* (Dues, 2010, p. 73).

When opponents frame issues in terms of moral conflicts, mutual understanding breaks down because the argument of one party simply does not resonate with the other party. Communication breaks down, emotions emerge,

---

10 Modernism represents a break from faith and duty that dominated the dark ages. Reason and rationality discovered through empirical and scientific methods guide our understanding of reality, not mere belief in a god.

11 Subjectivity is dependent on our own individual experiences, beliefs, values, attitudes, and point-of-view. Objectivity is based on that which can be observed, measured and evaluated independent of personal experiences, beliefs, values, attitudes, and point-of-view.

12 The principle that all people and institutions are subject to and accountable to law that is fairly applied and enforced.

13 Objective means not based on personal feelings, interpretations, bias or prejudice. Rationality means based on facts, reason or logic.

14 Exchange relationships reflect common understandings of obligations and benefits to be received in exchange for actions, behaviors or restraint among people.

and conflict results. The problem is that each side comprehends the issue differently and since there is no common basis for negotiation, one side views the other side as an enemy.

The essence of the disagreement and conflict rests on the assumption that there are absolute standards of conduct. For example, a police officer may correctly state that there is no *legal* justification for resisting arrest. The other party may, or may not, accept that premise, but counters with a statement that there is a *moral* responsibility to resist the efforts of those who represent a corrupt moral order, one that has historically marginalized, abused, and exploited people based on their race.

We don't have to look far today to find examples of moral conflict; abortion, universal health care, conflict in the Middle East, etc. Today the police are faced with moral conflicts over whenever an officer is justified in employing deadly force against an unarmed American citizen. The emotions on both sides can quickly overwhelm any effort to seek mutual understanding. Stating that the police kill many more white people under these conditions than blacks only intensifies the moral conflict because the standard itself is unjust in the eyes of one party.

From a rational point-of-view, modernist thought, individuals who fight with the police are morally wrong for doing so. The law backs the police through statutory prohibitions for resisting arrest, i.e., the law. Conversely, postmodernist though states that the police are representatives of an unjust system, therefore resisting arrest for violations of unjust laws is morally courageous.

> Intractable conflicts are exceedingly difficult to manage as one side views the other as the enemy and morally corrupt. They grow over time and take on a life of their own.

MORAL CONFLICT IS INTRACTABLE

Moral conflicts are always *intractable*, they take on a life of their own, and draw the involvement of other parties. They grow and spread with time and become complicated, never ending well for either party. A common example for the police is the prolonged marital dispute where each party views the other as evil and uncompromising. The strong emotional attachments can overwhelm the best mitigation efforts, especially when one party seeks to make the other suffer as much as possible. Conversely, *tractable conflicts* can be resolved and negotiated to the relative satisfaction of the parties. The solutions are never perfect, but the conflict can be managed and often resolved.

Intractable conflicts persist because they are viewed by all parties as impossible to resolve. In most cases, the lack of solid conflict management techniques over time has contributed to the escalation. What once may have been manageable has resulted in hostile interaction and bad feelings.

Most intractable conflicts do not begin as such, but become so as escalation, hostile interactions, sentiments, and time change the quality of the conflict. They can be triggered and emerge from a wide variety of factors and events, but often involve important issues such as moral and identity differences, high stakes resources, and/or struggles for power and self-determination (Burgess, 1996).

Race in America—The Common Characteristics of Intractable Conflict

Each conflict is unique in terms of the context and issues involved. None-the-less, there are a few common characteristics that are present in some degree in all persistent conflicts that have endured over time.

Protesters portraying Chicago police as evil and corrupt*

Context

The ongoing conflict between the police and the African American community provides insight into the importance of context in what can certainly be framed as a moral, intractable conflict.

> Intractable conflict is often driven by real or imagined differences in power between individuals or between groups, i.e., one party feel helpless or at the mercy of the other group.

Intractable conflicts regularly occur in situations where there exists a severe imbalance of power between the parties in which the more powerful exploit, control, or abuse the less powerful. Often, the power holders in such settings will

* Image labeled for unrestricted use.

use the existence of salient intergroup distinctions (such as ethnicity or class) as a means of maintaining or strengthening their power base (Staub, 2001).

Race has been an enduring distinction between the ruling elite in the United States, who are primarily represented by European Caucasians, and the minority black population. Over time this conflict has grown and new groups have joined, spurred on by issues and events that illustrate the imbalance of power between these groups. The white majority openly exercises its control over social institutions, sometimes resulting in devastating outcomes for poor people of color who are much less powerful.

The moral conflict is based in the widely held belief that this social control is used by white people as a way to maintain and strengthen a diminishing power base. Our sad history of racism and the use of the police by the status quo to control black people feed this moral narrative and drive the ongoing conflict. This legacy has propagated ideologies, practices, and behaviors that have taken on a cultural dimension that has served to perpetuate the conflict.

> Establishing a common basis of understanding or framework is important to managing intractable conflict.

Issue

Problems that can be divided and integrated into a common framework are manageable and can often be resolved to the satisfaction of all parties. The key is finding that common framework. This is not true of intractable conflicts because they lack a common framework as well as a sense of beginning, middle, and end; they just seem to have gone on forever.

Seeking a common framework has been elusive in the conflict between the white majority and the black community. There is fundamental disagreement about the beginning of the conflict, with those who understand that this conflict dates back 400 years and those who believe it merely dates to the end of the American civil war, when the rights of African American citizens were first recognized in law, or even to the dawn of the civil rights movement when lawful discrimination—Jim Crow—was ended.

Symbols of this pervasive conflict have taken the form of black lynchings, the police using firehoses and dogs to control black protestors, and the killing of unarmed black men. Despite the passage of time, these issues just seem to endure, i.e., the wounds are just not being allowed to heal.

Relationships

In the effort to build better relationships between the police and the African American community, the nature of contact becomes critical. In this regard, white police officers are at a distinct disadvantage compared to black police officers. *White officers have been isolated-segregated-from black culture and are therefore ignorant of the subtle nuances, mannerisms, gestures, and verbiage that define it.* Many black police officers understand the cultural differences that exist and this knowledge can give them an advantage.

In many intractable conflicts, the relations between the parties develop in settings where exclusive social structures limit intergroup contact and isolate the in-group across family, work, and community domains. This lack of contact facilitates the development of abstract, stereotypical images of the other, autistic hostilities, and intergroup violence (Deutsch, 2006).

> The legacy of racism is the social isolation of Whites from Blacks due to segregation, by government policy or individual choice that allowed the development of separate and distinct cultures.

Herein lies the *legacy of racism.* The social isolation of the past allows the parties to grow and develop apart. Each group is isolated, one by generational poverty and the other by white privilege, to the extent that distinct and seemingly insurmountable cultural divisions now exist in neighborhoods and communities that have predominantly black residents.

However, the relationships are also typically experienced as inescapable by the parties, where they see no way of extricating themselves without becoming vulnerable to an unacceptable loss. This may be due to a variety of constraints including geographical, financial, moral, or psychological factors. When destructive conflicts persist under these conditions, they tend to damage or destroy the trust, faith, and cooperative potential necessary for constructive or tolerant relations. In such relationships, the negative aspects remain salient, and any positive encounters are forgotten or viewed with suspicion and misconstrued as aberrations or attempts at deception (Deutsch, 2006, p. 538).

Consider the African American police recruit who is viewed by his family, friends, and neighbors as a traitor to his or her race. Consider the white police officer who seeks to build a better relationship with poor people of color on his or her assigned beat who is viewed with suspicion by those in the community. Even the most compassionate actions on the part of the police will be set aside in the wake of some horrific tragedy resulting from a violent police citizen interaction.

In-groups include those whom an individual shares an identity and culture that they can relate to. Out-groups are those with whom an individual does not share an identity or perceived commonality. Oppositional identities develop to a point where there is an emotional attachment with the in-group and the out-groups is viewed as the enemy.

In-group refers to a social, cultural or ethnic group with which an individual relates to. Conversely, an *out-group* is a social group to which an individual does not share an identity. Human beings, by nature, strive for inclusion. People tend to define themselves in terms of social groupings and are quick to denigrate others who don't fit into those groups.

In these conflict situations a sense of in-group and out-group affiliations develops where the opposing groups become increasingly polarized as the result of in-group interactions and discourse as well as out-group hostility. Oppositional identities develop where the out-group is disparaged and an emotional attachment to the in-group grows to the point that these polarized identities stand in the way of any efforts toward conflict management (Deutsch, 2006).

Social Processes

What we may accept as fair and just processes can be viewed very differently by those who consider themselves as members of a marginalized and discriminated against out-group. Group pressure to conform to in-group standards of behavior can lead to destructive behaviors regarding the out-group.

Stereotyping, prejudice and ethnocentrism (belief in the superiority of one's group) fuel dehumanization of the enemy—the out-group—to the extent that violence can result.

Cognitive process such as stereotyping, ethnocentrism, selective perception, self-fulfilling prophecies, and cognitive rigidity can fuel processes of de-individualization and dehumanization of the enemy, leading to moral disengagement and moral exclusion (Optow, 1990), that is, the development of rigid moral boundaries between groups, which exclude out-group members from typical standards of moral treatment, can lead to violence (Deutsch, 2006, p. 540).

One of the most pervasive problems within the police subculture is the tendency to dehumanize certain groups of people based upon stereotypes. When a police officer is bombarded day after day with situations that call into question the very humanity of those that he or she interacts with stereotyping of groups, ethnocentrism and de-individualization become the paths of least resistance. Objectivity is undermined by evidence confirming the selective perceptions related to the out-group and the results of these processes can make headlines.

Solutions to intractable conflict situations are elusive. For the police the best approach is the establishment of early warning systems that provide intervention strategies, i.e., conflict management before one party begins to see the other party as something less than human. These kinds of conflicts often have a long history and come to the surface in the face of specific events that garner intense media and public attention. The best hope of management occurs when *both sides can still see the humanity of the other side* and seek to understand their needs, aspirations, and point-of-view. Once the conflict reaches the level of destructiveness and violence, the only course of action is to contain the damage, stop the violence, and then begin the process of repairing the destruction.

MORAL CONFLICT MANAGEMENT TECHNIQUES

Managing moral conflicts presents a unique challenge for the police because the police can rarely claim to be objective and therefore, the role of a neutral fact-finding mediator is simply not available. Those who seek to intervene in moral conflicts, such as the common protracted marital dispute, requires the ability to arm themselves with the ability to see beyond one's own perspective and point-of-view. The ability to see the world as others see it is a fundamental skill. Listening and questioning should be directed at the source of the moral conflict with an eye toward finding some area of commonality between the parties.

> The police are rarely viewed as neutral by those whose group affiliation demands that the police are the enemy. The police represent the status quo and to those who feel marginalized, ignored, or repressed the police are easily viewed as evil.

Reframing

For any effort in conflict management to have a chance of success there must be a commitment on the part of all parties to maintaining the relationship. If one party does not feel that they have a stake in maintaining the relationship the effort at conflict management and subsequent negotiation will be futile. Herein lies a huge problem in modern policing when police officials do not recognize the value of maintaining good community relations, or when they feel the relationship is purely one-sided. *Reframing the conflict as a mutual problem to be resolved, or at least managed, through joint cooperative efforts is an effective strategy for overcoming the emotion and returning the discourse to a more manageable level.* What we are looking for here is a cooperative orientation even when the goals are unspecified or seem to be mutually exclusive. Here is where officers can attack the idea of resolving the conflict in the favor of one party over the other, win-lose. *What is actually desired is to reframe the conflict so that each party refuses to accept a resolution that means the other party is somehow diminished.*

> Reframing intractable conflict is the process of shifting focus and seeking commonality. Both parties must recognize the value of the relationship and be willing to not simply view the other party as evil and morally corrupt.

Chapter Summary

In this chapter we explored the basics of conflict management in the law enforcement and policing functions. The nature of law enforcement dictates that officers will face conflict situations regularly. It is incumbent upon them to mitigate whenever possible by employing proactive interpersonal skills consistent with self-awareness and emotional intelligence. In the policing role, officers are frequently called upon to intervene in conflict situations, serving as mediators. In these cases finding a reason to arrest and resolving conflicts with arrest does not serve the needs of the parties nor does it do anything to enhance the police community relationship.

Some basic tactics to mitigate conflict in the law enforcement role include listening, asking great questions, reflective statements, and shifting the focus of disputants.

Police officers are often called upon to intervene in conflict situations that do not involve law violations. In these cases there is usually a breakdown in the exchange relationships that exist between people. There is a misunderstanding of the relationship, a disagreement about the roles individuals should play, or simply a violation of the rules (formal or informal) that people expect to be followed. Someone wishes to bring the coercive power of the sate-police-down on their side to resolve the conflict. In order to maintain legitimacy in these cases officers need to remain carefully neutral. This is particularly true when the police are dealing with disputes involving racial issues. The questions of race are discussed in more detail in a following chapter.

Considerations for the Police Officers when called on to intervene include having sufficient time to invest; officers running from call-to-call may not have this opportunity. Self-awareness as to whether the officer has the necessary communication skill—especially listening skill. The absence of a selfish reason to get involved. Officers should never take advantage of a situations to feed their own ego or for other selfish purposes. Emotional control, emotions are contagious and officers cannot succumb to these emotionally charged situations.

Self-awareness is the ability to see ourselves as others see us. Police officers are charged with the duty of maintaining order in society, in order to accomplish this mission a basic understanding of what drives human behavior is necessary. Of even greater importance to their ability to manage conflict is an understanding of what drives their own behavior.

Tactics for conflict management in the policing role include listening, asking great questions, making reflective statements and engaging in behavior that is likely to mitigate the impact of emotion. The steps of conflict management include:

1. Make the Offer—Expressing a willingness to engage.
2. Build Rapport—Establish a commonality with the parties, a basis for sameness. Discover the common interests.
3. Define the Problem (Conflict) as Behavior—Attitudes and character are not negotiable, behavior is.
4. Identify Specific Behavior and Negotiate—Identify what it will take for one or both parties to change their behavior and secure a commitment to do so for the sake of the relationship.

Managing moral conflicts where parties view their adversaries as evil are particularly challenging. These kinds of conflicts are very difficult to resolve and can easily escalate to violence. Understanding that the parties may view the world very differently is a critical first step. Framing the conflict in a manner that helps them agree on common goals can help mitigate the negative feelings.

Moral conflicts are always *intractable*, they take on a life of their own and draw the involvement of other parties. They grow and spread with time and become complicated, never ending well for either party. The parties identify with a particular group that is at odd with the out-group, they tend to view the out-group as evil and immoral, disparaging the whenever possible.

Intractable conflicts need to be identified in advance using a type of early warning system. The potential for these conflicts should be mitigated with efforts to build a better foundation for understanding between the groups. Once the tendency to see the other group as something less than human develops tragedy, including repression and violence, may result. Managing moral conflict demands that each party value the relationship and see the validity of the other group's needs. One effective way to bring this about is to reframe the problem in such a way as to make the problem mutual, something that both sides need to work on for their mutual benefit or for a higher purpose.

Bibliography

Alexander, M. (2011). *The New Jim Crow: Mass Incarceration in the Age of Colorblindness.* New York: The New Press.

Bitner, E. (1970). *The Functions of the Police in Modern Society.* National Institute of Mental Health.

Burgess, H.A. (1996). Constructive Confrontation: A Transformative Approach to Intractable Conflicts. *Mediation Quarterly*, 305–322.

Coleman, P. (2003). Characteristics of Protracted, Intractable Conflict: Towards the Development of a Meta-Framework. *Peace and Conflict: Journal of Peace Psychology*, 1–37.

Covey, S.R. (1989). *The 7 Habits of Highly Effective People.* New York: Simon & Schuster.

Crank, J.P. (2004). *Understanding Police Culture, 2nd ed.* Routledge.

Deutsch, M.C. (2006). *The Handbook of Conflict Resolution: Theory and Practice, 3rd ed.* San Francisco: Jossey-Bass.

DeVito, J. (2003). *The Interpersonal Communication Book, 10th ed.* Boston: Allyn & Bacon.

Dues, M. (2010). *The Art of Conflict Management: Achieving Solutions for Life, Work, and Beyond.* Chantilly, VA: The Great Courses.

Duignan, B. (2010). *Postmodernism.* Encyclopedia Britannica.

Fitch, B.D. (2016). *Law Enforcement Interpersonal Communication and Conflict Management. The IMPACT Model.* Sage.

Freud, S. (1923). *The Ego and the Id.* London: Oxford University Press.

Goldstein, H. (1977). *Policing a Free Society.* Cambridge, MA: Ballinger.

Goleman, D. (1995). *Emotional Intelligence: Why It Can Matter More than IQ.* Bantam.

Goleman, D. (1998). *Working with Emotional Intelligence.* New York: Bantam.

Hunter, R.D. (2011). *Police Community Relations and the Administration of Justice, 8th ed.* Saddle River, NJ: Pearson.

Lavender, N.J. (2016, December 17). Enter the Age of the Pristine Self. *Psychology Today.*

Lewis, O. (1971). The Culture of Poverty. In E. Penchef, *Four Horsemen: Pollution, Poverty, Famine, Violence.* San Francisco, CA: Canfield Press.

Mann, T., Ornstein, N. (2016). *It's Even Worse than It Looks: How the American Constitutional System Collided with the New Politics of Extremism.* New York: Basic Books.

Montano-Harmon, M. (1991). Discourse Features of Written Mexican Spanish: Current Research in Contrastive Rhetoric and Its Implications. *Hispania, 74(2)*, 417–425.

Final Report of the President's Task Force on 21st Century Policing. (2015). *President's Task Force on 21st Century Policing.* Washington, DC: Office of Community Oriented Policing Services.

Optow, S. (1990). Moral Exclusion and Injustice: An Introduction. *Journal of Social Issues*, 1–20.

Payne, R. (1996). *A Framework for Understanding Poverty, 4th ed.* Highlands, TX: aha! Process, Inc.

Pew Research Center. (2016). *Partisanship and Political Animosity in 2016.* Pew Research Center.

Phillips, K.W. (2014). How Diversity Makes Us Smarter. *Scientific American.*

Police Executive Research Forum. (2016). *Use of Force: Taking Policing to a Higher Standard.* Washington: PERF.

Schwartz, H. (2016). *Political Correctness and the Destruction of Social Order.* New York: Macmillan.

Sirolli, E. (1999). *Ripples from the Zambezi.* Gabriola Island, Canada: New Society.

Solar, P.J. (2015). Law Enforcement v. Policing: What's the Difference. *ACJS Police Forum*, 3–10.

Staub, E. (2001). Genocide and Mass Killing: Their Roots and Prevention. In R.W. and J.D. Christe (eds), *Peace, Conflict and Violence: Peace Psychology for the 21st Century.* Upper Saddle River, NJ: Prentice Hall.

Stein, S. (2009). *Emotional Intelligence for Dummies.* Mississauga, ON: Wiley & Sons.

CHAPTER 9

Perspectives of the African American Community

■ ■ ■

Contemplation*

"The community, it's vital, caring, resourceful; it wants what any community wants: to be safe, to prosper, for its sons and daughters to prosper. It's not happening. It's not safe, and they're not prospering. The community looks around, at the poverty, the violence, the drugs, and asks, why? And it has an answer. Many in the black community believe that this is all happening because we-the outsiders, the cops, the white folks, the powerful-want it to happen."

"This is just conventional wisdom in the neighborhoods I work in: the government brings the drugs in so they can put our kids in jail so the cops will have work and the cracker prison guards upstate can make union wages."

* Image labeled for unrestricted use.

"As long as the community sees the police, the government, as a race enemy, there will be no rightful place for law. There can be no working together, no partnership, no common purpose" (Kennedy, 2011).

Learning Outcomes

Upon successful completion of this chapter the student will be able to:

- Briefly discuss the history of black Americans in the United States.
- Describe the impact of slave codes, the convict lease system, Southern "Jim Crow" and Northern segregation as mechanism of black oppression and discrimination.
- Identify the impact of mass incarceration in furthering a racial caste system in the United States.
- Describe what is meant by "residual" discrimination and how it impacts the lives of black Americans today.
- Identify specific conditions that are faced by inner-city African Americans that hinder equal opportunity.
- Describe specific strategies that officers can use to serve, support, and build better relationships with men of color.

Important Concepts

- Slave Codes
- Convict Lease System
- Segregation
- Equality of Opportunity
- White Supremacy, Black Subjugation
- Residual Discrimination
- Hyper-sensitivity
- Paternalism
- Patronizing
- Appropriate Disclosure

Questions for Discussion

- What would be some of the reasonable implications for modern police officers to be mindful of with regard to the history of the black experience in the United States?
- Characterize the historical relationship between African Americans and the police.
- What is "white supremacy" and how has it manifested itself historically and today?
- What does mass incarceration have to do with the historical treatment of black Americans?
- What is the difference between structural and cultural issues regarding race? How do they interact to disadvantage African Americans?
- What is meant by "white policing syndrome" and how is it recognized today?

INTRODUCTION

This chapter presents research documenting the perceptions of the African American community with regard to the police. Any effort to manage conflict and build better relationships requires an understanding of why the parties are in conflict. This chapter presents a few of the most prominent perspectives that can be found in the scholarly research that may be useful for this purpose.

The chapter begins with a brief history of black Americans, this is the context of historical discrimination and segregation that may provide a basic level of understanding of modern attitudes, and points-of-view that have an impact on the relationships between the police and black Americans. The next section presents the evolution of efforts to maintain segregation and discrimination, the structural and cultural aspects of modern race relations including the topic of mass incarceration.

Residual discrimination is what is left over once overt, explicit discrimination and racism has faded away and become reprehensible; the more subtle forms of discrimination, marginalization and exclusion are explored in an effort to get at what is really meant by "implicit" bias. Finally, specific strategies regarding how the modern police officer can build better relationships with people of color are explored. These strategies come to us from the work of J.L. Wood and Frank Harris III and their research on supporting men of color, adopted for policing.

I see race relations as a journey requiring vigilance and humility.

More powerfully—police officers, especially white police officers, must understand and accept that the Black experience vis-à-vis the police is a personal one and most often that experience has been negative.

The goal is to appreciate this fact and attempt in each encounter to be the exception in that series of experiences in that it is respectful and positive.

—Dennis J. Shields, Chancellor

> Conflict has its foundation in the lack of understanding, or the lack of willingness to understand, the other point-of-view.

A BRIEF HISTORY OF THE BLACK EXPERIENCE IN AMERICA

The conflict that often erupts between the police and the African American community, and between individual police officers and individual African Americans, has its roots in the bleak history of slavery and white supremacy in the United States. Managing conflict requires that police officers gain a deeper understanding of this history so that they can better understand, and empathize with the conditions that many African Americans find themselves in today.

African Americans today *encounter difficulties due to race that white people do not.* There are hurdles to equality of opportunity that simply do not exist for white people and taking a colorblind approach denies their negative racial experiences, rejects their cultural heritage, and invalidates their unique perspectives (Williams, 2011). Poor people—the principal victims and perpetrators of crime—are primarily people of color, and building better relationships with them requires that competent police officers understand their unique point-of-view.

Economic prosperity and growth in what would become the United States required **cheap labor**. The first choice available to sustain the new colonies was the system of indentured servitude that allowed for wealthy landowners and merchants to acquire labor by contracting with poor white and West Africans. Their work was exchanged for transportation to the new world where they served a term of indenture to reimburse the patron[1] for his expense.

The colonists considered enslaving the natives or indigenous people, but it was felt that indigenous people were not well suited for agricultural work and

---

1 A "patron" is a person who provides support for others. Indentured servants owed the individual who paid for their passage to America, their "patron," someone to whom something is owed.

would not hold up under slave conditions, especially in the south. They settled on the practice of enslaving Blacks because they were better suited for the work and they had a lower standing in society generally. Prior to 1619 Africans were not considered slaves; they enjoyed the same standing as indentured whites. It was only after 1660 that colonial legislation made it clear that Africans were to be considered slaves (Gabbidon, 2016). Whites had power in early American society because they had the option to appeal matters to the British monarchy. Blacks did not enjoy this same status and did not have a favorable public opinion among the majority white population (McIntyre, 1992).

> The interests and power of poor people in early America was undermined when whites were separated and given higher status than blacks, "divide and conquer." Whites were allowed to own land, called upon to police blacks, and were given a personal stake in slavery.

The elite class in the early United States recognized the threat from poor people, both whites and slaves. The threat was exemplified in **Bacon's Rebellion** (1670s) where slaves, indentured servants, free Blacks, and poor whites united against the planter class in Virginia. The response to this threat was a "divide and conquer" strategy where alliances based on the common interests of poor people against the powerful rich elites could be subverted. The tactic is known as the **"racial bribe"** where poor whites were allowed access to land, indentured whites were given the responsibility for policing slaves, and other tactics were used to reduce the chance of any future alliances between black slaves and poor whites.

> Poor whites suddenly had a direct, personal stake in the existence of a race-based system of slavery. Their own plight had not improved by much, but at least they were not slaves. Once the planter elite split the labor force, poor whites responded to the logic of their situation and sought ways to expand their racially privileged position (Alexander M., 2011, p. 25).

The Slave Codes

The concept of justice, as defined in law, was different depending on the color of one's skin. The slave codes emerged as a **formal** mechanism to promote and preserve slavery as well as the supremacy of white people, particularly in the south where their labor was viewed as an economic necessity.

> Slave codes embodied the criminal law and procedure applied against enslaved Africans. The codes, which regulated slave life from cradle to grave, were virtually uniform across states—each with the overriding goal of upholding chattel slavery. The codes not only enumerated the applicable law but also prescribed the social boundaries for slaves—

where they could go, what types of activity they could engage in, and what type of contracts they could enter into. Under the codes, the harshest criminal penalties were reserved for those acts that threatened the institution of slavers (e.g., the murder of someone white or slave insurrection). The slave codes also penalized whites who opposed slavery (Russell, 1998, pp. 14–15).

To enforce the slave codes slaveholders enlisted the *slave patrol* to hunt down and return runaway Africans and to put down slave revolts. The police in America have their origin in the need for the wealthy to protect their property from the lower classes, in the north the threat came from poor immigrants; in the south the threat to the economic prosperity of the rich was the property itself, i.e., slaves. The mission of the slave patrol was to ensure that slaves were quickly captured and returned to face the wrath of their primarily white masters.

In the south cheap labor in the form of slave labor was viewed as an economic necessity. To be without slaves for those who depended upon agriculture for their livelihood meant economic ruin, to be reduced in status to that of a poor white. For poor whites the road to prosperity was to own land along with slaves to work it more profitably.

There was a collective psychological impact of the slave codes that lingers through today including:

- Indoctrinating Blacks into the White social system, cutting Blacks off from their history and culture.
- Instilling an enduring sense of Black inferiority to Whites.
- A belief in the superior power of Whites.
- A deep sense of hopelessness (Anderson C., 1994).

Convict Lease System

Convict labor*

When an end was finally put to slavery in the United States the lingering impact of the psychology of slavery was reinforced through "Black Codes," laws that targeted poor Whites and African Americans. The drive to institutionalize the concept of White supremacy was profound and this was accomplished through a system of legal discrimination that came to be known as "Jim Crow."

The status of freed blacks in the South after the civil war and the passage of the 13th amendment was a significant social and legal problem for Southerners. Into the void created after the war stepped white southerners who reasserted their civil authority. The mechanism for reestablishing their legitimacy and power was a series of restrictive laws designed to oppress freed blacks and ensure their availability as a cheap source of labor. For example, blacks were required to sign long term labor contracts for very low wages and if they refused to do so they were adjudicated as vagrants and subjected to arrest.

Many southern states ran notorious state prisons where poor blacks, and whites, were leased out to wealthy landowners as convict labor. In this way a significant number of African Americans could be legally returned to their former status as slaves with the full backing of the law (DuBois, 1901).

White Supremacy and Racial Hate

The supposed psychological supremacy of white people was reinforced by hate groups such as the Ku Klux Klan who targeted free blacks; and, to a lesser extent, Native Americans and Spanish speaking minorities. Fear was generated by

* Image labeled for unrestricted use.

indiscriminate killings numbering more than 3000 between 1882 and 1930. Blacks were targeted by white gangs in an effort to suppress economic equality and pride, actions that were met with acceptance and even the occasional active participation of local law enforcement. Police precipitated[2] race riots which also served to undermine trust in the law and justice system throughout the early 20th century (Beck, 1995).

The separation of the Black race from the white majority was affirmed in law by the case of *Plessy vs. Ferguson* (1896) that put forth the standard of "separate but equal." The racist belief in the supremacy of the white race and the inferiority of the black race became the standard paradigm upon which public policy was based. Law enforcement was charged with furthering this paradigm through its policing of the black population. The danger of this state-sponsored segregation was first put forth by DuBois (1899) speaking about black crime.

> [Another] cause of Negro crime is the exaggerated and unnatural separation in the South of the best classes of Whites and Blacks. A drawing of the color line, that extends to street cars, elevators, and cemeteries, which leaves no common ground of meeting, no medium for communication, no ties of sympathy between the two races who live together, and whose interests are at the bottom one-such a discrimination is more than silly, it is dangerous (DuBois, 1899, p. 1357) as quoted in (Gabbidon, 2016, p. 16).

The despised status of southern blacks can also be understood through the lens of poor southern whites who viewed them as something less than human. The iconic image of Elizabeth Eckford, a 15-year-old black student entering Little Rock Arkansas Central High School in 1957 is a powerful illustration of the **raw hatred** of blacks by poor whites.

---

2 Precipitated in the sense that police action was the spark that ignited a tense situation.

Elizabeth Eckford challenging white supremacy*

Hazel Bryan is the white girl in the background with the short hair, clearly voicing her disdain for the black girl entering her high school. What is interesting about Hazel is the fact that she grew up in a house without plumbing, with parents who never graduated high school, and a father who beat her. She would go on in life to drop out of high school, get married, and live the life of the quintessential poor white southerner—white trash—including living in a trailer (Isenberg, 2016).

White fear of blacks was not limited to the south. As blacks migrated north at the beginning of the 20th century, they found competition for jobs and economic opportunity in the form of European immigrants who were seeking the same opportunities in primarily low skill jobs. Many of the white Europeans were already established in these jobs and they saw the black migration as a threat resulting in profound racial tensions in the already overcrowded urban areas such as Chicago (Massey, 1993).

Overt violence against blacks contributed to an overall atmosphere of racial hostility that was bolstered by the police acting on behalf of the white majority. Observations of racial inequities in the criminal justice system came to light as early as 1947 when one of the first text books addressed the topic of race and crime. Fueling the racial divide then and now is the data supporting the fact that blacks were arrested, convicted and sentenced to prison three times as frequently as whites (Sutherland, 1947, p. 121) as cited in (Gabbidon, 2016).

> The police, as representatives of the white majority, had a duty to carry out racist policies and enforce discriminatory laws. Sometimes this was done willingly, sometimes not with many blatantly discriminatory and racist laws being ignored by the police.

The police, as servants of the white majority, had been obligated to carryout discriminatory legislation, sometime willingly, sometimes not, the National

* Will Counts Collection: Indiana University Archives.

Coalition of Law Enforcement Officers for Justice, Reform and Accountability is dedicated to fighting the battle to free professional law enforcement officers from similar corrupting influences.[3] The fact is that there has never been a time in our national history when there existed a consensus that everyone should be equally valued in all areas of life. Overt racism is rare today, but its legacy persists in the covert attitudes, beliefs, and points of view of those in power, even in police agencies themselves.[4]

African Americans and the Police

Blacks in America first encountered the police in the form of the **slave patrols**. Slaves were unprotected by the law, especially when they were victims of crimes perpetrated by their owners and white people generally. Black people were arbitrarily stopped by white patterrollers[5] and questioned about their absence from the plantation merely because of their race, they were routinely searched, and the slave patrols also administered whippings (Websdale, 2001). Even free blacks were treated like slaves as in Virginia where blacks had to be employed in order to remain in the state, if not employed within 12 months they were threatened with the loss of their freedom if they remained (Taylor Green, 2000).

> You see de City policemen walkin' his beat? Well, dats de way de patty-rollin' was, only each county had dere patty-rollers, an' dey had to serve three months at a time, den dey would gib you thirty-nine lashes, 'ca'se dat was the law. De patty-rollers knowed nearly all de slaves, an'it wurn't very often dey ever beat them.
>
> —Frank Gill, Mobile, Alabama

> De paterollers was se law, kind od like de policeman now.
>
> —Polly Colbert, Colbert, Oklahoma (Dulaney W. M., 1996, p. 1).

African Americans were not employed as police officers until the mid-1800s when blacks began to appear in some larger cities during reconstruction, even in the south. However, by the last decade of the 19th century their presence in southern cities had been eliminated (Dulaney W., 1996). Eliminating black police

---

3 The National Coalition of Law Enforcement Officers for Justice, Reform and Accountability is a new coalition of current and former law enforcement officers from around the nation. Its mission is to fight institutional racism in our criminal justice system and police culture, and to push for accountability for police officers that abuse their power.

4 Commonly referred to implicit bias, the attitudes, stereotypes, that exist in all of us without our conscious knowledge.

5 Patterollers were organized groups of white men who hunted down runaways and disciplined slaves in the antebellum south.

officers from southern cities may have been accomplished as part of an overt racist agenda or simply a result of the difficulty black police officers faced in an environment that essentially prohibited them from enforcing the law on white offenders, but the standing of African Americans in the eyes of the police in those years is best illustrated by the following quote from Gunnar Myrdal (1944):

> The average Southern policeman is a promoted poor White with a legal sanction to use a weapon. His social heritage has taught him to despise the Negros, and he has had little education which could have changed him . . . the result is that probably no group of Whites in America have a lower opinion of the Negro people and are more fixed in their views than Southern policemen (Myrdal, 1944, pp. 540–541) as cited in (Gabbidon, 2016, p. 118).

Another enduring image is that of southern police officers on the front lines protecting the white status quo from challenges to their power and authority by African Americans.

A march for civil rights*

Blacks did not begin to join the ranks of the police in significant numbers until the 1960s. In the early days of the civil rights movement, three-fourths of the black population lived in the south. Those southern states with the largest black populations had no black police officers (Rudwick, 1960). The face of law enforcement was unmistakably a *White* one.

In writing about the lack of an Afrocentric perspective in policing literature, Cooper (2015) states the following:

> What the reader is not told by most Eurocentric writers, for example, is how blacks were often excluded from becoming police officers and that

* Photograph by Rowland Scherman for USIA—U.S. National Archives.

> in many communities the Ku Klux Klan and police were either complicit or one in the same (Cooper, 2015, p. 334).

What kept blacks out of policing all these years since the demise of the Ku Klux Klan is an **unwelcoming** atmosphere reflected in the following quote from a white police officer as reported by a black police officer. One might ask the question as to what individual, black or white, would choose to subject themselves to an environment in which such attitudes are prevalent, especially when other more lucrative and less demanding options are available.

> My [white] riding partner and I learned something. He said to me one time, we were riding along one day and just out of the clear, blue sky just talking about a whole lot of things and he says "You know what I've learned since you and I've been riding together?" And I said "What's that?" And he said, "You know, I found out that you have a family and you feel about them just about the same way I do about mine." He says, "I've also found out you have about the same moral values that I have, but I was raised to think that you were different." He said, "I've felt like black people were stupid and dumb and, you know, didn't know anything about anything," And he says, "You know, you and I talk about all kinds of things and a lot of times you know a lot more about it than I do." And I said, "Well you see that's the problem in this world. A lot of times kids grow up listening to what people tell them and they never question it and, unless they have an opportunity to actually get to know somebody one on one, they never know the difference. They just go through life taking their attitudes out on other people, and most of the time if you ask them why, a plain old answer: that's the way it's always been. That's the way my mother and father or whatever taught me." You see? [Black police officer] (Bolton, 2004, p. 11).

In a nation that prides itself on equality of opportunity, structural forces have been at work, sometimes overtly as in the case of slave codes, the convict lease system, and legal discrimination—"Jim Crow." Today overt discrimination is not only unlawful but widely viewed as morally repugnant, but that does not mean that it does not exist. There are structural forces at work that continue to challenge the resiliency of people of color, obstacles to equality of opportunity that present themselves within the confines of the modern police agency itself.

THE NEW FACE OF SEGREGATION

A black man in jail*

Discrimination is still legal! It simply changed form.

Following the civil war the north embarked upon a process of reconstruction that sought to inject the south with "northern" values. African Americans were suddenly vested with political and economic power and began their "brief moment in the sun" as declared by Martin Luther King Jr. many decades later. Southern whites reacted with panic and outrage and sought ways to redeem the south, in many cases through the use of terrorism to cower the emergent black influence and liberty. The northern influence ended in the south with the end of reconstruction when the evolving social order was struck down and blacks were relegated to their former status on the bottom of the southern caste system. The north abandoned any efforts to enforce the new federal civil rights legislation and southern blacks were left to the mercy of southern elites.

What later became known as the "Jim Crow" era emerged as a way to maintain legal discrimination. The landmark case of **Plessy v. Ferguson** set the legal precedence of *separate but equal* into law. Segregation of the races was maintained through local laws that were police enforced and intended to relegate American blacks to what was considered their appropriate place in southern society. The separation of the races was the priority; equality of opportunity, especially in education, was conveniently ignored by the southern elite in their zest to maintain their supreme status in the social order.

> After a brief period of progress during Reconstruction, African Americans found themselves, once again, virtually defenseless. The criminal justice system was strategically employed to force African

* Image labeled for unrestricted use.

> Americans back into a system of extreme repression and control, a tactic that would continue to prove successful for generations to come. Even as convict labor faded away, strategic forms of exploitation and repression emerged anew. As Blackmon notes: "the apparent demise . . . of leasing prisoners seemed a harbinger of a new day. But the harsher reality of the South was that the new, post-Civil War neo-slavery was evolving, not disappearing[6] (Alexander M., 2011, p. 32).

Over subsequent years and generations, blacks began to acquire political power in the North and the ability to organize against segregation, a northern system of legal discrimination. The National Association for the Advancement of Colored People (NAACP) engaged in successful challenges to the Jim Crow laws and the Supreme Court decision in **Brown v. Board of Education** ended the fallacy of separate but equal.

The landmark decision was met by new efforts to enact black codes and the reemergence of terrorism by the Ku Klux Klan and other hate groups in an effort to maintain white supremacy in the south. However, these efforts were challenged by a new tactic of non-violent resistance that captured the sympathy of *people of good will* throughout the nation. In arguing against violent resistance King said the following (1958):

> If one is in search of a better job, it does not help to burn down the factory. If one needs more adequate education, shooting the principal will not help, or if housing is the goal, only building and construction will produce that end. To destroy anything, person or property, can't bring us closer to the goal that we seek (Washington, 1986, p. 58).

The inherent injustice of the racial caste system advocated by white southerners and reinforced by Jim Crow laws in the south and segregation in the north was laid bare for the nation to see. ***What the nation saw it did not like.***

> The nonviolent strategy has been to dramatize the evils of our society in such a way that pressure is brought to bear against those evils by the forces of good will in the community and change is produced.
>
> The student sit-ins of 1960 are a classic illustration of this method. Students were denied the right to eat at a lunch counter, so they deliberately sat down to protest their denial. They were arrested, but this made their parents mad and so they began to close their charge accounts. The students continued to sit-in, and this further embarrassed the city, scared away shoppers and soon produced an economic threat to

6 Douglas Blackmon, "A Different Kind of Slavery," Wall Street Journal online, Mar. 29, 2008.

business life of the city. Amid this type of pressure, it is not hard to get people to agree to change (Washington, 1986, p. 58).

The era of legal discrimination was finally ended as the result of a groundswell of support for the civil rights act of 1964, a bill that ended the "Jim Crow" laws. The goal put forth by President Johnson was the full assimilation of the more than twenty-million Negros into American life.

The proponents of segregation and white supremacy in the south found themselves thrown back into a new kind of reconstruction era with federal troops and Department of Justice lawyers enforcing this new legislation. The old ways of maintaining the social order were no longer effective. A new way had to be found to keep the back man in his place and they found it in the call for law and order.

The Era of Mass Incarceration

The non-violent approach to social change advocated by King continued beyond the **Civil Rights Act of 1964** as African Americans sought to break down the barriers to economic inequality and integration. This happened to coincide with rapidly rising rates of crime in the late 1960s and early 1970s that provided a justification for crack-downs on lawlessness.

Diehard segregationists insisted that integration caused crime, laying the fault for public fear directly at the feet of the black man and his push for civil rights. Urban riots created enormous pressure for "get tough on crime policies" with issues of police brutality, primarily directed against blacks, being dismissed by those more concerned with civil disorder.

> *If [blacks] conduct themselves in an orderly way, they will not have to worry about police brutality.*
>
> —Senator Robert Byrd[7]

Rising crime rates, increasing poverty, and deteriorating urban environments fed the fire for new laws primarily aimed at a growing drug problem. Even black activists in the North joined in the call for a war on drugs including harsh mandatory sentencing guidelines (Barker, 2009).

The **Anti-Drug Abuse Act of 1986** called for harsh penalties, including mandatory minimum sentences for the distribution of cocaine, but far more severe punishments for the distribution of crack, a drug more associated with blacks (Alexander M., 2011).

---

[7] "Poverty: Phony Excuse for Riots? Yes, Says a Key Senator," U.S. News and World Report, July 31, 1967, p. 14.

After the civil rights act, Jim Crow was gone in the south, but white southerners saw a new way to resurrect segregation in the form of anti-crime proposals that appealed to the race-crime argument. The war on poverty, with its emphasis on integration, bussing, fair housing, education, and civil rights was transformed to a war on crime; specifically drug crime occurring in urban centers primarily populated by African Americans.

> As the rules of acceptable discourse changed, however, segregationists distanced themselves from an *explicitly*[8] racist agenda. They developed instead the racially sanitized rhetoric of "cracking down on crime," rhetoric that is now used freely by politicians of every stripe. Conservative politicians who embraced this rhetoric purposefully failed to distinguish between the direct action tactics of civil rights activists, violent rebellions in inner cities, and traditional crimes of an economic or violent nature. Instead, as Marc Mauer of the sentencing Project has noted, "all of these phenomenon were subsumed under the heading of 'crime in the streets" (Mauer, 1999) as quoted in (Alexander M., 2011, p. 43).

Adopting the rhetoric of the "**War on Crime**" enabled political actors to resurrect the racist policies of segregation in a way that struck fear in both the white and black populations. As the crack cocaine epidemic hit the large urban centers, the call went out for mandatory sentencing laws in response to the genocide that was occurring in the ghettos of the largest cities by leaders in the black community itself. However, Alexander's assertion that the war on drugs was merely a way to re-establish a racial caste system reminiscent of Jim Crow falls short. The fact is that many of those who supported the 1994 crime bill included the black Mayors of large cities and black activists who viewed the bill as an imperfect but necessary measure to combat pervasive violence in poor black urban neighborhoods (Neyfakh, 2016).

The impact-outcomes-of these efforts were that ninety-percent of those admitted to prison for drug offenses in many states were black or Latino. Even though this mass incarceration was explained in race-neutral terms, a new kind of race-based discrimination was born, what Alexander calls "The New Jim Crow" (Alexander M., 2011).

---

[8] Explicit refers to behavior that can be observed, that which is directly stated, or observed, such as refusing to hire someone because of their race. Conversely, Implicit is that which is implied but not stated or observable. In some cases those who practice bias that is implicit are not even aware that they are influenced by it.

Once a person is labeled as a felon, legal discrimination is allowed. Privileges of citizenship, such as jury service and voting, are not available to those who are convicted felons under the auspices of the war on drugs. Those convictions result from economic disadvantage that has its roots in structural inequalities that define life in the ghetto (Alexander M., 2011).

> Where incentives to make arrests exist the police, based on their human nature, seek out the easiest way to generate those arrests; in poor neighborhoods where drug use is out in the open and the citizens have the least ability to defend themselves legally.

Aggressive law enforcement and prosecutions became common, spurred on by generous monetary incentives provided by the **1994 crime bill**. Subsequent grants to local government police agencies were based partly on the numbers of arrests: the more arrests that were made, the better the prospects for more federal money. The best place to seek out those arrests was the ghetto where drug use and dealing were out in the open and the poor inhabitants lacked the resources to defend themselves in court. The arrests numbers increased, the federal money flowed, and the politicians could claim success in driving down the rates of violent crime. Unfortunately, the casualties—black men—were relegated to second-class status, again.

The attitude of the general—mostly white—population was that poor people of color had a choice, that they were responsible for their own actions, and if they chose a life of drug dealing they deserve what they got, i.e., prison and no voice in the political process.

The next section poses a question: whether the claim that poor people of color really did have a choice was actually true.

STRUCTURAL AND CULTURAL ISSUES IN MODERN TIMES

Institutional racism runs throughout our criminal justice system. ***Its presence in police culture, though often denied in the media by many police apologists, has been central to the breakdown in police-community relationships for decades in spite of good people doing police work*** *(Redditt Hudson, emphasis added).*

The race based problems that are occurring in urban areas are the result of *Social Structures* and *Culture Forces* that dominate these regions. Social structures are the ways in which social relationships are arranged and exist in our institutions such as schools, commercial enterprises, the economy generally, markets, governmental organizations, political organizations and any other organization or institution that provides order to social interaction. These structures and institutions carry power, influence, and privilege that are independent of the individuals who occupy positions within them (Alexander J.C., 2008) as referenced in (Wilson, 2009).

> Individual behavior is often driven by a shared understanding of social life and outlooks on the world. Common subjective views of reality, such as the legitimacy of the police, are powerful behavioral influences.

Cultural forces are the shared points-of-view among those individuals who occupy common places, such as poor inner-city neighborhoods and schools, or who have shared experiences and circumstances such as generational poverty, perceived victimizations, advantages, or personal associations. Individual behavior is often driven by **cultural scripts**; these are shared understandings of social life, a shared outlook, common views of reality or traditions, and practices and beliefs that are common to those who live and interact in the same physical and social environment (Hannerz, 1991) as referenced in (Wilson, 2009).

Inequality of outcome is driven by forces that are imbedded in the social structures that govern society, such as the criminal justice system, and the cultural forces that influence group behavior, such as the patterns of beliefs, norms, attitudes, and behaviors that become part of what it means to be a member of a particular group, i.e., inner-city black. Social structures include structural issues and social processes that contribute to unequal outcomes such as racial inequality.

Structural Issues

Social acts are structural forces that include behaviors on the part of individuals within a group holding power over another group. Examples include stereotyping, discrimination in housing and employment, and biased policing practices. These acts create unequal outcomes that are based on the standing of one group over another, such as race.

> A deeper understanding on the part of the police concerning the common perceptions of people of color can go a long way toward repairing the relationship. Discuss.

Social processes are structural forces that include laws, formal practices, and public policies that directly contribute to unequal racial group outcomes due to the characteristics of that group. When the decision makers do not understand the basis for the standing of one group relative to another, these forces can further damage the distribution of wealth, opportunity, and influence-social justice-in the larger society (Wilson, 2009).

The black migration of the 1950s provides an example of these forces at work. The migration was driven by the promise of greater economic opportunity for blacks in northern cities. When they arrived they found urban population centers inhabited by established and newly arrived European immigrants who were employed, or actively seeking employment, as unskilled laborers. These individuals saw the arriving blacks as a threat and engaged in acts such as employment discrimination, exclusion from unions, employee associations, and even clubs resulting in adverse outcomes. These are examples of *direct forces* of racism and under these conditions the only opportunities left to blacks were in the most menial and lowest paying jobs such as domestic service, trash collection, and hard labor; jobs that the more established, white, immigrants didn't want. These direct forces have since then been mitigated by a more progressive and enlightened understanding of human character and value.

> When particular groups are more vulnerable than others those groups are more likely to suffer the unintended consequences of what appear to be sound public policies.

However, *indirect* structural forces are more insidious because they go largely unnoticed until the results come to light. For example, the political forces that drove the war on drugs were an indirect force that led to the outcome of mass incarceration. Even though the war on drugs was not explicitly designed to result in mass incarceration, the indirect impact was racial injustice. *The point that this example illustrates is that some political decisions have a greater adverse impact on some social-racial-groups than others not by design, but because of the vulnerability of the group itself* (Wilson, 2009).

> In recent years, the growth and spread of new technologies and the growing internationalization of economic activity have changed the relative demand for different types of workers. The wedding of emerging technologies and international competition has eroded the basic institutions of the mass production system and eradicated related manufacturing jobs in the United States. In the last several decades, almost all of the improvements in productivity have been associated with technology and human capital, thereby drastically reducing the importance of physical capital and natural resources. The changes in technology that are producing new jobs are making many others obsolete (Wilson, 2009, p. 6).

The kind of labor necessary for success in the new economy is highly educated and well-trained men and women. Low skilled workers, including African Americans as a group, are at a distinct disadvantage due to the social stratification that leaves blacks vulnerable to economic conditions because they are at the lowest rung of the economic ladder. This means that they will be the first to be let go when the overall economy slows down. *A decline in the demand for low skilled labor has a bigger impact on people of color because so many more of them are low-skilled.* In addition, their relative position in the labor force perpetuates the stereotype that blacks are only suited for the most menial of jobs (Wilson, 2009).

The sharp economic decline of 2008 exacerbated another problem for poor people of color: their access to well-paying jobs is limited by geography. As the better jobs move out of the urban centers, black inner city residents find their opportunities limited to low paying service jobs because they **lack mobility**. Poor people of color become isolated, not only from the places of employment, but to the informal networks that alert them to job opportunities.

Cultural Issues

There is a distinct set of cultural traits that police officers quickly pick-up on and associate with African Americans today. The natural process of stereotyping creates a kind of cognitive shorthand that causes police officers, regardless of race, to apply generalizations that may not be accurate with regard to individual traits, attitudes and points-of-view. Sometimes this cognitive shorthand results in tragedies, tragedies that could be avoided if officers better understood the cultural forces at work in black neighborhoods.

> Cultural traits consist of shared outlooks, behaviors, traditions beliefs, and worldviews common to a group.

Cultural traits include shared outlooks, modes of behavior, traditions, belief systems, and worldviews that emerge from patterns of intergroup interaction. Black American culture has its roots in the history of black people in America and consists of attitudes, beliefs and traditions passed down from previous generations of blacks. These cultural traits also include skills, preferences, styles of self-preservation, etiquette, and linguistic patterns that may be completely foreign to a police officer who is unfamiliar with the patterns of normal discourse existing in certain areas due to their own segregation from it (Wilson, 2009).

The police also have a unique culture that emerges from patterns of intergroup interactions that have been passed down in the form of attitudes, beliefs, and traditions that place them into conflict with the black culture (Crank, 2004).

Understanding the impact of these cultural forces begins with understanding that much of the black American culture was created **as the result** of past discrimination, segregation, and blatantly unjust practices perpetrated, in many cases, by the police themselves.

> Racism has historically been one of the most prominent American cultural frames and has played a major role in determining how whites perceive and act toward blacks. At its core, racism is an ideology of racial domination with two key features: 1) beliefs that one race is either biologically or culturally inferior to another and 2) the use of such beliefs to rationalize or prescribe the way that the "inferior" race should be treated in this society, as well as to explain its social position as a group and its collective accomplishments. In the United States today, there is no question that the more categorical forms of racist ideology—in particular, those that assert the biogenetic inferiority of blacks—have declined significantly, even though they still may be embedded in institutional norms and practices (Wilson, 2009, p. 15).

One of the manifestations of living in culturally segregated groups such as the inner city is the continual exposure to what Wilson (2009) refers to as group-specific cultural traits (cultural frames, orientations, habits, and worldviews, as well as styles of behavior and particular skills) that emerge from patterns of *social exclusion*. One of these manifestations is related to the constant threat of physical attack that comes from living in high crime areas. "Street smarts" is a term used to describe the kind of behavior that is exhibited. Examples include avoiding contact with others, making oneself as small as possible so as to not be noticed, and viewing every new situation with suspicion and distrust. These characteristics can easily be interpreted by those unfamiliar with these living conditions as antisocial, distancing, and "suspicious" (p. 18).

> Patterns of behavior indicative of inner city life can easily be interpreted as antisocial, distancing, and suspicious.

Ironically, police officers working in inner city neighborhoods will display similar behaviors that can easily be interpreted as antisocial, distancing, and "untrustworthy" (Crank, 2004), but there are burdens on black Americans that simply do not resonate in the white population. Understanding these burdens may be of use in building better relations in these communities.

The Code of the Street

Anderson (1999) speaks to the "Code of the Street" that consists of **informal rules** that govern interactions and shape how people interact with one another and make decisions.

> This decision making is influenced partly by how people come to view their world over time—what we call "**meaning making**." It is important to remember that the processes of meaning making and decision making evolve in situations imposed by poverty and racial segregation—situations that place severe constraints on social mobility. Over time, these processes lead to the development of informal codes that regulate behavior.
>
> In a context of limited opportunities for self-actualization and success, some individuals in the community, most notably young black males, devise alternative ways to gain respect that emphasize manly pride, ranging from simply wearing brand-name clothing to have the "right look" and talking the right way, to developing a predatory attitude (Anderson E., 1999, p. 18).

Poverty places severe limitations on social mobility. Limited opportunity for success and self-actualization lead to alternative ways to gain respect and status such as adopting a predatory attitude.

Social integration and assimilation is hindered by these cultural forces, creating a huge chasm between inner-city blacks and the police, but culture is not the primary source of adverse and inequitable outcomes; rather, it is the *interaction of structural and cultural forces* that explains black disadvantage with structural forces claiming the larger share of responsibility.

For example, consider the segregation policies of Northern cities such as Chicago in the 1950s in response to black migration. Poor blacks and poor white immigrants were segregated into different schools with the white schools inarguably receiving more and better resources than the black schools. As a result, generations of black students were denied educational opportunities when compared to their white counterparts, an outcome resulting from both direct and indirect structural forces—political decision making—with implications that plainly resonate today.

White privilege refers to the advantages that those of European dissent enjoy when compared to Blacks. Unfortunately this term is most often used to illustrate how black Americans continue to be disadvantages thus perpetuating the idea that Blacks are somehow inferior breeding a sense of hopelessness.

The Burden on Black Americans

Due to no fault of their own, black Americans face unique obstacles that white people do not face. *White privilege* is the term that is popular with those who would seek to enhance white guilt, but the problem for black Americans goes well beyond any advantage enjoyed by those of European dissent. Speaking about the crisis in race relations back in 1958, Martin Luther King, Jr. put it this way.

> The crisis has been precipitated, on the other hand, by the radical change in the Negro's evaluation of himself. There would probably be no crisis in race relations if the Negro continued to think of himself in inferior terms and patiently accepted injustice and exploitation. But it is at this very point that the change has come. For many years the Negro tacitly accepted segregation. It not only harms one physically, but it injures one spiritually. It scars the soul and distorts the personality. It inflicts the segregator with a false sense of superiority while inflicting the segregated with a false sense of inferiority. But through the forces of history something happened to the Negro. He came to feel that he was somebody. He came to feel that the important thing about a man is not the color of his skin or the texture of his hair, but the texture and quality of his soul. With this new sense of dignity and new self-respect, a new Negro emerged (Washington, 1986, p. 85).

Unfortunately, the new Negro, as King put it, emerged into a society that was not ready to address the chronic systems of injustice that permeate it. The black American was used as a pawn by the elites in a continuing effort to solidify power over public policy. There were, and still are, advantages to separating whites and blacks by social status.

> *I'll tell you what's at the bottom of it. If you can convince the lowest white man he's better than the best colored man, he won't notice you're picking his pocket. Hell, give him somebody to look down on, and he'll empty his pockets for you.*[9] Lyndon Johnson (Isenberg, 2016, p. 264).

One of the best examples of how the racial divide is maintained is the impact of our most recent crime control polices. The disproportionate impact on black Americans was not anticipated in the rush to suppress a growing crime problem in the early 1990s, but the disparate impact of the anti-crime efforts cannot be ignored. One author claims that this impact was foreseen.

> Throughout this century, black Americans, especially men but increasingly also women, have been more likely than whites to commit violent and property crimes. They have also been more likely to be in jail or prison, on probation or parole. People of goodwill, from W.E.B. Du Bois at the turn of the century through Gunnar Myrdal in the 1940s,

---

[9] Bill Moyers, "What a Real President Was Like: to Lyndon Johnson the Great Society Meant Hope and Dignity, *The Washington Post,* Nov. 13, 1988.

> to most contemporary scholars of crime, agree the disproportionate black criminality is the product of social and economic disadvantage, much of it traceable to racial bias and discrimination, more overt in earlier times than today (Tonry, 1995, p. 1).

> Black Americans have been more likely than whites to commit crime, be convicted, and incarcerated. This results from social and economic disadvantage that can be traced back to past racial bias and discrimination.

These sources of social and racial bias include, but are not limited to, bias in police arrests, a lack of sympathy for black victims of crime, the exaggerated sympathy for white victims, and different patterns of criminality based on race. Criminal justice practitioners disagree about the extent of these problems, but they are in agreement that they exist and amount to chronic, as opposed to *acute*, social problems.[10]

To illustrate the difference Tonry (1995) offers the following in speaking about the alarming number of blacks that were under the control of the criminal justice system in 1991, over 50%.

> Those numbers are, or ought to be, shocking to every American. It is not hard to understand why many interpret them as prima facie evidence of a racist criminal justice system. Disturbing though the numbers are on the surface, what lies below is even more disturbing, for three reasons. First, the rising levels of black incarceration did not just happen; they were the foreseeable effects of deliberate policies spearheaded by the Reagan and Bush administrations and implemented in many states. Anyone with knowledge of drug-trafficking patterns and of police arrest policies and incentives could have foreseen that the enemy troops in the War on Drugs would consist largely of young, inner-city minority males. Blacks in particular are arrested and imprisoned for drug crimes in numbers far out of line with their proportions of the general population, of drug users, and drug traffickers (Tonry, 1995, p. 4).

> Black criminality is viewed as a chronic problem, one highly resistant to a cure. Its basis however rests upon acute social conditions that can be fixed if only society, Black and White, had the will to do so.

This situation has only gotten worse and illustrates, in Tonry's view, the willingness of our society to treat an acute social problem as if it were a chronic problem, meaning that they are problems highly resistant to any systematic

---

10 A chronic problem is one that is persistent over time. An acute problem is one that has only recently emerged.

intervention. The noble goal of full and complete integration of black Americans into the fabric of American life is being hindered by the short-sided efforts of those primarily concerned with political and economic expediency. These individuals hindering complete integration include *both* white and black individuals.

The relationship between the police and the black community has never been a good one, but public policy on crime control and the new war on drugs has had a devastating impact on black men. The effects have trickled down to the black family structure, undermined black resiliency, and contributed to a sense of hopelessness in inner-city black neighborhoods that has trapped these communities into a downward spiral of despair.

It is important, too, at this point to add yet another major contributor to the current plight of the black community: the breakdown of the black family, especially in inner city neighborhoods, and the resulting loss of a father's influence in black homes. First reported by a young researcher in the Kennedy-Johnson administration who went on to become a very influential senior U.S. Senator from New York, Daniel Patrick Moynihan's identification of the deterioration of the black family caused by the nation's public assistance (welfare) programs has been long ignored, but it has nonetheless been reinforced by current data that show that a child raised in a fatherless home is statistically far more likely to drop out of school, spend time incarcerated in prison, and live a life of poverty than are children raised in a home with the presence of both a mother and a father (Moynihan, 1965).

> Overt or explicit discrimination based upon race has been outlawed. What remains is a much more insidious problem consisting of implicit stereo-types, prejudice, and bias. This includes biased police attitudes toward Blacks and Black animosity toward the police.

RESIDUAL DISCRIMINATION

The direct forces of discrimination have been recognized, outlawed, and are now widely considered morally reprehensible. However, the residual effects remain in the form of stereo-types, prejudice, and bias. Wise policing requires that officers seek a deeper understanding of what can be perceived as *black animosity toward the institution of policing* as a structural force in American society.

> Researchers examining the history of U.S. policing have shown how powerful groups of whites developed police forces as a means of ensuring their power over the less powerful. For two centuries now, white authorities and citizens have viewed a police force as the first line of defense against, as some have said, the black "hordes" and therefore

> authorized the use of coercion and violence to keep black Americans subordinated in segregated communities. Thus, after the civil War, the white elites in the South authorized the use of naked violence and police power to subordinate the newly freed black citizens. By the end of reconstruction, unofficial (for example, Ku Klux Klan) and official white violence virtually re-enslaved most black southerners. Moreover, between the late nineteenth century and the 1960s, many white police officials and officers continued to aid white mobs who attacked or killed (often, lynched) black citizens. White Americans have long exercised a monopoly over physical force as authorized by law. From the seventeenth century to the present, the justice system has frequently failed to provide legal protection and social justice for African Americans and other darker-skinned Americans.
>
> Today, black communities and other communities of color are still disproportionately the focal point of much of the policing effort in the United States (Bolton, 2004, p. 12).

The argument has been made that there exists a number of structural, cultural, and ideological forces arrayed against black Americans in the United States, see Wilson (2009), Alexander (2011), Tonry (1995) and others. These forces have relegated them to secondary status behind whites; and the origin, development, and institutionalization of policing has been instrumental in this process. The legacy of past discrimination lives on in the subjective perceptions of black Americans regarding the police.

The White Policing Syndrome

The behaviors, attitudes and points-of-view reflected in the police are a function of the same attitudes and points-of-view that exists in the community at-large. Each law enforcement agency is unique as a function of an uncoordinated and decentralized system of policing here in the United States. As a result, one police agency may make extensive use of alternatives to arrest in a community that is very sensitive to social justice issues while a neighboring agency may maintain a 'crack-down" attitude toward what can easily be considered minor infractions.

> White policing syndrome is the routinely negative perceptions and treatment of black citizens by white police officers. When the majority of the population harbors negative perceptions of Blacks that same attitude will be reflected in police behavior.

Hawkins and Thomas (1992) identify what they refer to as the "white policing syndrome" that has been defined as the routinely **negative perceptions** and treatment of black citizens by white police officers (Hawkins, 1992). As representatives of the existing power structures or status quo, police officers tend to demonstrate the attitudes and points-of-view of those in power. For example, if the President of the local bank voices his anger about the teenagers who skateboard in the bank parking lot, who spray-paint graffiti on the curb, and scare away ATM customers; the beat officer is likely to display an antagonistic attitude when confronting these troublemakers.

According to Hawkins and Thomas, the white policing syndrome reflects the same tendencies related to race. If the majority of the population has negative dominant attitudes toward blacks, considering them more likely to be involved in crime, officers are more likely to treat blacks harshly because harsh treatment of blacks reflects community stereo-types and bias (Hawkins, 1992).

> A major social function of policing is to maintain existing group-based hierarchies, and white officers tend to hold stereo-types and prejudices that are linked to or shaped by their policing role. One illustration of this point is commonplace, racial profiling; many white officers today believe that the racial marker "black" is a sufficient reason to suspect, detain, or search blacks, and particularly black men (Bayley, 1969).

> The cure for the white policing syndrome is for the police to adopt a service orientation. The less social distance that exists between the police and black citizens the more likely it is that the police will adopt a service orientation. Segregation cuts both ways. Discuss.

The other problem that whites face related to the white policing syndrome is segregation. White officers are more likely to be less antagonistic when working in white neighborhoods. According to Banton (1964) police officers are more likely to adopt a service orientation in neighborhoods that are similar to their own. *Research confirms that the less social distance that exists between a police officer and the citizens that they police, the more likely that the officer will adopt a friendly and helpful orientation* (Banton, 1964) (Brown, 1981). Conversely, officers will be less likely to adopt an aggressive or antagonistic orientation when they view the citizens as holding the same attitudes, beliefs and points-of-view as they themselves.

The implication here is that *police officers should be required to live where they work because the social interaction will decrease the distance in terms of attitudes, culture, and point-of-view that exists between themselves and those that they police.* Better relationships occur naturally between those who are familiar with one another, segregation promotes those conditions in which white officers lack the ability to understand the behavior of citizens of color (Bolton, 2004).

In urban black communities, how the police are viewed by citizens is also critical to the police community relationship. In many cases the police are the most visible representatives of governmental authority. Further, most often they also reflect the white power structure, even if they are black. Recent studies about how the police are viewed by communities of color mirror the findings of the 1968 National Advisory Commission on Civil Disorders, in that many black Americans believed that police brutality and harassment is common in their communities (Commission, 1968) (Alpert, 1988).

The negative perceptions of police are the result of shared perceptions in the black community and the cumulative effect of consistent negative encounters with police over time. "There is no reason to suppose that anti-black hostility is a new development brought on by recent conflicts between the police and the black community. What appears to have changed is not police attitudes, but the fact that black people are fighting back" (Skolnick J., 1968).

Reducing the tension between the black community and the police may begin with the police recognizing the unique challenges of the black community and becoming more sensitive to these challenges. The other aspect of relationship building is how the police are viewed by the population that they serve. This can be a complicated matter depending on the level of diversity that exists in the community—the differing types of communities as was discussed in an earlier chapter. However, with regard to the black community in general, there is a suggestion that one of the best ways to improve the relationship is to have more black police officers working the street and in leadership positions in the police department. The presence of black officers and executives does not eliminate discrimination within the agency or biased enforcement practices, but black executives are usually more deliberate in their efforts to solicit black community support than their white colleagues (Dulaney W., 1996).

> Recruiting more black police officers offers two advantages; black citizens will feel the police are more representative, and the behavior of white officers will be tempered by the presence of black officers. Discuss.

The Value of Black Police Officers

Numerous arguments have been made about the effectiveness of employing more black police officers in reducing tensions between the police and the black community. These arguments are based on two specific premises: first, community members see black officers and then feel that the police agency is more representative of their community. Second, the presence of black officers has a direct impact on the behavior of white officers in that the black presence *makes white officers more sensitive* to black perspectives.

Even though the policing styles of white and black officers are essentially the same, the expectation is that black officers will be better in dealing with citizens of color on a day-to-day basis (Skolnick J. F., 1992). Support for this view is found in a study that concluded that black police officers were less social-dominance-oriented in their attitudes than white officers (Sidaius, 1994).

It just makes sense that black officers would reflect more positively in the eyes of black citizens because they have much better knowledge of the black community, its values and norms. However, black officers report that they felt more respected by white citizens than they do by black citizens. It could be that the difference rests not in race, but in socio-economic status. Both white and black officers are solidly middle-class and most choose to live outside of the communities that they police. However, the most frequent victims and perpetrators of crime are poor, generally poor people of color. The idea that the attitudes toward the police by citizens is often shaped by the different socioeconomic conditions, as discussed in a previous chapter, is also worthy of consideration. The negative image of the police in black communities may be explained more by the general role and perceptions of the police than by the behaviors or actions of individual officers (Criminal Justice Institute, 1985).

> Why is it difficult to recruit qualified black officers today? Discuss.

The implications of the research indicate that segregation has disadvantaged both Blacks and Whites in policing. Black police officers have most certainly been segregated from policing and discriminated against in hiring and promotion. This places them at a historical disadvantage as individuals, but the segregation of white officers from black neighborhoods has undermined the ability of white officers' to police these areas effectively. *Highly effective policing demands that officers have the desire and willingness to engage in the communities that they police.* This leads to greater knowledge of the attitudes, values, beliefs, and points-of-view of the citizens that they serve. Because black officers are more easily viewed as part of the inner city black communities, they are at a distinct advantage in relationship building and conflict management in those areas. However, they still face challenges within police agencies themselves that are reflections of residual discrimination in the society generally.

> Discrimination today consists of avoidance, exclusion, and generally insensitive acts.

The Character of Everyday Racism

Many individuals today, and white individuals in particular, assume that racism and discrimination are problems of the past. This leads them to advocate a "color blind" perspective on race relations. Such a perspective ignores the unique aspects of the African American experience as well as the obvious historical determinants of black disadvantage. Since such a perspective also assumes that black Americans should no longer *feel* discriminated against, this perspective is itself a part of the foundation of racial conflict today.

> Today, experiential racism continues to have an impact on the lives of all Americans of color, and especially on the lives of African Americans, the longest term (with Native Americans) racially oppressed group within this white dominated society. This discrimination ranges from intentional and easily documented acts, to less obvious and subtler forms of discrimination, to covert discrimination that takes place behind the scenes. Discriminatory acts by whites range from avoidance maneuvers, to exclusion and rejection, to verbal or physical attacks, to insults and insensitivity. Racial discrimination also varies in character and impact, depending on the site and location. For, example, black Americans often encounter different forms of discrimination in the workplace than they do in impersonal public locations such as malls and on the streets (Bolton, 2004, p. 28).

Critics of the *color blind* view will often state that racism, although clearly illegal and immoral in its overt forms, still exists. And it does: as the following paragraphs explain, it exists in both a systematic and experiential conceptual framework.

Systematic Racism

Systematic means that racism is inherent as part of societies' institutional processes. Structural factors in society, as put forth by Wilson (2009), contain racist elements. As an illustration of this, consider the words of Frederick Douglass, an early and eminently prominent black scholar and activist who commented on the racism faced by black Americans. "In nearly every department of American life they are confronted by this insidious influence. It fills the air. It meets them at the workshop and factory, when they apply for work. It meets them at church, at the hotel, at the ballot-box, and worst of all, it meets them in the jury box . . . He [the black American] has *ceased to be a slave of an individual*, but has in some sense become *the slave of society*" (Douglass, 1881) as referenced in (Bolton, 2004, p. 24).

> Systematic or systemic racism means that racism is an inherent part of our institutional processes. Discriminatory treatment is built into and supported by social institutions. Is this the case? Discuss.

Institutional or systematic racism can be best understood as the patterns of racial discrimination and discriminatory treatment that are built into and supported by social institutions. It is a centuries old system of racial oppression that was created by white people consisting of racialized emotions, ideologies, and attitudes that white people hold, consciously and unconsciously, about people of color.

> In everyday operation, a complex array of discriminatory and other racialized relationships distort what could be fully egalitarian[11] societal relationships into relationships that are in fact harmful, separating, and alienating. This means that racism is fully experiential as well as systematic. Constantly at work, systematic racism categorizes and divides human beings from each other and thus severely restricts the development of common human consciousness and egalitarian society. Everyday life under this system of racism involves an ongoing struggle between racially defined human communities—one community whose members are generally seeking to preserve unjustly derived privileges and power, and other communities whose members are seeking to overthrow racial oppression and garner a fair share of societal resources and opportunities (Bolton, 2004, p. 26).

Experiential Racism

The experiences of black Americans who function within society today illustrate the real meaning of everyday racism. For example, consider the impact of walking into a crowded room and having every face in that room turn to look in your direction, perhaps with whispered comments between individuals. This experience would be quite different if you were the President of the United States, or an otherwise famous individual as opposed to a black person walking into a room populated only by white faces. The attention received by the former would be based on individual notoriety, the attention in the latter case would be based on race and the collective generalizations attributed to persons who look like you.

Blacks simply face challenges that white people simply cannot relate to in everyday situations.

The perception of white superiority has deep roots in this country. Consider the words of the Chief Justice of the Supreme Court in the case of Dred Scott v. Sandford in 1857. Black Americans "had for more than a century before [the U.S. Constitution] been regarded as beings of an inferior order, and altogether unfit to

[11] An egalitarian is someone who believe in the equality of all persons. An egalitarian society recognizes this equality and affords all persons equal rights.

associate with the white race, either in social or political relations; and so far inferior, that they had no rights which the white man was bound to respect."[12]

Racial segregation was officially endorsed by the Supreme Court in the case of **Plessy v. Ferguson** (1896), a case that established the separate by equal principle for the separation of the races. The court in this case ignored the views of black people by stating that "the forced separation of the two races stamps the colored race with a badge of inferiority" but this is not worthy of consideration under the law because "this sense of inferiority is only a notion in black minds," presumably because of the equality with which they were then required to be treated with regard to the law, economic, and educational opportunity as ordered by the court in this case.

It wasn't until the 1950s that social scientists began to realize the implications of black experiences of every-day racism. Racial discrimination is experienced as a routine, recurring, and everyday reality for black Americans. It is motivated by racial stereotypes and racial images that have been long engrained into the fabric of society, so-much-so that they are not even noticeable to white Americans (Bolton, 2004).

The foundation of experiential racism is best explained by a black police officer in the following quote:

> You process information based on your experiences, your education, what you've been exposed to. And if you hadn't been exposed to certain kinds of things, you're going to process information a little bit differently. If you have cultural beliefs, philosophical beliefs that have been ingrained in you for years by your parents, your neighbors, your associates, your school, your friends, your whole socialization process—that makes you who you are and who you are determines how you make decisions and process information (Bolton, 2004, p. 43).

The perspectives of black Americans are formed by living in a world of limited opportunities: opportunities limited by race as opposed to any objective criteria. Under such conditions, a sense of **collective identification** forms that links members of the group with a shared consciousness or sense of solidarity. In the same way, police officers share a world of constant threat and physical danger, enduring social institutions that limit opportunities for blacks teach them how to survive in a world that is hostile to them merely because of the color of their skin.

Because of the way whites perceive them, blacks face challenges that white people simply cannot relate to. The following quote illustrates how white

[12] Dred Scott v. Sanford, 60 U.S. 393, 407 (1857).

stereotypes result in behavior on the part of police officers that contribute to black hostility toward whites, in this case resulting in lifelong impediments to building better police community relations.

> I was, must have been, like 12 or 13, and I'm trying to play recreational football, so I came out of the theater and I said to myself, "I'm going to see if I can just jog home," if I had the endurance to do it. I got down to right where the old [TV station] used to be, I said "Gees, I'm not even tired." I was on the last stretch so I picked up and I really started to sprint when a cop come up behind me, siren on, pulled over, and said, "Get up against the wall, get up against the wall!" the guy says, "What are you running for, what are you running for?" I told him, I said, "Just running, you know, felt like running" (Bolton, 2004, p. 45).

Through their experiences with police and through interactions with their peers, black children learn that the police are not their friends, they exist as a mechanism to control their lives as representatives and servants of an oppressive white dominated society. "It just seems like in our neighborhoods, they was always taking somebody to jail. They weren't there to do any good, or what I would call good." Black Americans have learned to fear the police and, if they wish to stay safe from police abuse, violence, and harassment, they learn to be careful (Bolton, 2004).

An understanding of experiential racism and its impact on self-esteem drove many wise black parents to avoid situations that perpetuated racism.

> Although things were segregated downtown, I never really paid it a whole lot of attention because of my mother. We went downtown shopping, and you said you had to go to the bathroom, Mom said, "Okay let's go home." And she put you in the car, and she took you home. I never used a colored bathroom, OK? You know, that type of thing. And if there was a lunch counter there and people were sitting down eating and you said, "Mom, I'm hungry," she said "Okay, let's go home." Put you in the car, and you go home and eat . . . My parents kind of stressed the importance of self-esteem. You know, you're not second to anybody. You're not less intelligent than anybody. Just, do the right thing. Always respect other people and they'll respect you (Bolton, 2004, p. 47).

Black Americans have been conditioned, first by overt racism and discrimination and now by the perpetuation of their victimized status, to be aware of the subtle signs of bias.

Hyper-Sensitivity

The experiences of black Americans during the era of Jim Crow in the South and segregation in the North were profound. Discrimination was an accepted part of the social landscape and even after that era ended with the Civil Rights Act of 1964 black Americans continued to experience racial hostility, sometimes blatant and sometimes subtle, through their everyday experiences.

> After so many years of overt racism and then watching the changeover years from those overt acts to covert acts, I can—and a lot of African Americans have developed an ability to—pick up on certain things. I mean, you can pretty much meet someone [and] within two or three minutes and know if they're sincere. And it's wrong, you can say, "Well that's prejudice, and you're prejudging someone," but the truth is the truth. After you've been treated a particular way so long and heard so many things, pretty soon, they come around full circle and you know what certain phrases mean. You know what certain mannerisms mean, because you've seen it thousands of times before and you've seen what it's attached to (Bolton, 2004, p. 65).

In the same way that police officers develop a hyper-sensitivity to danger, black Americans have developed a hyper-sensitivity to racism. They are alerted to potential hostility due to a long history of white hostility experienced personally or through stories passed down from relatives and friends that are much less obvious to white people.

Consider the following situation: Nearly twenty police applicants are lined up in anticipation of the physical agility test. They walk up to the officer in charge to check-in. The officer asks, "Name?" the reply is "Anthony, Michael J." the next applicant in line is approached, "Name" "Phillips, Thomas M." ". . . Name?" the applicants all reply as the officer goes down the line "Burton, Harold C." Then the officer approaches the only black applicant in the group and says, "You must be Dillon, right?" he replies "Yeah, how'd you know?" the officer replies "It's a cultural thing."

The context of being a police applicant in a room full of other police applicants who are all white triggers the hyper-sensitivity of the only black applicant. The actual intent of the officer was to be friendly and make Dillion feel welcome, but this back-fired badly due to the officer's ignorance and Dillon's hyper-sensitivity.

In an era of increasing racial hostility, police officers need to develop a better understanding of not only the historical context of the black American experience with the police, but also an understanding of where the perceptions of the police by black Americans comes from. Building better relationships depends on a new set of cultural skills as well as the wisdom to avoid behaviors that are counter-productive in this effort.

UNDERSTANDING MEN OF COLOR

The law enforcement function is one that generates conflict, especially in those who have a negative impression of the police. The reasons for this negative impression on the part of black Americans relates to the *history of how black Americans have been treated, the structural and cultural factors that divide white from black, and the legacy of discrimination that persists in the form of residual discrimination.*

The wise police officer knows how to mitigate conflict in the law enforcement role, but the policing role offers abundant opportunities to bridge the divide between the police—regardless of whether the officer is white or black—and the African American Community. It is in this role where the techniques of conflict management can be employed to fulfill the policing mission of order maintenance. However, there are unique characteristics of "Men of Color" that should also be considered in any genuine effort to support these individuals and build trust in these communities.

The Arch Enemies of Relationship Building

Police officers often frame their responses to non-critical situations and events under the assumption that the involved individuals suffer from a lack of guidance, usually a lack of proper parenting or authoritative intervention. This leads to crafting police responses that tend to demean, subordinate, or subjugate others.

> *"No human race is superior; no religious faith is inferior. All collective judgments are wrong. Only racists make them."*
>
> —Elie Wiesel

Collective judgements based on an individual's characteristics such as race are the essence of racism. People deserve to be recognized and valued as individuals.

Paternalism—To Act Like a Parent

The community caretaking role of the police is a long-established principle in law and in policing practice. Officers learn through their formal and informal training to frame their activity in the context of parenting the community.

> Police officers often come across as behaving like a stern parent. This is the basis of the resentment many people, both black and white, feel toward the police.

This practice can arguably run counter to fundamental American values such as freedom and liberty, making police action driven by this community caretaking function subject to intense scrutiny when such action involves privacy interests. Justice Brandeis (1928) spoke of the constitutional limitations of the community caretaking function in a famous dissenting opinion:

> "[e]xperience should teach us to be most on our guard to protect liberty when the government's purposes are beneficent. . . . The greatest dangers to liberty lurk in insidious encroachment by men of zeal, well-meaning but without understanding."[13]

The right of people to be free from governmental intrusion (privacy), a right established by the fourth amendment to the U.S. constitution and interpreted by the courts, provides specific guidance to the police in their community caretaking function. In deciding the appropriate role for the police, the courts routinely apply a balance test that seeks to determine whether the police action is reasonable based upon an overriding public need for public safety and security.

Over the years "men of zeal," in the words of Brandeis—women are also to be included—have pushed the limits of governmental authority in the interests of what they *subjectively* viewed as a legitimate public need. Such action on the part of governmental actors generates resentment from citizens, especially when those citizens feel as if they have been victimized by past governmental actions.

Paternalism is the policy or practice on the part of people in positions of power and authority that is aimed at restricting the freedom and responsibility of those subordinate to them "for their own good." It is the practice of dealing benevolently, but intrusively, with those who are deemed in need of this intrusive supervision or direction in the same way that a father deals with his children.

Police officers, regardless of gender, are often thrust into situations that demand acting like a benevolent parent. Some *men and women of zeal* take this role too seriously, sometimes violating the constitutional rights of individuals, but in other cases generating resentment from those who do not feel that they need parenting. This resentment makes it very difficult to gain the trust of disadvantaged individuals and communities no matter how desperate the need.

---

[13] Olmstead v. United States, 277 U.S. 438, 479 (1928) (Brandeis, J., dissenting), overruled by Katz v. United States, 389 U.S. 347 (1967), and Berger v. New York, 388 U.S. 41 (1967). President Reagan similarly quipped that the most terrifying words in the English language are "I'm from the government and I'm here to help."

Ernesto Sirolli (1999), a community development and entrepreneurship facilitator, provides profound insight into the more appropriate role of the modern police officer with regard to the community care-taking function:

> I began to conceive a vision of a society that facilitates personal growth by assisting individuals in achieving what they wish to achieve. A Taoist bureaucracy which does nothing until asked, and a great deal afterwards. A "humble" public servant who doesn't plan how to build the ideal society but who is enchanted by the unique, idiosyncratic needs and abilities of the people that he serves and whose task would be to respond to individual requests for assistance and provide the elements needed for that person to flower (Sirolli, 1999, p. 22).

What would a wise police officer look like if we were to ask Sirolli? One that accepts people as they are and offers assistance where ever possible to help them succeed. But, if those people don't want help, leave them alone!

In borrowing from the cutting edge literature of economic development, clues can be found to overcoming the resentment that undermines trust and legitimacy in policing. The desire of all good cops is to help people; that is best accomplished by allowing them to " 'heal themselves' by simply "being there, listening, facilitating, and responding to the client's needs for communicating and finding values to live by" (Sirolli, 1999, p. 22).

Simply being there to listen, facilitate, and respond may be beyond the capacity of the action oriented police officer who is frustrated with continual instances of self-destructive behavior. However, having the ability to simply listen to people with compassion and understanding is the mark of highly competent and wise police officers in the same way that these behaviors are the mark of the best parents. Some people simply don't want help and when this is readily apparent they should just be left alone.

In reflecting on the writing of E.F. Schumacher's words (1973), Sirolli offers the following advice:

> By writing "If people do not want to better themselves, they are best left alone," he challenged the view that helping others, whether as individuals or nations, is a moral injunction and that by doing "good work" we are somehow bringing civilization to those who "don't have it" (Schumacher, 1967).

The following words are particularly profound advice for the modern police officer who truly seeks to help impoverished communities of color.

> The message for me was to respect other cultures: we have to wait to be invited to share other people's problems, we have to listen with an open mind, and we have to leave behind our own prejudices and assumptions of superiority (Sirolli, 1999, p. 15).

The resentment that develops when governmental actors act as benevolent parents reinforces the perceptions of supremacy, *but also reinforces feelings of inferiority* that are already prevalent in these communities. When people feel the need for help they will ask for it, and governmental institutions such as the police should be ready to respond. However, to force themselves on people out of a misplaced or politically driven arrogant *desire to help* the disadvantaged breeds contempt, resistance, and undermines trust and legitimacy.

Patronizing—To Act as Patron

The other enemy of relationship building is to patronize others. The hallmark of the political era of policing was dominated by this concept, to owe allegiance and loyalty to a powerful political actor was the framework of corruption that undermined the legitimacy of nineteenth and early twentieth century police.

When officers communicate expectations in the form of specific behaviors that will be rewarded though, for example, a lack of enforcement action they run the risk of acting as a patron. A loyalty relationship is often created where an individual can infer that the police officer will look favorably on certain behavior and reward it. Other behaviors may weaken or undermine the relationship, but maintaining the relationship becomes the goal rather than compliance with the law.

> A complaint of an officer having a "condescending attitude" speaks to a patronizing demeanor.

Patronage allows people to look down on others and this comes across as an "air of condescension" that makes the victims feel small. It undermines their self-esteem and self-worth and seeks to relegate them to a permanent underclass status just like Jim Crow in the South and segregation policies in the north.

Today we see the symptoms of this problem in the sexual harassment allegations that are a part of the daily news cycle. The powerful elites, primarily men, act as patrons to aspiring actors, journalists, and public officials demanding *favors* for their continued patronage. The power that they exert over vulnerable individuals sometimes results in victimization and the loss of self-esteem.

When those who are willing to acquiesce to the wishes and demands of a patron gain influence, those with higher levels of competency are left behind, loyalty becomes more important than merit, *patronage breeds incompetency*.

Police officers can often find themselves in positions and situations where their services as a patron are sought-out. People rarely call the police out of a benevolent sense of civic duty, but rather they seek to gain the assistance of a powerful government actor to their own advantage, generally to the detriment of someone else. Police officers learn to be very careful with regard to the need to appear objectively neutral, getting both sides of a story and carefully weighing facts and the credibility of individuals. This is important, but is often very time consuming and emotionally demanding. The path of least resistance can often lead to a patronizing demeanor that comes across to others as indifference and condescension.[14] To act in a condescending manner is to treat others as if they are servants. This does not resonate well with most people, but it is a particularly serious issue to Black communities given the history of systematic oppression.

A wholly **professional** demeanor is the police officers best defense against appearing to patronize others. As opposed to an attitude of indifference, offering polite service and listening carefully are specific behaviors that the wise officer may employ to avoid this enemy of relationship building.

> Having a wholly professional demeanor is the best defense against behaving in a paternalistic or patronizing manner. However, a professional attitude can easily be perceived as indifferent or uncaring.

Building Better Relationships with Men of Color

In addition to the structural factors that have a devastating impact on African American communities, there are lesser cultural aspects of being a black male that should guide any efforts to support them (Wilson, 2009). Much of what is known about men of color comes from recent literature from the education field put forth by Wood and Harris (2017). Their work provides insight that police officers can use in their efforts to understand and support communities of color.

> If police officers truly wish to build better relationships with men of color they can adopt a supportive attitude as part of their service orientation.

Environmental Factors

The culture of poverty as it exists in inner-city neighborhoods creates incredible challenges for men of color. Police officers, especially white police

[14] Condescension means to display superiority and distain for others, i.e., white supremacy.

officers, have little understanding of these environmental conditions or of the economic pressures of poverty because they are white and predominantly middle-class. Compounding this lack of understanding is the fact that few police officers, white or black, choose to live where they police. This self-segregation undermines their ability to identify with the inner-city black culture. They have a tendency to frame the behaviors they observe through their middle-class frame of reference and judge the observed behaviors as rude, disrespectful, intimidating, and even threatening. Such views lead to behaviors on the part of the police that undermine trust such as those identified in the previous section.

One of the principal challenges for inner-city men of color is employment. Like most Americans men of color possess only the most basic job skills, but this impacts them to a much larger degree due to the environment of the inner city. The lack of low skilled jobs in this environment make them particularly vulnerable to economic downturns when they are the first to be laid off, see Wilson (2009).

The other big problem for men of color is the impact of residual discrimination. "Due to stereotypes of men of color as being lazy, indolent, deviant, and brutish, there are many challenges in gaining work opportunities" (Wood, 2017, p. 16).

Transportation problems severely limit the opportunity for men of color to gain stable employment. Work opportunities that men of color are suited for no longer exist in the inner-cities, transportation to the suburbs requires a car and the economic demands of automobile ownership are well beyond the means of the majority of these individuals. The alternative is the utilization of public transportation systems that are usually inconvenient and inconsistent with the transportation needs of inner-city residents.

The work opportunities that are typically available to inner-city men of color are also overwhelmingly temporary in nature. This breeds a constant sense of economic uncertainty, they don't know where their next meal is coming from. Developing linkages to the underground economy and engaging in illegal enterprises are often the most viable alternatives to stable sources of income and this, of course, makes them prime targets for law enforcement attention. They also make easy targets of themselves by driving poorly maintained, unlicensed, and uninsured "borrowed" vehicles when they can find them.

The illustration in the box describes a true and an all-too frequent scenario of how a traffic offense lands a poor person—particularly a poor person of color—in prison.

How can a traffic offense get you a ticket to prison?

by David Couper

The answer is, "Quite easily if you're poor!"

Let's take a look at the system of court fines and then correct it, our criminal justice system is rigged against poor people—and a big part of the Ferguson problem was how this system was working against the poor.

Professor Karin Martin at John Jay College of Criminal Justice had some interesting things to say about these disparities in a recent letter to *The New York Times*:[15]

> *"My research on the use of monetary penalties indicates that the widespread system of assessing interconnected fines, fees, penalty assessments and the like raises challenging questions of fairness. For a public institution to be the originator and the beneficiary of fines provides a troublesome incentive to direct resources away from other critical but less lucrative law-enforcing or adjudicating tasks (clearing backlogs of DNA analysis or testing rape kits). In fact, collection rates nationwide are abysmal: far below 50 percent in some jurisdictions. Most problematic is the tendency of fines and fees to be self-perpetuating (failure to pay prompts additional fees) and net-widening (subjecting more offenses to fines). A result is that the system of fines violates the fundamental tenet of proportionality in our criminal justice system.*
>
> *"A good solution would be to follow the European model of day fines, in which monetary sanctions are calculated as a percentage of income. This approach takes into account offense severity in addition to ability to pay. As such, it is an effective punishment that generates income, but it does so without sacrificing justice."*

She presents a reasonable solution—fines should be based on income not some legislated sum of money.

So how does a traffic ticket get you to prison? It goes like this: You are poor and looking for work. This morning you are driving to a new job. You're late and you are driving too fast. You need get to work on time. Now you are stopped by police.

You don't consider yourself a criminal and certainly not a person who could ever end up in prison. Prison is for bad people and you're not a bad person. Sure, you might smoke a little dope, but would never steal anything or hurt anyone. People who do that should go to prison, but that's not you.

15 Martin, Karen "In Ferguson, a System of Injustice through Fines" *The New York Times*, Sept. 15, 2014.

You have now just been handed a $200 speeding ticket. You can't pay it. You have no money. So you don't show up in court and now a warrant for your arrest is out there in cyberspace. Still, you don't consider yourself to be a criminal.

Now you need to avoid police at all costs. You can't afford to go to jail and lose this new job. Your driver's license is now suspended. Public transportation in your city will not get you to where you work. You continue to drive your car.

You must not get stopped by police. But an optical-scanning device reads your vehicle plates and you are stopped by police. You have three options, speed away, dump the car and run, or submit to arrest. Either option will eventually get you in jail.

You submit to arrest. You're now in jail and have lost the job that took you three months to find. A job, incidentally, needed to support not only you but your family. Fees and more fees are tagged on to that original $200 fine.

When you get out of jail you still need to find a job and you need transportation.

The next time you are stopped you vow not to be arrested. You simply cannot afford it. So you run and are caught and physically arrested, you try to get away. The end result is that you are charged with resisting arrest and, possibly, battery to a police officer as a result of your resistance.

State prison is now just a matter of time.

Campbell Robertson and Joseph Goldstein reported in the New York Times that this problem has been very present in St Louis County, Mo. and Ferguson. However, this situation is not restricted to St Louis County; it is a situation that exists in almost every city in America.

> *"Young black men, who in many towns in St. Louis County are pulled over at a rate greater than whites, routinely find themselves in the patchwork of municipal courts here, without lawyers and unable to pay the fines levied for their traffic violations. Many end up being passed from jail to jail around the county until they can pay their fines and in some cases other administrative fees, a revenue source on which some towns are growing increasingly reliant.*
>
> *" 'It angers people, because it seems like they're just messing with you,' said Cameron Lester, a 22-year-old college student who knew Mr. Brown, and days earlier was protesting his death. He described how an unpaid $75 ticket once turned into days behind bars in two different police stations and hundreds of dollars in fees. He was skeptical about change . . .*

"When a person fails to appear and pay, here as in many other places, a warrant is issued and that person's license is suspended. In the hodgepodge of cities that make up St. Louis County, some drivers may have multiple warrants. ***In Ferguson, more than one and a half warrants have been issued for every resident*** *(emphasis added). And as the warrants stack up, so do the fines: Not showing up to pay a $90 taillight violation means a failure-to-appear warrant with its own fee of $100 or more; each successive failure-to-appear warrant adds to that; and if there is a stop, there are incarceration fees and towing fees.*

" 'In the end,' said Brendan Roediger, an assistant professor at St. Louis University Law School, 'a person who had trouble coming up with $90 might owe a jurisdiction well over a thousand dollars . . .' "[16]

Stressful life events that are another byproduct of financial pressures plague men of color such as deaths, both in the family and in their personal relationships, divorce, eviction, major relationship breakups, job loss, and, of course, incarceration.

One might ask why these problems should be of concern to police officers who would, like educators, be tempted to dismiss them as beyond their control.

> It is harmful if inequalities are rationalized as beyond the control of practitioners. [Instead] we must focus on what is within the control of educators in terms of changing their own practices to meet the needs and circumstances of "men of color" (Harris, 2010).
>
> While educators have little control over the external pressures described here, they do have control over the environment they create and the support they provide while on campus (Wood, 2017).

By substituting the word "educators" with "police;" and "campus" for "urban neighborhoods;" and applying a bit of innovative thinking, a strategy of how to build better relations with communities of color may materialize.

Specific Relationship Building Techniques for Police Officers

Calls for service and emergency situations rarely allow the time to engage in relationship building, but when time allows or at their own initiative the best officers recognize the value of getting to know their community or neighborhood better. This is done one individual at a time and it also has the dual propose of

[16] Couper, David C., 2014, Sept. 14, "How a Traffic Offense Can Be a Ticket to Prison" https://improvingpolice.wordpress.com/2014/09/18/how-a-traffic-offense-can-be-a-ticket-to-prison/.

intelligence gathering for problem solving. The following suggestions can make these efforts very productive.

1. Get to know individuals by name and refer to them by name. This affirms their personhood and is a sign of respect. When engaged in law enforcement interactions, allow them to maintain their dignity whenever possible. Since men will fight to maintain their dignity, there is no benefit from causing them to lose it. Praise people in public, allow them to save face, and be ready to assist them in making a fresh start.

   Map the neighborhood, know where people live and their relationship to others. Having an understanding of how people relate to others geographically provides insight into neighborhood relationships and other linkages.

2. Be "intrusive" but with a non-confrontational tone. This means to engage proactively and seek out opportunities to engage in non-enforcement contacts. Avoid dis-engagement or creating the perception that individuals should approach you first or that the police have more important things to do. Don't erect walls; there are enough of those already.

3. Be fully present. This means focusing on the individual and treating each person as important. Ignore or set-aside interruptions to demonstrate a commitment to this individual right now. Be conscious of race and use a non-confrontational tone.

4. Make use of "appropriate" disclosure by revealing things about yourself. Tell a brief story to let individuals know that the police are human, too, and sometimes vulnerable.

5. When there is an opportunity to provide more formal assistance, connect individuals to people directly. Perhaps there is a job available at a business down the street, walk or drive the individual to the location, and personally introduce them to the owner.

6. Demonstrate a personal commitment to the individual's wellbeing. A business card with a phone number is a good start, but other symbols may become appropriate and available with time and experience (Adopted to policing from the work of Dr. J. Luke Wood and Dr. Frank Harris III).

Chapter Summary

African Americans today encounter difficulties due to race that white people do not. They face hurdles to equality of opportunity that simply do not exist for white people, and taking a colorblind approach denies their negative racial experiences, rejects their cultural heritage, and invalidates their unique perspectives (Williams, 2011). Poor people—the principal victims and perpetrators of crime—are primarily people of color, and building better relationships with them requires that competent police officers understand their unique point-of-view.

The elite class in the early United States recognized the threat from poor people, both whites and slaves. The concept of justice, as defined in law, was different depending on the color of one's skin. The slave codes emerged as a formal mechanism to promote and preserve slavery. To enforce the slave codes, slaveholders enlisted the *slave patrol* to hunt down and return runaway Africans and to put down slave revolts.

The police in America have their origin in the need for the wealthy to protect their property from the lower classes. In the north the threat came from poor immigrants; in the south the threat to the economic prosperity of the rich was the property itself, i.e., slaves. The mission of the slave patrol was to ensure that slaves were quickly captured and returned to face the wrath of their primarily white masters.

When an end was finally put to slavery in the United States, the lingering impact of the psychology of slavery was reinforced through "Black Codes," laws that targeted poor whites and African Americans. The impact on institutionalizing the concept of white supremacy was profound and this was accomplished through a system of oppression that came to be known as "Jim Crow." Blacks who violated the law, in many cases for minor crimes such as vagrancy, were sentenced to serve time in prison camps where their labor was cheaply sold by state officials through the convict lease system that essentially returned blacks to their former status as slaves.

The psychological supremacy of white people was reinforced by hate groups such as the Ku Klux Klan who targeted free blacks, and, to a lesser extent, Native Americans, and Spanish speaking minorities. Fear was generated by indiscriminate killings numbering more than 3000 between 1882 and 1930. Blacks were targeted by white gangs in an effort to suppress economic equality and pride, actions that were met with acceptance and even the occasional active participation of local law enforcement.

Blacks in America first encountered the police in the form of the slave patrol. Slaves were unprotected by the law, especially as victims of crimes perpetrated by their owners and white people generally. Black people were arbitrarily stopped by these white patterrollers[17] and questioned about their absence from the plantation, they were routinely searched and the slave patrols also administered whippings (Websdale, 2001). Even free blacks were treated like slaves as in Virginia where blacks had to be employed in order to remain in the state, if not employed within 12 months there were threatened with the loss of their freedom (Taylor Green, 2000).

Blacks did not begin to join the ranks of the police in significant numbers until the 1960s. What kept blacks out of policing was an unwelcoming atmosphere perpetrated by white officers, supervisors, and the majority white population generally. The face of law enforcement was unmistakably a *white* one.

The direct forces of discrimination have been recognized, outlawed, and are now widely considered morally reprehensible. However, the residual effects remain in the form of stereo-types, prejudice, and bias. Wise policing requires that officers seek a deeper understanding of what can be perceived as black animosity toward the institution of policing as a structural force in American society.

The argument has been made that there exists a number of structural, cultural, and ideological forces arrayed against black Americans in the United States, see Wilson (2009), Alexander (2011), Tonry (1995) and others. These forces have relegated them to secondary status behind whites and the origin, development, and institutionalization of policing has been instrumental in this process. The legacy of past discrimination lives on in the subjective perceptions of black Americans regarding the police.

The behaviors, attitudes, and points-of-view reflected in the police are a function of the same attitudes and points-of-view that exists in the community at-large. Each law enforcement agency is unique as a function of the uncoordinated and decentralized system of policing here in the United States.

The race based problems that are occurring in urban areas are the result of *Social structures* and *culture forces* that dominate these areas. Social structures are the ways in which social relationships are arranged and exist in institutions such as schools, commercial enterprises, the economy generally, markets, governmental organizations, political organizations, and any other organization or institution that provides order to social interaction.

---

[17] Patterollers were organized groups of white men who hunted down runaways and disciplined slaves in the antebellum south.

Cultural forces are the shared points-of-view among those individuals who occupy common places such as poor inner-city neighborhoods and schools; or who have shared experiences and circumstances such as generational poverty, perceived victimization, advantages, or personal associations.

Due to no fault of their own, black Americans face unique obstacles that white people do not face. *White privilege* is the term that is popular with those who would seek to enhance white guilt, but the problem for black Americans goes well beyond any advantage enjoyed by those of European dissent.

The direct forces of discrimination have been recognized, outlawed, and are now widely considered morally reprehensible. However, the residual effects remain in the form of stereo-types, prejudice, and bias. Wise policing requires that officers seek a deeper understanding of what can be perceived as black animosity toward the institution of policing as a structural force in American society.

The law enforcement function is one that generates conflict, especially in those who have a negative impression of the police. The reasons for this negative impression on the part of black Americans relates to the history black Americans, the structural and cultural factors that divide white from black, and the legacy of discrimination that persists in the form of residual discrimination.

The wise police officer knows how to mitigate conflict in the law enforcement role, but the policing role offers abundant opportunities to bridge the divide between the police—regardless of whether the officer is white or black—and the African American Community. It is in this role where the techniques of conflict management can be employed to fulfill the policing mission of order maintenance. However, there are unique characteristics of "Men of Color" that should also be considered in any genuine effort to support and build trust in these communities.

Bibliography

Alexander, J.C. (2008). *A Contemporary Introduction to Sociology: Culture and Society in Transition.* St. Paul, MN: Paradigm.

Alexander, M. (2011). *The New Jim Crow: Mass Incarceration in the Age of Colorblindness.* New York: The New Press.

Alpert, G.A. (1988). *Policing Multi-Ethnic Neighborhoods: The Miami Study and Findings for Law Enforcement in the United States.* New York: Greenwood Press.

Anderson, C. (1994). *Black Labor, White Wealth.* Edgewood, MD: Duncan & Duncan.

Anderson, E. (1999). *Code of the Street: Decency, Violence, and the Moral Life of the Inner City*. New York: W.W. Norton.

Banton, M. (1964). *The Policeman in the Community*. New York: Basic Books.

Barker, V. (2009). *The Politics of Imprisonment: How the Democratic Process Shapes the Way Americans Punish Offenders*. New York: Oxford University Press.

Bayley, D.A. (1969). *Minorities and the Police: Confrontation in America*. New York: Free Press.

Beck, E.A. (1995). Violence Toward African Americans in the Era of the White Lynch Mob. In D.E. Hawkins, *Ethnicity Race and Crime: Perspectives Across Time and Place* (pp. 121–144). New York: University of New York Press.

Bolton, K., Feagin, J.R. (2004). *Black in Blue*. New York: Routledge.

Brown, M. (1981). *Working the Street: Police Discretion and the Dilemmas of Reform*. New York: Sage.

Commission, N.A. (1968). *National Advisory Commission on Civil Disorders, Report*. New York: Bantam Books.

Cooper, C. (2015). An Afrocentric Perspective on Policing. In R. Dunham and G. Alpert, *Critical Issues in Policing, 7th ed.* (pp. 331–351). Long Grove, IL: Waveland Press.

Crank, J.P. (2004). *Understanding Police Culture, 2nd ed.* Routledge.

Criminal Justice Institute. (1985). Black Police Officers: Do They Really Make a Difference??? The Empirical Evidence. *Blacks in Criminal Justice*, 37–39.

Douglass, F. (1881). The Color Line. *North American Review*.

DuBois, W. (1899). The Negro and Crime. *The Independent,* 51.

DuBois, W. (1901). The Spawn of Slavery: The Convict Lease System in the South. In H.G. Gabbidon, *African American Classics in Criminology and Criminal Justice* (pp. 83–88). Thousand Oaks, CA: Sage.

Dulaney, W. (1996). *Black Police in America*. Bloomington: Indiana University Press.

Gabbidon, S.A. (2016). *Race and Crime*. Los Angeles, CA: Sage.

Hannerz, U. (1991). *Soulside: Inquiries into Ghetto Culture and Community*. New York: Columbia University Press.

Harris, F.I. (2010). The Equity Scorecard: A Process for Building Institutional Capacity to Educate Young Men of Color. In C.J. Edley, *Changing Places: How*

Communities Will Improve the Health of Boys of Color (pp. 277–308). Berkeley, CA: University of California Press.

Hawkins, H.A. (1992). White Policing of Black Populations: A History of Race and Social Control in America. In C.A. McLaughlin, *Out of Order* (pp. 65–86). Boston: Little, Brown.

Isenberg, N. (2016). *White Trash: The 400-Year Untold History of Class in America.* New York: Penguin Books.

Kennedy, D. (2011). *Don't Shoot: One Man, a Street Fellowship and the End of Violence in Inner-City America.* New York: Bloomsbury.

Massey, D.D. (1993). *American Apartheid.* Cambridge, MA: Harvard University Press.

Mauer, M. (1999). *Race to Incarcerate.* New York: The New Press.

McIntyre, C. (1992). *Criminalizing a Race: Free Blacks During Slavery.* New York: Kayode.

Myrdal, G. (1944). *An American Dilemma: The Negro Problem and Modern Democracy.* New York: Harper & Brothers.

Neyfakh, L. (2016). Black Americans Supported the 1994 Crime Bill, Too. *Slate.*

Rudwick, E. (1960). The Negro Policemen in the South. *Journal of Criminal Law, Criminology, and Police Science, 51*, 273–276.

Russell, K. (1998). *The Color of Crime: Racial Hoaxes, White Fear, Black Protectionism, Police Harassment, and Other Macroaggressions.* New York: New York University Press.

Schumacher, E. (1967). Economic Development and Poverty. *Manas, 20*, 1–8.

Sidaius, L.S. (1994). Social Dominance Theory and the Criminal Justice System. *Journal of Applied Social Psychology*, 338–66.

Sirolli, E. (1999). *Ripples from the Zambezi.* Gabriola Island, BC: New Society Publishers.

Skolnick, J. (1968). *The Politics of Protest.* National Commission on the Causes and Prevention of Violence.

Skolnick, J.F. (1992). Above the Law: A Plan for New Cops. *Black Enterprise*, 42.

Sutherland, E. (1947). *Principles of Criminology, 4th ed.* Philadelphia: Lippincott.

Taylor-Green, H.A. (2000). *African American Criminological Thought.* Albany: State University of New York.

Tonry, M. (1995). *Malign Neglect.* New York: Oxford University Press.

Washington, J. (1986). *The Essential Writings and Speeches of Martin Luther King Jr.* New York: HarperCollins.

Websdale, N. (2001). *Policing the Poor: From Slave Plantation to Public Housing.* Boston: Northeastern University Press.

Williams, M. (2011). Colorblind Ideology Is a Form of Racism. *Psychology Today.*

Wilson, W. (2009). *More than Just Race.* New York: W.W. Norton & Company.

Wood, L.J. (2017). *Supporting Men of Color in the Community College: A Guidebook.* San Diego, CA: Montezuma Publishing.

CHAPTER 10

Perspectives of the Police: Why the Police Do What They Do

by Danny McGuire, Ed.D.

■ ■ ■

The police role is extremely diverse, ambiguous, and dynamic. Egon Bitner has stated that, from its earliest origins, police work has been a 'tainted' occupation: "The taint that attaches to police work refers to the fact that policemen are viewed as the fire it takes to fight fire, that in the natural course of their duties they inflict harm, albeit deserved, and that their very existence attests that the nobler aspirations of mankind do not contain the means necessary to insure survival" (Dempsey, 2014, p. 135).

New police officers in Chicago*

Learning Outcomes

Upon successful completion of this chapter the student will be able to:

- Identify the various types of crimes.

* Image labeled for unrestricted use.

- Differentiate between common calls for police service.
- Explain a few of the various policing strategies.
- Explain the common police perspectives on responding to citizen calls for service.
- Identify the factors that justify citizen stops by police.

Important Concepts

- Violent vs. Nonviolent Crimes
- Police Deployment
- Call Prioritization
- Response Perspectives

Questions for Discussion

- How are police assets deployed?
- What is the difference between violent and nonviolent crimes?
- How are calls for police service prioritized?
- Is there a difference in police response to calls for service?
- What goes into the decision-making process for officers as it relates to stopping individuals?

INTRODUCTION

Police work within particular communities is a complicated phenomenon that can often lead to misunderstanding and conflict. Police officers are often scrutinized for their actions regarding individuals that they stop based on ethnicity, race, or culture. The legal basis for a police stop is a clearly settled matter of law, stops are based on direct violations of law (e.g. traffic violations), or reasonable suspicion of criminal activity and behavior. Race, ethnicity, or culture are, by law and practice, only to be considered when these characteristics are relevant in the particular situation.

In recent years there has been substantial criticism of the police regarding their use of certain strategies—such as stop, question, and frisk—as well as their presumed use of racial profiling and other assumed justifications for police stops. As a result, uninformed analysis of raw data has been used to label the police as biased and even racist. In this chapter the perspectives of actual officers working in a large urban area are offered in an effort to further public understanding of why the police do what they do in response to citizen calls for assistance.

Police agencies classify calls for service by priority. Priority designations have a profound impact on how individual police officers respond, including their attitude toward citizens and the effort that they put forth on a given call. Police officers are deployed and assigned to geographic areas based on need, as determined solely by the number of calls for help coming from each area: more police are assigned in areas where higher levels of citizen calls' for service originate. Such areas have a "higher priority" for police resources.

Policing technology/strategies used in responding to such calls have had various levels of effectiveness in controlling crime and disorder. The kinds of strategies employed in any given area is based upon the types of crime problems reported by citizens as opposed to arbitrary motives or political considerations. Some of these strategies will be explored in this chapter.

The chapter concludes with interview data obtained from working police officers themselves, providing a perspective on actual police work that is seldom available or understood. These interviews provide a real-life perspective from individual officers, dispatchers, and police deployment experts who experience the "real world" of responding to emergency service calls every working day.

TYPES OF CRIME

Understanding the different types of crimes is important when judging why and how police resources are deployed. Police officers cannot enforce all the laws all the time; they must make choices because police time and resources are limited. Those choices are based on rational criteria such as the severity of the crimes reported. For example, residents and business owners have a legitimate complaint when gang members spray-paint graffiti on their homes and businesses; this is a crime called criminal damage to property and it is important, but it is not as important as gang related shootings in the area.

Criminologists—people who study crime—commonly categorize crimes into several major groupings: violent crime; property crime; white-collar crime; organized crime; and consensual or victimless crime (Barkan, 2014).

Violent Crimes

According to Barkan (2014), the news media exaggerate the problem of violent crime because violent crimes capture the attention of Americans, i.e., homicides are more exciting than theft and drug dealing. Violent crimes are actually a rare event in most places; however, the densely populated urban areas, such as those existing in the inner city of Chicago, are an exception. Violent crime is all too real for the people who live in these areas; it traps them inside their homes and makes them afraid to let their children out to play or even to walk to school. They live in constant fear and they have a right to expect the police to be able to help.

> Violent crime is a rare event, but of the highest priority for police.

The Federal Bureau of Investigation defines violent crime in this way:

". . . violent crime is composed of four offenses: murder and non-negligent manslaughter, forcible rape, robbery, and aggravated assault. Violent crimes are defined in the UCR[1] *Program as those offenses which involve force or threat of force . . ."*

Table 10.1 provides listings of the part I and part II offenses recognized by the FBI for crime reporting purposes. However, some part I offenses are not violent crimes, for example, many people confuse robbery and burglary. A robbery occurs when someone physically takes something from someone by the use or threat of force with the intent to permanently deprive that person of the benefit or use of that property. Robbery is a violent crime because the use of force is threatened, implied, or undertaken. It makes no difference whether the crime is committed at gunpoint, knifepoint, or through the use of "strong arm" tactics. It makes no difference whether such tactics are actually used or only implied. Burglary, on the other hand, is entering into a residence or building with the intent to commit a theft or other felony, no force or violence is implied; both of these crimes are part I offenses but only robbery is a violent crime.

In some cases, a nonviolent crime can lead to a violent crime. For example, drug possessing and low-level dealing is generally considered to be a non-violent crime. However, consider the individual who is desperate to acquire illicit drugs due to physiological distress associated with withdrawal. Such an individual may approach a low-level, non-violent, drug dealer in an effort to acquire the drugs that they need, but may not be able to pay for them. Suddenly the nonviolent drug offender becomes violent by pulling out a knife and stabbing the drug dealer, robbing him or her of the drugs. This is a common occurrence in areas plagued by the illicit drug trade where non-violent "victimless" crimes evolve into crimes of violence. This outcome is most common in areas generally inhabited by poor

---

1 UCR stands for the Uniform Crime Reporting program.

people—people who have no choice but to depend on the police for security and protection.

> Poor people cannot hire their own security, purchase alarms, or relocate to safer areas. They are at the mercy of inner city crime and can only rely on the police to protect them.

The broken-windows theory of crime control is often criticized today because of its impact on poor people of color. This tactic of crime control—attacking the non-violent petty crimes in order to prevent more serious crimes—has been most effective in curtailing instances of crime escalation. Consider the minor, victimless crime of gambling. Skeptics of the broken window policing theory state that gambling, which is commonplace among poor people, is a victimless crime not worthy of police attention, especially since enforcing gambling laws primarily impacts poor people of color. From the authors' personal experience, something as simple as an alley dice game in the inner city of Chicago can escalate into a homicide merely because of a dispute about whose turn it is to roll the dice.

Non-Violent Crimes

The Federal Bureau of Investigation describes non-violent or property crimes as:

> *". . . property crime includes the offenses of burglary, larceny-theft, motor vehicle theft, and arson. The object of the theft-type offenses is the taking of money or property, but there is no force or threat of force against the victims. The property crime category includes arson because the offense involves the destruction of property; however, arson victims may be subjected to force . . ."*

Part I and Part II Offenses

> The uniform crime reporting system divides crime into Part I and Part II offenses. Part I offenses include violent crime and serious non-violent crimes. All other crimes are Part II offenses.

Table 10.1 (below) describes in detail the separation between Part I and Part II offenses. Part I offenses, as described, include more violent crimes such as homicide, rape, and aggravated assault but also include nonviolent crimes such as burglary, larceny, and motor vehicle theft. Part II offenses are generally less severe and include vandalism, drunkenness, disorderly conduct, and other types of crimes that are initially less violent or life-threatening.

Table 10.1—Part I and Part II Offenses

Part I Offenses	
Criminal Homicide	Larceny—Theft (Except Motor Vehicle Theft)
Rape	Motor Vehicle Theft
Robbery	Arson
Aggravated Assault	Human Trafficking, Commercial Sex Acts
Burglary	Human Trafficking, Involuntary Servitude
Part II Offenses	
Other Assault, Simple	Gambling
Forgery and Counterfeiting	Offenses Against the Family and Children
Fraud	Driving Under the Influence
Embezzlement	Liquor Laws
Stolen Property: Buying, Receiving, Possessing	Drunkenness
Vandalism	Disorderly Conduct
Weapons: Carrying, Possessing, etc.	Vagrancy
Prostitution	All Other Offenses
Sex Offenses: (except Rape and Prostitution offenses)	Suspicion
Drug Abuse Violations	Curfew, Loitering Laws, and Runaways—(Persons under 18)

Source: Federal Bureau of Investigation, Criminal Justice Information Services Division, Uniform Crime Reporting Program. (2013). Summary Reporting System (SRS) user manual. Washington, DC: U.S. Department of Justice, pp. 20–22.

The difference between violent and nonviolent crime is important, but an understanding of how and why non-violent crime can evolve into violent crime is critical to understanding how and why police resources are allocated in greater numbers in certain geographic areas than in others.

> Relatively minor non-violent crimes like drug dealing can, and often do, evolve into serious violent crimes.

CALLS FOR POLICE SERVICE

All calls for police service are categorized by priority. Many police agencies pride themselves on responding to calls for service on a first come—first assigned basis. In the City of Chicago, the sheer number of calls received on a daily basis requires that they be assigned by priority. For example, in a particular geographical area or district of the city there may be 400 calls for service in an eight-hour tour of duty. In many cases, there are only 15 patrol units available to answer those 400 calls; in the same way a hospital emergency room must triage patients based on the severity of their injuries, the police should be expected to deal with the most serious and life threatening cases first, leaving the less serious and non-life threatening cases for later.

> Police cannot respond to calls for service on a first come first serve basis in a large city like Chicago. Calls for service must be prioritized and the level of priority dictates how the police respond and how they interact with people when they arrive.

A veteran Chicago dispatcher describes the system this way. When a call comes into the dispatch center, a call taker answers the phone and asks a series of standard questions of the caller. Included in this list of standard questions is the nature of the problem and a description of the persons involved. In a crime related call, the suspect description—including race—is essential for police officers in establishing reasonable suspicion to stop potential suspects. Police officers cannot stop people arbitrarily, they must have a factual justification for this action and race is very often a part of that justification. By the same logic, whether the suspect is tall or short, thin or obese, male or female, young or old will also be a part of the same factual description of the person to be sought.

Other information that can be obtained from the caller includes location information, the type of crime or exact offense, whether the crime is "in-progress" or has already occurred, suspect descriptions i.e., including gender, age, race, clothing, unusual characteristics, last known direction of travel, means of travel, etc., the identification of witnesses, circumstance information, the nature of relationships, i.e., spouse, siblings, cousins, friends, etc., and any other information that may be useful in properly classifying the crime and identifying the perpetrator.

This information is collected, organized, and processed in an effort to properly and accurately establish the call's priority ranking.

Examples of calls by priority actually used by Chicago:

Priority One:

- Shots fired in progress (occurring now)
- Robbery in progress (occurring now)
- Sexual assaults in progress (occurring now)
- Person with a gun
- Battery in progress (occurring now)

- Domestic disturbance in progress (occurring now)
- Person shot
- Other types of violent crimes or calls requiring an immediate police response.

An example of a priority one dispatch is as follows:

"units in 8 and units on citywide. Shots fired at 62nd and Rockwell. Caller states approximately 10 shots fired into a crowd by a male black subject wearing a black hoodie with blue jeans running northbound on Rockwell. No further information at this time."[2]

The city is divided into police districts geographically (i.e., 8 or 8th district), with police units assigned to those districts and the sub-unit designations called beats in a manner that will be described later. Priority one calls are broadcasted over the district wide radio frequency with the intention that they alert all police units in the district to the priority one call.

Priority Two:

Priority two calls are non-life-threatening calls for service, crimes that have just occurred, or calls where the offender is no longer present but may be in close proximity. Priority two calls include calls that do not demand an emergency police response. Examples include:

- Suspicious persons
- Gang disturbances
- Robberies that just occurred
- Domestic disturbances where the offender is no longer on the scene
- Traffic crashes with injuries (dispatchers have the ability to upgrade this to a priority one call if the injuries are life-threatening).

Priority two calls are the second level of priority because they are not related to incidents that constitute an immediate threat to life, but they are still urgent and demand a prompt police response.

Lastly are priority three calls: these calls are non-emergency and do not require a prompt police response. The majority of police calls for service are priority three; they are the least urgent and can be set aside in favor of priority two or certainly priority one calls.

---

2 Information courtesy a veteran Chicago police dispatcher in December 2017.

Examples of priority three calls include:

- Traffic crashes with no injuries
- Loud music complaints
- Noise complaints
- Barking dogs
- Neighbor disputes
- Property crimes
- Drug dealing calls

Priority three calls, although non-life-threatening, may escalate into a priority two or even a priority one call depending on the evolving situation. For example, a call of dealing drugs in a specific district may turn into a robbery "just occurred" when the drug dealer gets robbed or even shot when the robbery goes bad. This additional information can come into the police dispatch center as a new call for service or as an update to the original priority three call.

When a district receives 400 calls in an eight-hour time period, the prioritization system is critical for managing the limited police resources.

Drug Dealing and Suspicious Occurrence Calls

Calls regarding drug dealing and suspicious persons are numerous, but not generally dispatched over the radio because many drug dealers carry police scanners for the purpose of monitoring police activity. These kinds of calls are more effectively communicated to police tactical units through computer terminals or by cell phone to avoid alerting potential suspects. Tactical teams are employed in situations where a more aggressive, pro-active, response is assumed to be more effective in actually catching individuals engaged in criminal activity. These kinds of calls, and the related police response, have the greatest potential for generating conflict due to their covert nature.

Most citizens know that when they call the police for drug dealing, suspicious activity, noise complaints, or other types of low priority events the police response is likely to be delayed due to the call's low priority. A veteran Chicago dispatcher reports that it has become common for people who are requesting low priority police service to report anonymously that shots are being fired in a specific area. They know that this gets the police there faster.

> Callers often exaggerate the severity of a situation to facilitate a more rapid police response. A gathering of disorderly subjects on the street is often called in as a drug deal "in progress", a fight, or even man with a gun. In this way a situation that may not even warrant a police response is escalated into a major violent crime event dictating aggressive police tactics that can easily be perceived as out of proportion to the problem.

Artificially inflating the priority of these calls has an impact on the police and can also be a source of conflict with citizens. The attitude and demeanor of an officer responding to a "shots fired" call is dramatically different than the attitude and demeanor of an officer responding to a noise complaint. When police respond to what they believe is a priority one call of shots fired or person with a gun they will be on high alert and they will be hyper-vigilant; it is also reasonable to expect that the officer(s) demeanor will be less than cooperative, conciliatory, or sympathetic regarding the citizen(s) that he or she will encounter. When the call is actually regarding a minor occurrence such as assumed gang members or drug dealers loitering on the street corner the responding officers' actions can easily be viewed as excessive or, to use a new phrase, "not proportionate" to the threat. This is particularly true for tactical officers who work in plain clothes and may not even be immediately identifiable as the police.

When people view the actions of the police as excessive, it is certainly reasonable to assume that their willingness to cooperate, offer witness information, and partner with the police will diminish; injuring the police community relationship.

> Police officers cannot assume that the nature of the call has been exaggerated, although they often do. Experiences teaches officers that violent crimes are more likely in some areas than others. Assuming that a "shots fired" call is exaggerated may be accurate, but it is not prudent for a police officer or his or her colleagues.

Tracking a Call Through the System

When a call comes in to dispatch, a call taker answers the phone and gathers information. Call takers are required to ask specific questions regarding the caller's information. For example, is the caller someone calling to report a crime that is occurring, a crime that has just occurred, or is the caller the actual victim of a crime. The call taker will ask questions to make an initial determination as to whether this caller is reporting a crime; whether they may have observed a subject fire shots and run from the scene, or whether they are victim of a crime (for instance whether, someone shot a gun at them). This is not always an easy determination to make.

They will also inquire about descriptions of offenders that include gender, ethnicity, approximate age, approximate height, approximate weight, and a clothing description. They may ask questions such as: Is the subject wearing a hat, if not what is the offender wearing? Black hoodie, blue jeans, etc.?

A critical piece of information is whether the offender committed a crime with a weapon and, if so, what that weapon looked like. Was the weapon a knife? A large knife? A small knife? Was the weapon a gun, was it a rifle? A pistol? A revolver? What color was this weapon? The call taker will ask a series of questions and then relay this information to the dispatcher who will then dispatch this information immediately to the police officers in the area in which the crime was reported.

An example of how the exchange between call taker, dispatcher, and the responding officer on the street is as follows:

The dispatched call:

"... units in 8, units on citywide, shots fired 63rd and Rockwell. Caller states that a male black wearing a black hoodie and blue jeans walked up to a crowd standing on the north east corner of 63rd and Rockwell and fired approximately five shots into the crowd. It is unknown if anyone was hit and the offender ran westbound on 63rd St. from Rockwell. Nothing further ...'

The street officer's response to this kind of call may be as follows:

When responding to the call I was at 61st and California. I did not activate my emergency equipment so I could possibly get close without being detected and hopefully catch the offender. I cut down the side streets and took a different route. It was 330 in the morning and I saw a male black with a black hoodie and blue jeans walking northbound down Talman at 62nd St.

I decided to stop him as he matched the description of the offender of the shooting. When I stopped him, I conducted a protective pat-down search, and noticed that the subject's heart was beating rapidly and he seemed out of breath. I asked him what was going on, and he said 'someone was shooting over there on 63rd St., you should go look for that mother fucker and quit fuckin' with me'. The subject became agitated and his movements were quite furtive (suspicious).

When I got to the portion of my pat-down in his waistband I felt a hard object on his right side. At that point the subject began to flee on foot and I started to chase him. I went on the radio for dispatch calling an emergency foot chase because I believed this individual had a gun and was part of the original dispatch of shooting.

The offender pulled an object from his waistband and the object appeared to be a gun that he threw into a gangway. At this point, more officers were involved in the foot chase and took on the role of chasing the subject while I located and secured the weapon in the gangway.

The subject was caught a short time later by assisting units and the weapon was recovered. This in fact was the individual who did the shooting and two people were struck by gunfire. We had the two individuals who were victims of an aggravated battery by handgun, an offender, the weapon he used in the offense, and a witness who was able to identify the individual as the offender in the shooting . . ."[3]

The above story illustrates how a typical call for service involving a violent crime works its way through the call prioritization and dispatch process. It shows how an officer, utilizing a description given from a crime, was able to stop an individual matching that description resulting in the apprehension of a violent offender. It also shows how a veteran officer's mind works when responding to a call of this type. It all begins with the information supplied by the caller as extracted and organized and categorized by a skilled call taker. In these cases, the call taker's protocol for extracting information from callers will be direct, assertive and indifferent with respect to the citizen caller and this can also undermine good police community relations.

POLICE DEPLOYMENT (HOW POLICE ARE DISTRIBUTED)

> Police resources are limited. Officers are deployed into specific geographic areas (areas, districts, beats) based on the number and type of calls for service.

The city is divided into geographic areas called districts. The number of police related calls for service varies by district with some districts receiving many more police calls than others. According to information received directly from a veteran dispatcher on a given weekend, some districts could receive over 500 calls while others experience less than 100. In addition, the kind of police calls for service varies by district with some receiving many more calls of violent crimes and in-progress crimes than others.

Table 10.2 is an illustration of reported crimes called into the Chicago Police Department between Friday, May 27, 2016 and Sunday, May 29, 2016 by district. This does not include the low priority calls for service which, according to a veteran Chicago police dispatcher, could triple the amount of calls for crimes reported.

---

3 A call personally experienced by the author.

Table 10.2—Chicago Police Calls to Report Crimes Citywide by District for the Weekend of Friday May 27, 2016–Sunday May 29, 2016

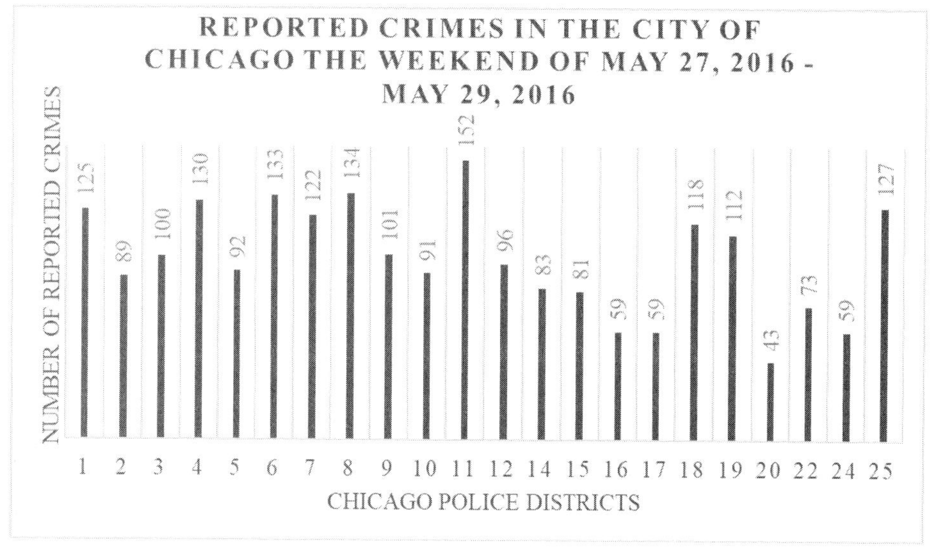

Source: Crimes—2001 to present City of Chicago Data Portal. (2017). Retrieved December 13, 2017, from https://data.cityofchicago.org/Public-Safety/Crimes-2001-to-present/ijzp-q8t2/data.

The above table is only reported crimes by district, it does not include the multitude of other calls for police assistance that do not involve crimes. A call for police service may involve a potential hazard, loud music, a group of disorderly subjects, a suspicious occurrence, a traffic accident, a complaint related to a city ordinance, garbage, problems with animals, or a multitude of other citizen concerns that cause citizens to reach out to the police because they simply don't know who else to call.

Crime data results from calls for service only when those calls involve crimes. Crimes are identified based on the facts of the call and are then categorized for reporting purposes based on the Uniform Crime Reporting standards (UCR) that have been established by the Federal Bureau of Investigation. When an officer responds to a crime related call for service, he or she is required to document the crime in a case report. The officer will ask for a "RD Number" or report number from dispatch and then categorize the crime in that report based on the UCR offense code that most closely matches the facts of the case. This is the foundation of the national crime reporting system in the United States. In the following radio transmission, the responding officer is identifying themselves and requesting that a report number be assigned to his or her call involving a battery to a person that occurred at 3200 W. 63rd.

". . . 820 can I get an RD Number for a 0486 which occurred at 3200 W. 63rd St.?"[4]

According to the data in Table 10.2, the busiest police district for calls during the specified time period was the 11th police district with 152 crimes reported while the district with the fewest calls was the 20th district with only 43.

In Chicago there are three general patrol/investigative geographic areas: Area North, Area Central and Area South. These areas contain districts, there are 22 police districts with some areas having more districts than others. For example, the 16th district, which is located by O'Hare Airport, falls under Area North patrol, while the 4th district which is close to the Illinois-Indiana border falls under Area South. Area North includes districts 011; 014; 015; 016; 017; 019; 020; 024; 025. Area Central includes districts 001; 002; 003; 008; 009; 010; 012; 018 and Area South includes districts 004; 005; 006; 007; 022.

Districts are headed by a commander who is similar to a mini-police chief for that district. The district commander reports to the area deputy chief and area deputy chiefs report to the chief of patrol who oversees all patrol operations in the city and reports to the police superintendent. For example, the 22nd district commander reports to the deputy chief of patrol of area South. That deputy chief reports to the chief of patrol and the chief of patrol reports to the superintendent who is appointed by the Mayor with the advice and consent of the city council. This bureaucratic organizational system is common in police organizations, it is intended to provide clear reporting relationships, command authority, control over police resources, and public accountability.

> Police officers are deployed into different roles such as uniformed patrol, plain clothes tactical units, uniformed saturation gun teams, detectives, SWAT officers and other roles that employ different tactics to combat the particular crime problem.

Patrol Resources

In addition to an allotment of uniformed patrol officers, each district also has "Flexible deployable resources" such as saturation or gun teams that may be utilized by area deputy chiefs to assist districts with particular crime problems. An area saturation team is a group of uniformed officers led by a Sergeant which is assigned temporarily to a district to provide a higher level of police visibility. A higher level of police visibility is assumed to deter many kinds of crime, but it also creates an ominous police presence that is sometimes uncomfortable for citizens.

Gun teams are generally plainclothes officers assigned to districts for the specific purpose of seeking out gun offenders. These officers utilize aggressive

[4] Information gained from an interview with a veteran Chicago police dispatcher.

tactics and operate covertly, relying on intelligence information that enables them to target individuals, groups, and specific locations. The goal of these teams is the arrest of serious, weapons-carrying criminals; as one might expect, their demeanor and tactics are not generally those associated with the goal of improving police community relations.

A flexible deployment gun team may be assigned to a particular district when there is an increase in shootings during a particular timeframe. For example, the area South deputy chief may deploy his/her area gun team to a district to assist his normal staff in responding to "shots fired" calls or other gun related calls for service. The alternative and sometime concurrent response is to deploy a uniformed saturation team to provide a high visibility deterrence to help quell the shootings. The two-pronged approach, apprehension by gun teams and deterrence by saturation teams, attacks the gun violence problem from two direction. These types of police resources are deployed in response to a crime problem, i.e., people calling the police for help.

In years past, the Chicago police department had many more specialized units to address the needs of district commanders making requests for more officers in their area. Units like Task Force teams, Gang Crimes, Special Operations Section (SOS), Targeted Response Unit (TRU), and Mobile Strike Force (MSF) were utilized and deployed upon request of district commanders to help combat crime surges in their respective districts. In those instances, much like today, a request was made of the deputy chief of special operations who then approved deployment of the specialized units to those areas.

These units pulled out of a central location and received daily assignments for the districts where they were to be deployed. For example, in the Special Operations Section or SOS, officers would report to roll call and were then told what district assignment they would be reporting to for that evening. On any given night there could be five teams consisting of a Sergeant and 8 to 10 police officers working over and above the normal officer staffing. The system of numerous specialized units has been streamlined for greater control and accountability.

The following map shows the current Chicago Police Department geographic mapping of police districts. This is citywide and includes all 22 Chicago police districts shown in heavy blue lines. Within each district there are beats, often referred to by name, representing smaller geographic areas or neighborhoods such as "Lake View," "Beverly," and "Englewood."

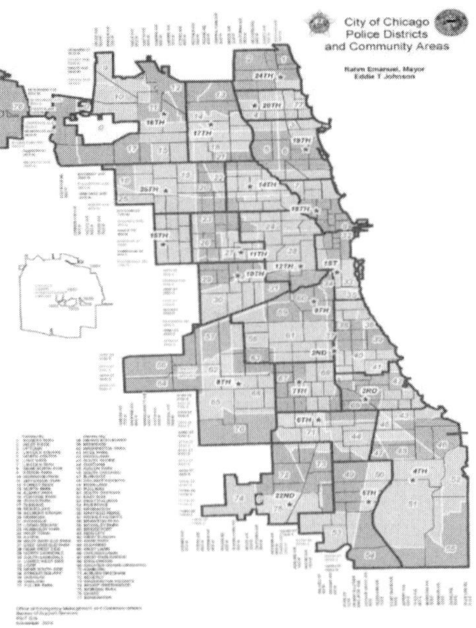

Current Chicago Police Department District Map*

Specialized and Investigative Resources

Investigations is a separate operational division from patrol and also contains specialized units. The investigative function can either be reactive or proactive depending on the nature of the calls for service and intelligence on an underlying crime problem. For example, the area North deputy chief may analyze the data from the 11th district where a spike in violent crime in the form of aggravated batteries with handguns is evident. Based upon his or her experience, these crimes are likely gang related. The deputy chief may then request supplementary gang investigative resources from the investigations division to deal with serious calls and investigations so that his or her district patrol officers may be freed-up to respond to low priority service calls that are often neglected when copious amounts of violent crime plague the district.

> Investigative resources are separate from patrol resources in that they do not normally provide the initial response to calls for service. Reactive investigative resources such as detectives conduct follow-up investigations; proactive investigative resources, such as drug units, gather intelligence and initiate investigations into criminal activity.

The narcotics unit may also be requested to assist district officers when specialized narcotics training and expertise is needed to combat increases in drug crime reported by citizens. Narcotics investigators may use different strategies

* Chicago Police Department—Home Page (2017).

such as covert (undercover) investigative tactics or the more aggressive street enforcement tactics that are often effective in addressing citizen anxiety.

A covert narcotics operation usually consists of undercover purchases of narcotics to build a case against a drug dealer or to supplement an investigation based upon a citizen complaint of drug dealing. Street enforcement involves officers engaging in street-level investigations and arrests based on their own direct observations of drug related offending. Street level enforcement attacks the problem directly and usually results in arrests for possession before a major drug dealing case can be built. This often has the impact of driving the criminal element out of a neighborhood as the result of complaints by citizens.

Tactical teams may also be called on by district commanders. Traditionally, tactical teams have been thought of as SWAT (Special Weapons and Tactics). Chicago has its own dedicated city-wide SWAT team; however, a district tactical unit consisting of plainclothes officers driving unmarked cars may be assigned special missions depending on the needs of the district. For example, if the 8th district has a rash of burglaries, the tactical team may be on a "burglary mission." This mission would be directed at attempting to stop burglaries in a geographical area where the crime statistics have shown an abundance of burglaries based on citizen complaints.

There is a profound difference between the district tactical team and the much more para-military city-wide **SWAT team**. The SWAT team is a highly trained group of officers who are called out during crisis situations to execute high risk search warrants, and to deal with other types of high risk activities. The SWAT team trains continuously for the most common scenarios that they may face and are identified by their military uniforms. They are a highly specialized group of individuals with highly specialized training in all different realms of hostage rescue, crisis intervention, high risk search warrant execution, and other types of situations that require a highly skilled and highly trained law enforcement response. They do not respond to routine calls for service and their function is strictly limited to the highest-level threats.

A district tactical team operates only within its own district. Its mission is to address violent crimes based upon information gathered within that district as the result of citizen crime reports combined with information from watch-commanders and other district resources. They receive direction from the district commander and may also be utilized for specialized details, but they are generally free from the duty to respond to routine calls for service.

A **patrol officer**, is the backbone of any Police Department. Patrol officers have the responsibility of responding to all calls for police service from "in progress" crime calls, to "just occurred" incident calls, and to low priority calls such as dogs barking and disorderly subjects. They write reports, they make arrests, they enforce traffic offenses, respond to traffic crashes, and take on any other assigned or self-initiated activities. They do the majority of the police work on a daily basis, serving citizens needs as best as they can in their district during their tour of duty.

The Chicago Police Department currently has 12,051 sworn members assigned to 22 police districts with more than 77 special units, including the narcotics division and marine operations unit. In an article by Cherone (2017) the author discussed how many police officers were currently serving with the Chicago Police Department and how they were deployed.

> *". . . About 60 percent of the Police Department's officers are assigned to one of 22 police districts, according to the data provided by the inspector general. The other 40 percent of officers are assigned to specialized units that are charged with a specific mission or duties, including the canine unit and detective bureau.*
>
> *Most officers are assigned to patrol the South and West Sides where, according to the data, the majority of crimes in Chicago are committed. For example, the Harrison and Englewood police districts on Chicago's West and South sides are home to about 5 percent of the city's population—but nearly a quarter of all crimes in 2016 took place there, officials said. Those two districts have the highest number of officers—888—assigned to patrol them, accounting for 12 percent of the total number of officers assigned to Chicago's police districts . . ."*

Just two police districts, Harrison and Englewood accounting for just 5% of the city's population account for over 25% of all crime in the city.

The information provided in the article shows that police officers have not necessarily been deployed on geographical considerations or even by population; they are deployed based on need. In other words, they are deployed where citizen calls for assistance are currently the highest and where intelligence and crime data say that they are needed the most.

Cherone (2017) continued:

> *". . . that strategy means that districts like Jefferson Park on the Far Northwest Side which, at 36 square miles, is the biggest in the city but has fewer officers per person, a source of frustration for many residents who fear they will be targeted by criminals who know that most officers are stationed on the South and West sides . . ."*

Mayor Rahm Emanuel promised to add 970 positions to the Police Department, including 516 police officers, and the new officers are to be deployed based on a statistical analysis compiled by a consultant based on crime data, calls for services and district geography according to Police Superintendent Eddie Johnson (Cherone, 2017).

This information would suggest that police officers are being deployed based on need as opposed to vague "political" considerations, a constant complaint that plagues Chicago. Districts receive an allotment of officers based on crime and call for service data, individual officers are allowed to bid for their assignments based upon seniority as per the union contract. Officers with the most years on the job have first choice on their assignment and this choice lasts for one year, new police officers get the left-over assignments for the duration of their 18 month "probationary" period. Once they successfully complete the probationary period they will be able to bid for assignments according to the union guidelines.

Table 10.3 presents officer deployment information by district (as of the time this is being written) including the total number of officers assigned to each district, the number of officers assigned per square mile, and the number of officers per citizen.

Table 10.3—Chicago Police District Manpower Distribution

District	Total Officers	Officers/ Sq. Mi.	Population/ Officer
1st (Central)	313	66.8	182
2nd (Wentworth)	323	43	343
3rd (Grand Crossing)	321	52.8	234
4th (South Chicago)	327	12	378
5th (Calumet)	332	26	224
6th (Gresham)	341	42.1	266
7th (Englewood)	426	65.4	167
8th (Chicago Lawn)	394	17.1	628
9th (Deering)	336	24.9	463
10th (Ogden)	356	45.3	332
11th (Harrison)	462	75.7	153
12th (Near West)	339	35	377
14th (Shakespeare)	243	40.5	485
15th (Austin)	350	91.7	170

16th (Jefferson Park)	266	8.4	750
17th (Albany Park)	246	25.6	586
18th (Near North)	360	76.8	325
19th (Town Hall)	389	45.3	516
20th (Lincoln)	247	56.6	370
22nd (Morgan Park)	271	20.1	376
24th (Rogers Park)	272	50.2	519
25th (Grand Central)	337	30.9	595

Source: Cherone, H. (2017, May 02). Here's How Many Officers Are Patrolling Your Neighborhood.

Analyzing Data

Utilizing the Chicago Police Department homepage, the author was able to locate current statistical information on the 11th district and 20th district. These districts were chosen because, earlier in this chapter, a weekend of crime reporting was provided showing that the 11th district had the most calls for reported crime while the 20th had the least. Accordingly, officer deployments Cherone (2017) identified the 11th district as having the most police officers, 426 while the 20th district had the 3rd least amount with 247.

The following graphic illustrates the geographical boundaries of the 11th district. The district itself is small when compared to other districts and contains 15 beats.

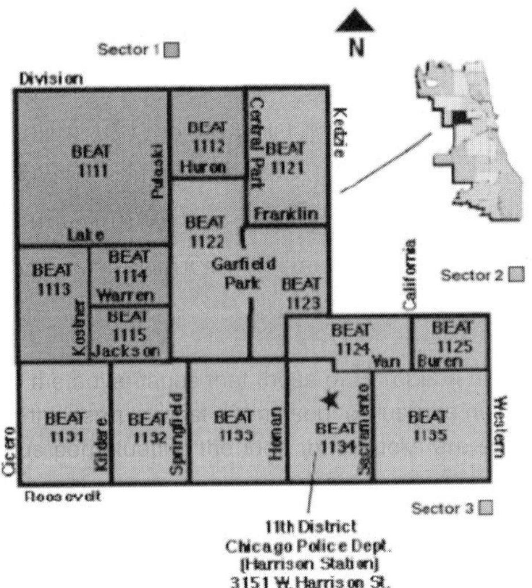

Chicago Police Department 11th District—Harrison*

* Chicago Police Department—Home Page (2017).

Table 10.4—Crime Complaints for the 11th District from December 4, 2017 through December 10, 2017

Rahm Emanuel
Mayor

Chicago
Police Department

Eddie T. Johnson
Superintendent

District 11

CompStat

Week 49

Geocoded for District Consolidation

District Reports

Report Covering the Week of 04-Dec-17 Through 10-Dec-17

	Last 7 Days			Last 28 Days			Year to Date			2 Yr.	3 Yr.	4 Yr.
	2017	2016	% Chg	2017	2016	% Chg	2017	2016	% Chg	% Chg	% Chg	% Chg
CRIME COMPLAINTS												
MURDER	1	3	-67%	4	10	-60%	63	93	-32%	29%	26%	85%
CRIM SEXUAL ASSLT	2	0	0%	9	12	-25%	107	120	-11%	3%	0%	47%
ROBBERY	11	14	-21%	85	79	8%	882	937	-6%	10%	27%	21%
AGG BATTERY	8	13	-38%	35	50	-30%	649	717	-9%	11%	23%	29%
BURGLARY	12	10	20%	36	35	3%	464	459	1%	8%	-10%	-28%
THEFT	6	11	-45%	36	36	0%	428	488	-12%	12%	-15%	-28%
MTR VEHICLE THEFT	16	26	-38%	52	80	-35%	677	724	-6%	23%	25%	4%
TOTAL	56	77	-27%	257	302	-15%	3270	3538	-8%	13%	11%	1%
SHOOTING INCIDENT	4	11	-64%	20	39	-49%	334	461	-28%	30%	81%	115%

HISTORICAL COMPARISON

	2017	2016	2015	2014	2013	% Change 2017 - 2016	% Change 2017 - 2015	% Change 2017 - 2014	% Change 2017 - 2013
MURDER	63	93	49	50	34	-32%	29%	26%	85%
CRIM SEXUAL ASSLT	107	120	104	107	73	-11%	3%	0%	47%
ROBBERY	882	937	803	695	726	-6%	10%	27%	21%
AGG BATTERY	649	717	585	529	502	-9%	11%	23%	29%
BURGLARY	464	459	431	514	644	1%	8%	-10%	-28%
THEFT	428	488	383	506	595	-12%	12%	-15%	-28%
MTR VEHICLE THEFT	677	724	549	540	648	-6%	23%	25%	4%
TOTAL	3270	3538	2904	2941	3222	-8%	13%	11%	1%

The above CompStat figures are posted on Monday, one week after closing date.

CompStat figures are preliminary and subject to further analysis and revision. Crime statistics reflect Illinois Compiled Statutes and differ from the crime categories of the F.B.I. Uniform Crime Reporting System. All degrees of Criminal Sexual Assault are included in the Criminal Sexual Assault category.

Source: https://home.chicagopolice.org/wp-content/uploads/2017/12/15_PDFsam_CompStat-Public-2017-Week-49.pdf.

The following graphic illustrates the geographical boundaries of the 20th police district which is larger geographically than the 11th district and contains only 9 beats.

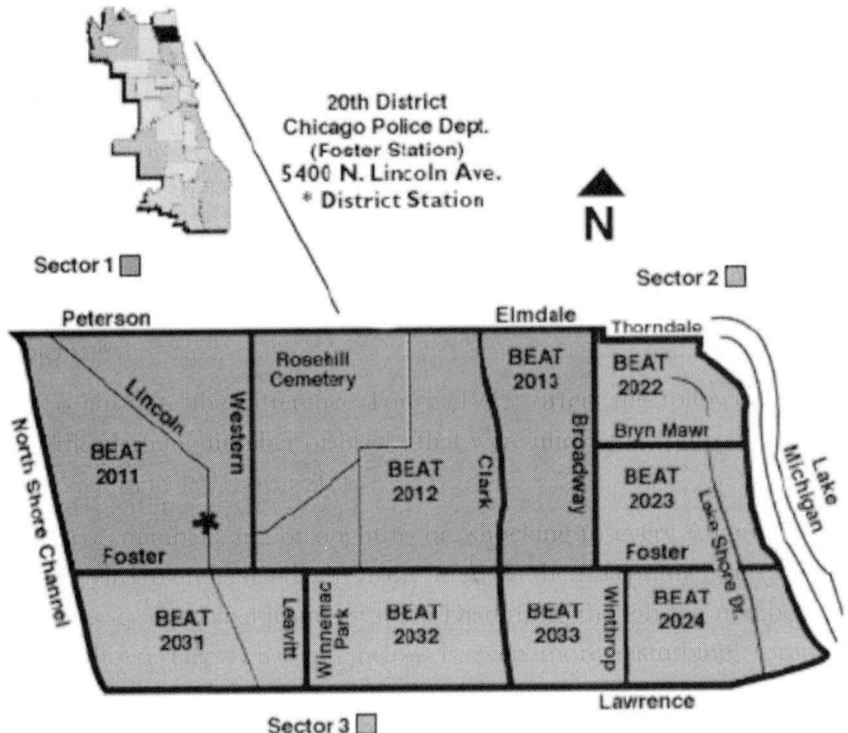

Chicago Police Department 20th District—Foster*

* Chicago Police Department—Home Page (2017).

Table 10.5—Crime Complaints for the 20th District from December 4, 2017 through December 10, 2017

Rahm Emanuel
Mayor

Chicago
Police Department

Eddie T. Johnson
Superintendent

District 20

CompStat
Week 49
Geocoded for District Consolidation

District Reports

Report Covering the Week of 04-Dec-17 Through 10-Dec-17

	Last 7 Days			Last 28 Days			Year to Date			2 Yr.	3 Yr.	4 Yr.
	2017	2016	% Chg	2017	2016	% Chg	2017	2016	% Chg	% Chg	% Chg	% Chg
CRIME COMPLAINTS												
MURDER	0	0	0%	0	0	0%	2	3	-33%	-67%	0%	-33%
CRIM SEXUAL ASSLT	2	1	100%	6	3	100%	48	53	-9%	109%	109%	243%
ROBBERY	0	1	-100%	10	7	43%	122	126	-3%	23%	26%	-20%
AGG BATTERY	3	0	0%	7	6	17%	60	74	-19%	-8%	7%	-10%
BURGLARY	3	8	-62%	9	25	-64%	194	212	-8%	11%	-6%	-29%
THEFT	3	5	-40%	19	21	-10%	298	272	10%	40%	15%	9%
MTR VEHICLE THEFT	3	3	0%	14	11	27%	159	171	-7%	-6%	5%	-22%
TOTAL	14	18	-22%	65	73	-11%	883	911	-3%	18%	11%	-11%
SHOOTING INCIDENT	0	0	0%	1	2	-50%	10	17	-41%	-44%	100%	43%

HISTORICAL COMPARISON

	2017	2016	2015	2014	2013	% Change 2017 - 2016	% Change 2017 - 2015	% Change 2017 - 2014	% Change 2017 - 2013
MURDER	2	3	6	2	3	-33%	-67%	0%	-33%
CRIM SEXUAL ASSLT	48	53	23	23	14	-9%	109%	109%	243%
ROBBERY	122	126	99	97	152	-3%	23%	26%	-20%
AGG BATTERY	60	74	65	56	67	-19%	-8%	7%	-10%
BURGLARY	194	212	174	206	274	-8%	11%	-6%	-29%
THEFT	298	272	213	259	273	10%	40%	15%	9%
MTR VEHICLE THEFT	159	171	170	151	204	-7%	-6%	5%	-22%
TOTAL	883	911	750	794	987	-3%	18%	11%	-11%

The above CompStat figures are posted on Monday, one week after closing date.

CompStat figures are preliminary and subject to further analysis and revision. Crime statistics reflect Illinois Compiled Statutes and differ from the crime categories of the F.B.I. Uniform Crime Reporting System. All degrees of Criminal Sexual Assault are included in the Criminal Sexual Assault category.

Source: https://home.chicagopolice.org/wp-content/uploads/2017/12/15_PDFsam_CompStat-Public-2017-Week-49.pdf.

The 20th police district has 247 officers assigned, the 11th district is much smaller and has nearly twice as many officers assigned, 462. The 20th district had 883 reported crimes from January 1, 2017 through December 10, 2017, the 11th district had 3270 reported crimes. Over three times the amount of crime was reported in the 11th district as was reported in the 20th district.

Clearly, police resources in the City of Chicago are deployed to geographic areas of the city based on need. That need is determined by the number of citizen calls for help. This data shows that the allotment of officers to these districts is driven, mostly if not solely, upon rational analysis of crime data; neither geographic size nor population has had a measurable impact on officer assignment.

POLICING STRATEGIES

Police agencies employ different crime control strategies all of which have differing impacts on the police community relationship. Generally, the goal is crime control with police community relations being of secondary importance.

The National Institute of Justice, crimesolutions.gov website (2017) identifies several different police crime control strategies and evidence of effectiveness for each strategy. Utilizing this information, some of the more popular past and present crime control strategies are broken down and explained, and the evidence of their success, or lack of success is presented.

Broken Windows Theory

The Broken Windows Theory was first presented by James Q. Wilson and George L. Kelling in the March 1982 issue of the Atlantic Monthly. In this seminal article, these two authors presented a way of thinking about disorder and its relationship to actual crime problems that can be summarized simply as taking care of the small nuisance offenses to prevent the larger crime problems from taking hold in a neighborhood.

The implication of this theory is that the best way for the police to keep a neighborhood safe was for officers to concentrate on neighborhood patrol duties which included foot patrol and arresting people for "quality of life crimes" such as drunkenness, loitering, pan-handling, and other minor nuisance crimes (Wilson, 1982).

The "broken windows" perspective, which shares many assumptions with routine activities and rational choice crime control theories, emphasizes the need for police to crack down on minor offenses to reduce major crimes (Schram, 2014).

The National Institute of Justice, CrimeSolutions.gov describes the Broken Windows Policing Theory as a:

". . . hot spots policing approach (which) is a disorder reduction tactic used by some law enforcement agencies in high crime neighborhoods. The strategy is based on the

'broken windows' theory of crime, which suggests that crime is likely to flourish in areas with high levels of physical and social disorder. It entails the use of broken windows policing, also known as disorder policing or order maintenance policing, which focuses resources on small areas with high crime rates (hot spots) to produce a crime-reduction effect throughout the larger area . . ." (National Institute of Justice Website).

This strategy was employed in major urban areas in the early 90s and was considered successful in reducing overall crime in New York:

"*. . . Many attribute New York's crime reduction to specific 'get-tough' policies carried out by former Mayor Rudolph Giuliani's administration. The most prominent of his policy changes was the aggressive policing of lower-level crimes, a policy which has been dubbed the "broken windows" approach to law enforcement. In this view, small disorders lead to larger ones and perhaps even to crime. As Mr. Giuliani told the press in 1998, "Obviously murder and graffiti are two vastly different crimes. But they are part of the same continuum, and a climate that tolerates one is more likely to tolerate the other. . .*" (Francis, 2003).

Many skeptics of the broken window theory have brought evidence forward to suggest that these practices lead to deeper issues relating to social justice. According to Childress (2016), these "minor offenses" for which people are being arrested give the perception that the people committing these offenses are truly bad people. More aggressive "broken windows" enforcement policies could lead the police to violate civil rights and have racially charged policing incidents because they tend to focus law enforcement attention on poor communities of color (Childress, 2016).

Although there are many skeptics of the broken windows policing strategy, it has been attributed, at least in New York, for driving down the crime rates during the Giuliani era in that city.

Community Policing

The U.S. Department of Justice describes Community Oriented Policing Services (COPS) as:

"*. . . Community policing emphasizes proactive problem solving in a systematic and routine fashion. Rather than responding to crime only after it occurs, community policing encourages agencies to proactively develop solutions to the immediate underlying conditions contributing to public safety problems. Problem solving must be infused into all police operations and guide decision making efforts. Agencies are encouraged to think innovatively about their responses and view making arrests as* *only one of a wide array of potential responses"* (Department of Justice: Community Oriented Policing Services Website).

Some of the activities utilized in community policing are foot patrols, community meetings, and specific reporting procedures for citizen complaint issues that may be more of a nuisance than a criminal act. Since these nuisance crimes may turn into larger criminal activity, community policing focuses on community service as a way to connect with the community and work with local residents to solve the underlying problems that cause crime.

In Chicago, the community policing strategy is known as Chicago Alternative Policing Strategies or CAPS. Each police district has its own CAPS office headed by a sergeant and staffed with specially trained officers. The number of officers assigned to this activity can vary from district to district. The mission for each district CAPS team is to address concerns of that particular district by working with the district's citizens, businesses, and other stakeholders.

Hot Spot Policing

Hotspot policing is defined as policing focused on small geographic places or areas where crime is concentrated. This strategy has arguably been one of the most important policing innovations of recent decades (Koper, 2014).

According to Braga & Wiesburg (2010), hotspot policing is one of the most effective policing strategies in the modern age. Crime is controlled by placing police in small geographic areas which are shown by data to be areas where crime occurs regularly. The police then employ high visibility tactics in an effort to deter crime in that small area.

Some skeptics of hotspot policing have stated that this strategy merely relocates or disperses crime to other areas. When hot spot policing is used in one area, these skeptics argue, criminals simply move their enterprises to other areas where the police are not as numerous or visible. Utilizing hot spots analysis to determine where crime rates are highest and then deploying an overwhelming police presence to those areas could be considered a primitive form of the next strategy, named Problem Oriented Policing or POP.

Problem Oriented Policing (POP)

> Problem oriented policing is not the same as community oriented policing. POP relies on precise analysis of problems that lead to crime, strategy development and implementation to combat the underlying problem, and evaluation of the effectiveness of the strategy.

Professor Herman Goldstein is considered the early founder of Problem Oriented Policing (POP). POP is described as:

> *". . . an approach to policing in which discrete pieces of police business (each consisting of a cluster of similar incidents, whether crime or acts of disorder, that the police are expected to handle) are subject to microscopic examination (drawing on the especially honed skills of crime analysis and the accumulated experience of operating field personnel) in hopes that what is freshly learned about each problem will lead to discovering a new and more effective strategy for dealing with it.*
>
> *"Problem-oriented policing places a high value on new responses that are preventive in nature, that are not dependent on the use of the criminal justice system, and that engage other public agencies, the community and the private sector when their involvement has the potential for significantly contributing to the reduction of the problem.*
>
> *"Problem-oriented policing carries a commitment to implementing the new strategy, rigorously evaluating its effectiveness, and, subsequently, reporting the results in ways that will benefit other police agencies and that will ultimately contribute to building a body of knowledge that supports the further professionalization of the police . . ."* (Center for Problem-Oriented Policing Website).

Many people have confused POP with community oriented policing and other strategies, but problem-oriented policing is its own distinct strategy. POP may encompass other strategies—such as community oriented policing or hotspot policing—it is a unique and distinct strategy for addressing crime issues in particular areas. Unlike the ambiguous concept of "community oriented policing," problem oriented policing has a demonstrated impact on driving down crime when properly implemented.

For example, if complaints about a lot of graffiti come to the attention of the district commanders by way of the local community policing officer, and that officer notes that the tags[5] on the graffiti suggests that it all seems to have been created by the same small group of individuals and it is limited to a specific general area, the area will then be identified as a hotspot for graffiti, the patrol division

[5] "Tags" are symbols of gang affiliation that sometimes identify gang turf. "Taggers" are usually wannabe gang members who spray-paint walls and garages with these symbols.

will be notified, and the district commander will notify his watch personnel (who are the people who work the specific tours of duty in the area) to be on the lookout for the perpetrators. He would also be expected to put a special "graffiti car" up and running in that area to attempt to apprehend the perpetrators. Then other factors can be addressed to identify underlying conditions that make that particular area susceptible to this problem.

POP might also be used, for instance, in an area where there is a problem of intimidation of young people by gang members. In one such actual situation, citizens were demanding help with the problem of gang members who would position themselves on a school route before or after school to attempt to recruit gang members from the ranks of grade school children. To combat this problem the city of Chicago implemented a strategy called "Operation Safe Passage." The program involved deploying police, civilian volunteers, and civilian crossing guards at strategic positions along the school route for the purpose of making these gang members feel "unwelcome." In this situation, the partnership formed between the police and the community was effective in solving that problem.

This successful effort exemplifies the way the POP system works. It involved a series of steps:

- a problem was identified through community relations or community policing;
- the community policing officers interacted with citizens and businesses in the area to clearly identify the problem;
- the officers worked together with concerned community members to come up with a strategy to combat the problem;
- the strategy was implemented by the police and community members working together; and, finally,
- the effort was assessed by the officers and cooperating community members to determine the effectiveness of the solution.

Accountability for dealing with these and similar problems is facilitated through a program known as COMPSTAT. This accountability mechanism takes the form of meetings where the commander of the district or his/her designee describe their crime reduction strategy for the benefit and critique of their peers.

COMPSTAT

This acronym is a label for the police practice and system of comparing crime statistics. It is a performance management system as opposed to a specific crime control strategy such as community policing or problem-oriented policing. The process consists of regular command staff meetings where district commanders present their crime statistics and brainstorm ideas on what strategies to employ to drive those stats down.

> Holding the police, specifically commanders, accountable for driving down crime has always been a problem in policing because the police actually have little control over those conditions that cause crime. COMPSTAT seeks to inject an element of accountability into policing, creating a learning environment where the best crime control practices can be identified and encouraged.

The program holds commanders accountable for crime increases and forces them to engage in problem solving sessions. Commanders take turns describing issues and problems in their area of responsibility and reporting successes, failures, and addressing future needs to combat crime. A fundamental aspect of this program is relentless follow-up on crime problems, the implication is that, should commanders fail to reduce crime, they will face consequences ranging from demotion and re-assignment to embarrassment among their peers.

According to a document produced by United States, Department of Justice, Bureau of Justice Assistance 2013, Compstat was born in New York in the 1990s and is explained as:

> "*. . . Compstat is a performance management system that is used to reduce crime and achieve other police department goals. Compstat emphasizes information-sharing, responsibility and accountability, and improving effectiveness. It includes four generally recognized core components: (1) Timely and accurate information or intelligence; (2) Rapid deployment of resources; (3) Effective tactics; and (4) Relentless follow-up . . .*" (p. 2).

The report continues:

> "*. . . The most widely recognized element of Compstat is its regularly occurring meetings where department executives and officers discuss and analyze crime problems and the strategies used to address those problems. Oftentimes, department leaders will select commanders from a specific geographic area to attend each Compstat meeting . . .*" (p. 2).

The essence of this program is the responsibility of command level personnel to deploy their personnel resources responsibly based on information they are gathering from citizens, crime reports, intelligence, trial and error, and other sources. Commanders are being held accountable by their bosses for effectiveness in combating crime and other problems reported by citizens in their area and this can be a powerful motivator to develop innovative solutions to crime problems.

For example, if there is an outbreak of shootings in a specific area of a district that have garnered media attention, the mayor's office will be calling the superintendent's office whose office will then be calling the district commander to find out what they are doing to address the shooting problem. Follow-up will take place at the next Compstat meeting where high-level command personnel from the police department, such as the chief of patrol, will hold their subordinate commanders accountable for the response and effective deployment of police resources.

Compstat has increased in popularity in large police departments throughout the nation because the system holds command level individuals accountable for the issues and crime problems that occur in their areas of responsibility. Pressure to perform is injected at the highest levels and several ranking members of the NYPD have moved on to command level jobs in different cities throughout America because of their success and knowledge of this system of accountability. Bill Bratton brought a calm step model to the Los Angeles Police Department, John Timoney brought it to Philadelphia and expanded it in Miami, and lastly Garry McCarthy enhanced Chicago's version of Compstat (United States, Department of Justice, Bureau of Justice Assistance, 2013).

Compstat is a system of accountability which holds department command level personnel responsible for specific geographic areas of the city based on citizen complaints of crime. They respond to issues that relate to crime in their areas and defend their decisions on how to deploy resources based on need.

INTELLIGENCE-LED POLICING

Intelligence-led policing is a policing evaluation model built around the assessment and management of risk. Crime, call for service information, and intelligence directs police operations rather than operations controlling, disseminating, and interpreting intelligence (Maguire & John, 2006).

> Intelligence led policing is a risk management crime control strategy. Unlike traditional criminology that focuses on offenders, intelligence led policing focuses on geographic locations where crime occurs and asks how the environment contributes to the crime problem.

Intelligence-led policing gained notoriety and forward momentum after the 9/11 terrorist attacks in New York City. Fusion centers were developed in major cities where information could be shared by different agencies with federal, state, and local agencies all having input on potential terrorist threats. This technology was later incorporated into regular law enforcement operations with fusion centers becoming intelligence sources for many different agencies regarding crime, crime patterns, and crime reduction strategies.

Intelligence-led policing is distinct from broken windows policing in that intelligence led policing uses emerging technologies to identify areas where crimes may be committed in the future. Once these areas are identified, law enforcement resources are deployed to those areas to help stop crime proactively.

This explanation was echoed by White (2012):

> *". . . Intelligence led policing is a strategic, future oriented and targeted approach to crime control focusing upon the identification, analysis and management of persisting developing problems or risks. In simpler terms, it is a model of policing which intelligence serves as a guide to operations rather than the reverse"* (White, 2012, p. 320).

Ratcliffe (2016) stated that several different policing strategies are incorporated into an overall intelligence-led policing effort. Community policing models, problem oriented policing models and other strategies such as COMPSTAT are blended together and this is what makes intelligence-led policing work.

POLICE PERSPECTIVES ON INITIATING CITIZEN CONTACTS AND RESPONDING TO CRIME AND CALLS FOR SERVICE

Police officers have a unique perspective as it relates to responding to calls for service and crime. Police officers are the front lines of response; they are the assets that are deployed in response to citizens calls for assistance. They have first-hand experience on responding to calls, performing field interviews, executing investigatory stops, and making arrests. Understanding their perspective is important in understanding how police response works and crime reduction happens.

Interviews

To help readers understand police response and perspectives, a series of personal interviews were conducted with 16 veteran Chicago police officers who have spent time in the patrol division. Some of the participants, in addition to their patrol experience, are currently assigned to, or have spent time Chicago police area mission teams, district tactical teams, and other specialized units that may have been charged with citywide response and deployment.

Their responses were recorded and transcribed and qualitative analysis was used to summarize the data and findings. According to Waters (2016), the goal of qualitative phenomenological research such as this is to describe a "lived experience." This research presentation employs a method to study the experiences of individuals in the first person, in other words, people who have first-hand experience in an area that others may not have experienced (Roth, 2012). Policing is a closed craft that does not lend itself well to direct observation; to understand policing fully, one has to have lived it. Extracting that "lived" data was the goal of these interviews.

The identity of the interview participants is protected; however, the author did record demographic information regarding them to demonstrate their subject-matter expertise. All of the interviews were voluntary and no participants received any benefit or remuneration for their participation in this project.

The police officers were instructed to describe their experience by naming the districts in which they worked, and whether or not they worked on a district tactical team; a citywide specialized unit (SU) such as gang investigations, gang enforcement, special operations section, tactical response unit, mobile strike force, or other specialized unit such as the SWAT team. They were also asked if they worked in an area gun team or mission team, which would be reported as a specialized team.

To clarify, a citywide team (CW) is a unit such as gang investigations that deploys from a centralized location but has city-wide responsibility. A specialized team (ST) consists of area saturation teams or an area gun team that may be deployed to districts based on needs presented by the district commander or at the behest of the area deputy chief. A tactical team (TT) is a district tactical team that is already located in the geographical district of responsibility to respond to the needs of that particular district.

Lastly, districts of assignment are reported as numbers; for example, if an individual worked in the 8th district, it would be reported as 008. The demographic and related data from the interviews are reported in Table 10.6.

Table 10.6—Interviewee Demographics

Source Title	Ethnicity	Gender	Age	Years of Service	Active or Retired	Date of Interview	Rank	Experience
Source 1	White	Male	52	28	Active	12/10/2017	Police Officer	007, 018, CW, ST, SU
Source 2	White	Female	40	15	Active	12/12/2017	Police Officer	011, 016, 017, TT
Source 3	Hispanic	Male	57	32	Retired	12/10/2017	Sergeant	015, CW, SU
Source 4	White	Male	55	30	Retired	12/12/2017	Detective	008, TT, Det.

Source 5	Black	Male	48	25	Active	12/12/2017	Detective	011, CW, Det.
Source 6	Hispanic	Female	36	8	Active	12/10/2017	Police Officer	004, ST
Source 7	White	Male	39	15	Active	12/9/2017	Sergeant	015, TT, ST, 003, SU
Source 8	White	Female	34	12	Active	12/8/2017	Police Officer	003, TT, CW, SU
Source 9	Black	Female	42	18	Active	12/12/2017	Police Officer	005, 006, 018
Source 10	Hispanic	Male	48	21	Active	12/15/2017	Police Officer	011, CW, SU, ST, 020
Source 11	White	Female	45	18	Active	12/10/2017	Police Officer	008, TT, ST
Source 12	White	Male	30	8	Active	11/30/2017	Police Officer	003, TT, ST
Source 13	Black	Male	50	25	Active	11/30/2017	Police Officer	009, CW, 008, TT, SU
Source 14	White	Male	43	19	Active	12/1/2017	Police Officer	011, 010, TT, CW, SU
Source 15	Hispanic	Male	45	16	Active	12/2/2017	Police Officer	010, TT, CW, 018, ST
Source 16	White	Female	32	10	Active	12/10/2017	Police Officer	015, 016

The interview guide for the interview was the same for all participants and included the following disclaimer which was read to the interviewee by the interviewer:

> "*. . . This interview is being conducted at your free will and of a volunteer nature. There is no gain, monetary or personal, for participation in this interview. The information gathered will solely be used for the purpose of generating articles for police periodicals and/or the investigators personal use for future research and/or scholastic materials. Participants will be kept anonymous and identified as 'Source' followed by the appropriate number . . .*"

The reason for the disclaimer is to let each participating police officer know that this process is strictly voluntary and done under the blanket of anonymity to provide a level of comfort for the participating officers who are generally reluctant to discuss the job outside of the confines of the police fraternity.

Each interview sought answers to the following questions:

1. Do you understand the aforementioned information read to you by this interviewer?

2. In your time on the job have you had an opportunity to work in various police assignments? Please explain. If you worked on a district tactical team you do not have to identify the district, just say tactical team. If you worked in an area mission team, you do not have to identify that area or what team, just say specialized team. By the same token if you worked in a city wide unit such as special operations, targeted response unit, or mobile strike force, just state city wide unit. Lastly if you worked in units such as gang investigations, gang enforcement, or narcotics, just state specialized unit.
3. While engaged in the assignments did you have the opportunity to respond to calls for police service via dispatch?
4. In your police career how many calls for service do you think you have responded to? It is okay to approximate a number.
5. Are the calls for police service different depending on the district? For example, are calls for police service different in districts like 7, 11, 15 then somewhere like 16, 18, or 1? Please explain.
6. Can you explain to me the factors that go into your decision to stop an individual while on your tour of duty?
7. Is there anything else you would like to add?

The interviews concluded with the interviewer reading the following statement:

". . . Thank you for your participation in this interview and especially your candor. This information once again will be used to generate articles and police periodicals, research and scholastic materials for the investigator. You will be identified as 'Source' followed by a number. Demographic information will only be kept for statistical purposes and reported in scholastic materials. In no way will the demographic information be used in an attempt to identify you . . ."

It was important for the researcher to establish a bond of trust with the participants even though the researcher in this case was a twenty-year veteran police officer. The aforementioned disclaimers were important to establishing and maintaining rapport throughout the interview process

"Cops trust cops" because police officers often believe that outsiders do not understand the critical issues cops face. One interviewee, in a side conversation, stated "people think that what we do is like what they see on TV, they have no idea the things we've seen, the places we've been, and the things that we've had to do to keep them safe."

Police culture is a unique aspect of this job. Misrepresentations in the media, misinformation reported as fact, and other issues often create glaring distortions of what police culture is. This often creates distrust of outsiders by law enforcement professionals.

To cops, the police subculture is not understood as a secretive counter-culture plagued by institutional wrongdoings; rather, it is one of honor that has been forged through years and decades of dealing with the depravity of man. Police officers trust their peers because they have a body of shared experiences and feelings, the things they've seen and the horrors that haunt them are shared by their police brothers and sisters.

Police Perspectives Analysis

Based on the information obtained from these interviews a perspective unique to these individuals was uncovered. The average age of the interviewees was 43.5 years old and the average time of service was 18.75 years (Table 10.7). Table 10.8 identifies the interviewee demographics in terms of race and gender, 10 males and 6 female interviewees with the ethnic breakdowns listed. Table 10.9 identifies the assignment history—number of different assignments—for the interviewees who took part in this process. It shows that 50% of the interviewees had three or four assignments during their career while 38% had five or more and only two interviewees had one or two assignments over the course of their police career to date.

With regard to age, time on the job, and assignments within the police function, this was a diverse group of officers.

Table 10.7—Interviewee Average Age and Time of Service

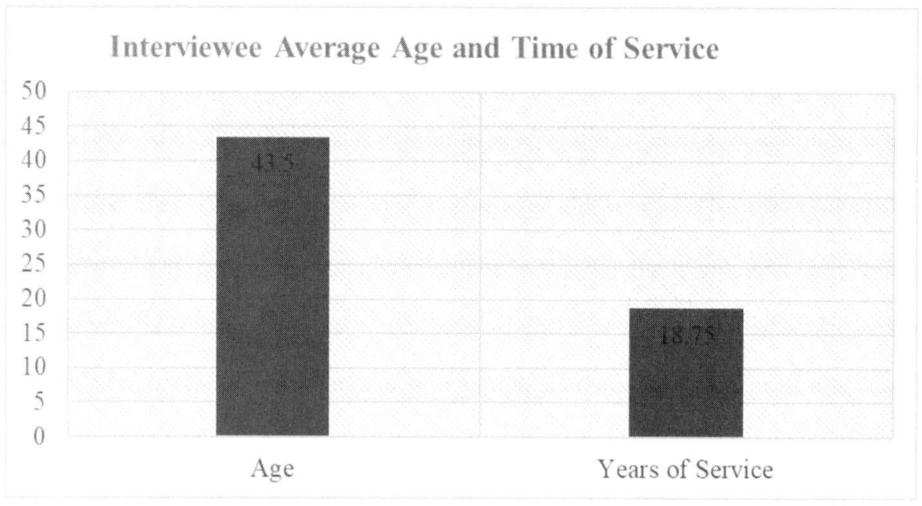

Table 10.8—Race & Gender

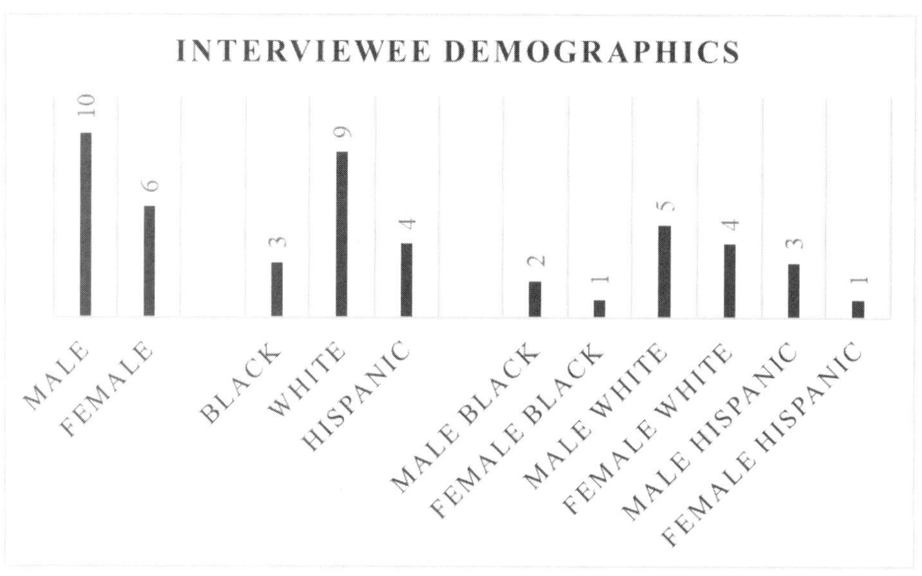

Table 10.9—Interviewee Assignment History

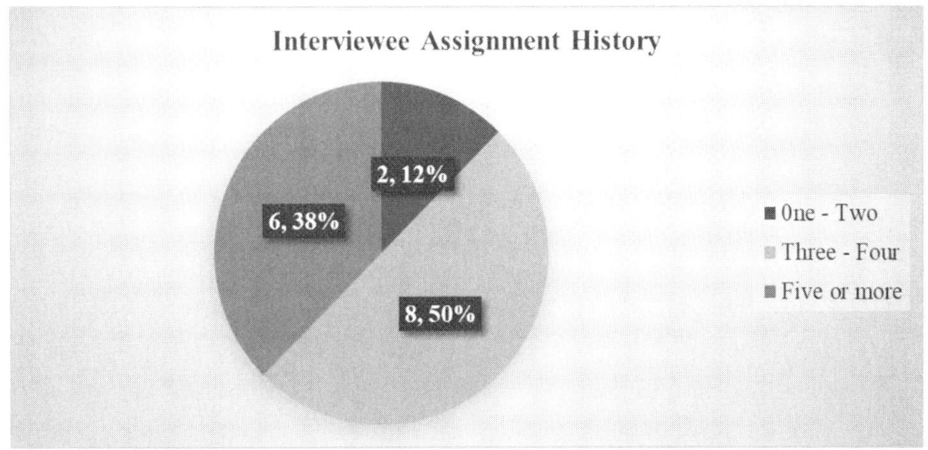

Open coding was used to highlight sections of the interview data and to provide initial organization. The next step was to use axial coding to further categorize the data in code sets of response data (Ravitch & Carl, 2016).

According to Seidel (1998), analyzing qualitative data is like putting a jigsaw puzzle together. From this frame of reference, codes were assigned to different responses.

Table 10.10—Qualitative Coding Matrix from Interviews

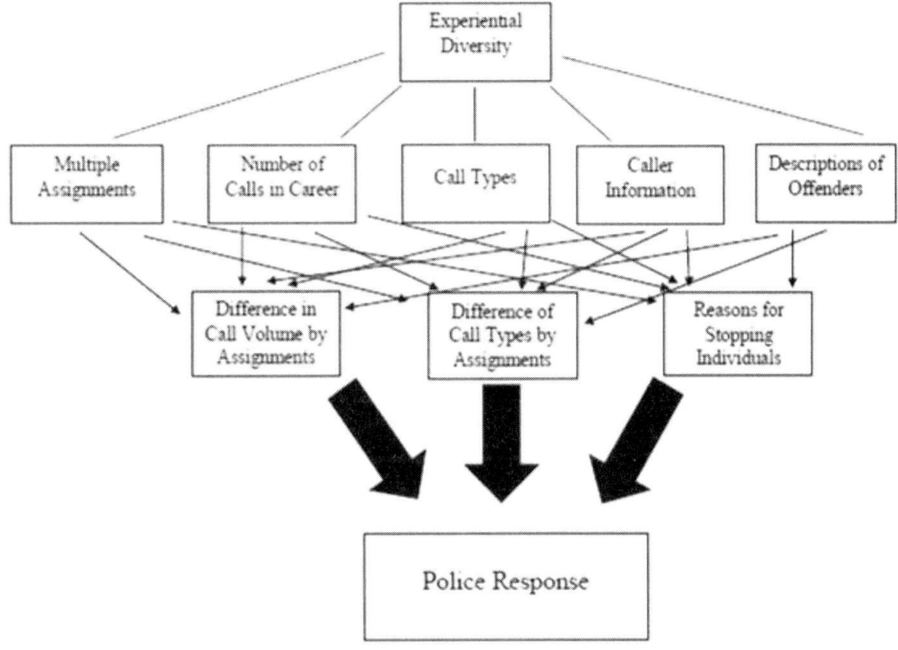

Table 10.10 illustrates the coding majors utilized by the author to disseminate the qualitative data and interview responses to the questions asked of the participants.

The first tier was experiential diversity which, when broken down, directed the researcher to the open coding codes of multiple assignments, number of calls responded to in a career, call types, caller information, and descriptions of offenders.

When that data was examined, utilizing axial coding, the interviewer was able to narrow the responses down to difference in call volume by assignment, difference in types of calls by assignment, and reasons for stopping individuals. All of this information impacted the police response. The second tier of coding with the titles of: multiple assignments; number of calls in career; call types; caller information; and descriptions of offenders all intersect with the next level of coding which is: difference and call volume by assignment, difference and call types by assignment, and reasons for stopping individuals. This intersection is important because it shows the information gathered in the interviews all relate to one another even though the officers all have had varying assignments.

To illustrate this in more detail, Table 10.11 shows the approximate number of calls the interviewees have responded to in their police career. The majority of interviewees, 56%, stated that they have responded to over 1000 calls for police service during their Chicago police career; while 31% of the interviewees stated that they have responded to between 500 and a thousand calls for service. This gives the participants in the interview a diverse experience perspective regarding police service calls and response.

Table 10.11—Participants Approximate Number of "Responded to" Police Service Calls

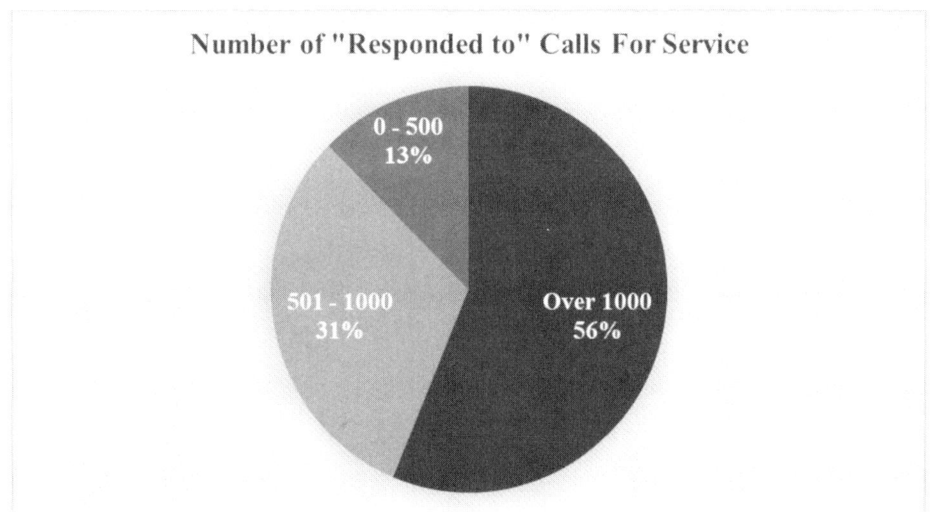

Table 10.12 shows the interviewee's perspectives on the difference of call volume and call type as it relates to the assignment. For example, in the interview the question was asked: "Are the calls different depending on district?" For example, "Are calls for police service different in a district like 7, 11, 15 than in districts 16, 18, 1? If so, please explain." Based on this question all 16 participants reported that there were differences in call volume and type in the various police districts.

Call Differences

Table 10.12—Reported Difference in Call Types and Volume for Respective Assignment/Area

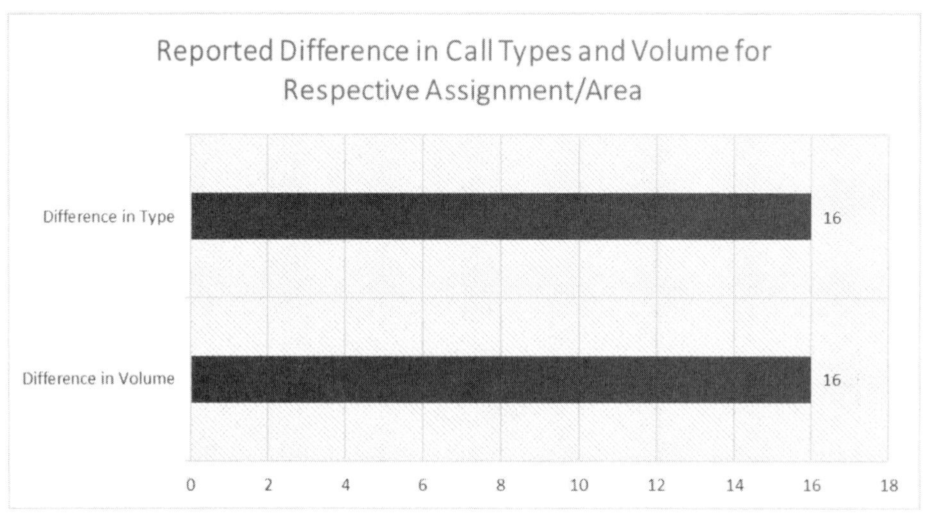

Descriptions of differences varied, however in response to this question, the subject of interview number one stated:

"Interviewee: "Yes and No. What I mean by that is the sheer call volume in a district like 7 as opposed to 18, and I have worked in both, is pretty big but . . ."

Interviewer: "can you explain what 'pretty big' means please?

Interviewee: "yes sir. In Englewood on a hot Saturday night, you may have 400 calls for service in the district during your tour. In 18, you may have about half that but the calls are similar.

What I mean by that is in 18 you may have a lot of in-progress calls such as battery in-progress, bar disturbance in-progress, robbery in-progress, battery just occurred, and your occasional noise disturbance; whereas in 7 you have in-progress calls or shots fired, person shot, domestic in progress, battery in progress, robbery just occurred."

Interviewer: "sounds pretty similar. Is there a difference?"

Interviewee: "yes. In Englewood there are a ton of shots fired calls, but many of them are not bona fide. Citizens seem to call the police because there's other types of disturbance and want them there fast so they report 'shots fired' as opposed to something that it really is.

In 18 if there's a 'shots fired' call you know that it's more than likely bona fide. Also in Englewood a report of 'robbery just occurred' could be someone being ripped off on the dope spot trying to buy drugs. They can't tell the police that but they can say that an individual took their stuff and their money at gunpoint. In 18 a robbery that occurs on the street is usually a purse snatch or a stick up.

Another factor that goes into calls being bona fide or not bona fide is the caller information. A true victim will leave their information so you can contact them or at least meet up with them to talk about what happened. Anonymous callers usually are not leaving their information because either they are reporting a falsehood or because they fear retaliation. That's the scenario that usually happens in Englewood (the Englewood district).

> **Responding to calls for service is different for police officers depending on where they are working, high violent crime areas compared to low violent crime areas.**

The interviewee stated that responding to calls in a district like Englewood, 11th, as opposed to the 18th district is different not only because of the amount of calls but also the types of calls and caller information. According to the interviewee people may misrepresent the type of call or issue reported because they want the police to respond faster, this is more prevalent in the Englewood district than it is in other districts. The interviewee also stated that a real crime victim will provide their name, anonymous callers are usually reporting a falsehood or fear retaliation from the individuals they are calling on.

In another interview, the interviewee stated that they worked in both one of the busier districts of the city as well as a slower district in the city, and in their perspective there was a difference between them also:

Interviewee: "while I have worked in both 11 and 16 so yeah there is a difference!"

Interviewer: "can you explain this difference please?"

Interviewee: "sure! In 11 it's calls for shots fired all night long, domestics all night long, dealing drugs all night long, and none of the callers leave their names or numbers. Everyone wants to be anonymous.

In 16 it's noise complaints and suspicious people all night long. Most people who call in 16 leave their name and you know those calls are more than likely bona fide. Also in 16 you don't have an abundance of gang bangers hanging out on a street corner, or parked in their car on the street smoking weed, or selling dope on a block."

Many of the other 15 interview participants reported similarities in their responses, stating that although the call types may be similar, calls are falsely reported-exaggerated-because the callers wants a faster police response to a low priority call. Callers used a higher priority type of call (shots fired—priority one) to get the police there faster when the situation was actually a priority-three drug call.

Stopping People

Table 10.13 illustrates responses to the question about why a police officer makes the decision to stop an individual. Many of the participants reported that they may stop individuals hanging out on a corner—behavior choices—where violent crimes have been committed in the past. They may also stop an individual because they display indications-behaviors-that they may be armed, officers are concerned for the safety of the neighborhood. In addition, some of the participants reported that they would stop people based on community policing complaints-generalized suspicion-from beat meetings or other types of citizen complaints where citizens express fear and concern about particular individuals.

> **The police stop people based upon descriptions of suspects as provided by callers and/or witnesses. They do not do so randomly or arbitrarily.**

Table 10.13—Reasons for Stopping Individuals

REASONS FOR STOPPING INDIVIDUALS DURING TOUR OF DUTY

Reason	Count
Description (Service Call)	16
Information Gathering/Warrant Service	16
Concerned for Safety/Community Information or Complaint	6

One of the interviewees stated the following:

Interviewee: "the decision to stop somebody was usually based on a description. An offender description. So like in 11 you'd have a shots fired call with the description of a male black running westbound on Polk from St. Louis, and you are coming east bound on Polk a couple blocks away, and you actually heard the shots being fired, so you stop the man running that matches the description. Simple as that."

Interviewer: "have you ever stopped anyone that wasn't matching the description and an in progress call? If so can you explain what determined that stop?"

Interviewee: "yeah, of course I have. Usually based on prior complaints or knowledge of the area. Like if you knew that a bunch of disciples were hanging out on a certain corner all the time, you might come up and stop them and tell them to get off the corner so they don't get shot tonight because there's a rash of shootings in that area and rival gangs have been shooting up the place."

Interviewer: "did any of those field interview stops turn into arrests? If so explain, please."

Interviewee: "yes a lot of the time they would. A lot of these people you are stopping and talking to are gang members. They are on the street or corner either looking out for a dope spot and call you out when you drive down the street so the drug dealer can run off before detected, or they are holding a gun to do a shooting

These aren't upstanding citizens just drinking lemonade on a hot summer day."

According to the information obtained in this interview, the decision to stop a black male subject, for example, is based upon the description provided of the offender by a victim or witness of the individual who committed the crime. Also, the decision to stop and speak with gang members was based on their observed behaviors. The example given was a rash of shootings in the area where rival gangs have been loitering and engaging in suspicions and criminal activity.

In another interview a veteran Chicago police officer stated the following:

Interviewee: "often times the stops are investigatory based on offender descriptions from calls or when I worked in the specialized unit a lot of times we had people identified or wanted for crimes and we would stop people who matched the description of that individual who the warrant was for."

Interviewer: "have you ever stopped anyone that wasn't matching the description and an in progress call? If so can you explain what determined that stop?"

Interviewee: "oh yes. A lot of times you would stop associates of someone wanted or you'd stop a large group of people because in that area there were a rash of violent crimes and you don't want them becoming victims of that."

Interviewer: "did any of those stops turn into arrests? If so explain, please."

Interviewee: "yes and no. Sometimes you get lucky and catch the offender from an in-progress crime as you're driving to the call. Other times you stop a group of people while looking for a particular suspect and someone ends up having a warrant when you run their name or they have some contraband during your protective pat down search."

According to this officer's interview, another reason that individuals are detained or arrested is because of information obtained by officers during their investigative stops.

An additional interviewee gave this response as to why he/she may stop an individual during their tour of duty:

Interviewee: ". . . you would always stop people during your tour of duty. It's what you're there for. You're there to prevent crime from happening. In a place like 11 or 15, even 7 or 8 there are gang bangers on the street messing around. People in those neighborhoods can't come out of their house and kids can't play because the gang-bangers have their block locked down as a dope spot.

Bullets don't have any eyes. These thugs start shooting it out and the poor girl skipping rope or the grandma sitting on the front porch gets hit . . ."

Interviewer: "What would you base those stops on?"

Interviewee: "probable cause. Either they are described in an in-progress call or you know that there's complaints about gangs loitering on a corner. Or to make sure that they're just not the victim of the next shooting. A lot of these gang bangers hang out on the corner and the rival gangs just drive by and start shooting up the place, they don't care who they hit, so you stop these dudes to make sure that innocent victims aren't a part of their nonsense.

Also you may have a citizen wave you down and say 'hey there's a dude with a gun over there,' so you're going stop that dude. Also me and my partner used to get the warrant list in the district and see who was wanted, and if we knew a dude on our beat was wanted we would look for him and maybe stop some of his associates to see where dude was at."

In the absence of a description of a suspect as provided by a caller or witness, police attention is drawn to particular individuals because of their behavior.

The responses during this interview pointed to another important conclusion, other than probable cause, police stop individuals based on the individual's behavior and not due to race or other factors.

According to Skolnick 2015:

". . . police officers, because their work requires them to be occupied continually with potential violence, develop a perceptual shorthand to identify certain kinds of people

as symbolic assailants, that is, as persons who use gesture, language, and attire that the police have come to recognize as a prelude to violence. This does not mean that violence by a symbolic assailant is necessarily predictable. On the contrary, the police officer responds to the vague indication of danger suggested by appearance . . ." (Skolnick, 2015, 1438–1457).

Given the information provided in the interviews, officers identify behavior of the individuals as reason for the initial stop, thereafter it is the general interaction of the potential offender with the police officer that drives the officer's decision to conduct a pat-down or to investigate further.

Skolnick 2015 stated that *". . . a young man may suggest the threat of violence to the police by his manner of walking or 'strutting,' the insolence in the demeanor being registered by the police as a possible preamble to attack . . ."* (Skolnick, 2015, 1510–1512).

The participant responses to question 6 were quite interesting, "Can you explain to me what factors go into your decision to stop an individual while on your tour of duty?" This particular interview participant gave this response:

Interviewee: "Well . . . when working in patrol and responding to an emergency call or even a specialized team like a district tactical team or an area team you rely on offender descriptions. Sometimes in these districts like 11 and 15 there's no descriptions of the offender because, as I stated earlier, someone is calling the police to report a man with a gun or shots fired just to get the police on their block.

In a place like 18 where a robbery just occurred or is in progress, you may have an offender description so based on that I would decide who to stop because of a matching description.

In the specialized unit I work in we have a lot of players identified who have committed crimes or are currently dirty. So we will go on that information to stop associates of that person or people where they may hang out to get information.

Another big reason to stop somebody is because of gang shootings. For example, if I'm working district 11 and there has been a rash of gang shootings in an area or a city block, and I see a bunch of players out there, I may stop them just to get them off the corner so they're not the next victim of a shooting. It's that simple."

The responses in this interview also indicated that behaviors and descriptions drive the decision to stop individuals. According to Alpert 2006:

Despite ethnicity, if someone is wearing all black clothing, this is an indication that they are up to no good. If an officer is well acquainted with people and places in his beat, he can tell based on appearance who "doesn't belong." Persons who look "different" raise suspicion (e.g., white person in black neighborhood). In contrast, officers who rated appearance to be of low priority typically provided one of two explanations: (1) that most people encountered looked similar enough to render appearance meaningless as a factor that might arouse suspicion, or, (2) that they did their best not to judge people based on their appearance (Alpert, 2006, p. 5).

In addition, Alpert in a 2006 study commented on "behavior" as significant, with nearly half of the officers reporting that it was a high priority in forming suspicion to make a stop. The following comments about behavior offered by Alpert, were significant because they mirrored comments made by participants in this study:

A Police officer stated that he watches out for the "felony stare" (i.e., getting nervous when they see a police car, making every effort to avoid the police).

A Police officer said that behavior is very important to him because he can tell when a person is lying to him. He can tell this by the way they act.

A Police officer said he can tell if someone has done something just by how they respond to him. "It is very important to tell if they are fidgeting" (Alpert, 2006, p. 6).

Another interviewee made a profound statement at the end of the interview when asked if there was anything else to add. The interviewee stated this:

". . . I never stopped anybody because they were black. I only stop people because of the information about the area that I was assigned to, and what I mean by that is if there were an abundance of gang complaints on my beat and a geographical area, I would stop the players in that area based on that information or they matched the description of an offender of a robbery that just occurred or some sort of in-progress call, not for any other reason.

Watching and listening to people who are uninformed about this absolutely turns my stomach. I love this job and love the city, and I cannot believe some of the things I hear and see . . ."

Individuals are not stopped by the police due to race. They are stopped because they match a suspect description as provided by a caller, or they are behaving in a manner that draws police attention, or when confronted by an officer they behave in a manner that necessitates a tactical police response such as a frisk for weapons, or a combination of factors that rarely includes their appearance, i.e., race.

Alpert stated that:

". . . once an officer became suspicious of an individual they were equally likely to stop the person whether or not the person was male or female, African American or

white, young or old or perceived to be of low or high economic status . . ." (Alpert, 2006, p. 7).

Officers are more likely to stop individuals based on suspicion and the suspect's behavior. Characteristics such as gender, socioeconomic status, ethnicity, and age did not influence the likelihood of stop after suspicion is formed (Alpert, 2006).

In conclusion, the police officers perspective on responses to calls varies from areas of assignment as it relates to call volume, call types, caller information and general activity in a given area. The police response may also vary based on caller information that may point to callers in certain areas fearing retaliation or just wanting the police to respond faster to a lower priority call.

The one constant in all the data was the decision to stop individuals from a police perspective. As it is reported by the interview participants, all seasoned veteran Chicago police officers who have responded to different calls for service in different areas of the city, justify their stop decisions on descriptions provided by callers, information given from crime statistics, community complaints, or investigation/warrant service. This means that the police, from the perspective of our interview participants, are stopping the individuals that meet the description of individuals who are reported to have committed crimes or who are behaving in a manner that draws police attention and suspicion.

Information that police dispatchers take during a call for service is dispatched to police officers working the street, the information that the officers use in determining who to stop is initially based on what the caller is reporting. If caller reports that an offender is committing a violent crime, yet the situation is truly some sort of lower priority disturbance, it does not make a difference to the responding police officer or the dispatcher who was taking the call. They are taking the information from the citizen who is making the complaint or requesting service.

Whether a caller is using anonymity or requesting to talk to the police, the responding units must proceed with the best information available. That means if a call is of "a person with a gun/shots fired" the officers must proceed with the description of the offender and under the assumption that the person described by the caller has a gun and constitutes a serious threat to the police. Responding officers will be on high alert and are likely to display a demeanor appropriate to the reported situation, to expect officers to behave differently is unrealistic.

Chapter Summary

This chapter established that police respond differently to different types of crime and that there is a large difference between violent and nonviolent crimes. Calls for service, from the perspective of a veteran police dispatcher for the Chicago Police Department, shows that there is a priority system for call response by the police and this also may contribute to people calling in and making false reports for priority of calls such as calling in "shots fired/man with a gun" when the call is really for a noise disturbance.

Deployment strategies for the Chicago Police Department, which in 2016 led the nation in homicides and shootings, are based on citizen calls for service and reported crime. A personal interview with a veteran Chicago police officer with a great amount of experience deploying officers in the Chicago Police Department, shows that officers are routinely deployed to areas on the basis of calls for service, crime reports, and information gathered in CompStat meetings.

There are several different types of policing strategies used by the Chicago police department and other agencies to control crime, with varying levels of success. These strategies include Broken Windows, Community Policing, Hot Spot policing, Problem Oriented policing, COMPSTAT and Intelligence-Led policing. Even with all these options, in the end crime control requires motivated police officers on the street to combat the crime and disorder.

The perspective of the law enforcement professional, or police officer, is often overlooked. From an academic standpoint, collecting data from current and former police officers of varying ages, varying years of service, different kinds of assignments, and wide ranging experiences, garnered interesting responses and data points. They tell a story of policing from the perspective of those who are "doing the job every day."

From this information the interviews were able to establish that police response may be different as a result of the kinds of call information provided by the citizens who are reporting crimes. The reasons for police to stop individuals during their tour of duty is largely based on offender descriptions provided by callers and by the observed behavior of potential suspects and offenders.

According to the information in this chapter and interviews with police officers who serve, individuals are not stopped by the police merely because of their appearance, i.e., race. Individuals are stopped because they match descriptions of offenders that have been provided by victims and witness of crime or because of the behavior choices that these individuals make, behaviors that attract the attention of the police and form the bases of the lawful justification for a stop under the constitution.

Bibliography

Alpert, G.D. (2006). *Police Officers' Decision Making and Discretion: Forming Suspicion and Making a Stop*. Washington: NCJRS.

Barkan, S.E. (2014). *Social Problems: Continuity and Change* (Vol. 1). Boston, MA: Flat World Knowledge.

Boundaries—Police Districts (current) City of Chicago Data Portal. (2017). Retrieved December 11, 2017, from https://data.cityofchicago.org/Public-Safety/Boundaries-Police-Districts-current-/fthy-xz3r/data.

Braga, A.A., Weisburd, D. (2010). *Policing Problem Places: Crime Hot Spots and Effective Prevention*. New York: Oxford University Press.

Center for Problem-Oriented Policing. (n.d.). Retrieved December 20, 2017, from http://www.popcenter.org/about/?p=whatiscpop.

Chicago Police Department—Home Page. (2017). Retrieved December 18, 2017, from https://home.chicagopolice.org/online-services/crime-statistics/.

Childress, S. (2016, June 28). The Problem with 'Broken Windows' Policing. Retrieved December 15, 2017, from https://www.pbs.org/wgbh/frontline/article/the-problem-with-broken-windows-policing/.

Crimes—2001 to present City of Chicago Data Portal. (2017). Retrieved December 13, 2017, from https://data.cityofchicago.org/Public-Safety/Crimes-2001-to-present/ijzp-q8t2/data.

Crime Statistics—Chicago Police Department. (2017). Retrieved December 17, 2017, from https://home.chicagopolice.org/online-services/crime-statistics/.

Cherone, H. (2017, May 02). Here's How Many Officers Are Patrolling Your Neighborhood. Retrieved December 12, 2017, from https://www.dnainfo.com/chicago/20170417/logan-square/heres-how-many-officers-are-patrolling-your-neighborhood-watchdog.

Department of Justice: Community Oriented Policing Services. (n.d.). Retrieved December 18, 2017, from https://cops.usdoj.gov/Default.asp?Item=2558.

Federal Bureau of Investigation, Property Crime. (2011, July 26). Retrieved December 13, 2017, from https://ucr.fbi.gov/crime-in-the-u.s/2010/crime-in-the-u.s.-2010/property crime.

Federal Bureau of Investigation, Criminal Justice Information Services Division, Uniform Crime Reporting Program. (2013). Summary Reporting System (SRS) User Manual. Washington, DC: U.S. Department of Justice, pp. 20–22.

Federal Bureau of Investigation, Violent Crime. (2011, July 25). Retrieved December 14, 2017, from https://ucr.fbi.gov/crime-in-the-u.s/2010/crime-in-the-u.s.-2010/violent-crime.

Francis, D.R. (2003, January). What Reduced Crime in New York City. Retrieved December 19, 2017, from http://www.nber.org/digest/jan03/w9061.html.

Koper, C.S. (2014). Assessing the Practice of Hot Spots Policing: Survey Results from a National Convenience Sample of Local Police Agencies. *Journal of Contemporary Criminal Justice, 30(2),* 123–146. doi:10.1177/1043986214525079.

Maguire, M., John, T. (2006). Intelligence Led Policing, Managerialism and Community Engagement: Competing Priorities and the Role of the National Intelligence Model in the UK. *Policing & Society, 16(1),* 67–85. doi:10.1080/10439460500399791.

National Institute of Justice, CrimeSolutions.gov. (n.d.). Retrieved December 16, 2017, from https://www.crimesolutions.gov/TopicDetails.aspx?ID=84.

Ratcliffe, J.H. (2016). *Intelligence-Led Policing, 2nd ed.* Abingdon, UK: Routledge.

Ravitch, S. M., Carl, N.M. (2016). *Qualitative Research: Bridging the Conceptual, Theoretical, and Methodological.* Los Angeles: SAGE.

Roth, W. (2012). First-Person Methods—Toward an Empirical Phenomenology. Wolff-Michael Roth Springer. Retrieved November 29, 2016, from http://www.springer.com/us/book/9789460918315.

Ruthhart, B., Gorner, J., Dardick, H. (2017, January 30). Chicago Police Expand Tech to Curb Shootings. Retrieved December 18, 2017, from https://www.policeone.com/police-products/Intelligence-Led-Policing/articles/284645006-Chicago-police-expand-tech-to-curb-shootings/.

Schram, Pamela J. *Introduction to Criminology: Why Do They Do It?* Interactive eBook, *2nd ed.* SAGE Publications, Inc, 02/2017. VitalBook file.

Seidel, J.V. (1998). Appendix E: Qualitative Data Analysis. Retrieved December 27, 2017, from ftp://ftp.qualisresearch.com/pub/qda.pdf.

Skolnick, J.H. (2015). *Justice Without Trial: Law Enforcement in Democratic Society, 4th ed.* [Kindle].

United States, Department of Justice, Bureau of Justice Assistance. (2013). COMPSTAT: Its Origins, Evolution, and Future in Law Enforcement Agencies. Washington, DC: Police Executive Research Forum.

Wagner, M. (2016, October 04). SEE IT: S.C. Cops Wear Superhero Shirts for Shooting Victim. Retrieved November 09, 2017, from http://www.nydailynews.com/news/national/s-cops-wear-superhero-shirts-shooting-victim-article-1.2817177.

Waters, J. (2016). Phenomenological Research Guidelines. Retrieved November 22, 2016, from https://www.capilanou.ca/psychology/student-resources/research-guidelines/Phenomenological-Research-Guidelines.

White, J.R. (2012). *Terrorism and Homeland Security*. Australia: Wadsworth Cengage Learning.

Wilson, J.Q., Kelling, G.L. (2014, February 19). Broken Windows. Retrieved December 19, 2017, from https://www.theatlantic.com/magazine/archive/1982/03/broken-windows/304465/.

PART 3

Managing Conflict by Building Better Relationships

■ ■ ■

Chapter 11: Building Better Relationships Through Restorative Justice (by Amy Nemmetz, Ph.D.)

This chapter introduces the concept of restorative justice as a way to seek better outcomes for victims of crime. As a way to manage conflict, Restorative Justice offers an opportunity for crime victims to have their voices heard. Crime perpetrators have the opportunity to learn, first hand, about the harm that they have caused. Rather than merely punishing criminals, restorative justice offers the opportunity for rehabilitation by helping perpetrators to understand the harm that they have caused.

Chapter 12: Building Better Relationships Through Youth Mentoring & Engagement

This chapter presents youth mentoring as a way that the police can actively engage with their communities. Mentoring offers the opportunity for police officers to serve as role models for young people, a way that the police can help build resilience and self-esteem that will help young people resist the corrupting influences that they are likely to face as they grow into adolescence and adulthood.

CHAPTER 11

Building Better Relationships Through Restorative Justice

by Amy Nemmetz, Ph.D.

■ ■ ■

We cannot do anything about the past, but can take steps to shape our future. Change happens at the level of the individual. —Scilla Elworthy

Learning Outcomes

Upon successful completion of this chapter the student will be able to:

- Define restorative justice.
- Identify and apply the three principles of restorative justice.
- Differentiate among restorative justice initiatives.
- Explain who can potentially benefit from restorative justice initiatives.
- Explain how restorative justice initiatives can mitigate conflict.
- Explain how theoretical perspectives have been linked to restorative justice.

Important Concepts

- Accountability
- Engagement
- Restoration
- Primary Victim

- Secondary Victim
- Zero Tolerance Policy

Questions for Discussion

- What are five objectives of punishment and how can each objective be defined?
- What is the significance of the Crime Victims' Rights Act of 2004?
- What are the three principles of restorative justice?
- What is the difference between primary and secondary victims?
- What is one theory that parallels well with restorative justice principles?
- What is one example of a restorative justice program and what does the program entail?
- Why are some people skeptical about restorative justice initiatives?
- Why may restorative justice initiatives not be appropriate in some circumstances?

INTRODUCTION

In this chapter the topic of restorative justice is explored as a strategy for reducing and managing conflict. Restorative justice is a new perspective when compared with the traditional concepts of retribution, incapacitation, restitution, and deterrence in dealing with criminal wrongdoing; the overall goal is to try to repair the harm to victims following a crime versus focusing primarily on punishing the offender. Restorative justice initiatives allow victims to have their voices heard. Although restorative justice initiatives vary in style and format, the majority of victims and offenders who participate share positive thoughts about the process and experience.

THE HISTORY OF EFFORTS TO CORRECT BEHAVIOR

Restorative justice is often misunderstood; several assumptions are incorrectly harbored by people in the community and professionals in the criminal justice system:

- Restorative justice programs and initiatives do not always replace punishment.

- Restorative justice initiatives may accompany a formal punishment or be offered in lieu of punishment.
- Participation in restorative justice initiatives does not equate to forgiveness and healing for the victim of a crime.
- Healing is a process; some victims may never feel fully recovered.

Forgiveness is unique to each crime victim; each victim gets to decide if or when forgiveness seems to make sense. Regardless of the restorative justice initiative, *restorative justice programming centers around the concept of restoring or repairing harm caused to victims following a crime.* Offenders are provided opportunities to acknowledge harm they have caused and explore ways to try to repair the harm with the assistance of those negatively affected by the crime.

Spot Check

Myth: Restorative justice initiatives result in healing for the victim.

Fact: Healing is a process; although some victims and survivors may disclose that they healed fairly quickly, others may experience the effects of the crime for years.

Spot Check

Myth: Restorative justice initiatives result in healing for the victim.

Fact: Healing is a process; although some victims and survivors may disclose that they healed fairly quickly, others may experience the effects of the crime for years.

Spot Check

Myth: When a victim of a crime agrees to engage in restorative justice it means the victim has forgiven the offender.

Fact: Forgiveness is a personal component for victims and survivors. A victim of a crime may choose to have a conversation with the offender to seek answers to questions. Although a victim of a crime may ultimately choose to forgive an offender, the goals of restorative justice are not centered around forgiveness.

Spot Check

Myth: Juveniles are not intellectually mature enough to really benefit from restorative justice initiatives.

Fact: Juveniles may act before considering the consequences of their actions. Additionally, juveniles may minimize the effects of their actions. Hearing and seeing a survivor tell their story can be very effective for the juvenile who failed to consider the ramifications of his/her actions.

Although, there has been a heavy focus on providing restorative justice initiatives for juvenile offenders and these efforts have been very successful, restorative justice programs and initiatives are not just reserved for juveniles in the system. Adults and juveniles around the globe are exploring restorative based opportunities to hold offenders accountable while also giving victims more power and a voice in the criminal justice system. According to Braithwaite (2007) "at the 2000 United Nations Congress on the Prevention of Crime and Treatment of Offenders, a resolution that encouraged all nations to promote restorative justice passed unanimously" (p. 289). With national leaders providing support for restorative justice nearly 20 years, it make sense for those working directly in the criminal justice system to explore restorative initiatives in more detail?

WHERE DOES RESTORATIVE JUSTICE FIT IN THE SCHEME OF CRIMINAL JUSTICE?

The concept of restorative justice is often associated with the corrections field. More specifically, restorative justice based initiatives can be something:

- A judge discusses when sentencing an offender;
- An initiative that is introduced by a community corrections agent;
- A program an inmate completes in a correctional institution following sentencing; or
- Even an alternative to formal court involvement in the juvenile justice system.

Properly used, a restorative justice program is not itself intended to be a punishment. Rather it should be considered one of the *objectives* of a program of punishment. A well designed punishment may include some of all of the following objectives:

Retribution

When someone falls victim to a crime, initial thoughts might include, "the offender will pay for this," "I demand justice," or, "I will get even!" The traditional saying, "an eye for an eye" sums up a traditional concept of retribution.

Real retribution is not always achieved by what is imposed on the offender. For instance, some states utilize the death penalty for offenders found guilty of first degree murder, but while "an eye for an eye" takes the life of the murderer, it does nothing to repair the emotional damage to those whose loved one was murdered. The purpose of retribution is to have the offender make some kind of effort to ease the consequences of his/her crime upon those who have been victimized.

Incapacitation

To incapacitate is literally to restrict or keep an offender from harming society. In the traditional "crime control model," jailing or imprisoning the guilty person may satisfy the "lock them up and throw away the key" mentality and serve the societal goal of keeping the offender off the streets and out of trouble, but that, by itself, does not prepare the jailed felon for a return to society when incarceration ends. Constructive use should be made of incarceration to prepare the jailed person for a better life after release. Job training and education while "doing time" can help improve the convicted felon's chances of leading a law abiding life when the felon returns to society.

Restitution

Restitution has been used interchangeably with the phrase "making amends" or the notion of paying a victim back after a crime has been committed. From a purely financial sense, restitution may include paying the victim back for property altered or taken, paying for medical bills directly related to the victimization, or paying for wages lost due to time the victim missed from work because of the criminal act.

Although, historically, offenders may have arranged for restitution on an informal basis with a victim, restitution is now commonly ordered by a judge at a sentencing hearing. Some correction departments assist the offenders with the restitution logistics if the offenders are ordered to community supervision or sentenced to serve time in a correctional institution. With the assistance of the corrections officers, restitution payments can be sent to the victim. Such payments are typically made over an extended period of time, either because the restitution payments are not ordered until the end of the judicial process, which can take months, or because it will take the offender a long period of time to acquire the funds needed to make restitution payments.

Deterrence

To 'deter' (prevent a crime) is an ongoing goal when working with adult and juvenile offenders. The magic question seems to be, how to deter effectively. Judges may take a variety of stances when considering deterrence at a juvenile adjudication hearing or an adult sentencing hearing. Judges who aim to send a message to the community about what may happen if one commits the offense, may strive for a **general deterrence** sentence. On the other hand, a sentencing judge may impose a sentence directed to specifically deter the specific offender from engaging in crime in the future. Thus, the goal is **specific deterrence**.

The goal of deterrence coincides with the objective of letting others know what may happen if they opt to commit a criminal act.

Restorative Justice

The United States criminal justice system focuses heavily on offenders. This makes sense as offenders commit crimes. However, harm accompanies crime. A crime against a person damages that person—the victim—emotionally and perhaps physically and financially as well.

Although victims receive less attention than offenders in the criminal justice system, there have been several legislative advances to recognize that crimes often result in harm. The federal Crime Victims' Rights Act (2004) is an excellent example of how concern for victims should be built into the criminal justice system.

The Crime Victims' Rights Act provides a framework of actions the criminal justice system should take on behalf of victims. These include:

- Informing victims of plea agreements,
- Providing court appearance notification to victims,
- Giving the victim an opportunity to talk to the prosecutor's office,
- Restitution, and
- The opportunity to be heard at the sentencing.

Restorative justice initiatives should direct attention both to the harm done to victims and to the offender taking accountability and attempting to repair the harm that they have caused. Victims of a crime should be given an opportunity to describe the harm they have experienced as a result of the crime and to suggest what actions the offender might or should take to try to repair some of the harm caused.

Crime Victims' Rights Act[1]

18 U.S.C. § 3771. Crime victims' rights

(a) RIGHTS OF CRIME VICTIMS.—A crime victim has the following rights:

(1) The right to be reasonably protected from the accused.

(2) The right to reasonable, accurate, and timely notice of any public court proceeding, or any parole proceeding, involving the crime or of any release or escape of the accused.

(3) The right not to be excluded from any such public court proceeding, unless the court, after receiving clear and convincing evidence, determines that testimony by the victim would be materially altered if the victim heard other testimony at that proceeding.

(4) The right to be reasonably heard at any public proceeding in the district court involving release, plea, sentencing, or any parole proceeding.

(5) The reasonable right to confer with the attorney for the Government in the case.

(6) The right to full and timely restitution as provided in law.

(7) The right to proceedings free from unreasonable delay.

(8) The right to be treated with fairness and with respect for the victim's dignity and privacy.

(9) The right to be informed in a timely manner of any plea bargain or deferred prosecution agreement.

(10) The right to be informed of the rights under this section and the services described in section 503(c) of the Victims' Rights and Restitution Act of 1990 (42 U.S.C. 10607(c)) and provided contact information for the Office of the Victims' Rights Ombudsman of the Department of Justice.

LIMITATIONS ON THE USE/EFFECTIVENESS OF RESTORATIVE JUSTICE

Restorative justice initiatives may not be the magic answer for all offenders:

Retribution may accomplish a desire to make an offender suffer for harm caused, but there is no way to ascertain if the offender truly understands the harm

1 https://www.justice.gov/usao/resources/crime-victims-rights-ombudsman/victims-rights-act.

caused and there is no certainly that the offender will consider repairing any harm to his or her victims.

While incarcerated the offender may or may not be offered opportunities to participate in retribution and restoration efforts.

When amends and restitution is made by someone else—the offender's family, for example—it may substantially help the victim of the crime, but is likely to have little or no effect on the offender.

When the offender is incarcerated, and thus removed from the community for an extensive period of time, he or she may have no opportunity to make restitution and, in any event, the offender is more likely to be focused solely on their own predicament and changed circumstances. Unless given counseling, retribution and restitution are likely to be the farthest thing from their mind.

Upon release from an institution, there is no guarantee that the offender has spent much time thinking about accountability and repairing harm caused by the crime.

It would be fabulous if Magic 8 balls could predict who will be deterred from future criminal behavior, but sentences that are intended to deter do not necessarily parallel restorative practices. *However, when an offender participates in a restorative justice initiative as part of a sentence or in lieu of a formal sentence, the offender is expected to think critically about harm caused, who has been impacted by the crime, and what can possibly be done to try to repair the corresponding harm caused by the crime.*

TRADITIONAL REHABILITATION IN COMPARISON TO RESTORATIVE JUSTICE

Rehabilitation continues to be a goal when working with offenders. More specifically, helping offenders address harmful past and current choices in order to prevent future criminal acts is essential.

But restorative justice initiatives differ slightly from traditional rehabilitative treatment approaches. Traditional offender treatment programs focus heavily on one on one talk therapy sessions. When providers opt to involve others in the treatment session, those in the room may have included offenders with similar treatment needs (group therapy) or family members who could provide additional insights about the offender's past behaviors and future needs. Traditional multi-systemic treatment approaches bring several people involved with the offender together for meetings or treatment sessions

Although restorative justice initiatives vary, in many instances the offender has the opportunity to hear from their victim(s) or a panel of victims. The offender is also invited to talk about the victimization and recognize the harm caused; victims and survivors assist the offender with this process by sharing the true extent of the harm they have endured. Together, victims and offenders can discuss ways to try to repair the harm.

Unlike traditional treatment providers, the restorative justice facilitator plays a much smaller role in the dialogs and conversations. The real work and conversation during a victim offender dialog or discussion circle stems from the offender and victims. The facilitator truly may resemble a passive guide at times.

Spot Check

Myth: Restorative justice initiatives cannot be facilitated unless the offender of the crime is able to meet with the primary victims of the corresponding crime.

Fact: Restorative justice is not a hard science. There are several ways and opportunities to be a part of restorative justice. For example, offenders can take accountability, try to repair harm caused to victims, and engage with those who have been affected by their crimes by working with secondary victims to include the offender's family members who have been negatively impacted by the offender's crime.

ORIGINS AND PRINCIPLES OF RESTORATIVE JUSTICE

Although it is unclear who is specifically responsible for restorative justice initiatives, Howard Zehr (2002) often points to indigenous people who resided in Canada and Mennonites in North America. People from these groups were practicing a healing approach following a wrongdoing; those negatively affected had the opportunity to engage in conversations with the person responsible for the harm. Solutions and opportunities to repair the harm were discussed via a team approach through conversations. Those responsible for the harm had to take accountability, apologize, and make amends.

Restorative justice initiatives come in many formats. Regardless of 'how' restorative justice programs or initiatives are delivered, the three principles of restorative justice remain the same. More specifically, the first principle, accountability, seems to be consistent with the criminal justice system, parenting practices, and school initiatives. Simply stated, someone acknowledges that they have caused harm and subsequently takes responsibility for his or her actions. The second principle is restoration; how may the person attempt to repair the harm that has been caused? The third restorative justice principle is engagement. When considering engagement, it is ideal to identify who has been harmed and invite those affected to come together to talk about how they have been harmed and what they may need to help repair the harm (Zehr, 2002).

Although, the criminal justice system may be considered a punitive, retribution based system by many, restorative justice initiatives focus on questions such as who has been hurt, what needs do they have, and whose obligation is it to address the corresponding needs (Zehr, 2002). As a result, the focus is on both the offender and the victim. Although restorative justice practices have been previously thought to be more appropriate for juveniles (Miller and Heffner, 2015), programming initiatives have been utilized nationwide with adult offenders, too.

TYPES OF RESTORATIVE JUSTICE INITIATIVES & PARTICIPATION

Restorative justice initiatives can positively impact offenders, primary and secondary victims, family and friends of victims, and family and friends of the offender. Primary offenders are those directly impacted by a crime (Karmen, 2013). Secondary victims are all the others who are harmed by a crime. They include, but are not necessarily limited to family members of the victim and offender, police officers, neighbors, and others in the community.

Although judges may encourage an offender to participate in restorative justice programming, participation should not be forced upon offenders, primary victims, and secondary victims. In some cases, an offender does not want to participate in a restorative justice program either because, for example, an offender is not willing to take responsibility for causing harm to a victim. In other instances, an offender's attorney may be opposed to the offender participating in the programming; this may stem from the reservations the attorney has about the offender publicly admitting guilt/taking accountability for harming others.

Victims of crimes may also have reservations about restorative justice initiatives. Umbriet and his colleagues (2002) discovered that approximately 50% of victims decline the option to participate in restorative justice programs or dialogs (Umbriet, Coates, & Vas, 2002). A victim may decline the offer to participate in restorative justice programming due to not wanting to meet with the offender, concerns that the crime is too petty to discuss, or feeling frustrated by the minimal/light case outcomes (light sentence the offender received).

However, victims and offenders who opt to participate in a restorative justice initiative, overwhelmingly report positive feelings about the restorative justice program or initiative following participation. Some studies even show that more than 80% of victims who participated in restorative justice based conversations with a facilitator and offender felt satisfied with the process and conversation (Umbriet, Coates, & Vas, 2002). Even though victim satisfaction rates seem to be slighter higher than offender satisfaction rates in most studies, more than 50% of offenders report positive feelings about speaking with the victim of their crime via a restorative justice initiative (Umbriet, Coates, & Vas, 2002).

Spot Check

Myth: Secondary victims of crime cannot send the same powerful message in a restorative justice initiative when compared to the primary victim.

Fact: Secondary victims are harmed by crime too. Offenders may not understand the ripple effect of their crimes. Subsequently hearing from others who have been negatively affected by a crime (secondary victim) is a powerful experience for offenders. For example, hearing from the primary victim's neighbor that her children have nightmares every night because they are afraid someone will break into their residence is likely something the offender had not considered.

Spot Check

Myth: Victims of crimes often disclosed that meeting with their offender via a victim-offender facilitator led dialog is an extremely painful and negative experience.

Fact: The majority of victims express satisfaction about the restorative justice program as they get to voice their thoughts. More specifically, victims get answers to their questions, get to talk candidly with the offender about how they have been impacted by the crime, and get an opportunity to express thoughts about how the offender can rectify the harm caused by the crime.

IMPACTS OF RESTORATIVE JUSTICE FROM A THEORETICAL PERSPECTIVE

Black and white television days may seem like an 'olden day' phenomenon, but the general concepts about crime have not changed. In the simplest sense, offenders commit crimes, police make arrests, prosecutors charge cases, judges sentence offenders, and offenders serve their sentence. Just like Sheriff Andy wanted to ascertain 'who' was responsible for crime in Mayberry and, subsequently, bring that person in to discuss the crime an its impact on others, the courts see criminal acts as a "crime against the state" and thus strive to hold offenders accountable. Every crime inflicts damages on others—its victims. Yet, victims may have very little input when it comes to the court proceedings (assuming an offender is arrested and charged) and the subsequent sentence. Restorative justice initiatives focus on a crime's victims, including all who have been adversely affected, and how the damage done to them can best be ameliorated.

RATIONAL CHOICE THEORY

Rational choice theorists posit that people make decisions about committing a crime after weighing risks and rewards or corresponding actions. For example, if a person walks past a residence late at night and discovers an open garage door with several pieces of equipment and motor vehicles in the garage, the person will make a decision regarding how to respond to the sighting. The person has several choices such as: walking by without disturbing anyone or anything on the property, unlawfully entering the garage to take a closer look at the property, or stealing items from the garage. Rational choice theorists would argue that the person would compare the rewards and benefits associated the risk walking away without taking anything of entering the garage and taking some items. If the person decides that the risks of taking the items and benefiting from having them outweigh the risks of possibly getting caught, arrested, charged, and sentenced, the person is more likely to choose a criminal path.

Understanding the extent of the harm caused by crime is a key component of restorative justice initiatives. In the example provided, taking items out of a garage probably resulted in more than simply a financial loss to the property owner. The harm may also have included children in the home having difficulty sleeping in the future; loss of items with deep sentimental value; financial losses stemming from the need to purchase another car, missed time away from work because their car was stolen, lost wages, and eventual job loss due to working with the police and court officials in lieu of being at work; and the constant feeling of uneasiness about someone accessing their personal property. By emphasizing such losses for the offender, restorative justice initiatives can serve as a future deterrent by making the offender more aware of the total costs of crime if criminal opportunities arise again.

Reintegrative Shaming

John Braithwaite's reintegrative shaming theory focuses on the need to address shame associated with crime in a positive way (Schmalleger, 2014). Unlike disintegrative shaming practices in which the focus is to shame an offender in front of others in the hopes of deterring future criminal acts, reintegrative shaming practices add a positive twist to shaming. More specifically, Braithwaite stresses the need for the criminal justice system to address formally the harm caused by a crime (shame the offender) and then follow-up with acceptance of an offender back into society or the community (restoration focus).

These notions parallel with restorative justice principles. An offender taking accountability is the first principle of restorative justice (Zehr, 2002). Taking accountability may include discussing factors that led up to a victimization, revealing decisions that were made at the time of the victimization, and sharing actions following the victimization. The restoration principle of restorative justice, delves into the offender trying to take steps to repair some of the harm. Attempts to repair the harm caused may include paying the victim for their physical losses (restitution), completing community service (repaying/restoring the community), and addressing unanswered questions the victim may have.

Social Control Theory

We often ask why people they choose a crime free lifestyle. Social control theorists posit that morals, ethics, and values may be effective factors in keeping people from choosing to engage in crime. Understanding the extent of crime and the ripple effect of criminal acts goes hand in hand with the social control theory notions. Victims of crime have been essential in outlining how deeply a crime victimization can impact their lives and the wellbeing of their friends and loved ones. More specifically, facilitators leading restorative justice programs may bring in several people who are affected by crime to address the harm they have experienced. Voicing these harms is essential to build upon 'why' people should not engage in criminal acts.

RESTORATIVE JUSTICE INITIATIVE EXAMPLES

Most criminal justice professionals and offenders who have heard something about restorative justice, think that restorative justice initiatives consist of a dialogue at some point between the offender and the corresponding victim. This is the goal for many restorative justice program facilitators. However, there are opportunities to engage in restorative justice initiatives without the offender having direct contact with a primary victim.

Restorative justice initiatives seem to fall along a spectrum depending on the circumstances and those involved (Zehr, 2002). For example, a victim of a crime may choose to talk to a group of offenders about the harm he endured and corresponding repercussions without talking directly to his offender. Additionally, an adult offender may choose to talk to a group of juvenile offenders about past crimes, take accountability for the crimes, identify and discuss corresponding victims of the crime, and share how the harm can possibly be repaired for victims.

One to One Victim Offender Conferencing

One to one victim offender conferencing usually involves a facilitator bringing together the offender and a primary victim. The facilitator meets independently with the offender to ascertain if he or she has taken accountability for his or her actions and if he or she would like to attempt to repair the harm caused. Additionally, the facilitator conducts individual meetings with a primary victim to ascertain if the victim seems to be truly ready to face the offender and engage in a conversation with the offender. The facilitator remains cognizant of the further trauma primary victims could experience when facing the offender during the one to one victim offender conference. Thus, some victimizations such as sexual assault crimes are not considered for victim offender conferencing. Unfortunately, trauma could also result from the setting in which the conference would ultimately take place such as a correctional institution (Moriarty & Roberts, 2008). Subsequently, there may be several additional meetings conducted to discuss whether the victim wants to move forward and if so, what kinds of questions may be addressed during the meeting.

The facilitator and victim may also consider discussing anticipated conferencing outcomes as a result of the victim offender dialog. In a perfect world, the actual one to one victim offender dialog takes place in a comfortable setting in which the facilitator, victim, and offender can sit comfortably in a circle. The facilitator serves as a guide during the dialog. Ultimately though, the victim is in charge and the victim and offender dominate the conversation.

The victim is able to provide commentary regarding how s/he felt when victimized and the emotional, physical, and financial repercussions of the victimization. The victim may also choose to ask questions that have went unanswered to often include a question regarding 'why?' The offender is provided an opportunity to apologize even though the victim may opt not to accept the apology. The offender may be able to provide details about circumstances that contributed to the victimization. The one to one victim offender conference may be a very emotionally charged session.

Discussion Circles

Similar to the one to one victim offender dialog, a restorative justice discussion circle usually consists of a group of people discussing victimizations, effects of victimizations, and corresponding steps to attempt to repair the harm that has been caused (Zehr, 2002). The circle may consist of the offender(s), primary victim(s), secondary victims, community members, facilitators, and support persons affiliated with the victim and offender. Although the facilitator may share suggested guidelines for the discussion circle and provide suggestions for how to pose questions, the facilitator does not dominate the discussion. Rather, the facilitator remains a fairly quiet, yet attentive discussion circle member.

Restorative justice based discussion circles also rely on a talking piece. More specifically, a tangible item is designated as a talking piece. The person holding the talking piece is the person who has the floor. The talking piece may be a simple common object such as a pen or a marker. Or, the talking piece can be a symbolic item such as a book to represent that there are many 'chapters' in life. A 'center piece' may also be part of the discussion circle session to represent a calming center focal point such as a bouquet of flowers or a picture of a waterfall.

Family Group Conferencing

Family group conferencing is a restorative practice that can take on several forms and purposes. For example, a family group conference coordinated by human service agencies serves as a conference to bring together family members and support networks to include treatment providers when trying to find strategies and solutions to family situations often following a family maltreatment issue or a family concern. For example, when a child is at risk of out of home placement, a family group conference may be scheduled with corresponding social workers, adult family members, treatment providers, and friends or other contacts who can identify the roots of the problem, identify goals to address the problems, identify who will assist the parent(s) in meeting the goals, list what resources are needed, and provide a prospective timeline for accomplishing the tasks.

The family group conference is not a finger pointing session. Nor, is the conference intended to be a hostile meeting. Rather, the goal is to create ways to reach solutions which are in the best interest of parents and children in the home.

A family group conference can also be scheduled following a crime. Attendees at the conference often include family members of the victim(s), the offender's family members, the offender, primary victims, and the facilitator (Umbreit, 2007). Similar to other restorative justice programs and initiatives, the offender and victims have an opportunity to share their stories, openly discuss the crime, share the multiple repercussions of the crime, and discuss what steps are needed to begin try to repair the harm caused.

RESTORATIVE JUSTICE AND POLICING

Restorative justice is not a formal lesson covered in the typical police academy. Nor, is restorative justice a component that police officers spend time studying extensively in a post high school academic setting. Yet, there are opportunities to bridge restorative based initiatives and policing. When police contact a juvenile who is not making good choices, police may ask the juvenile to take accountability for his or her actions, ask the juvenile what s/he needs to do to rectify the situation, and then follow up to assure that the juvenile follows through. Officers engaging in a school resource officer role likely employ these strategies more often than they realize. Although, police are not likely to scream, "Hey, I just practiced restorative justice based initiatives with a juvenile," they have asked the juvenile to take accountability, attempt to repair the harm that was caused, and asked the juvenile to consider all who were affected by the bad choice.

For example, Dubuque, Iowa Police Department has adopted several restorative based practices without formally thinking about how closely their practices align with restorative justice based philosophies!

Dubuque Police Department officers visit with females in the community who decided to show their appreciation for officers by baking some treats and delivering the goodies to the station. Officers Thomas Warner, Mike McTague, Ryan Scherrman and Jon Brokens are pictured with the girls.*

* Image courtesy of Dubuque Police Department

Chief Mark Dalsing*

> Police Chief Mark Dalsing is a hands on administrator and role model for his officers. Whenever possible, he promotes learning opportunities for juveniles in the City of Dubuque. Although, Dubuque Police Department does not have a program specifically entitled: Restorative Justice, many of the programs initiated with juveniles in the Dubuque community are restorative based.

Examples of programs offered by the Dubuque Police include:

Interventions. An intervention is a one on one meeting between a school resource officer and a student following a rule violation in the school. The officer works with the juvenile to ascertain what they did wrong and the officer explains the possible corresponding legal ramifications. Then the officer and juvenile discuss what steps need to be taken to rectify the situation. After a plan is in place, the officer works with the juvenile to see that the juvenile follows through with the Intervention/plan. Although interventions are completed in an official capacity, there is not a formal juvenile justice system involvement.

Mediations. Dubuque Police Department school resource officers also facilitate several mediations annually in the middle schools and high schools. The session consists of a conversation between the school resource officer, school staff member, and two or more students when information is received regarding an unresolved problem that could lead to a physical altercation. Ultimately, the mediation serves as a preventative initiative as the goal is assessing the root of the

* Image courtesy of Dubuque Police Department.

problem and deciphering an acceptable agreement between the students. Interventions are completed in an official capacity but without formal action.

Fight Diversion. At times students admit to being mutually at fault when a physical altercation occurs. If the students have not previously engaged in a physical fight, the students may be invited to participate in a series of diversion classes facilitated by Dubuque police officers in lieu of facing criminal charges. It should be noted that one-sided physical attacks are addressed as assaults and subsequently not eligible for the fight diversion program. Students who successfully complete the fight diversion program will not face criminal charges for the physical altercation.

Weapons Diversion. The weapons diversion program has been established as a diversion based program for students who are caught with BB guns, Airsoft guns, or other weapons that do not fall in the category of "illegal carrying of firearms. Similar to the fight diversion program, Dubuque police officers lead sessions to help the juveniles take accountability for the actions, identify ramifications of their behavior, and understand the impact of their choices on the school community, their family, and the Dubuque community. Students who successfully complete the weapons diversion program will not face criminal charges for the corresponding weapon violation.

Shoplifting Diversion. The shoplifting diversion program is a Dubuque Police Department program facilitated in the community; the program is not part of the Dubuque schools. Similar to the other diversion programs, individuals caught shoplifting for the first time are provided with the option of completing a series of sessions facilitated by Dubuque Police Department in lieu of facing criminal charges. Participants are expected to take accountability for the shoplifting, identify the ramifications to include legal system, effect on the business owners, others negatively impacted by the shoplifting, and discuss options for repairing the harm caused.

Chief Dalsing and his staff also take pride in several initiatives that have provided channels for youth to make connections with members of the Dubuque community to include officers. The popular Explorer program consists of Boys Scouts of America for boys and girls 14–21 who have an interest in law enforcement careers. The Explorers assist the department with community events. The Dubuque Police Department has been elated to see the positive results; in addition to building strong relationships, many of the Explorers have completed high school and college, and applied for positions with Dubuque Police!

Building Trust and Legitimacy in the Dubuque Community

Dubuque Police Department members strive to provide education to the community while also keeping members abreast of areas of concern. Annual talks and trainings have included: Safe internet use, Dangers of Sexting, Domestic Violence, Youth Violence, Search & Seizure, and related policing topics topping out at nearly 400 annually! The 911 in Schools program is facilitated by the 911 Center as a way to teach the youngest elementary students about proper use of 911. DARE remains a continued positive program in the elementary and middle schools. "The Black Girls Blues" is a program facilitated in the high school setting. The program focuses on young African American girls breaking from the stereotype of needing street credibility to settle things through fighting; "Changing Lives Through Literature" is a program where kids read specific books based on true stories about youth successes and failures. It is intended to be a diversion option. Although the program is fairly new, evaluations revealed positive results! Additionally, the teen court program is still gaining momentum.

IDENTIFYING AND WORKING WITH AT-RISK YOUTH

In a perfect world, juveniles would not engage in criminal acts. Criminologists, sociologists, psychologists, and related scholars and practitioners spend countless hours trying to ascertain what factors and theoretical explanations account for the majority of juvenile crime. Simply stated, there is not a magic wand to address all juvenile crime and delinquency. Initiatives such as zero tolerance policies in which a juvenile is expelled for verbally threating another student for example, often draw criticism (Teasley, 2014). Fortunately, there are opportunities to try to reduce the likelihood of future crime and delinquency.

Several school officials, court professionals, human service workers, and related professionals have adopted restorative based practices to help juveniles hone in on the three principles of restorative justice—accountability, engagement, and restoration. Juveniles in schools that have been labeled as "tough" and "troubled" have even requested to "circle up" when the juveniles see trouble brewing. Time and time again, positive relationships and respect for one other follows restorative practices (Teasley, 2014).

Researchers have continued to find that when juvenile offenders meet with their victims, the crime becomes personalized for the juvenile as the juveniles see and hear the impact of their actions and they truly begin to understand the depth of the harm they caused their victims (Choi, Green, & Gilbert, 2011). Furthermore, engaging in restorative justice initiatives seems to aid the victim as well as the offender as both feel more satisfied with case decisions, feel heard by the system, and see the system as operating in a more just manner overall (Leonard & Kenny, 2011). And perhaps most importantly, several researchers have found a drop in juvenile crime when studying the relationship between participating in restorative justice initiatives and crime among juveniles (Bergseth & Bouffard, 2012, Braithwaite, 2007).

Although no two juvenile circumstances are the same, researchers have found a drop-in recidivism rates for juveniles who participated in restorative justice initiatives even among male juveniles who had engaged in violent crimes (Bergseth & Bouffard, 2012). Communities can get creative in restorative programming for juveniles. More specifically, not for profit community entities may opt to engage in restorative practices and enter into an agreement with formal agencies—police departments, juvenile court, and correctional programs. An undergraduate intern had the opportunity to see the Madison, Wisconsin YWCA restorative juvenile programs in action.

A Step in the Right Direction: Creative Restorative Practices with Juveniles

The Madison YWCA has worked diligently to develop restorative justice based initiatives with juveniles in the Madison community. In addition to working directly in schools to engage in restorative initiatives, the YWCA has developed the community center program.

The community center program has served as an alternative to formal juvenile justice court involvement. Referrals are sent to the YWCA from the Dane County Department of Human Services juvenile justice division. Successful completion of the community center program will result in the juvenile justice judge and the human services staff dropping the juvenile's ticket and closing juvenile court involvement for the corresponding case. The decision to refer a juvenile justice case to the YWCA rests with the juvenile justice social worker and juvenile judge. Although the offenses/tickets seem to vary, referrals include tickets for non-felony cases such as curfew violations, trespassing, disorderly conduct, possession of marijuana, possession of a bb gun, retail theft, and other ordinance violations or criminal misdemeanors.

Upon receiving the referral from the juvenile justice social worker, the YWCA intake worker contacts the juvenile's parent to provide information about the YWCA community centers program. The parents are also asked to share their concerns about the juvenile and corresponding concerns. A conversation is also held with the juvenile to gather additional details about what transpired. Then a pretrial conference is scheduled. At the pretrial conference the juvenile completes a questionnaire and shares their version of what led to the ticket. Then, a circle is scheduled.

A YWCA facilitated circle is held at a local library, community center, or the YWCA. Attendees include the facilitator, the juvenile, and ideally friends, family members, or mentors selected by the juvenile. School members or others involved in the incident may also be a part of the circle. The facilitator commences the circle by introducing the talking piece to serve as a reminder for who gets to talk/ have the floor (the person holding the talking piece is the only one who should be talking at that time) and the center piece object to serve as a warm focal object at the center of the circle. Introductions are conducted next; each attendee shares their name and affiliation to the juvenile or process. The juvenile is then directed to select one of the quotes that appear on an index card in the center of the circle. Once a card/ quote is selected, the juvenile reads the quote and everyone in the circle takes a turn holding the talking piece and stating what the quote means to them. Next, participants are asked to address a deeper truth seeking question such as, "tell us about a time that you made a choice you later regretted even though you did not get caught or in trouble for the incident." Then the conversation leads into the juvenile and others sharing thoughts about the ticket the juvenile received, thoughts about the police contact, and future actions that are necessary to prevent the situation from reoccurring. The circle concludes with a discussion about an appropriate plan for the juvenile to appropriately rectify the situation.

One of the components that makes the community circles so unique is the creativity woven into each juvenile agreement. For example, a female juvenile was issued a ticket for violating the city established curfew. The juvenile had shared with the group that she enjoys music. Subsequently, her 90-day agreement/plan discussed at the conclusion of the circle consisted of writing a song about what she did and why curfews are important in addition to agreeing to address school obligations. The school obligations in the agreement included providing routine progress reports and preparing a goals report. Another juvenile shared that he was interested in possibly being a lawyer. Subsequently, his 90-day agreement focused heavily on conducting research regarding requirements for becoming a lawyer, a handful of law schools, and corresponding goals for the juvenile to make the dream a reality. In each juvenile case, the YWCA community center facilitator continually checks in with the juvenile to empower the juvenile to complete the commitments outlined in the agreement to assure each component is completed within the specified 90-day window. Upon successful completion, the YWCA staff members enthusiastically provide a report to the juvenile judge. As a result, the juvenile's curfew ticket is dismissed and the juvenile court involvement is terminated for the corresponding case.[2]

CORRECTIONS AND RESTORATIVE JUSTICE

Textbooks often break the correctional system into two main components: community corrections and correctional institutions. Although, community corrections may consist of several types of entities, correctional institutions are

[2] The information was obtained from Y employees via a verbal conversation.

often viewed as simply a place to house those who should be removed from the community for a judicially established period of time.

Community Based Corrections

People who are under formal court ordered supervision by a correctional agency while residing in the community are essentially participating in community based corrections. As a result, the offenders are able to maintain relationships with others residing in the community and avoid the stigmatization of being incarcerated. Community supervision programs also save money as housing offenders in prison is extremely costly. There are several types of community based supervision programs to include probation supervision, parole and extended supervision, day report centers, and intensive supervision programs.

The most common form of community corrections is probation supervision. Someone who has committed a crime or violated a statute may be placed on probation supervision via a judge or other court official ruling. Like adults, juveniles may be placed on probation supervision as well. Offenders must comply with several rules while on probation supervision. Standard rules of supervision include: reporting to the department of corrections office for scheduled appointments with the probation agent, complying with urinalysis testing for the purpose of drug screening, obtaining and maintaining employment, complying with treatment or programming, being available for home visits, and controlled substance usage restrictions. Additionally, offenders on probation supervision may be subjected to punitive rules based on the seriousness of the act or due to a supervision violation. For example, a punitive rule would be house arrest; compliance is tracked via a tracking device such as a GPS monitoring bracelet.

Several other forms of community supervision programs are utilized in the United States. Parole release or extended supervision are programs established to monitor those who have been released from a correctional institution. Offenders on parole or extended release are subjected to many of the same rules as offenders on probation supervision—obtain and maintain employment, comply with recommended or court ordered treatment, refrain from engaging in criminal activity, refrain from using controlled substances, comply with drug testing, report for office visits, comply with home visits, and provide supervising worker with changes or updates in status (housing/relationship/employment).

Day reporting centers and intensive supervision programs ae additional community supervision options available to probation, parole, and extended supervision workers. For example, and offender's supervision rules may include, providing a urine sample for the purpose of drug screening at a day report center three days/week. An offender on community supervision may also be required to wear a tracking devise such as a GPS ankle bracelet to allow the supervising agent to establish restricted areas in the community and add restrictions regarding when the offender may leave their residence.

Correctional Institutions

The words jail and prison are often used interchangeably with the term correctional institution. County jails within each state are typically managed by the corresponding county sheriff's department. Jails house people who have recently arrested and are being detained for a short period of time, those ordered to remain in jail pending the completion of their criminal case, and offenders who have been sentenced to serve typically one year or less for a crime in which the person has been convicted. On the other hand, state or federal correctional institutions (often referred to as "prisons") are operated by the state, federal government, or private entities in which the state or federal government maintains a contract. Offenders housed in a correctional institution reside among other offenders, may be offered vocational training based programming, and work toward educational goals such as finishing a high school equivalency diploma or completing a 2-year post high school degree program. Offenders are often allowed limited time with loved ones via institution established on-site visiting guidelines.

Recidivism is a constant concern in communities as there is a large fear that an offender will commit a new crime or violate a supervision rule that will later be deemed worthy of spending time in a correctional institution. The phrases "repeat offending" or "messed up again" have often been used in place of 'recidivism.' As depicted by several department of corrections reports, recidivism may include offenders who are revoked from community supervision for technical violations such as failure to comply with face to face appointments with supervising agents and failure to notify an agent of housing (Clear, Cole, Reisig, 2016). Subsequently, community members, victims, and family members of victims and loved ones may ask, "what are we supposed to do with these offenders who keep messing up?" Fortunately, restorative justice based initiatives can be completed with offenders involved in community corrections and those housed in correctional institutions. Restorative justice initiatives allow offenders to formally take accountability for harm they have caused via their criminal actions while also taking subsequent steps to try to repair the harm caused when applicable.

A rural medium security correctional institution has opted to engage in a variety of restorative justice based programs without breaking the budget! The program seems to be a win-win for the inmates who voluntarily sign up for the program, the undergraduate student facilitators, and the correctional staff members who continually hear positive feedback!

Fall 2017 Victimology Restorative Justice students assisted inmates in making the fleece tie blankets for victims.*

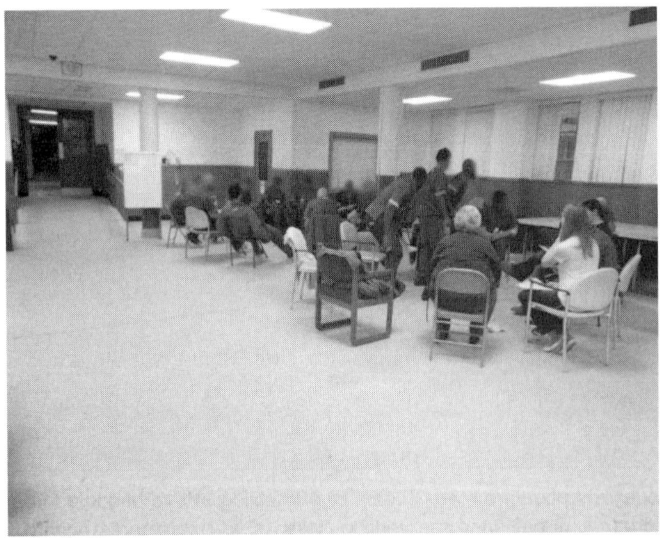

The fall 2017 UW–Platteville Victimology Restorative Justice students are leading victim impact discussion circles and reflection exercises with inmates enrolled in the restorative justice victim impact program.*

* Photo provided by Prairie du Chien Correctional.

* Photo provided by Prairie du Chien Correctional.

The inmates participating in the victim impact program are making the fleece tie blankets for victims of crimes.[3]

Students Conduct Victim Impact Programming

"Don't judge an inmate by his jumpsuit. People can change, and if you give them the resources they need, they will try all they can to reform and change other people's lives as well."

These are the words of Clay Spooner, a sophomore criminal justice major at the University of Wisconsin-Platteville, who, along with 17 of his criminal justice and forensic investigation classmates, recently helped facilitate three sessions of victim impact programming for 50 inmates at Prairie du Chien Correctional Institution in Prairie du Chien, Wisconsin. The goal of the program, now in its fourth year, is to help inmates take accountability for the people and communities who have been affected by their crimes, understand the hurdles victims face following a crime, and participate in opportunities for repairing harm.

Students participating in the program are enrolled in the Victimology and Restorative Justice course, taught by Dr. Amy Nemmetz, assistant professor of criminal justice at UW–Platteville. Restorative justice is a theory of justice that emphasizes repairing the harm caused by criminal behavior, and is accomplished through cooperative processes that include the victim, the offender, family members of the victim and the offender as well as members of the community.

[3] Photo provided by Prairie du Chien Correctional. Students included in these photos at UW–P have signed a release authorizing the use of their images for this book.

Prior to the sessions, students toured the inmate housing unit, visiting area, chapel, restrictive housing, recreation area, on-site health services and a large programming area at Prairie du Chien Correctional Institution then attended a Choices panel, where inmates talked openly about their past, what led them to prison and their lives in prison.

Session One: Impact of Alcohol

At the first session, students and inmates watched a video about a man who was sentenced to 22 years in prison for killing two 20-year-old women. While in prison, the man wrote letters of apology to the victims' families and in time, both families forgave him. One of the women's mother was instrumental in getting his sentence reduced to concurrent 11 year sentences and the two of them now travel to tell their story and discuss drinking and driving.

Following the video, students and inmates discussed the power of restorative justice, forgiveness and healing. Afterward, Mayda Crites, the mother of a drunk driving victim, shared her son's story as well as her own personal experience with the criminal justice system and how she has found healing through restorative justice initiatives.

One of the inmates said that for him, the most significant part of the victim impact programming was hearing Crites share her story. "As a person who has put a mother/family through similar suffering, I am motivated to do everything in my power to make amends," he said. "Even if not to my victim's family, then to others affected by harm. I've learned not to be defined by my past actions/choices, rather to allow my present to prepare my future endeavors."

Session Two: Victims and Intimate Partner Violence

At the second session, students watched a video about a woman who had been severely injured by two offenders committing a violent crime. The woman, despite protests from her children, ultimately forgave both offenders and, for more than a decade, visited with one of the men annually at the prison where he was serving his sentence.

Following the video, students led small group discussions about the three principles of restorative justice: accountability—taking responsibility for causing harm; restoration—trying to repair the harm caused by the crime; and engagement—inviting everyone who has been impacted by the crime to provide thoughts about the harm caused. Inmates then wrote down their thoughts about whether they had taken accountability for the crimes they committed and tried to repair the harm they had caused.

Students also led small group discussions about intimate partner violence and domestic violence. Inmates, many of whom witnessed intimate partner violence and domestic violence in their homes as children, shared their thoughts on why victims may stay in the home.

Session Three: Alcohol and Other Drug Abuse, Victims, and Paying It Forward

At the final session, students and inmates watched an inspirational video, "Pay It Forward," then participated in small group activities that emphasized the importance of showing kindness to others. Inmates discussed people who had had a positive impact on their lives as they were growing up and shared times in their lives when someone had done or said something kind to them. Students and inmates then discussed positive steps people can take every day to make someone's day better. Inmates named the crimes they had committed, thought about the primary and secondary victims of their crimes and shared what they hoped someone did for the victims to make their situations better.

Students also led small group discussion about the difficulties that victims face after a crime has been committed against them.

As a way to help inmates give back to victims, students and inmates made fleece tie blankets together. While the inmates cut the fabric and tied the knots, they talked about the types of hardships victims at domestic abuse shelters experience, why children in foster care and juvenile homes may be victims of the system and what kinds of feelings these children may have. When the project was finished, the inmates voted to give the 30 blankets they had made to Family Advocates, a domestic and intimate partner violence shelter, as well as victims in the community via the police and maltreated children via human services.

"This experience changed me," said Spooner, an Albany, Wisconsin native. "It opened my eyes and gave me some insight into life and how one little mistake can tear people and their families apart," said Spooner. "I also learned that some people genuinely want to change and be a positive impact to friends and family. I really think that we, as a society, need to give people who are incarcerated more chances to prove themselves and give them a second chance—after all, they are still humans."

Spooner said the experience at the prison helped prepare him for his future career in corrections, either as a correctional officer or a probation officer. "The experience allowed me to expand my knowledge of the Department of Corrections and made me realize how much knowledge I can learn from many different people," said Spooner. "It also helped me realize that people who are in prison are still people and to not judge them based on what we hear in the media."

"Every semester, I am impressed with the offenders' ability to truly analyze the impact of their crimes on their direct victims, secondary victims and their community," said Nemmetz. "I continue to be impressed by the students who walk into the institution with hesitation and leave feeling proud and accomplished by the hard work they put into facilitating the discussion circles and activities."

"The collaboration with UW–Platteville has become one of the most sought-after programs we offer to inmates—it's to the point that inmates write year-round, asking to participate, though it's only offered twice a year," said Lisa Pettera, program supervisor at Prairie du Chien Correctional Institution. "They hear about it from men who have completed the program. They seem to understand that their thinking is going to be challenged, but they hope to come away with something that will help them in the future. Inmates really respect the students and appreciate that they are willing to spend this time with them."

Students who participated in the program included Spooner, Octavia Bogan, Alex Breuer, Riley Gallagher, Cheyenne Gilbert, Monika Glodowski, Kyle Gregory, Leah Hoeksema, Amber Hoffman, Madeline Kingsley, Cole McGraw, Alexis Ostrum, Renee Peters, Mitchell Pfohl, Courtney Pryce, Izzy Stanosek-Rockwood, Cassandra Story and Nicole Willenbring.

The hands-on, experiential learning experience at Prairie du Chien Correctional Institution was made possible with the support of the university's Office of Research and Sponsored Programs, a UW–Platteville initiative and funding source for campus-wide coordination, integration and leadership of community-based scholarship of engagement projects and internships that involve students, faculty, staff and community partners.[4]

THE FUTURE AND RESTORATIVE JUSTICE: WHAT DOES THE FUTURE LOOK LIKE THROUGH A RESTORATIVE JUSTICE LENS?

Accountability. Engagement. Restoration. Ideally juveniles and adults who have completed restorative justice initiatives will have a much better understanding of the many lives and communities criminal offending can negatively impact. Suddenly, the focus is not on 'what is in it for me' rather, who will be harmed by my actions. Primary and secondary victims will hopefully not just be something that sounds like a textbook chapter heading. Rather, offenders will be able to consider how their actions affect their own family members, people interacting with them, and their communities.

---

4 Written by: Laurie A. Hamer, University Relations Specialist, College of Liberal Arts and Education, 608-342-6191, hamerl@uwplatt.edu. Link to Laurie Hamer's article: https://www.uwplatt.edu/news/students-conduct-victim-impact-programming. * * * Reprinted with permission from UW–Platteville and pictured students.

Reservations About Restorative Justice

Through a restorative justice based lens, criminal justice and related professionals can see that the 'state' may be the heading on a case file, but the restoration and engagement list extends far beyond what is named in a corresponding file. Additionally, restorative practices can be initiated and facilitated with a limited or nonexistent budget. The operating costs may simply consist of time away from other activities and commitments to work with those who have harmed others to address: accountability, restoration needs, and engagement of those impacted.

Yet, there are community members, victims, scholars, and criminal justice and related professionals taking a strong stance against restorative justice. For example, a police officer replied very negatively to an email invite announcing an upcoming restorative justice conference scheduled to take place at the university in which he had previously attended. The officer candidly replied that the academic program was clearly not the same program that he had graduated from and he wondered how victims of crime would feel about the "ridiculous" restorative justice conference. Perhaps, the officer was personally impacted by a crime? Or, the maybe the officer assumes that restorative justice programming will replace punishment for offenders?

Greene (2013) expresses several concerns about restorative justice programs and initiatives. One concern is the exclusion of certain types of offenders. Although all states in the United States had adopted at least some form of restorative justice programming in the state by 2004, restorative justice facilitators have frowned up accepting sexual abuse cases and intimate partner violence cases for restorative justice initiatives due to the power the offender may exert during a dialog and the concern of further trauma to the victim. Furthermore, Greene (2013) argues that restorative justice initiatives have been housed primarily in juvenile system via school programs and juvenile justice directed programs. Thus, adult offenders who may commit more serious crimes than juveniles may be given less opportunities despite the strong need for deterrence based programs.

An additional argument seems to center around the 'tip of the iceberg' argument. More specifically, restorative justice programs focus on taking accountability and repairing harm in order to reduce the possibility of future crime without necessarily addressing 'why' the offender engaged in the crime initially and/or if additional support is needed to address underlying issues. Furthermore, restorative justice program facilitators should give consideration to system inequalities such as race, socioeconomic status, and gender (Greene, 2013). More specifically, are individuals being overlooked from programming opportunities because of marginalization problems? And, are these factors being considered when discussing 'why' the offender may have opted to commit a crime that ultimately harmed someone?

Finally, it is pertinent to at least mention financial reservations. Budget conversations seem to infiltrate every programming conversation. If a criminal justice professional is engaging restorative justice programming as part of their job responsibilities, they are spending less time on other important duties such as direct supervision of inmates on the cell block for correctional staff members working in a correctional institution.

Chapter Summary

Restorative justice is not the silver bullet answer for addressing all crime. Nor, will all offenders and victims be excited about the opportunity to participate in restorative justice based initiatives. Offenders and victims may decline an invitation to participate in restorative justice initiatives.

Victims and offenders have a minimal role during the court process. Victims and offenders may not have an opportunity to share their story, their pain, or their needs during the sentencing stage of the judicial system. The majority of victims and offenders who opt to participate in a restorative justice program report feelings of satisfaction after the process. More specifically, victims get the opportunity to hear and see the offender take accountability for the crime, the victim gets to share with the offender how deeply the crime affected them, and victims and offenders discuss steps the offender may be able to take to try to repair some of the harm caused.

Restorative justice initiatives can be overwhelming from a logistical sense even though the programs often are not a big burden to tight budgets. The process takes time; the 'behind the scenes' scheduling and prepping with offenders and victims is not a quick task. For example, making logistical arrangements for dialogs in institutional settings such as a correctional institution requires extra steps such as background investigations and special permission from administrators. Related expenses are often very minimal especially considering the financial and emotional toll associated with recidivism and housing offenders in correctional institutions.

Restorative justice programs are being utilized in every state in the nation. Worldwide, communities have adopted restorative practices in some sense. The cost effective programming seems to be a 'win' for the offender and a 'win' for criminal justice when considering the cost of crime on victims and society.

Bibliography

Choi J.J., Green, D., Gilbert, M.J. (2011). Putting a Human Face on Crimes: A Qualitative Study on Restorative Justice Processes for Youths. *Child Adolescent Social Work Journal, 28(5),* 335–355.

Bergseth, K.J., Bouffard, J.A. (2012). Examining the Effectiveness of a Restorative Justice Program for Various Types of Juvenile Offenders. *International Journal of Offender Therapy and Comparative Criminology, 57,* 1054–1075.

Braithwaite, J. (2007). Encourage Restorative Justice. *Criminology & Public Policy, 6(4),* 689–696.

Bouffard, J., Cooper, M., Bergseth, K. (2016). The Effectiveness of Various Restorative Justice Interventions on Recidivism Outcomes Among Juvenile Offenders. *Youth Violence and Juvenile Justice, 15(4),* 465–480.

Clear, T.R., Cole, G.F., Reisig, M.D. (2016). *American Corrections, 11th ed.* Belmont, CA: Wadsworth, Cengage.

Greene, D. (2013). Repeat Performance: Is Restorative Justice Another Good Reform Gone Bad? *Contemporary Justice Review, 16(3),* 359–390.

Karmen, A. (2013). *Crime Victims: An Introduction to Victimology, 8th ed.* Belmont, CA: Wadsworth, Cengage.

Leonard, L., Kenny, P. (2011). Measuring the Effectiveness of Restorative Justice Practices in the Republic of Ireland Through a Meta-Analysis of Functionalist Exchange. *The Prison Journal, 91(1),* 57–80.

Miller, S.L., Hefner, M.K. (2015). Procedural Justice for Victims and Offenders: Exploring Restorative Justice Processes in Australia and the U.S. *Justice Quarterly, 32(1),* 142–167.

Moriarty, L., Roberts, A.R. (2008). Controversial and Critical Issues with Crime Victims: Current Research Begins to Reconcile the Debates. *Victims and Offenders, 3(2/3),* 127–130

Schmalleger, F.J. (2014). *Criminology Today: An Integrative Introduction, 7th ed.* Upper Saddle River, NJ: Prentice Hall.

Teasley, M. (2014). Shifting from Zero Tolerance to Restorative Justice in Schools. *Children & Schools, 36(3),* 131–133.

Umbreit, M., Coates, R.B., Vos, B. (2002). The Impact of Restorative Justice Conferencing: A Multinational Perspective. *British Journal of Community Justice, Summer(1),* 210–24.

Zehr, H. (2002). *The Little Book of Restorative Justice*. Epsom, England: Good Books Publishing.

CHAPTER 12

Building Better Relationships Through Youth Mentoring & Engagement

■ ■ ■

Learning Outcomes

Upon successful completion of this section the student will be able to:

- Describe the value of youth mentoring in furthering the mission of the police.
- Describe the basic elements of a youth mentoring program.
- Identify potential outcome measures that can be used in evaluating the effectiveness of a youth mentoring program.

Important Concepts

- Labeling Theory

INTRODUCTION

Some of the most progressive police agencies have recognized that building better relationships with their community requires a planned, strategic effort to build a sense of trust between police officers and the young people in the community they serve. A deliberate, conscious effort to build and maintain such a relationship between police officers and the youth of the community is the best way to minimize conflict and tensions when the inevitable times of stress create conflict between them.

YOUTH MENTORING

Youth mentoring is one way that progressive police agencies can build better relationships on a personal level. Most young people have an interest in policing and law enforcement and this presents an advantage to officers willing to make a commitment to building a foundation of trust with young people.

The term "mentoring" originated in the ancient Greek tradition put forth in the Homeric poem, *The Odyssey*. It refers to someone who supplements parental efforts by providing a young person with additional guidance, helping the parents by serving as an additional teacher, protector, and counselor for the young person.

The themes identified with mentorship include:

- Mentorships are enduring personal relationships
- Mentorships are reciprocal relationships
- Mentors demonstrate greater achievement and experience
- Mentors provide protégés with direct career assistance
- Mentors provide protégés with social and emotional support
- *Mentors serve as models*
- Mentoring results in an identity transformation
- Mentorships offer a safe harbor for self-exploration (Johnson, 2007).

The benefits of mentoring programs do not reside solely with the mentee or protégé, but also with those who choose to serve in this capacity. *Mentors, in this case police officers assigned to youth mentoring programs, enjoy higher levels of job satisfaction and career success as a result of their commitment to mentoring youth in the community* (Valencis, 2009).

UNDERSTANDING THE YOUNG

Children entering the teen years are impressionable, they are beginning to emerge from childhood into a new world of adolescence on the way to adulthood. The pre-teen and teen years present an ideal opportunity for positive interactions between the police and young people. Careful attention to the quality of those interactions is an important foundational aspect of police community relations.

> For many children, police can be a role model, a powerful authority figure, a protector, an adult friend, a hero, and an avenue to adventure and excitement (Hunter, 2011, p. 242).

"Wise" police officers are **sensitive** to the quality of their interactions with youth. One of the greatest pitfalls to police-youth interactions has its foundation in "*labeling theory*:" many, perhaps most, first-time interactions between a young person and the police occur when the police are responding to a call for service, and most such calls unfortunately involve a minor criminal complaint. In such a context, there is often an explicit assumption of criminality. *When this explicit—or even an implicit—labeling bias is communicated to the young person, it can easily become a self-fulfilling prophesy for the youth.*

The essence of labeling theory is that people tend to behave in ways that reflect how they believe others perceive them. Labeling is a social process that manifests itself in the behaviors of others toward the individual. For example, if a young person is treated like an adult, he or she is more apt to act like an adult, at least in your presence. Conversely, if you treat a person like an adolescent, they are likely to act like an adolescent; if you treat a person like a criminal . . . ? (and so it goes, a self-fulfilling prophesy).[1]

Police officers are powerful authority figures. Despite what many cops will think, young people admire the police and want to be like them. This admiration presents a unique opportunity for the wise police officer, but such opportunities can vanish quickly if the officer is not astute enough to recognize them. *An antagonistic encounter where the cop clearly signals distain, disapproval, or labels the youth as a deviant or criminal will destroy any hope of rapport or a productive relationship.* Unfortunately, the dysfunctional actions of one officer will reflect on all officers. One can be sure that the stories told by a mistreated youth will quickly spread among his or her peers.

Even when an arrest of a young person is necessary, it can be accomplished in a manner that is sensitive to the unique status of youthful offenders. Indeed, such sensitivity is fundamental to the juvenile law system: that system is based on the idea that the police, prosecutors, and courts must be sensitive to those who are not yet mature; that these officers of the law must recognize that youth are both less blameworthy and have a greater capacity for change than do adults.

Police officers dedicated to community service and crime prevention must, when dealing with youths, ask themselves the following questions:

---

[1] Labeling theory is rooted in the idea of the social construction of reality, which is central to the field of sociology, and is linked to the symbolic interactionist perspective. As an area of focus, it flourished within American sociology during the 1960s, thanks in large part to sociologist Howard Becker. However, the ideas at the center of it can be traced back to the work of founding French sociologist Emile Durkheim. The theory of American sociologist George Herbert Mead, which focused on the social construction of the self as a process involving interactions with others, was also influential in its development (Becker, 1964).

- How can I deal with youthful misbehavior in a way that both protects the public, discourages the behavior, and yet does not negatively label the youth?
- How can I help a youth to master the tasks of adolescence and encourage mature behavior?
- How can I help a youth to satisfy his or her need for excitement, risk and the chance to "prove" himself or herself in positive, constructive ways (Hunter, 2011, p. 244)?

YOUTH MENTORING—AN INTRODUCTION

The goal of youth mentoring programs is to improve the well-being of the youth by providing a role model whose behavior they can be encouraged to copy. Such mentoring is especially important when dealing with youth from homes where there is neither a father nor a man capable and willing to serve as a male role model. Male role models—mentors—can be effective in improving the behavior, responsibility, social development, and academic performance of youth.

Youth mentoring programs involve matching police officers to young people who need or want a caring, responsible adult in their lives. In some cases, youth already have a caring adult in their lives, relegating the police officer to the role of a "back-up," providing the kind of caring presence the parent may not be capable of providing for any number of reasons. But in far too many instances today, young people are being raised in homes lacking either a male or female role model, or, even worse, no meaningful role model at all. The police officer, in such situations, has a unique opportunity to provide the only positive role model that such children will ever experience while growing up.

For the police officer, then, every contact with young people puts him or her in a position where his or her behavior (or mentoring) can be viewed as a kind of "target hardening" that arms youths with skills and knowledge that can make them more resilient and resistant to the kinds of peer pressures that may lead to conflict with the police.

The purpose of police mentoring programs, then, is to build positive, trustworthy, cooperative, and beneficial relationships between officers and young people. This provides direct benefits for both the police and the youngsters; the police enjoy less antagonism, fewer explicit indicators of contempt and disrespect, more cooperation, and perhaps even gain reliable sources of information pertaining to neighborhood problems. Youth gain a positive role-model, someone to look-up-to, emulate, and pattern their behavior after as they explore the new world of emerging adulthood.

Participation in youth mentoring programs has been proven to produce benefits for participants, particularly in cases where the youth participant is from a background that places them "at-risk." Careful planning, implementation, and selection of police participants improves the success of these programs significantly. According to DeBois et al. (2002), mentoring programs are most successful when:

- Participating youth have either had preexisting difficulties or been exposed to significant levels of environmental risk,
- Evaluation samples have included greater proportions of male youth,
- There has been a good fit between the educational or occupational backgrounds of mentors and the goals of the program,
- Mentors and youth have been paired based on similarity of interest, and
- Programs have been structured to support mentors in assuming teaching or advocacy roles with youth (DuBois, 2002, p. 58).

Specific benefits for youth included emotional and psychological well-being, problem solving skills, better resistance to high-risk behavior, greater levels of social competency, improved academic achievement, and higher levels of workplace and employment success.

Those who make the best mentors include individuals with a background in a "helping" profession or those who have a demonstrated propensity and desire for this kind of work. Service oriented officers—guardians, as opposed to law enforcement oriented officers-warrior cops—make the best mentors.

There is a potential for long lasting relationships between officers engaged in mentoring programs and participants. Higley et al. (2014) discovered that the length of the relationship between mentors and mentees was associated with positive outcomes, but a broken relationship between the parties foreshadowed negative outcomes for the youth. A short relationship lasting less than 6 months was associated with increases in alcohol abuse, lowered self-esteem, and lowered academic performance. The implications for longstanding relationships were not addressed in this study, but the negative implications of short-lived mentoring relationships are profound. This indicates that police agencies seeking to develop these programs, and officers who express a willingness to participate, need to be committed for the long-run (Higley, 2014).

The decision to develop mentoring programs, to devote police resources and make long-term personnel commitments, reflects a "leap of faith" on the part of the agency and the local governmental authority. Research does not overwhelmingly support the effectiveness of these programs; only modest positive outcomes have been uncovered for reducing juvenile delinquency and aggressive youth behavior. Positive outcomes related to academic performance and substance abuse were even smaller, recidivism rates for youthful offenders engaged in mentoring programs showed no improvement over-all (Developmental Services Group, Inc., 2011).

The real question for police leaders is whether a youth mentoring program is a better use of an officer's time than other areas of responsibility such as routine preventative patrol, criminal investigations, or crime prevention work. This was the crux of the decision whether or not to discontinue the DARE[2] program. In the wake of studies that failed to substantiate the effectiveness of drug abuse resistance education in reducing drug abuse on the part of adolescents and young adults who participated, questions were raised: "Why are we continuing to devote resources to an ineffective program?" The answer, "Because, despite the research findings, it is a better use of an officer's time than driving around writing tickets and occasionally arresting people." *The benefits of such programs go well beyond what is measurable in terms of reducing adolescent drug abuse; the benefit that is important is the benefit to the police and the community of building the long-lasting relationships that will still exist between the former students and "their" DARE officer. These benefits should not be overlooked.*

Mentoring Best Practices

Research has uncovered some of the ways mentoring programs can be structured so that the benefits to youth are most likely. These programs, like DARE, struggle for the clear indicators of effectiveness needed to justify their existence in the face of scarce police and community resources. For those communities willing to devote the substantial resources required for such programs, the following "best practices" have been identified:

- Mentoring programs require careful planning, implementation, and continuous monitoring.

---

2 DARE stands for Drug Abuse Resistance Education, a program initially developed in Los Angeles by Chief Darrell Gates in the 1980s that placed police officers in the elementary schools teaching children about the dangers of drug abuse and strategies on how to resist peer pressure.

- Mentors need to have a demonstrated commitment to mentoring and need to be screened for their "service" and "helping" orientation.
- Mentors need to be matched to mentees based on common characteristics, interests, and character. There must be rapport between the mentor and mentee.
- Mentors and mentees need initial and ongoing training in topics such as relationship building, emotional intelligence development, and warning signs.
- Mentors need a support group, individuals to whom they can turn with questions and concerns.
- Mentors need to recognize the importance of their relationship with the parent or guardians and to be sensitive to concerns that parents or guardians may have about intrusiveness, and even replacement, as a dominant influence with the child.

Behavioral expectations need to be made perfectly clear for both the mentor and mentee. This can even take the form of a signed contract shared among all parties, including the parent and guardian, outlining everyone's expectations and responsibilities (Keating, 2002) (Rhodes, 2005).

CURRENT PROGRAM EXAMPLES

MADISON POLICE DEPARTMENT COMMUNITY OUTREACH AND RESOURCE EDUCATION (CORE) PROGRAM DESCRIPTIONS

Madison Metropolitan School District (MMSD) and
Madison Schools and Community Recreation (MSCR)[3]

Working in Partnership with the Community

The Madison Police Department hosts a number of innovative programs in partnership with various public and private community stakeholders. Each of these programs have a youth mentoring component, but the variety of programs incorporated under the CORE banner offer opportunities for police community interaction that may appeal to youth participants, depending on their area of interest.

Relationship Building Emphasis

The Madison Police Department has gone to great lengths to engage with the community that it serves. Rather than embarking upon various programs or initiatives under the ambiguous heading of "Community Oriented Policing," the Madison Police Department grabs this concept by the throat, establishes a specific mission for this group of initiatives, and establishes specific, measurable program objectives as part of their operational planning.

The culture of community service and mentorship is reinforced as an element of this police agency's culture as evidenced below in the concept and strategy of community outreach statements.

MISSON

The Community Outreach and Resource Education (CORE) Team mission is to enhance the Madison Police Department's efforts to reduce disproportionate

[3] Courtesy City of Madison, Wisconsin and the Madison Police Department.

arrests related to racial disparities and improve trust and perception of fairness through procedural justice, community outreach, education, and problem solving.

VISION

Build, strengthen and sustain community relationships and open communications with respect, equity and trust.

OBJECTIVES

- Enhance department's efforts to reduce arrest racial disparities and improve trust through procedural justice, community outreach, and problem solving
- Build relationships with youth in order to foster mutual trust and positive police interactions, resolve conflicts, and better understand the criminal justice system
- Break down barriers between youth and police through mentoring and leadership building
- Create opportunities to engage with communities of color in a non-enforcement capacity and facilitate conversation about the role of police and its impact on these communities
- Create and expand programs to divert youth from the criminal justice system
- Encourage the involvement of parents
- Work collaboratively across districts and with outside agencies and citizens to address quality of life and public safety issues.

CONCEPT OF COMMUNITY OUTREACH

The Madison Police Department's longstanding reputation as a pioneer in community policing carries with it a tradition of innovation and a commitment to continuous improvement. We strive to identify trust gaps and challenges to our service mission in order to uphold our stated promise and to put into daily action its ideological underpinnings. In this ongoing effort, the Department seeks to establish new and strengthen existing community outreach initiatives aimed at building relationships with those being served.

COMMUNITY OUTREACH STRATEGY

The CORE team will focus on centralized coordination of our various community-policing strategies and in ensuring consistent program facilitation throughout the city. Working collaboratively with district resources and partner agencies such as Centro Hispano, Urban League, MMSD, MSCR, YMCA, Boys and Girls Club, and others, CORE team objectives include initiatives that seek to break down barriers between youth and police; to create better understanding—particularly in communities of color—regarding the role and limitations of police; to reduce racial disparities reflected in our arrest rates; create and expand programs to divert youth from the criminal justice system (restorative justice, community courts, etc.); and to enlist parents, educators, advocates, and community leaders to promote wrap-around support for youth throughout their growth and development. CORE coordination will hopefully better connect all officers to available resources and opportunities, and establish structured assessment and evaluation of our various outreach programs, cultivate broader community reach, and minimize the potential for some of our challenged youth to "fall through the cracks."

CORE collaborates with MMSD/MSCR throughout the academic year and summer months to host programming for middle school youth. This collaboration allows MPD to connect with youth to break down barriers through mentorship and help build relationships to foster mutual trust and positive police interactions. Programming focuses on what police do and why and career exploration. Activities include the Mobile Mini Police Academy and "See It To Be It" tours where youth visit local Madison businesses.

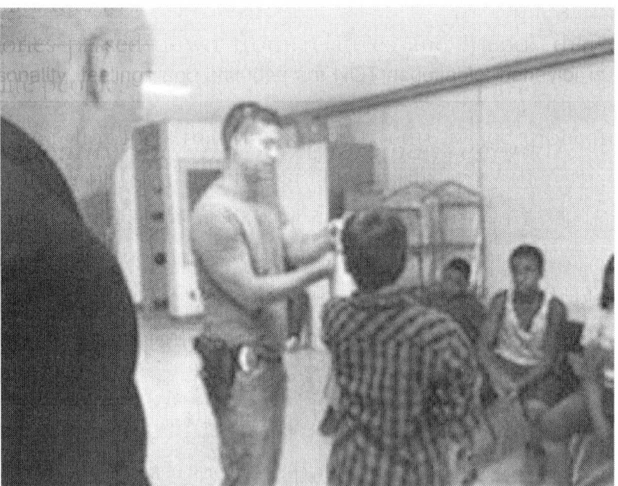

Madison Police officers interacting with youth as part of the CORE program*

* Courtesy Madison Police Department.

"See It To Be It" Career Tours

"See It To Be It" is a grassroots initiative where CORE partners with area businesses to plan and facilitate tours that provide youth the opportunity to visit local businesses and gain insight into many different career choices. These tours provide an all-encompassing plan for future success where children see it to believe it. Tours have included visits to Dane County Airport, MG&E, UW-Health, MFD Stations, MPD Stations, MATC, and WMTV.

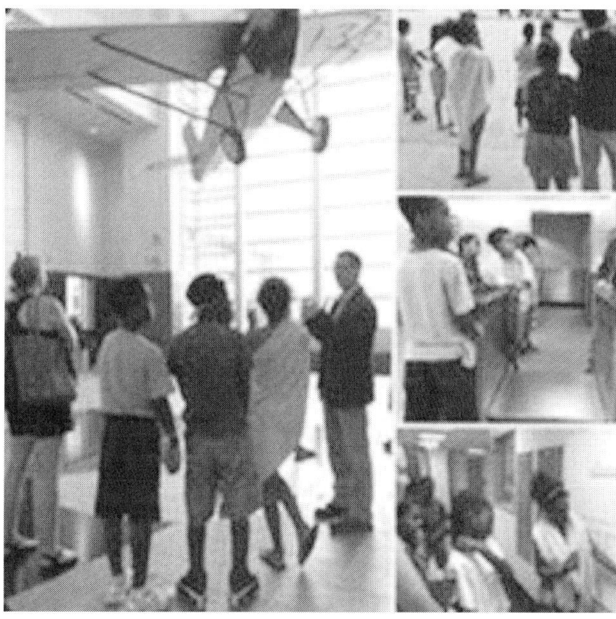

Madison Police working in partnership with area youth organizations, businesses, and officials*

"Bigs In Blue"

The Madison Police Department has developed a new partnership with Big Brothers Big Sisters of Dane County with a unique program called "Bigs in Blue." MPD is one of the first departments in the nation to start this type of program in which an officer is partnered with a "Little." This is a long-term mentoring programing where Bigs and Littles meet once a week inside school. Current partnering schools are Lakeview, Randall, and Emerson.

* Courtesy Madison Police Department.

A little brother to a Madison Police officer*

"Lifting to Inspire Future Trainers" (LIFT)

The Madison Police Department has partnered with Carbon World Health to develop an incredible new mentoring program that focuses on highly marginalized youth. LIFT offers youths an alternative way of achieving their dreams by inspiring them to achieve greatness and success through health and wellness.

---

* Courtesy Madison Police Department.

Madison Police officers promoting fitness with area youth*

Explorer Post 911

The Madison Police Explorer program offers young adults the unique experience of working "hands-on" with officers to develop a personal awareness of the criminal justice system through training, practical experiences, competition, and other activities. Explorers experience comprehensive career focused training, character development, improved physical and mental fitness, and interpersonal growth through self-discipline, teamwork, challenging experiences, and high standards of performance and personal conduct. The Explorer program is an excellent way for youth to gain insight on law enforcement careers, network with various individuals throughout the nation, and serve their community by assisting in a supplementary law enforcement and liaison capacity. MPD's Explorer Post 911 meets at our state of the art training facility twice a month. Youth who are between the ages of 14 and 21 and maintain a GPA of 2.0 are encouraged to join.

* Courtesy Madison Police Department.

Introducing young people to policing the "Madison Way"*

Youth Academies

Black Youth Academy and Latino Youth Academy are offered each summer and are held at our Training Center. While these weeklong academies strive to break down barriers and to cultivate a better understanding—particularly within communities of color—regarding the role and function of police, they are intended to be inclusive and open to all kids. Through these youth academies we hope to foster trust and establish positive relationships with community youth and their families. In addition, our youth academies are designed to instill and nurture leadership qualities and provide participating youth with opportunities to challenge themselves and work together as a team.

During the academy, the students are exposed to a variety of topics and are given opportunities to apply what they've learned during scenario-based portions of the academy. The programming is as hands-on and interactive as possible, but the students get a flavor for some of the more mundane but equally important administrative paperwork that comes along with a career in policing as well. Students hear from officers about the paths that led them to a career in policing and share their personal stories and photographs with the students. This is always a highlight as it provides an opportunity for the students to see the human beings behind the badge.

* Courtesy Madison Police Department.

The Youth Academy*

Madison Officers Reflecting on the Benefits of Youth Outreach

The following comments from Madison officers provide insight into what these efforts mean to them.

"Outreach in the community is a lot like the concept of "paying it forward," you hope that your one positive contact trickles down to the person's family, friends, teachers, etc."

—Officer Jodi Nelson

"Outreach opens doors to conversations within the community with people you might not have had the opportunity to interact with otherwise."

—Sergeant Scott Kleinfeldt

"Sometimes you have to allow yourself to be vulnerable when dealing with the community, it makes the contact more genuine or real."

—Officer Jodi Nelson

"Community engagement really helps to humanize our profession."

—Sergeant Scott Kleinfeldt

"Our Amigos en Azul is a grass roots program that was started by Patrol Officers assigned to the South District who wanted to do more for our Latino community in Madison."

—Officer Jared Prado

* Courtesy Madison Police Department.

"Our partnership with different groups (community partners and non-profits) has strengthened because of our commitment to positive outreach. We realize that it is much easier to build and strengthen our community if we can do it together."

—Sergeant Scott Kleinfeldt

"Community engagement is the most successful crime prevention tool that Police Departments have available to them."

—Sergeant Scott Kleinfeldt

"I've found that positively engaging with our community through CORE programs, especially youth, has fostered an open environment where deeper discussions regarding policing in our society can take place. Policing in the 21st century is more than just responding to calls for service. It's about understanding our youth and their needs and helping them to make smarter life choices. That's crime prevention 101."

—Officer Tyler Grigg

"The most rewarding part of my community outreach position is helping to create community partnerships with local organizations, schools, and businesses to make Madison a safer and happier place to live. #InThisTogether"

—Officer Tyler Grigg[4]

Kansas City Missouri Police Athletic League

Courtesy Police Athletic League of Kansas City, Inc.

The Police Athletic League is not a new concept in police community interaction, but it is one that focuses on building relationships at an early age, at a time in the life of a young person prior to them being exposed to the often corrupting influences of youth culture. It can be thought of as a kind of target hardening against the self-destructive forces that often emerge in adolescence.

National History

The National Police Athletic League (PAL) started in 1912 when Lt. Flynn of the New York Police Department offered inner city youth some positive experiences with police officers. These police officers volunteered their time to coach baseball, play stick ball in the streets, and mentor youth. Today, PAL serves

[4] The above information was provided by the City of Madison Wisconsin Police Department, reprinted here with permission.

more than 1.5 million youth ages 5 to 18. PAL has over 300 chapters and 1700 centers worldwide.

Local History

The mission of the Police Athletic League of the Kansas City, Missouri Police Department is to offer youth the opportunity to interact with police officers in a positive setting while participating in cultural, mentoring and sports programs with the main emphasis being placed on academics. The PAL program serves as a constructive alternative to anti-social behavior and boredom during the developmental years and into adulthood. The mission is facilitated through the daily operation of the PAL centers, through the operation of sports leagues and through cultural activities, such as field trips. In all PAL activities, a life skills curriculum is presented by PAL officers and all PAL youth are required to maintain a 2.0 grade point average in school or attend tutoring and make a good faith effort to raise their GPA.

The Kansas City Missouri Police Department PAL program started as a community-oriented policing project in 1994 through the Westside CAN Center in CPD. In 1998, PAL obtained membership in the National Association of Police Athletic Leagues and incorporated as a not for profit 501(c)3 organization (PAL, Inc.) with a board of directors and certification in the state of Missouri. As a not-for-profit corporation, all PAL activities are funded through private donations and grants. No PAL activities are funded by the department. Through an agreement with PAL Inc., the department has agreed to provide law enforcement personnel as staff, and office space only as available.

The PAL Section was formed and centralized in April 2000 and is assigned under the Investigations Bureau, Investigations Support Division, Youth Services Unit with the D.A.R.E., G.R.E.A.T. and Juvenile Sections. Currently, two sergeants and seven officers are assigned to the PAL Section. PAL offers at-risk youth in high crime areas the opportunity to interact with police officers in positive after school activities in an effort to reduce juvenile crime.

The PAL Section currently operates three PAL Centers in the Kansas City metro area: The CPD PAL Center, located in the Clymer Center at 1301 Vine in the Theron B. Watkins Housing complex; the MPD PAL Center, located at 7575 Monroe in East Hills Apartments Community Center; and the EPD PAL Center opened in the Summer 2001, located at 1801 White in the Blue Valley Recreation Center. The KCMO Parks and Recreation Department closed this center in April 2000. Since reopening the Center, substantial renovations have been made funded by private donations, grants and countless volunteer hours performed by the community and police officers.

PAL offers police officers and other department members not assigned to the PAL Section the opportunity to support PAL programming in several different ways. The sale of PAL merchandise, fundraising events and an annual golf tournament all are open to members to participate with the proceeds benefiting PAL programming. Members can volunteer to assist in program activities or in coaching of teams involved in league play. Members can make monetary donations to PAL at any time, or during the annual United Way campaign, by specifically directing their donation to PAL. To date, a significant amount of volunteer hours are credited to the police department offices and members.

Specific programs include:

- After School Programming
- Baseball
- Boxing
- Cheerleading
- Football
- PAL Gardening
- Trail Blazers Mountain Bike Club
- Softball
- Futsal[5]

HUMANIZING POLICE OFFICERS

Lieutenant Shawn Hill
Santa Barbara Police Department
Courtesy Santa Barbara Police Department, Chief Lori Luhnow

Affinity Cards: A project designed to bridge divides between communities and police

The Santa Barbara Police Department in Collaboration with The Executive Session on Police Leadership

Labeling Theory (as previously explored) identifies some of the difficulties in creating enduring relationships between police and civilians. As a result, youths

[5] The above information was provided by the *Police Athletic League of Kansas City, Inc. reprinted here with permission.*

oftentimes have difficulties identifying with police officers, thus hampering the ability for the two groups (police and youth) to forge bonds and create the mentor/mentee relationship. These difficulties could be further explained by considering Benedict's *worldview* theory.

According to Benedict (1934) a worldview is the concept that refers how a culture sees the world, and how that culture views its relationship with the world. This concept can be applied to different social groups, as well as occupational groups. Viewed as an occupational group, police officers can have a working personality. Because police officers are distinguished as sworn members of law enforcement, they are set apart both literally and mentally from the civilian population. The Police officer's working personality can be described as an Us-Versus-Them mentality (Kappeler et al., 1998). The us versus them mentality has been often used to describe how law enforcement and civilian community members feel as though they are "against" each other.

This sentiment, similar to other beliefs and traditions, can be passed down culturally from adults to youths, especially within those groups who are historically marginalized. These groups are often those most in need of positive non-enforcement contacts with the police. Additionally, police often feel as though the public doesn't understand their job and associated risks. According to a PEW survey Behind the Badge, 86% of police officers surveyed believe that the public doesn't understand the risks they face while on duty. Further evidence of the divide between the police and public worldview is the significant disparity in the responses to the understanding of police work. According to Morin et al. (2017), 86% of police officers say the public does not understand the challenges of their job, while 83% percent of the public say they do. Despite these disparities, 72% of Officers say it is very important for officers to have detailed knowledge of the community they police, including the people and culture (Morin et al., 2017).

In considering programs to engage police officers and youth, and manage the conflicts discussed above, consideration should be given to programs and initiatives that humanize police officers to the public they serve. The President's Task Force on 21st Century Policing identified the use of technology as a pillar for public education, and to build trust and legitimacy in our communities. The Santa Barbara Police Department, in collaboration with The Executive Session on Police Leadership, have developed a product to provide a low cost and effective way for departments to engage community through technology. The Affinity Card project focused on creating a platform to highlight *commonalities* between officers and the local communities they serve, emphasizing the importance of *humanizing* police officers.

Affinity can be defined as a feeling of closeness and understanding that someone has for another person because of similar qualities, ideas, or interests (Merriam-Webster, 2017). By Officers sharing life experiences with people in the community through stories, rifts between police and community can be diminished, and trust and legitimacy can begin where it has be absent and accelerate where it has been present. Affinity Cards, borrowing from the traditional trading card concept, provide links to videos of the officer through the use of QR codes or a traditional web browser address. The card itself provides a picture of the officer and some "fun facts" such as their favorite children's book, or superhero for the younger children, and links to videos for older youth and adults to learn about the officer who provides them service in their neighborhood. Affinity cards are designed as a voluntary option for officers, and the individual officer decides what information they are comfortable sharing.

Affinity cards

- A sports style trading card with an officer's picture on front.
- Personalized information on back featuring officer's early life experiences (favorite teacher, favorite book, sport hobbies, etc.).
- Smartphone scanning QR code on back with a link to video of officer discussing experiences in their childhood and young adult lives, unrelated to policing. These experiences emphasize commonalities between officers and community members, and humanize the officer.

Use QR code scanner on smartphone to link to video of officer

Officers can share pictures from their past

Project Potential

Affinity cards can:

- Be transformative vessels to humanize police officers to the communities they serve.
- Provide a platform for informal leaders in the department to engage with the community and take ownership of community policing, creating change in organizational subculture.
- Provide a *complimentary strategy* (indirect contact) to improve intergroup relations between police and community (Vezzali et al., 2014).
- Use technology to engage youth, and allow for department to engage public in educational opportunities. Varieties of cards can be created as vessels for public education (use of force, etc.).
- Partnerships can be created with local schools using videos relating to curriculum topics. Officers can be in the classroom and answering calls for service simultaneously.

- Internships can be created with local college film departments to film and produce video.
- Partnerships with local businesses can be made, where businesses sponsor the cost of an officer's card to pay for production costs in exchange for a logo or website on the card.

It is important to recognize that this product is not intended to permit an agency to claim its success in community engagement. Instead, it offers police leadership a product that embraces the spirit of community policing by infusing a bond between the officers and the people in their community through the sharing of human experience. The card concept can also be expanded to include public education by recording educational videos related to police policy and procedure to promote transparency.

Chapter Summary

Youth mentoring is a way that police agencies can take affirmative steps to build better relationships with their community. The key is to build a foundation of trust and this is easiest to do when young people are exposed to the police in a positive context at an early age.

Youth mentoring requires a significant commitment on the part of the police agency and this commitment involves allocating resources for this purpose. Taking officers off the street and deploying them to non-crime related duties can be difficult to justify, especially when there is a lack of clear evidence that such programs are effective in reducing crime and disorder. However, one can argue that past efforts have looked in the wrong place for this evidence. Program evaluations collect and analyze data, but a better place to look for evidence of the effectiveness of these programs is in the faces of the young people affected by them and in the faces and comments of the police officers themselves. Young people may not remember the content of lessons from the DARE program, but they do remember *their* DARE officer.

The de-humanizing aspects of police work and the subsequent alienation of the police from the communities that they serve can be mitigated by programs such as affinity cards. When young people have a chance to get to know their police officers as real people, one of the unrecognized benefits of the DARE program—ongoing relationships—can develop. At the same time, police officers learn to understand the value that appropriate disclosures and the sharing of information about themselves can have when building understanding and trust between the police and the people they serve.

In the final analysis, it is through programs such as those described herein that police community relations can be improved.

Bibliography

Becker, H.S. (1964). *The Other Side: Perspectives on Deviance.* New York: The Free Press.

Developmental Services Group, Inc. (2011). *Mentoring: A Literature Review.* Washington, DC: Office of Juvenile Justice and Delinquency Prevention.

DuBois, D.L. (2002). Effectiveness of Mentoring Programs for Youth: A Meta-Analytic Review. *American Journal of Community Psychology, 30(2)*, 157–197.

Higley, E.W. (2014). Achieving High Quality and Long-Lasting Matches in Youth Mentoring Programs: A Case Study of 4Results Mentoring. *Child & Family Social Work, 21(2)*, 240–248.

Hunter, R.D. (2011). *Police Community Relations and the Administration of Justice, 8th ed.* Saddle River, NJ: Pearson.

Johnson, W. (2007). *On Being a Mentor.* Mahwah, NJ: Lawrence Erlbaum.

Keating, L.T. (2002). The Effects of a Mentoring Program on At-Risk Youth. *Adolescence, 37.*

Rhodes, J.R. (2005). The Protective Influence of Mentoring on Adolescents' Substance Use. *Applied Development Science*, 31–47.

Valencis, L. (2009). *A Guide for Mentoring Programs in Police Departments.* Denver, CO: Regis University.

Index